Study Guide

for

Kalat's

Introduction to Psychology
Seventh Edition

Mark R. Ludorf
Stephen F. Austin State University

with a Guide for Nonnative Speakers by
Eric Bohman
William Rainey Harper College

THOMSON
™
WADSWORTH

Australia • Canada • Mexico • Singapore • Spain • United Kingdom • United States

For more information about our products,
contact us at:
Thomson Learning Academic Resource Center
1-800-423-0563

For permission to use material from this text or
product, submit a request online at
http://www.thomsonrights.com.
Any additional questions about permissions can be
submitted by email to **thomsonrights@thomson.com.**

Thomson Wadsworth
10 Davis Drive
Belmont, CA 94002-3098
USA

Asia
Thomson Learning
5 Shenton Way #01-01
UIC Building
Singapore 068808

Australia/New Zealand
Thomson Learning
102 Dodds Street
Southbank, Victoria 3006
Australia

Canada
Nelson
1120 Birchmount Road
Toronto, Ontario M1K 5G4
Canada

Europe/Middle East/South Africa
Thomson Learning
High Holborn House
50/51 Bedford Row
London WC1R 4LR
United Kingdom

Latin America
Thomson Learning
Seneca, 53
Colonia Polanco
11560 Mexico D.F.
Mexico

Spain/Portugal
Paraninfo
Calle/Magallanes, 25
28015 Madrid, Spain

CONTENTS

GETTING THE MOST OUT OF YOUR STUDY GUIDE

Chapter Learning Objectives and Outline

A list of learning objectives and an extensive outline are provided at the beginning of each chapter. This is a great place to start each chapter. Review both the learning objectives and outline before reading the chapter and before it is discussed in class. The learning objectives provide broad ideas of what you should expect to learn in the chapter. The outline follows the text's learning module format and includes text page numbers for detailed information on any topic. Reviewing the objectives and outline will provide a framework for you as you read and process the chapter. Also, consider making notations in the outline based on your readings. You can revisit the outline following your class.

Related Websites and Lecture Material

Each chapter contains the URL for the text website. From this website you can link to the Student Book Companion site. Each chapter at the companion site includes an interactive crossword puzzle, flashcards, a glossary, online quizzing, a Pre-test and Post-test, a link to vMentor, and other beneficial links. These tools will allow you to become an active learner leading to better performance in the course. In this study guide, study tips are provided in each chapter. You can use these throughout the course as well as in other courses. Reviewing all of the chapter tips early is recommended.

Module and Comprehensive Assessments

Like the text, the study guide chapters are partitioned into anywhere from 2-5 modules. Each module contains several types of assessment questions including fill in the blank, short answer, multiple choice, and true/false. The modular assessments can be used two ways. The first method would be to use the module assessments in a "real-time" fashion. That is, as you are learning each module you can take the assessments to determine how well you understand the information. You can use your performance to gauge your understanding and review topics you did not do well on. A related strategy would be to complete only half of each question type. Then after reviewing those topics you didn't do well on you can use the other half of the questions to once again assess your understanding. A second method, which could be used in combination with the first, is to use the module assessments as a review tool in preparation for an upcoming test.

In addition to the module assessments, at the end of each chapter is a Final Chapter Comprehensive Assessment Test covering topics from all of the chapter modules. Both of the strategies suggested for the module assessments can be slightly modified and employed with this assessment.

GETTING THE MOST OUT OF YOUR PSYCHOLOGY COURSE (AND COLLEGE)

You are about to begin to study a fascinating subject--psychology. In some ways, you have been studying psychology for years. You have always been observing, predicting, and trying to control human behavior. Now, however, you are going to learn about how psychologists study behavior using scientific methods. Psychology is inherently an interesting topic, so you should be motivated to learn more about it. This introduction is designed to help you get the most out of your psychology course and out of your college experience.

BEFORE THE COURSE BEGINS

Select the "Right" Professor

Not all professors are created equal. Selecting the "right" professor is one of the most important things you can do to increase your chances of success. You should try to select a professor that fits your self-assessed learning style. Students now have the opportunity to anonymously evaluate professors at

www.ratemyprofessor.com. You can use these evaluations to review professors you are considering taking a course from. **BE CAUTIOUS** however, since there is virtually no quality control at this site and anyone can post their opinions. One way to get a better idea of the validity of the reviews is to select a professor that you have had and to review comments students have made about him or her. Are they consistent with your perceptions? Most likely you will find statements you consider accurate and those you consider inaccurate. Keep this in mind when you examine the reviews of other professors you are reviewing.

Selecting the "Right" Course

Just like professors, not all sections of the same course are alike. Students today have a variety of modes from which to select when choosing a course. It is likely that you can take an introductory psychology course in a traditional lecture format, in a completely web-based format, or some mixture of the two. It is also likely that you can take the course at any time during the day or at night. Selecting the right course at the right time can be key to you doing well in the course. Are you a person who needs personal interaction with the instructor and other students? Then a traditional lecture course will likely be best for you. If, however, you do not need that in person interaction and you enjoy working on a computer, you might want to consider taking a web-based or mixed course. Also, selecting a course time and day that fits your schedule, needs, and preferences will also benefit you.

Start with a Positive Attitude

What you believe can influence how well you do. In an experiment by Greenwald, Spangenberg, Pratkanis, and Eskanazi (1991) students listened to tapes that were supposed to have subliminal (below threshold for perception) messages. The messages were about losing weight or about increasing self-esteem. The subliminal messages themselves had no effect, but students' expectancies did produce changes. Those students who thought that the tape should increase self-esteem did increase in self-esteem (even when the tapes contained no messages). So, thinking that they would be more self-confident made the students feel more self-confident.

Set Difficult, but Realistic, Goals

Expecting that you will do well in a course is the first step to doing well. But, thinking about doing well isn't enough. You need to produce a good study plan and stick to it to actually do well. Make a pronouncement at the beginning of the term that you will work as hard as possible to succeed in your courses. But, that's not enough. Set specific, difficult, but realistic, goals for each of your courses (getting all A's, a B average, or a C average--whatever is reasonable for you). In addition, set up a specific short-term goal for each test and assignment that you do for each course. Such goals will both help to increase your self-confidence and your performance (Locke and Latham, 1990). College instructors tend to give lower grades than high-school instructors, and the competition is much tougher. And yes, college instructors give Fs to students, even those who take all the tests (if, of course, they fail most of them). So, don't take success for granted. On the other hand, don't become discouraged. Set up realistic goals and work to meet them. Plan to reward yourself at the end of the term if you achieve your goal. The reward could be something like going on a camping trip to a favorite place, buying new clothes, or whatever might work to motivate you. Then, stick to your contingency plan. That is, give yourself the reward only if you meet your goal. Setting up smaller rewards for your short-term goals, such as getting a B on a test, is also a good idea.

Look Through Your Textbook.

You have already purchased your book, so you have accomplished the first step to succeeding in your introductory psychology course. Take a look at your text. Although you may think that you already know what psychology is, you probably don't have a good idea of what this course will be about (even if you took a course in high school). In college, psychology is generally taught as a scientific discipline. So, you will observe as you look through your text that there is a chapter on research methodology early in the book. That chapter is critical for you to understand how psychological research is done and why it is important to do research in psychology. Start with an open mind; you are about to study behavior in a way that you never have before. Look at the various chapters in your book so that you can see the range of topics that it covers. Yes, there is biology in psychology; understanding the biological underpinnings of behavior is an important component of the area of psychology known as psychobiology. Other psychologists study learning, memory, development, and language. As you look at your text, you will discover that personality and mental disorders are covered toward the end of the book. You can understand those topics much better after you understand the biology of behavior, the principles of learning, and the development of behavior. So, read through the chapter objectives in your book to prepare yourself for the topics that you will study in the course. Knowing what is coming will make you better able to integrate and understand the topics.

Find Some Friends (or Make Some) Who Are Taking the Course

One of the best ways to study is with a study group. Interteaching is a relatively new idea related to group study except that it involves pairs of students. Boyce and Hineline (2002) define interteaching as a "mutually probing, mutually informing conversation between two people." Learning in a small group is a very effective way to learn (Druckman & Bjork, 1994). Such a group can force you to read the material and to understand it well enough to be able to present it to others. Four people is about the right number for your study group. Contact three other students and find a time once a week when you can meet for about 2 hours. Put this time into your schedule for the term and stick to it; plan to meet with your study group every week at the prearranged time. Make sure that you have serious students who are willing to spend the time both in and out of the study group to prepare for the course. Don't let anyone have a free ride. Everyone in the study group must be committed to learning as much as possible in the course.

Make a Practical Schedule

At most universities, you are expected to spend about 2-3 hours a week studying for every 1 hour a week that you are in class. This means that you should study about 6-9 hours a week for a course that meets 3 hours a week. If you are taking five such courses, this translates into a "workweek" of 35-45 hours. Think of studying as your job. (If you have another job, think of studying as a second job.) Be sure that you are able to schedule enough hours to do the "job" that you are actually paying to do. Yes, college is different from other types of jobs in that you are paying to do it (or someone else is, if you are fortunate enough to have financial assistance). The fact that you are paying to be in college makes it doubly important that you take it seriously and do your studying "job" competently.

So before classes begin, set up a schedule that you are likely to be able to follow. Put in all the things that you must do at specific times--classes, the times when your study groups for various classes have agreed to meet, your other job for which you are paid (if you have one), meetings that you must attend, time for family obligations, social activities, and so on. Then, see where you can schedule blocks of time for study. Unlike high school, you will probably have lots of free time between classes during the day. USE IT! Don't look at those 2 hours between classes and assume that it is time to waste, or time to sit around and talk with friends. Assume that your psychology class meets 2 hours after another class 3 days a week. Schedule those 2 hours to go to the library and study for psychology on those 3 days. If you use those 2 hours to study for psychology 3 times a week, you have arranged for almost all the time that you need to study for the course. Add 2 hours for a study group for psychology, plus an hour to review one night a week, and you have provided enough study time for one of your courses, psychology. Set up a similar schedule for your other courses. It is important that you set up a studying schedule **that will work for you**. If you always get hungry and eat lunch, don't put study time in the library from 11 to 1. You simply won't stick to it. Also, if you cannot sit still very long, don't schedule a block of 4 hours straight for study. Put a study place in your schedule and stick to it. For most students, going to your Union's dining center and planning to study will not work. Friends will join you, and soon you will be talking and not studying. So, before classes even begin, work up a schedule that fits your life-style, including both specific times for study and also places where you will study. Try your schedule for a while; if some part of it is not working, rearrange it and try the new schedule for a while. The important aspect of setting up such a schedule is that you end up studying at a constant rate. You will be "up" on the readings and you will not need to cram for tests.

If you've tried to set up a schedule based on 3 hours of studying per course and you simply could not fit in enough hours because of your other commitments, you should think about changing your course schedule. Don't take more courses than you have time for. It is better to take longer to get through college with good grades than either to fail your courses or to squeak through with a minimal GPA. Too easy a schedule can be a mistake also. So, before the term begins, you need to assess your situation accurately and decide whether you will have the time to handle the course schedule that you have set for yourself.

WHAT TO DO DURING CLASS

Go to Class

In most college courses, your instructor won't take attendance, and he or she may not even know whether you're there or not. Still, it is important to attend every class. One reason is that many instructors present material in class that is not in the textbook, and that material is often included on tests. If you miss classes, you miss important material, and you will miss more test questions. Even if your instructor does not ask test questions that are directly related to lecture, but not covered in the book, he or she still probably uses the lecture to emphasize certain topics. There is a huge amount of material covered in your introductory psychology textbook. No one could possibly learn it all in one, or even two, academic terms. Thus, students can use the lecture to determine which topics the instructor finds most important (and probably most interesting). Those topics are likely to be overrepresented on tests relative to topics that your instructor did not discuss in class. You cannot know which specific topics will be emphasized on the test unless you attend every class and listen to what is being covered.

What to Do (and Not to Do) in the Classroom

You should attend class in order to learn. Hearing material, as well as reading it, will help you to understand and remember it better. If this is why you are attending class, why sit in the back of the room where both hearing and seeing will be more difficult? The backs of large classrooms are often noisy with students talking and otherwise disrupting the class. So, avoid the back. You have taken the time to come to class (and you have paid for it!), so sit in the front and make the most of it. Most of the best students sit in the front and they interact with the instructor. Sitting in front and being an active learner will both help you to learn better and help make the class more interesting to you. Even in very large classes, instructors usually get to know a few students who sit near the front and who interact with them.

Don't sit with your friends if you will end up talking with them during class. You should have "talk with friends" time in your schedule, and the middle of class isn't the time. Talking in class distracts the instructor, distracts your fellow students (who have also paid to attend the course), and means that you get less out of the course. If sitting with your friends means talking with them, sit somewhere else. And don't go to class either to read the newspaper or to study for tests in other classes. If those are your goals, go somewhere else where the lecturer won't distract you, and you won't distract the lecturer.

So, you are in class, and you have chosen a seat near the front where you can both see and hear well. You are all ready to pay attention and learn all you can. What do you do in class?

Listen, and *Understand* What Is Being Said

Listen carefully and ask questions if you do not understand what is being presented. If you are embarrassed to raise your hand in class, ask your instructor before or after class or during office hours. Or if you have a teaching assistant, find him or her during office hours. Another alternative is to write out your question and hand it to the instructor or leave it on the podium before the next class. Most instructors will make every effort to answer students' questions. Don't let material that is unclear go by--make every effort to understand it.

Take Notes

Taking notes improves class performance, and taking notes and reviewing those notes helps even more (See Chapter 5 Study Tip in this study guide). Students take better notes with more experience in college. Notes become more organized, more selective, and more accurate (Van Meter, Yokoi, & Pressley, 1994). Your notes should differ depending upon what you will need to know for tests. If your instructor will want you to know definitions on a multiple-choice or a matching test, then you need to take down more verbatim facts. If, however, concepts will be stressed either on multiple-choice or essay tests, then you will need to write more general concepts in your notes (Van Meter et al., 1994). Whatever the final purpose of your notes, never try to write down everything verbatim without thinking about it. Try to pick out important points. After you understand a point, write it in your own words (unless it's a definition and you will need to know it verbatim for the test). Go back over your notes soon after class and put comments on them. While the lecture is still fresh in your mind, fill in gaps that you missed and clarify points that are fuzzy in your notes. Try to add some other examples or apply the concepts to other situations, and jot those down in your comments. Later, your notes, plus comments written very soon after the lecture, will make a great source to review for your tests.

An example of a good set of notes with comments written on them is shown on p. xi. The student put the line down the left side before class. The class notes were written on the right side. The purpose of the left column is to add comments after class. The printed comments in the left column were added after the lecture to clarify the notes.

Make Up Missed Classes

If you have to miss class, get the notes from someone who takes good notes. (But do not miss class unless missing it is really necessary.) Don't assume that the material you missed won't be on the test; it surely will! Make an agreement in your study group that you will share notes with each other (but only when one member has a good reason for missing class). Even getting notes from someone won't be as good as being there yourself. Notes are personalized with material that the notetaker thought was important and material that the notetaker did not know before (Van Meter et al., 1994). Therefore, looking at two sets of notes would be a good idea. Go through one set of notes and write out your own notes in your own words. Then look at the other set of notes and fill in things that were missing from the first set and write in clarifications for the first set. Put in question marks where you don't understand something and be sure to have that clarified either in your study group or by your instructor or your teaching assistant.

Access Course Website

If your instructor has a course website you should access this site frequently (at least once a week) to see whether there is any new information available. The more often your instructor mentions the website, the more often you should visit it.

Sample Notes for Improving Memory Lecture

Date: *Wednesday, Oct. 17*	*Improving Memory by Using Mnemonic Devices* Text: *Chap. 7*
Mnemonic means memory in Greek	*1. Useful mnemonics*
Also called peg system	*A. Pegword*
	How does it work?
Need to be able to imagine thing you want to remember	*Uses words that rhyme with numbers (1 is a bun, 2 is a shoe)*
Imagery plus verbal code puts it into memory twice	*Make interacting image of rhyme and thing to be remembered*
	Go through rhyme at retrieval, pulling out images
	Useful for remembering imageable things in order (up to 10)
Originated by Greek speech-givers	*B. Method of loci (locations)*
	How does it work?
Can use rooms in home	*Uses well-learned locations along a route*
So, imagine what you want to buy in each place	*Make interacting image of location and thing to be remembered*
This is the retrieval plan	*Imagine walking though locations at retrieval, pulling out images*
	Useful for remembering imageable things in order (many)
	C. First-letter mnemonic
	How does it work?
Like "Every good boy does fine"	*Take first letter of words to form a sentence or story*
	Use the sentence or story to retrieve the first letters
	Useful for memorizing in order (many things)
Need to watch that you don't remember rhyme, but not real items	*May be difficult to get from first letter to term*
	D. Keyword mnemonic
	How does it work?
Need to be able to imagine keyword	*Turn unfamiliar term into English keyword that sounds similar*
	Make an image of keyword and meaning of term
	Unfamiliar term should result in retrieval of keyword plus image
	When can it be used?
Think of Russian word delo as jello	*Foreign language vocabulary*
Imagine a "cap race" with the leader changing often, for capricious	*English vocabulary*
Use for plant species in hierarchy-imagine angel for angiosperm	*Biological taxonomies*
	2. Why do mnemonics work?
A. and B. are the two main points about memory	*A. They promote a deep level of processing*
To remember well, you need to	*1. Many use visual images which forces one to think of meaning*
1) get it in (encode) well	
2) get it out (retrieve)	*2. Most tie new material to already known material*
	B. They give a good retrieval scheme to pull memory out

GET THE MOST OUT OF YOUR STUDY TIME

The goal of studying is to understand and remember information so that it can be used at some later time: first, for tests in your course; later, as knowledge to help you better understand your experiences and solve real-world problems. If this broader goal is to be met, you need to understand material; simply memorizing terms and definitions is not enough. Most instructors will try to tap your understanding of material on tests. Understanding and applying material takes time, but the methods described below will make your studying more efficient and more effective than simply reading the textbook several times. As a student, your main job is to learn and apply information, so you should have already planned your time so that this can be accomplished on a regular basis, several times a week. Learning the material presented in your courses is a matter of getting information into memory and later getting it out. Chapter 7 of your textbook contains an entire chapter on memory processes, but those aspects that are specifically relevant to studying will be described below.

Memory is Dependent Upon a High Level of Learning and Good Retrieval Cues

Research on memory has shown that the amount of time that information can be retained in memory is directly related to the level of learning. *Information that is overlearned* (learned perfectly and then studied beyond that point) *is remembered longer* than information that is just barely learned (Krueger, 1929). One way to ensure that material is learned well is to *process the information to a deep or meaningful level* (Craik & Tulving, 1975). Material that you thought of only in terms of surface structure (e.g., what do the words sound like?) is not as well remembered as information that you thought of in terms of its meaning (how is this concept similar to one that I already know?). Students often repeat a definition over and over to themselves with the idea that this will strengthen the concept in memory. Memorizing a definition word for word is unimportant; being able to use the word is much more important. Furthermore, experimental studies have shown that mere repetition does not increase the likelihood that the material will be recalled later. Craik and Watkins (1973) showed that words that had been repeated over and over for 12 seconds or more were not remembered any better than words that had been repeated for only 1 second. On the other hand, *repetition that involves thinking about the meaning of material and connecting it with information that is already known is effective in increasing memory.*

Effective Ways of Producing High Levels of Learning

Material that is understood is remembered better than material that is not understood (Bransford & Johnson, 1973). Understanding material means that you have tied it into concepts that you already know, and this is one of the ways to produce a meaningful memory. If you do not understand material, don't simply try to memorize it by repetition. This is not effective. It is almost certain that the material you do not understand will appear on the test, so spend the time to ask someone to help you understand it. A good test of understanding is to try to apply the material to real-life situations or to come up with some examples of your own.

Making images of concepts can help memory. Images may help because they result in both a visual and a verbal memory code (Paivio, Walsh, & Bons, 1994). Try to visualize concepts whenever possible! Making bizarre images can also help. Use bizarreness sparingly, however, because bizarre images are only remembered better when they are mixed in with common images (McDaniel, Einstein, DeLosh, May, & Brady, 1995) and when you will have to remember without many cues on your test (Riefer & LaMay, 1998).

Generating information can increase memory. Jacoby (1978) showed that generating answers, even if they were simple, led to better memory for the answers than simply reading them. Foos, Mora, and Tkacz (1994) found that generating outlines, questions, and answers led to better test performance than reading instructor-prepared materials. However, make sure your questions and outlines hit most of the main points because generating helps only on test questions directly related to what you generate. Anything that you can do to produce material rather than being a passive reader should help (Linden & Wittrock, 1981).

Repetitions of material should be distributed, not massed. Many experiments, using many different types of materials, have shown that repeating material immediately after the first presentation (massed presentation) does little to help memory. *Repeating material after other material has been presented* (distributed presentation) *does help memory* (e.g., Melton, 1970). Studying once a day for a week will lead to better memory later than studying the same material seven times during a single day (Bahrick Bahrick, Bahrick, & Bahrick, 1993). For example, reading your text twice with 24 hours between the first reading and the rereading will produce better memory than reading it twice with no time between the readings (Krug, Davis, & Glover, 1990). So, a good plan would be to read a chapter before your instructor is going to lecture on it and then to reread it 2-3 days later, after hearing the lecture. Plan your study time so that you can take advantage of the effects of distributed study. Don't put off studying until the last minute so that all you can do is massed study (otherwise known as cramming). It won't be very effective in the long run.

Retrieval Cues are Important to Get Information Out of Memory

Practice retrieving rather than spending all your time trying to input material into memory. Material that has been tested is remembered longer than material that wasn't tested (Runquist, 1983). Furthermore, testing yourself in a distributed way is also helpful. Gradually increasing the intervals at which you test yourself is better than always testing yourself after the same amount of time. For example, you might study material and then test yourself on it after one hour, then after three more hours, and then after a day has passed (Cull, Shaughnessy, & Zechmeister, 1996).

Retrieval is best when the conditions of testing match the conditions of learning (Tulving & Thomson, 1973). No matter how well you know material, you must ultimately show your knowledge by pulling the material out of memory. Simply getting it into memory is not enough; retrieval is also necessary. Many experiments have shown that if you think of a concept in one way while learning it, you will need to think of it in the same way when your memory is tested. Otherwise, you may not be able to remember it. If you are going to have essay tests, plan how you would answer a question. Learn a series of key words that will help you to recall each point. You might find that a mnemonic system, such as the method of loci described in Chapter 7, could be helpful. If you are going to take a multiple-choice test, try to think of the concept in as many different ways as possible. *The more ways that you store a concept in memory, the more likely that your understanding will match one of the alternatives on the test.* Nitsch (1977/1979) has shown that people can better recognize a concept that is tested in a new way if they have learned with varied examples. So, try to think of as many different examples and ways of understanding a concept as you can.

Similar physical conditions at encoding and retrieval help. The match between study and test is also true for environmental conditions. There is some evidence that studying and being tested in the same room might help (Smith, Glenberg, & Bjork, 1978). However, don't worry if your tests are in a different place from your lectures. Saufley, Otaka, and Bavaresco (1985) found that students who took tests in rooms that were different from their classrooms did not do any worse than students who took tests in their classrooms. If you learn material well and in several different environments, you will probably be able to remember the material in any setting. However, there is some interesting recent evidence that suggests that the music you listen to may affect your ability to learn and remember on tests. Balch, Bowman, and Mohler (1992) found that students who read text material while listening to music that had words remembered less of what they read than students who either listened to no music or who listened to music without words. They also found that students who listened to either classical music or jazz while studying did better on tests when listening to that same music during the tests. Your instructor probably won't want you to listen to tape recorded music during your tests (he or she may become suspicious about what you're listening to if you have an ear phone in your ear). So, your best bet is to study without music. This is particularly true if you are introverted. Music is distracting to introverts and listening while reading results in poorer memory for material (Furnham & Bradley, 1997). Instead of listening to music while studying, use music as a reward. After you have studied for an hour with no music, take a 15- minute music and refreshment break and listen to your favorite music, undisturbed by studying.

Using Your Study Group

Each week your study group should meet for about 2 hours; that time should be used for studying, not visiting. (You may plan to all go out afterward for an hour to visit, but visiting should be avoided during the study-group time itself.) Groups will need to work out their own study procedures, but here is a schedule that will make the group efficient in studying.

Last Week's Material

1. Each member should have written questions over a part of the material as assigned at the last meeting. During the week, group members should write answers to all question. The study session should begin by trading the written answers to questions and having everyone "grade" someone else's questions. The textbook and notes should be used to ensure accurate grading.

2. A discussion about any difficult concepts or frequently missed questions should follow until everyone understands each answer.

This Week's Material

3. Each group member will have been assigned a topic to "teach" (perhaps a section from the chapter, or from a recent lecture). How you break up the material may depend upon how much the instructor takes out of the book on tests and how much he or she takes out of lecture.

4. Each group member should "teach" the other members his or her assigned material. All group members should feel free both to ask questions and to clarify concepts as each person teaches.

Next Week's Assignments

5. Everyone should have looked at what is coming next week and have an idea about what topic he or she would like to teach next. Part of the assignment will be to write about five questions on the topic; the other part of the assignment will be to prepare to teach it. Study groups may find other procedures that work for them. However, using the group to provide tests for each other is an essential aspect of the study plan. Use of the study group is incorporated into the SPAR system described below

SPAR: A Method of Studying

The SPAR method is a study method that should help you to incorporate the guidelines described above. It was developed by Rusche (1984) and is similar to the SQ3R method (presented in Chapter 7), but it is easier to remember the key words that go with SPAR than with SQ3R (people forget the three Rs). **SPAR** stands for **S**urvey, **P**rocess meaningfully, **A**sk questions, and **R**eview and self-test. Application of this method, with your textbook and study guide, lecture material, and study group, will be described.

Survey

The main goal here is to ask "What am I to learn?" Having a general idea of the topics will help you to tie the material in with concepts that you already know.

Textbook and Study Guide

First, look at the Learning objectives and Outline in this study guide and the information at the beginning of each chapter your book. This gives you an overview of the contents of the chapter. Next, read through the introductory material in the chapter to give you some idea about how the ideas presented in the chapter are relevant in everyday life. At the beginning of each section, there are questions that will be answered in the section. Think about how you would answer them before reading the chapter. There is a Summary at the end of each section. Read each point in the summary and think about what type of information would be needed to understand that point. The last part of each section in the text contains *The message*. These are good summaries of the main points of a chapter.

Lecture

Look at your course outline or syllabus so you know what your instructor will cover each day. Read the relevant material in your textbook before going to class so that you will have the background for the topic.

Study Group

At the end of each weekly meeting, assignments of topics should be made for the next week. Looking over the upcoming material in order to agree on topic assignments will also serve the Survey function in SPAR. Each member should be assigned a specific topic to teach the next week and also to emphasize in writing questions.

Process Meaningfully

The main goal here is to understand the material in a meaningful way, that is, to process it deeply and produce a high level of learning.

Textbook and Study Guide

Read the chapter carefully. Do your first reading of the chapter before your instructor lectures on the topic. Stop and think about what you have read at the end of each section. Don't just try to recite what is in each section-- understanding is critical. Try to relate material to what you already know. Think of other examples of the concepts. If you can form visual images of the concepts, do so. Answer the questions that are asked in the Concept Check sections of each chapter. Try to answer the questions in the Something to Think About sections. Remember, it is better to generate answers than simply to read. If your instructor has assigned more than one section, it would probably be better to work with only one section at a time.

Lecture

Go back over your notes soon after class and put comments in the left column. While the lecture is still fresh in your mind, fill in gaps that you missed and clarify points that are fuzzy in your notes. Try to add some other examples or apply the concepts to other situations, and jot those down in your comments. See the sample notes given earlier.

Study Group

One of the best ways to learn is to teach others. Presenting material to other individuals forces one to process it meaningfully. Each member of the study group will need to process some of the material very meaningfully in order to "teach" the other members. "Knowing" something requires far less processing than "teaching" something. However, everyone should read all of the material and process it meaningfully as described above.

Ask Questions

The goal here is to anticipate the types of questions that you will be asked later, so you will have practice in picking out the main concepts.

<u>Textbook and Study Guide</u>

The study guide will make this portion of SPAR easy because the questions are provided. Complete the module assessments portion of the study guide soon after reading the relevant module. The questions are similar to those that are likely to appear on an objective test. The questions, alternatives, and explanations include the terms that are described at the back of each textbook chapter. Select the answer to each question without looking at your text. Check your answer. If your answer is wrong, write the correct answer and think about why it was the correct answer. Look up the concept on the page in your text indicated beside the correct answer. Write why your answer was wrong. Check your reason against that given in the study guide. If you want to remember the concept better, it is important that you generate the reason rather than simply reading it in the study guide. Also, look at why the other alternatives are wrong to be sure that you understand the concepts tested in the question. If you still do not understand, reread the section of text that is associated with the objective tested in the question. If that does not help, ask your instructor or teaching assistant to explain the concept to you.

<u>Lecture</u>

Go back over your lecture notes. Write questions of the type given under the Short-Answer section of your study guide. Try to write one question for each main point discussed in lecture. It is important that you write the questions, so you can use them later. Be sure that your questions are relevant to the material and that they are not too general, but also not too specific. Examples of good questions over the notes on memory are given below.

Sample Questions from Memory Improvement Lecture

1. *How does the pegword system work? How is it similar to and different from the Method of Loci?*

2. *Describe how the keyword system can be used to remember definitions for abstract words?*

3. *How do all mnemonic systems encourage a deep level of processing?*

4. *In what ways do mnemonic systems work as effective retrieval schemes?*

<u>Study Group</u>

Here's where the study group really comes in. You can answer not only your own questions, but those written by the other members of your group. Each member of the group should be responsible for a specific topic. Part of the responsibility should be to write at least five questions on that topic that could be answered by the other group members. Short-answer questions are probably best. Because you have the study guide with questions covering text material, you should mostly write questions that focus on lecture material. After each group member has "taught" his or her topic, the questions prepared by group members should be passed out. Actually, simply preparing the written questions is a great way to learn.

Review and Self-Test

The main goal here is to test your memory and understanding of the material by answering questions of the type that will appear on a test.

Textbook and Study Guide

Presumably you have already read all of the assigned sections in a chapter and all of the assessments in the study guide. Wait at least 24 hours before going on. This will allow you to forget material that was not processed meaningfully enough. It is important that you find out which material was not well learned before the actual test in your course. Now, return to the study guide. Write out answers to the short-answer essay questions for the chapter. The questions require retrieval from memory with few cues, so that your level of learning can be tested. If you can write answers under these conditions, you know the material well enough to do well on any kind of test. The study guide provides answers to these questions so you can check yourself. It also provides the page in the textbook where the answer appears. Don't simply read the answers. You know by now that generating answers is important for later memory. Once you have checked your answer, keep trying to answer the questions yourself until you can produce a correct answer from memory without the textbook or your notes. Now take the Final Comprehensive Chapter Assessment Test and check your answers using the page references to look up errors.

Lecture

Write answers to the questions that you wrote over lecture material. Check your answers against your notes. If you cannot produce a good answer to a question, get some help. Once you have a good answer to each question, keep trying to produce that answer from memory without using your notes or text.

Study Group

During the week, each group member should write answers to the questions prepared by other group members, as well as those he or she wrote, without looking at the book or notes. This should be done during the week between your meetings. At the beginning of the next meeting, you can exchange your answers, and everyone can "grade" someone else's. The group should discuss errors and make sure that everyone understands the concepts, especially those that were missed on the "test." Groups can also review the other questions and discuss their answers to these questions.

PREPARING FOR TESTS

If you have followed all of the above advice, you will be almost ready for the test when it comes. There should be no need to do massive cramming on the night before the test. However, you should add an extra hour or two to review the material. Use the materials produced in your study group. Take out those short-answer questions that the members of your group wrote and write answers again. Write the answers to the short-answer questions in the study guide again. Spend some time scoring your answers and also look back at your original answers. What have you forgotten this time that you knew before? Have you corrected earlier mistakes, as judged by the answers that were "graded" by your study group? Look over your notes, paying specific attention to your comments. Did you get the answers to issues that you had questions about? Look at the chapter outlines in the study guide and in the textbook.

Can you give a sentence or two explaining each topic? When you know all of the answers well, take the Final Comprehensive Assessment tests for the appropriate chapters without using your book or notes. Score the test. If you made an error, look up the correct answer on the page given. Look back and see if you understood those questions and why the alternatives were wrong. It would be a good idea to review the Final Comprehensive Assessment test questions, the outline in the study guide, and the summary in the text just before you take the test in your course.

Watch Out for Overconfidence

There are many studies in psychology (e.g., Fischhoff, Slovic, & Lichtenstein, 1977) that show that college students tend to be overconfident. This is particularly true when tests are difficult (Schraw & Roedel, 1994). This means that you may go into a test thinking that you know more than you do. One of the best ways to combat overconfidence is to take a practice test that is as similar as possible to the actual test (Glover, 1989). However, make sure that the practice test is very similar; just answering a few questions may not predict how well you will do on an actual test (Maki & Serra, 1992). Probably, the best way to ensure against overconfidence is to take a test that is more demanding than the actual test. For example, if your test will be multiple-choice and you practice with short-answer essays, you probably won't be overconfident because essay tests demand more knowledge than multiple-choice tests. If your actual test will be short-answer essay, then using multiple-choice practice tests to gauge your level of knowledge would not be a good idea. Multiple-choice tests would be fine to use as part of your study, but do not assume that if you get everything correct on a multiple-choice practice test that you will be able to do well on a short-answer essay test. Write some essay questions for yourself or use essay questions produced by your study group, and use your performance on those to judge how well you will do on the actual test. Try to make your practice-test experience as similar as you can to the actual test, and better yet, make your practice-test experience more demanding than the actual test is likely to be.

TAKING TESTS

General Advice for All Types of Tests

<u>Be Prepared and Arrive Early at the Test Site</u>

Have everything that you need for the test. If you are to use a special ID number, make sure that you have found that before the test. If you need to use a special pencil or test booklet, make sure to have those with you. Arrive a few minutes early for the test. If you are allowed to select a seat, find a seat where distractions will be minimal. One way to minimize auditory distractions, even minor ones, is to wear earplugs during the test. In fact, it might be a good idea to wear them while you are studying. If students turn in their tests when they are finished, sit in a place where they will not be walking around you. In an auditorium, the best seats are in the middle of a row where students will not step over you. Don't sit near the place where the tests are to be turned in and don't sit near the door. If other students do begin to leave and you are not finished yet, don't panic. You will be allowed the full test time and if you do the test carefully and check your answers, you will probably need most of the time. Assume that those "early birds" did not know the material and guessed at most of the answers.

<u>Begin the Test By Surveying It</u>

You will probably have a time limit on your test. Still, begin by reading the test instructions and listening to any instructions or corrections given in class. Knowing what you are doing will save time in the end. Get an idea of how long the test is. Make sure that you have all the pages by checking that the question numbers are sequential.

Ask Questions

If you really don't understand a question, either put up your hand or walk up and ask the instructor or teaching assistant. Don't just answer the question based on one interpretation when there is another reasonable interpretation. Ask for clarification. If you don't know a word in a question, ask for a definition. If it is a word that you should know, your instructor probably won't give you the definition, but it doesn't hurt to ask.

Pace Yourself

If the room does not have a clock, wear a watch. Allow yourself enough time to finish the test. For example, if you are supposed to answer 50 questions in 50 minutes, you should average no more than 1 minute per question. Periodically, check yourself to be sure that your pace is right.

Don't Cheat

Learning the material in your courses will have lifelong benefits to you. The knowledge that you gain from your college courses will allow you to better understand and solve a lifetime's worth of problems. Doing well on tests by looking at your "brilliant" friend's answers or by using cheat sheets will gyp you of useful knowledge. Cheating also degrades the value of an education for everyone. If college graduates have not learned the knowledge expected of them because they cheated, the value of a college education is lessened. Furthermore, most universities have severe penalties for cheating. You could fail the test, fail the course, or even be suspended from school. So, don't be tempted to cheat. Instead, learn the material, and there is no need to consider being dishonest.

Taking Multiple-Choice Tests

Watch the Wording of Questions

Words like always and never mean there are no exceptions. Something always occurs or it never occurs. Such alternatives are usually (although not always) wrong. Few facts in psychology are that absolute.

Pick the Best Answer

One answer may be correct under most circumstances and another answer may be correct under a more general set of circumstances. Select the answer that is most generally correct and that has the fewest exceptions. If you can, before reading the possible answers, write down what you think the answer is. That way when you go to the possible answers you will already have an idea of what you think the correct answer should be. Don't immediately choose a, if a seems correct. Answer b may be correct also and perhaps even better. You are supposed to choose the best answer, not just one that is partly or possibly correct. Also, some instructors use double-answer questions. Both **a** and **b** may be correct and the correct answer is e, both a and b. Always read all of the alternatives before selecting the best one.

Watch for Negative Questions

Read the question carefully and note if it contains a negative, such as "not" or "isn't." Many students miss that little word and select an alternative that is true. What they don't notice is that the question asked the student to select the alternative that is <u>not</u> true. Allow yourself some extra time to answer "not" questions and be sure to double-check your answer carefully.

Mark out Incorrect Alternatives

Read each question and mark off the alternatives that you know are wrong. Don't be hasty about this. Read each alternative carefully, filling it in as the answer. If you're sure the answer is wrong, mark it out. Then, select the best choice among the items you did not eliminate.

Skip the Difficult Questions

If you are not certain about your answer, skip the question and go back to it later when you will know how much time you can afford to spend on it. (But don't forget to come back to the ones you omitted!)

Avoid Interference from Incorrect Alternatives

Research on memory has shown that it is sometimes harder to recognize (select) an answer that is embedded in other similar answers than to simply recall it from memory (Tulving & Thomson, 1973). Thus, for those difficult questions that you skipped, you might do better to turn the multiple-choice test into a short-answer test. When you go back to those questions, cover the alternatives and try to write what you think should be the correct answer. Then, look at the alternatives that you haven't eliminated as being wrong, and see which one best matches what you wrote. Choose that answer.

Make your Best Guess

After you have gone through the test twice and eliminated wrong alternatives, make your best guess among the remaining choices. Because you have already marked out alternatives that you know are wrong, your chance of getting the question correct has improved. It's 50% if there are only two remaining alternatives.

Don't Pay Attention to Patterns

Instructors usually don't look at the pattern of correct answers until after the test is printed. Some intentionally use a random-number sequence to determine the order of answers, so it's possible that the correct answer might be the same alternative on many consecutive questions, or that the correct answers might accidentally form some pattern. Select the best answer for each item and don't worry if there seems to be too many of one alternative or if the alternatives form a pattern.

Put your Answers on the Answer Sheet Carefully

If your answers need to go on a special answer sheet, it is probably a good idea to wait until you have circled the answers to all questions before transferring them to the answer sheet. Make sure that you are on the right question as you mark the answer sheet. After you have transferred your answers, take an extra minute to check to ensure that the circled answer for each question is what you placed on the answer sheet.

Check your Answers

When you finish, if you have time available, check your answers to each question. You may catch some mistakes.

Taking Essay Tests

Take a Few Minutes to Read all the Questions

This is particularly important if your instructor allows you to choose which of several questions you can answer. Look over all the questions and make a decision about which item you know the best. Start by answering your best questions. They will go quickly and allow you to build confidence.

Outline your Answers

Many essay questions have several parts. Jot down each part. Some instructors grade by assigning specific numbers of points to specific parts of the essay. Whether or not this is the case with your instructor, you will probably get more credit for your answer if you specifically address each point in your answer. It is probably a good idea to write a short heading and underline it for each part. This will force you to organize your answer in line with the question and it will also make grading easier for your instructor. He or she will see that you have answered all parts.

Don't Add Irrelevant Material

The point of essay answers is not to write everything you know that is tangentially related to a topic. The point is to write what you know that is directly related to the topic. Going off on tangents won't impress the graders with your knowledge. Such extraneous material is likely to annoy them because they have to search for the correct answer. Make it easy for graders by just giving relevant information in an organized form.

Don't Answer Questions that Weren't Asked

This is related to the irrelevant material discussed above. If you really know nothing about a topic, then you are in trouble and, chances are, you have not followed the guidelines listed above. Don't try to weasel out by answering some question other than what was asked. Write whatever you know about the topic and leave it at that. And study harder the next time!

Write Legibly

Some instructors simply give up if they have difficulty reading an answer (and they are unlikely to assume that the correct answer is really there without reading it). Thus, try to write as legibly as possible. If you have poor handwriting, try printing your answers or try to write larger than usual. Whatever you can do to make your handwriting more legible will help you in the long run.

Taking Matching Tests

Understand the Rules

The most important point here is to understand the rules of the matching tests. If your instructor did not tell you, then ask. (You do have a right to know the constraints on the test.) Is each alternative used only once, or can some be used multiple times? Is there, in fact, a match for each item? Find out these things before you start.

Write in the Answers that You Know

The whole matching item might look overwhelming, but once you have written answers that you are sure of, you may do much better on the rest. This is much easier if each alternative is used only once. You can simply cross off those that you are sure of and you greatly reduce the number that you need to use for the remaining items. If alternatives can be used more than once, then you might look for items that are similar to those that you know and put in the same alternatives.

Work with one item at a time

Take a single item on the matching test and compare it with each alternative individually. You might even put the number of the item beside an alternative if you think it might match. Then go through those that you have put the item number beside and make it a multiple-choice test. Mark out the alternatives that seem less likely until you are left with only one in ideal circumstances, or more in less-than-ideal circumstances. If you cannot decide among several alternatives, simply guess. You have already improved your chances by eliminating many of the potential match items.

Taking Online Tests

Special Considerations

Many instructors are moving to some form of web-based or online testing. Taking web-based tests are similar to traditional paper and pencil tests, but they do present some unique challenges. First, you should familiarize yourself with the testing process and procedures associated with the system. Your instructor may offer a "practice" or "fun" quiz which does not count towards your grade so that you can become familiar with the process. Second, most online tests have time limits associated with them. You should always be aware of the amount of time remaining. Some systems will update the timing only when each question is answered. For example, after submitting your answer to a question the clock may show the time remaining as 24:55 and this will be displayed until you submit your next answer. If you then take 2:35 seconds to answer the next question when you submit your answer the clock will change from 24:55 to 22:20. This method of timing can be disconcerting if you are not familiar with it. Other systems will keep a real time clock. That is, it will display the second by second countdown while you are answering your question. Related to timing is the submission of your test. Some systems will not allow you to submit your test AFTER the time has ended. Thus, you need to keep track of how much time you have left. Third, make sure you have "saved" your answers and any changed answers before submitting your test. Finally, make sure you have a reliable connection to the internet before starting a test. Check with your instructor regarding how to handle testing issues and problems.

Learn from Your Errors

Use the Pre-Test and Post-Test

In preparing for a test a very effective method is to take the Pre-Test available at the Student Companion Site. Based on your performance a study plan will be developed for you. Using the study plan you can revisit topics you need to master. Following your studying you can then reassess yourself with the Post-Test to determine whether you have mastered the material. There are also several other online quizzes available at the same website.

Understand Your Wrong Answers

Always look over your test when you get it back (or go and look at the key if your instructor posts one). Check your test and make yourself aware of which items you have gotten right and which are wrong. Don't be "sick of it" and not look at a test after it's over and graded. The test provides a great learning experience, particularly if your instructor gives a cumulative final. The material that you missed will probably be back on the final, so keep your tests to study for the final exam.

Use the Test Experience to Analyze Your Study Plan

If you met your goal on the test, then you know that you are studying appropriately. Keep doing what you have been doing; your study plan works! If you did worse than you realistically expected, then you either need to change your study plan, find more time for study, or change your goal. Changing your study plan should be the first step. Go back over your plan and see whether you could use some of your time more efficiently. Is your study group working or do they spend half the study time visiting? Are you really using those hours between classes? Are you following through on your study plan? For example, are you writing answers to questions or are you just looking at them and assuming that you know them? When you make an error on a question while studying, are you going back to really understand why you were wrong and why another answer is correct? If you really are giving the course all the time that you can and if you really have an efficient study plan that you are following, you may have to reset your goals. Perhaps, getting an A in the course is not realistic. Change your expectations to settle for a B (but don't settle for much less--there is always a way to improve your study plan).

IF YOU HAVE PROBLEMS

There are a number of things to do if you find you are not doing as well on your tests as you wish. Visit your instructor or your teaching assistant during office hours. They may have some specific ideas about how you can do better in the course you are taking. Don't be afraid to go to your instructor's office during office hours. Even when they are teaching large classes, most instructors are alone during office hours. Students rarely go to see them. Even if things aren't going badly, you should always feel free to visit your instructor and discuss either your progress in the course or an issue that is of interest to you. If you still have problems with a course, try your university's counseling center. They have a staff who is trained to help you. Use them, even if your problem is not severe. You probably have an advisor who can help you also. Go and talk with him or her when you begin to have difficulty. Find out about your school's drop policy. Can you still drop the course that is causing the problems without penalty? If you are overloaded (which you should know before classes start when you make up your schedule), drop the excess courses immediately. Don't think that you will start with more courses than you have time for and later drop the worst one. By that time, you have already spread yourself too thin and hurt your performance in all of your courses. Set up a reasonable load and then stick with it.

FINAL NOTE

It is true that all of this takes a long time. However, learning a great deal of new material, as is necessary in any college-level course, is not easy. The procedures suggested here will make you much more efficient than if you simply read and reread your text. These studying techniques will pay off, and as you get better at using them, they will become easier. The key point in all of this is to BE ACTIVE. The less time you spend passively reading and the more time you spend actively generating answers and testing yourself, the better you will do on tests in your course. And generating answers makes studying much more interesting than simply reading and reading and reading. The topics covered in this textbook are exciting and useful in everyday life. May you learn them well and use them for your entire lifetime!

REFERENCES

Bahrick, H. P., Bahrick, L. E., Bahrick, A. S., and Bahrick, P. E. (1993). Maintenance of foreign language vocabulary and the spacing effect. *Psychological Science, 4,* 316-322.

Balch, W. R., Bowman, K., and Mohler, L. A. (1992). Music-dependent memory in immediate and delayed word recall. *Memory and Cognition, 20,* 21-28.

Bransford, J. D., and Johnson, M. K. (1973). Consideration of some problems of comprehension. In William G. Chase (Ed.), *Visual information processing.* New York: Academic Press.

Boyce, T. E., & Hineline, P.N. (2002). Interteaching: A strategy for enhancing the user-friendliness of behavioral arrangements in the college classroom. *The Behavior Analyst, 25,* 215-226.

Craik, F. I. M., and Tulving, E. (1975). Depth of processing and the retention of words in episodic memory. *Journal of Experimental Psychology: General, 104,* 268-294.

Craik, F. I. M., and Watkins, M. J. (1973). The role of rehearsal in short-term memory. *Journal of Verbal Learning and Verbal Behavior, 12,* 599-607.

Cull, W. L., Shaughnessy, J. J., & Zechmeister, E. B. (1996). Expanding understanding of the expanding-pattern-of-retrieval mnemonic: Toward confidence in applicability. *Journal of Experimental Psychology: Applied, 2,* 365-378.

Druckman, D., and Bjork, R. A. (Eds.). (1994). *Learning, remembering, believing: Enhancing human performance.* Washington, D. C.: National Academy Press.

Fischhoff, B., Slovic, P., and Lichtenstein, S. (1977). Knowing with certainty: The appropriateness of extreme confidence. *Journal of Experimental Psychology: Human Perception and Performance, 3,* 552-564.

Foos, P. W., Mora, J. J., Tkacz, S. (1994). Student study techniques and the generation effect. *Journal of Educational Psychology, 86,* 567-576.

Furnham, A., & Bradley, A. (1997). Music while you work: The differential distraction of background music on the cognitive test performance of introverts and extraverts. *Applied Cognitive Psychology, 11,* 445-455.

Glover, J. A. (1989). Improving readers' estimates of learning from text: The role of inserted questions. *Reading Research Quarterly, 28,* 68-75.

Greenwald, A. G., Spangenberg, E. R., Pratkanis, A. R., and Eskenazi, J. (1991). Double-blind tests of subliminal self-help audiotapes. *Psychological Science, 2,* 119-122.

Haenggi, D., and Perfetti, C. A. (1992). Individual differences in reprocessing of text. *Journal of Educational Psychology, 84,* 182-192.

Jacoby, L. L. (1978). On interpreting the effects of repetition: Solving problems versus remembering solutions. *Journal of Verbal Learning and Verbal Behavior, 17,* 649-667.

Krueger, W. C. F. (1929). The effects of overlearning on retention. *Journal of Experimental Psychology, 12,* 71-78.

Krug, D., Davis, T. B., and Glover, J. A. (1990). Massed versus distributed repeated reading: A case of forgetting helping recall? *Journal of Educational Psychology, 82,* 366-371.

Linden, M., and Wittrock, M. C. (1981). The teaching of reading comprehension according to the model of generative learning. *Reading Research Quarterly, 17,* 45-57.

Locke, E. A., and Latham, G. P. (1990). *A theory of goal setting and task performance.* New York: Prentice-Hall.

McDaniel, M. A., Einstein, G. O., DeLosh, E. L., May, C. P., Brady, P. (1995). The bizarreness effect: It's not surprising, it's complex. *Journal of Experimental Psychology: Learning, Memory, and Cognition, 21,* 422-425.

Maki, R. H., and Serra, M. (1992). Role of practice tests in the prediction of test performance over text material. *Journal of Educational Psychology, 84,* 200-210.

Melton, A. W. (1970). The situation with respect to the spacing of repetitions and memory. *Journal of Verbal Learning and Verbal Behavior, 9,* 596-606.

Nitsch, K. E. (1977). Structuring de-contextualized forms of knowledge. (Doctoral dissertation, Vanderbilt University) as cited in J. D. Bransford. (1979). *Human cognition.* Belmont, Calif.: Wadsworth.

Paivio, A., Walsh, M., and Bons, T. (1994). Concreteness effects on memory: When and why? *Journal of Experimental Psychology: Learning, Memory, and Cognition, 20,* 1196-124.

Riefer, D. M.; & LaMay, M. L. (1998). Memory for common and bizarre stimuli: A storage-retrieval analysis. *Psychonomic Bulletin & Review, 5,* 312-317.

Runquist, W. (1983). Some effects of remembering on forgetting. *Memory and Cognition,, 11,* 641-650.

Rusche, K. M. (1984). The effectiveness of study skills training for students of different personality types and achievement levels. (Doctoral dissertation, Loyola University).

Saufley, W. H., Jr., Otaka, S. R., and Bavaresco, J. L. (1985). Context effects: Classroom tests and context independence. *Memory and Cognition, 13,* 522-528.

Schraw, G., and Roedel, T. D. (1994). Test difficulty and judgment bias. *Memory and Cognition, 22,* 63-69.

Smith, S. M., Glenberg, A., and Bjork, R. A. (1978). Environmental context and human memory. *Memory and Cognition, 6,* 342-353.

Tulving, E., and Thomson, D. M. (1973). Encoding specificity and retrieval processes in episodic memory. *Psychological Review, 80,* 352-373.

Van Meter, P., Yokoi, L., Pressley, M. (1994). College students' theory of note-taking derived from their perceptions of note-taking. *Journal of Educational Psychology, 86,* 323-338.

CHAPTER 1

WHAT IS PSYCHOLOGY?

CHAPTER OVERVIEW INFORMATION

LEARNING OBJECTIVES

By the end of Chapter 1 you should

- ✓ Be capable of defining psychology as a science
- ✓ Be interested in learning about psychology
- ✓ Be aquainted with the history of psychology as a science
- ✓ Be informed about recent trends and developments in psychology
- ✓ Be capable of understanding the philosphical themes of Mind/Body, Nature/Nurture, and Free Will/Determinism

CHAPTER 1 OUTLINE

Chapter 1 provides the foundation for your understanding of the entire text. Topics explored in Chapter 1 include the Philosphical Issues in Psychology, What Psychologists Do, and the History of Psychology.

Chapter 1 is presented below in outline format to assist you in understanding the information presented in the chapter. More detailed information on any topic can be found using the page references to the right of the topic.

Module 1.1 The Goals of Psychology

I. Psychology had its start in philosophy, and some philosophical issues are still important in psychology (p. 4)
    A. Free will vs. determinism (p. 5)
        1. Does behavior have predictable natural causes or are some choices unpredictable? (pp. 5-6)
    B. Mind-brain problem (p. 6)
        1. How does brain activity relate to behavior and experience? (p. 7)
    C. Nature-nurture issue (p. 7)
        1. Are differences in behavior due to heredity or environment? (p. 8)

II. What psychologists do (p. 8, Figure 1.4)
    A. Some psychologists teach and do research in universities (p. 8)
        1. Biopsychologists are interested in the nervous system, effects of drugs and hormones, genetics, effects of brain damage, and drugs (p. 8)
        2. Psychologists interested in learning and motivation focus on how the outcomes of past behavior affects present behavior (p. 9)
        3. Cognitive psychologists study how people think and acquire knowledge (p. 10)
        4. Developmental psychologists study behavioral capacities typical of different ages (p. 10)
        5. Social psychologists study how individuals influence each other (p. 10)
    B. Clinical psychologists and psychotherapists usually work in practice settings (p. 11)
        1. Clinical psychologists specialize in understanding and helping people with problems (p. 11)
        2. Psychiatrists are medical doctors who deal with emotional disturbance (p. 11)
        3. Psychoanalysts emphasize the methods of Freud (p. 11)

C. There are other types of non-clinical applied psychologists (p. 11, Table. 1.1)
    1. Industrial/organizational psychologists study people at work (p. 12)
    2. Ergonomics (human factors) psychologists study people-machine interactions (p.13)
    3. School psychologists deal with the psychology of students (p. 13)

III. Psychology is a good major to prepare for many careers (p. 14)
    A. Women receive over half of the doctorates in psychology (p. 15)
    B. Minority representation in psychology is growing, but the percentage is still small (p. 15)

The message: *Psychologists do very different things but they are dedicated to understanding psychological processes through research. (p. 15)*

Module 1.2 Psychology Then and Now
IV. The early era of psychology was 1879 to 1920 (p. 17)
    A. Wundt founded the first psychology laboratory in 1879 (p. 17)
        1. Psychological experience is composed of compounds (p. 17)
    B. Titchener tried to describe the structures of mind (p. 19)
    C. William James focused on how the mind produces useful behavior (p. 20)
    D. Early psychologists studied psychophysics, the relationship between perceived stimulus intensity and actual physical intensity (p. 20)
    E. Darwin's theory spurred the study of animal intelligence (p. 20)
    F. Galton focused on human intelligence (p. 22)

The message: *Psychologists don't have all the answers but they continue to search through research. (p. 25)*

RELATED WEBSITES AND ACTIVITIES
Visit http://psychology.wadsworth.com/kalat_intro7e/ for text online quizzing, glossary flashcards, crossword puzzles, annotated web links, and more.

LECTURE MATERIAL
Information from the text is only half of the picture. Don't forget to review your lecture material. Process each topic meaningfully. Most importantly, be sure that you understand the material in each lecture-if you don't, ask your instructor or teaching assistant.

**STUDY TIP # 1: Each chapter is divided into smaller sections called modules. Instead of reading the entire chapter in the text at one time, read one module at a time. Then complete the same module in the study guide. Then repeat for each subsequent module.

**TIP: Associate the lecture material with the information from the text, with things that you already know, with your personal experiences, or with real-life applications. Type or neatly re-write your notes. Make sure they are detailed and organized. Make comments on your notes. Then write questions to cover each concept.

Module 1.1 The Goals of Psychology
Answer these questions soon after reading the **Module 1.1: The Goals of Psychology**. There are several formats to the assessments. Answers to all questions appear on pp. 12-15.

Fill in the Blank
Provide a term(s) which best completes the statement below. Answers appear on p. 12.

1. _____ psychology is the study of people at work.

2. The idea that the mind is somehow separate from the brain but controls the brain and therefore the rest of the body is known as _____.

3. A _____ psychologist studies how we think and acquire knowledge.

4. _____ is the belief that behavior is caused by a person's independent decisions.

5. _____ psychologists usually work with students in kindergarten through 12th grade to identify their educational needs and develop plans to meet them.

6. A _____ tries to explain behavior in terms of biological factors such as brain activity and genetics.

7. _____ psychologists study human behavior from "womb to tomb" or the behavioral capacities typical of different ages and how behavior changes with age.

8. _____ psychologists usually have a Ph.D. or a Psy.D. and specialize in understanding and helping people with psychological problems.

Short Answer
The following questions require a short written answer (3-7 sentences). Answers appear on pp. 12-13.

1. Explain how chaos theory can explain apparently unpredictable events.

2. Research studies cannot solve the mind-brain problem, but they can shed light on it. How?

3. Some psychological disorders are more common in large cities than in the country. Describe how the nature and the nurture viewpoints might explain this.

4. How do biopsychologists and cognitive psychologists differ?

5. How does the approach taken by learning psychologists differ from the approach taken by social psychologists?

6. Describe how the acceptance of women in psychology has changed from the 1890s to today.

7. Describe the types of settings in which psychologists work.

Multiple Choice
Circle the best answer below. Check your answers on pp. 13-14. If your answer was incorrect, try to write why it was incorrect. Check your reasons on pp. 13-14.

1. Psychology is the systematic study of:
   a. conscious thought
   b. human behavior
   c. abnormal behavior
   d. behavior and experience
   e. techniques for manipulating and tricking people

2. According to determinism:
   a. choices cannot be predicted
   b. unpredictability implies a lack of causes
   c. everything people do has a physical cause
   d. much of human behavior is caused by random factors
   e. physical events have natural causes, but human decisions are guided by free will

3. What do research studies, such as those measuring brain activity, say about the mind-brain problem?
   a. they show how mind controls the brain
   b. they constrain the answers that philosophers can give to this problem
   c. they show that mind and brain are two names for the same thing
   d. they indicate the independence of mind and brain
   e. they show that brain activity causes thoughts

4. A researcher attempts to determine whether a personality trait is inherited or learned. Which philosophical issue is she addressing?
   a. nature vs. nurture
   b. chaos theory versus indeterminism
   c. free will vs. determinism
   d. mind-brain problem

5. What does a biopsychologist study?
   a. the influence of the nervous system, drugs, genetics, and brain damage on behavior
   b. thinking and acquiring knowledge
   c. behavioral capabilities at different ages
   d. the influence of experience on behavior

6. A psychologist taking which approach would argue that "people differ from one another because some of them know more than others about a particular topic"?
   a. social
   b. clinical
   c. behavioral neuroscientist
   d. cognitive

7. A child's parents believe that boys are aggressive. Indeed, the son is aggressive. To what would a social psychologist attribute the child's aggressiveness?
   a. the child is living up to (or down to) the expectations of his parents
   b. the child's behavior is part of his nature
   c. the child has been rewarded for past aggression
   d. the child has some subtle damage in a specific part of the brain

8. Which type of psychologist would try to help a person who has emotional difficulties?
   a. human factors psychologist
   b. developmental psychologist
   c. clinical psychologist
   d. school psychologist

9. Dr. Psyche has an M.D. degree and his specialty is helping people with emotional problems. He sometimes prescribes drugs for his patients. He is a:
   a. clinical psychologist
   b. psychiatrist
   c. psychoanalyst
   d. experimental psychologist

10. Women constitute:
    a. 16% of all psychologists
    b. just over 80% of all graduate students in psychology
    c. over 65% of all graduate students in psychology
    d. less than 30% of all psychologists, and the number is declining

True/False
Select the best answer by circling *T for True* or *F for False*. Check your answers on pp. 14-15.

1. **T or F** Determinism suggests that we can make choices independent of external causes.

2. **T or F** An evolutionary psychologist would examine sexual jealousy in males in terms of the evolutionary history of humans.

3. **T or F** Women comprise a majority of the Psychologists in North America receiving Ph.D.s

4. **T or F** Forensic psychologists provide assistance in understanding behavior by examining autopsy reports.

5. **T or F** Counseling psychologists help people understand psychological problems.

6. **T or F** The daily activities of a cognitive psychologist, a clinical psychologist, an ergonomist, and an industrial/organizational psychologist have a lot in common.

7. **T or F** During the history of psychology, researchers' opinions have remained constant about what constitutes an interesting, important, and answerable question.

8. **T or F** One of the major differences between clinical psychologists and psychiatrists is that only clinical psychologists can prescribe medication to treat psychological problems.

Module 1.2 Psychology Then and Now
Answer these questions soon after reading the **Module 1.2: Psychology Then and Now**.
There are several formats to the assessments. Answers to all questions appear on pp. 15-17.

Fill in the Blank
Provide a term(s) which best completes the statement below. Answers appear on p. 15.

1. _____ set up the first psychology laboratory in Leipzig, Germany.

2. _____ is generally considered the father of American psychology. His interests were in the area of how the mind produces useful behavior.

3. While _____ popularized psychotherapy, his methods are far less popular today and have mostly been replaced by other methods.

4. _____ is credited with systemizing the approach to behaviorism, popularizing it, and stating its assumptions.

5. In 1905 Binet developed one of the first functional _____ tests.

Chapter 1

6. Edward Tichener developed the study of _____ which was an attempt to describe the structures of the mind.

7. _____ psychology compares the behavior of people from various cultures.

8. Specialists who compare the behaviors of different animal species are known as _____ psychologists.

9. _____ is the field of psychology that concentrates on observable and measurable processes.

Short Answer

The following questions require a short written answer (3-7 sentences). Answers appear on pp. 15-16.

1. Describe the approach taken by most psychologists from about 1920 to 1970.

2. Why did early psychologists study sensation?

3. Describe the term "functionalism" and give an example of what may be of interest to a psychologist working within the functional approach.

4. Why has cross-cultural study become so important in psychology?

5. Explain why Edward Titchener's research methods were virtually abandoned after his death in 1927.

6. What did Darwin contribute to the field of psychology?

7. Why were early psychologists so interested in sensation?

Multiple Choice
Circle the best answer below. Check your answers on p. 16. If your answer was incorrect, try to write why it was incorrect. Check your reasons on p. 16.

1. Wundt's main question was:
   a. what are the components of experience?
   b. can questions about mind be answered philosophically?
   c. how does the mind produce useful behavior?
   d. how do the consequences of behavior strengthen behavior?
   e. why do some men become eminent?

2. How did Darwin's theory affect psychology?
   a. his work showed Hull that mathematical equations could be used to describe learning
   b. his finding that physical stimuli and perceived stimuli are not directly proportional began the study of psychophysics
   c. his work implied that animals have intelligence, and comparative psychologists began to study it
   d. his work showed that it was easy to measure animal intelligence
   e. women were finally allowed to earn Ph.D. degrees because of his theory

3. Wilhelm Wundt is known for:
   a. studying rats in mazes
   b. being the founder of behaviorism
   c. setting up the first psychology laboratory
   d. asking whether intellectual variations were based on heredity
   e. being the founder of American psychology

4. Who was among the first investigators to try to measure intelligence and to ask whether intellectual variations were based on heredity?
   a. John B. Watson
   b. Clark Hull
   c. Francis Galton
   d. William James

5. The mathematical description of the relationship between the physical property of a stimulus and its perceived properties is called _____.
   a. cognition
   b. functionalism
   c. psychophysical function
   d. the principle of compatibility

6. William James preferred to learn how the mind produces useful behaviors. His approach was termed?
   a. introspection
   b. principle of compatibility
   c. functionalism
   d. cross-cultural study

True/False
Select the best answer by circling *T for True* or *F for False*. Check your answers on p. 17.

1. **T or F** Behaviorism is a field of psychology that concentrates on observable, measurable behaviors and not on mental processes.

2. **T or F** Cross-cultural study has become increasingly influential in modern psychology.

3. **T or F** Wilhelm Wundt studied changes in participants' experiences by using introspection.

4. **T or F** The perceived intensity of a stimulus is directly proportional to the actual physical intensity of a stimulus.

5. **T or F** William James's book *The Principles of Psychology* defined the questions that dominated psychology for years afterward and even to some extent today.

6. **T or F** Charles Darwin revolutionized and popularized psychotherapy with his methods of analyzing patients' dreams and memories.

FINAL COMPREHENSIVE CHAPTER ASSESSMENT TEST

Check your answers on p. 17.

1. Psychology is best defined as the study of:
   a. abnormality
   b. social influences
   c. consciousness
   d. human behavior
   e. behavior and experience

2. Prof. R is engaged in a debate with Prof. S. Prof. R argues that people are free to make choices and that their choices are unpredictable. Prof. S argues that choices are made because of past experience and that each choice could be predicted if we knew enough. Prof. R's arguments support _____ and Prof. S's arguments support _____.
   a. free will; determinism
   b. mind controls brain; brain controls mind
   c. determinism; free will
   d. brain controls mind; mind controls brain
   e. nurture; nature

3. Boys generally spend more time playing with toy guns and trucks than girls do. Which of the following reasons for this is consistent with the <u>nature</u> point of view?
   a. boys watch more violent television shows than girls do
   b. boys like to do what their fathers do and many fathers use guns and trucks
   c. boys have genes that make them prefer such toys
   d. society discourages girls from playing with such toys
   e. boys are given such toys so they have more opportunities to play with them

4. A clinical psychologist is:
   a. the same as a psychiatrist
   b. the same as a psychoanalyst
   c. any psychologist with a Ph.D.
   d. a psychologist who helps people with emotional problems
   e. any psychologist who administers and interprets tests

5. A psychoanalyst:
   a. is the same as a clinical psychologist
   b. is the same as a psychiatrist
   c. adheres to Freud's methods and theories
   d. has fewer years of formal training than a clinical psychologist
   e. always hold the Ph.D. degree

6. How is a psychologist different from a psychiatrist?
   a. there is no difference
   b. psychiatrists deal with helping people; psychologists do research in universities
   c. psychiatrists have M.D. degrees; psychologists have Ph.D. degrees
   d. psychologists use methods developed by Freud; psychiatrists do not
   e. psychologists can prescribe drugs; psychiatrists cannot

7. Which type of psychologist would be most interested in the genetic makeup of an individual?
   a. cognitive
   b. behaviorist
   c. biological
   d. psychoanalytic
   e. clinical

8. A child is constantly in trouble at school for disrupting the class. How would a learning psychologist view this situation?
   a. there is conflict in the child's home, and he unconsciously wants to hurt his parents
   b. the child may have damage to a specific part of his brain
   c. the child's diet is lacking in essential minerals and vitamins
   d. the child only receives attention (which is reinforcing) when he is disruptive
   e. other students expect the child to be disruptive, so he is

9. A psychologist believes that differences between males and females are due to society's expectations about how boys and girls behave. This psychologist takes which viewpoint?
   a. social
   b. cognitive
   c. physiological
   d. clinical
   e. behaviorist

10. African Americans, Hispanics, Asian Americans, and other minorities constitute:
    a. about 16% of all doctorates in psychology
    b. about 50% of all psychologists
    c. 25% of all clinical psychologists
    d. about 50% of all doctorates in clinical psychology
    e. 5% of all psychologists today, but the percentage is declining

11. What was Wundt's most lasting impact on psychology?
    a. his discovery that it takes time to shift attention
    b. he set the precedent for studying psychological questions with scientific data
    c. he correctly described the elements of mind
    d. he made self-observation into an exact science
    e. he mapped out the psychophysical functions relating psychology to physical stimuli

12. Mary Calkins, the first woman psychologist:
    a. received her Ph.D. degree from Harvard
    b. was never allowed to attend graduate classes
    c. performed poorly on her final examination for the Ph.D., so she never received her Ph.D.
    d. never received her Ph.D. because Harvard would not grant a Ph.D. to a woman
    e. completed a Ph.D. at Harvard, but was unable to find a job because she was a woman

13. How does the psychology advocated by the behaviorists differ from the psychology advocated by the structuralists?
    a. the behaviorists were more interested in sensation than the structuralists
    b. the behaviorists emphasized the study of animal intelligence, and the structuralists developed a psychology of human intelligence
    c. the behaviorists developed mathematical models of intelligence, and the structuralists developed nonmathematical models
    d. behaviorists emphasized learning, and the structuralists emphasized sensation

14. A researcher is trying to understand cognitive processing of stimuli by examining PET scans. The answers she finds will likely add to clarifying
    a. the mind/brain problem
    b. the nature/nurture problem
    c. the free will/determinism problem
    d. the psychology/philosophy problem

15. If you need assistance with your mental health due to stress in your life. Which of the following are you least likely to get some assistance from?
    a. psychiatrist
    b. clinical psychologist
    c. clinical social worker
    d. developmental psychologist

ANSWERS AND EXPLANATIONS FOR CHAPTER MODULE ASSESSMENTS

Answers to the Fill in the Blank Questions – Module 1.1

1. Industrial/Organizational (p. 12)

2. dualism (p. 6)

3. Cognitive (p. 10)

4. Free will (p. 5)

5. School (p. 13)

6. biopsychologist (p. 8)

7. Developmental (p. 10)

8. Clinical (p. 11)

Answers to the Short Answer Questions – Module 1.1

1. Researchers can look for links between behavior and brain activity. For example, studies using PET scans show that different tasks result in different patterns of brain activity. This puts constraints on how philosophers should think about the mind-body problem. (p. 7)

2. *Nature:* People have a genetic predisposition to the psychological disorder. As the disorder worsens, they move to the big city to find a job and use the welfare services. *Nurture:* Life in crowded, impersonal cities causes the psychological disorder. (p. 8)

3. Psychologists with Ph.D. degrees may concentrate in many different areas. One type of psychologist, a clinical psychologist, usually works with people who have emotional problems. Psychiatrists have M.D. degrees, but they are only psychoanalysts if they complete specialized training at an institute of psychoanalysis. Relatively few clinical psychologists and psychiatrists are psychoanalysts. (pp. 8-9)

4. The biological psychologist looks for relationships between the nervous system and other biological systems and behavior. The cognitive psychologist studies the specific thought processes and knowledge necessary to perform various tasks. (pp. 8-10)

5. The learning psychologist is interested in studying observable behavior. Behavior occurs because of what consequences follow it in a given situation. The social psychologist stresses the role of others in influencing behavior. Social norms and expectations are important. (pp. 9-11)

6. In 1895, Mary Calkins completed her graduate work at Harvard University, but they would not grant a Ph.D. to a woman. Today, women receive over two thirds of the psychology Ph.D.s. (pp. 15, 24).

7. The largest percentage of psychologists work in settings that provide health care, such as hospitals, clinics, and independent private practices. A little over 33% work in academic institutions, including colleges, universities, and medical schools. Others work in a variety of settings: businesses, government, schools, and counseling centers. (p. 9, Fig. 1.4)

Answers to the Multiple Choice Questions – Module 1.1

1. a. Incorrect. Unconscious thought is studied too, especially by psychoanalysts
    b. Incorrect. Animals are studied, especially by biological psychologists
    c. Incorrect. Normal behavior is studied too, e.g., do people have several kinds of memory
    d. Correct! (p. 3)
    e. Incorrect. Psychologists try to understand why people act as they do, not to develop techniques for tricking them

2. a. Incorrect. If enough could be known, choices would be predictable
    b. Incorrect. Many small causes may result in complex effects that seem unpredictable
    c. Correct! (pp. 5-6)
    d. Incorrect. Causes are not random; they are orderly and can be known
    e. Incorrect. Determinism says that human behavior results from predictable causes

3. a. Incorrect. Research cannot resolve the mind-brain problem
    b. Correct! (pp. 6-7)
    c. Incorrect. Research cannot resolve the mind-brain problem
    d. Incorrect. Research cannot resolve the mind-brain problem
    e. Incorrect. Research cannot resolve the mind-brain problem

4. a. Correct! (p. 8)
    b. Incorrect. Asks whether apparently unpredictable events result from many small causes
    c. Incorrect. Asks whether behavior has identifiable causes
    d. Incorrect. Studies the relationship between mind and brain

5. a. Correct! (p. 8)
   b. Incorrect. Cognitive psychologist
   c. Incorrect. Developmental psychologist
   d. Incorrect. Learning psychologist

6. a. Incorrect. Would emphasize influence of others, not knowledge
   b. Incorrect. Emphasizes emotional influences, not knowledge
   c. Incorrect. Would emphasize biological influences, not knowledge
   d. Correct! (p. 9)

7. a. Correct! (pp. 10-11)
   b. Incorrect. It is not part of his inherited traits, it is probably learned
   c. Incorrect. A learning explanation in terms of consequences
   d. Incorrect. This is a biological explanation

8. a. Incorrect. Studies interactions between humans and machines
   b. Incorrect. Studies changes with age
   c. Correct! (p. 11)
   d. Incorrect. Works with children with academic difficulties

9. a. Incorrect. An M.D. is needed to prescribe drugs; a clinical psychologist has a Ph.D.
   b. Correct! (p. 11)
   c. Incorrect. No indication that he trained at a psychoanalytic institute
   d. Incorrect. Experimental psychologists don't help people with emotional problems; they study perception, learning, memory, and thinking

10. a. Incorrect. Only 16% of the doctorates in clinical psychology are awarded to ethnic minorities
    b. Incorrect. Just over 65% of graduate students are women
    c. Correct! (p. 15)
    d. Incorrect. Over 65% with the percentage increasing

Answers to the True/False Questions – Module 1.1

1. **False**: Determinism suggests that everything that happens, including making choices, has a cause. (p. 5)

2. **True**: Evolutionary psychologists try to understand how behavior and experience is affected by the evolutionary history of the species. (p. 9)

3. **True**: Women receive about two thirds of the psychology Ph.D.s. (p. 15)

4. **False**: Forensic psychologists provide assistance to professionals in the criminal justice system. (p. 12)

5. **False**: Counseling psychologists help people make decisions dealing with health, marriage, and education. Clinical psychologists help people experiencing psychological problems. (p. 12)

6. **False**: Though these are all psychologists their daily activities can be very different. (p. 14)

7. **False**: Researchers have changed their opinions several times about what constitutes an interesting, important, answerable question. (p. 17)

8. **False**: Psychiatrists are medical doctors and can therefore prescribe drugs. Most clinical psychologists cannot. (p. 11)

Answers to the Fill in the Blank Questions – Module 1.2

1. Wilhelm Wundt (p. 17)

2. William James (p. 20)

3. Sigmund Freud (p. 23)

4. John B. Watson (p. 22)

5. intelligence (p. 21)

6. structuralism (p. 19)

7. Cross-cultural (p. 24)

8. comparative (p. 21)

9. Behaviorism (p. 22)

Answers to the Short Answer Questions – Module 1.2

1. Behaviorism was the dominant school of psychology. The idea was that observable behavior, rather than elements of mind, should be studied. The main research question was: What do people and other animals do under various conditions? (pp. 22-23)

2. The philosophical reason was that they wanted to understand mental experience, and experience is primarily composed of sensations. The strategic reason was that they wanted to create a scientific psychology, and they began with questions that could be answered. (p. 20)

3. Functionalism is concerned with learning how the mind produces useful behaviors. Good psychological issues to be addressed using functionalism - How can people strengthen good habits? Are people able to attend to more than one item at a time? How do people recognize that they have seen something before? How does an intention lead to action? (p. 20)

4. Cross culture study, which compares people from various cultures, has become important because different cultures and ethnic groups have different beliefs and experiences which could add to understanding a broader range of behavior and experience. (p. 24)

5. Titchener's questions about the elements of the mind were not answerable, and he could not determine the accuracy of his observer's experiences. His frustrating approach turned many other psychologists against studying the mind, and toward studying observable behaviors. (pp. 19-20)

6. According to his theory, humans and other species share a remote common ancestor, but that each species evolved in a different way, adapting to its surroundings and way of life. He also believed that all vertebrate species have other basic features in common, and that nonhuman animals should exhibit some degree of human characteristics, such as intelligence. (p. 21)

7. They wanted to understand mental experience which they believed is composed mostly of sensations. Also, a scientific psychology had to begin with answerable questions and many questions about sensations are answerable. (p. 20)

Answers to the Multiple Choice Questions – Module 1.2

1. a. Correct! (pp. 17-18)
    b. Incorrect. Asked by philosophers prior to Wundt; Wundt tried to answer the questions experimentally
    c. Incorrect. Asked by the functionalist, William James
    d. Incorrect. Asked by the behaviorists
    e. Incorrect. Asked by Francis Galton

2. a. Incorrect. Darwin influenced Hull's use of animals, but not Hull's use of mathematics
    b. Incorrect. Darwin didn't study sensations
    c. Correct! (p. 21)
    d. Incorrect. Later psychologists tried to do this but not very successfully
    e. Incorrect. Darwin's theory did not help to improve the lot of women in psychology

3. a. Incorrect. Clark Hull is known for studying rats in maze
    b. Incorrect. John B Watson is known for being the founder of behaviorism
    c. Correct! (p. 17)
    d. Incorrect. Francis Galton is known for asking whether intellectual variations were based on heredity
    e. Incorrect. William James is known for being the founder of American psychology

4. a. Incorrect. John B. Watson was the founder of behaviorism
    b. Incorrect. Clark Hull studied maze learning
    c. Correct! (p. 22)
    d. Incorrect. William James is knows as the founder of American Psychology

5. a. Incorrect. Cognition is thinking and acquiring knowledge
    b. Incorrect. Functionalism is an attempt to understand how mental processes produce useful behaviors
    c. Correct! (p. 20)
    d. Incorrect. The principle of compatibility is the concept that people's built-in or learned expectations enable them to learn certain procedures more easily than others

6. a. Incorrect. To look within themselves
    b. Incorrect. The concept that people's built-in or learned expectations enable them to learn certain procedures more easily than other procedures
    c. Correct! (p. 20)
    d. Incorrect. Research that compares people from various cultures

Answers to the True/False Questions – Module 1.2

1. **True**: Behaviorism was a dominant force for nearly 50 years. (p. 22)

2. **True**: By studying other cultures, we can better understand aspects of our own behavior. (p. 24)

3. **True**: Although he did use introspect it was not very successful because he couldn't determine the accuracy of his studies. (p. 17)

4. **False**: The perceived intensity is not directly proportional to the physical intensity of a stimulus. (p. 20)

5. **True**: James's book was called "The Principles of Psychology". (p. 20)

6. **False**: Sigmund Freud was the man credited with this; Darwin's interest was more in the area of evolution. (p. 23)

Answers to Final Comprehensive Assessment

1. e (p. 3)
2. a (pp. 5-6)
3. c (p. 7)
4. d (p. 11, Table 1.1)
5. c (p. 11)
6. c (pp. 10-11, Table 1.1)
7. c (p. 8, Table 1.2)
8. d (p. 9)
9. a (p. 10)
10. a (p. 15, Fig. 1.4)
11. b (p. 19)
12. d (p. 24)
13. d (pp. 19-20, 22-23)
14. a (pp. 6- 7, Fig. 1.1)
15. d (p. 10, Table 1.1)

CHAPTER 2

SCIENTIFIC METHODS IN PSYCHOLOGY

CHAPTER OVERVIEW INFORMATION

LEARNING OBJECTIVES

By the end of Chapter 2 you should

- ✓ Understand the protocols and processes of science
- ✓ Develop an ability to think critically about claims
- ✓ Be familiar with the different research methods and their strengths and weaknesses
- ✓ Be familiar with descriptive and inferential statistics and the role statistics play in psychological research

CHAPTER 2 OUTLINE

Chapter 2 is a very important chapter (you already figured that out given it is the second chapter in the text) because it introduces the tools that psychologists use to understand the science of psychology. You may be asking "why do I need to know about methods and methodology to understand psychology?" Comprehension and appreciation of the process of science are essential in understanding and evaluating psychology.

Chapter 2 is presented below in outline format to assist you in understanding the information presented in the chapter. More detailed information on any topic can be found using the page references to the right of the topic.

Module 2.1 Thinking Critically and Evaluating Evidence

I. Scientists generally agree on how to evaluate competing theories (p. 31)
    A. The goal of research is to establish theories (p. 31)
        1. Theories should be comprehensive explanations of observable events, make new predictions, and be falsifiable (pp. 31-32)
    B. There are ordered steps for gathering evidence (pp. 32-33, Fig. 2.1)
        1. Developing a hypothesis (p. 32)
        2. Devising a method to test the hypothesis (p. 33)
        3. Measuring the results (p. 33)
        4. Interpreting the results (p. 33)
    C. Experiments should be replicable (p. 33)
        1. A meta-analysis combines many studies and can discover small effects (p. 34)
    D. Theories should be parsimonious, that is, fit known facts with the simplest assumptions (p. 34)
        1. A simple, or parsimonious, explanation for Clever Hans' arithmetic skills is that he watched his trainer and received cues (pp. 35-36)
        2. There is no scientific evidence for extrasensory perception (p. 36)
            a. Evidence is often based on anecdotes (pp. 36-37, Fig. 2.3)
            b. Psychic stage performers use tricks and illusions (pp. 37-38)
            c. Experiments have produced mixed results and positive results may not be replicable (p. 38, Fig. 2.4)

The message: *Scientific conclusions are tentative, subject to revision, and parsimonious. (p. 39)*

Module 2.2 Conducting Psychological Research

II. Research follows some general principles (p. 40)
    A. Variables should be operationally defined (pp. 40-41)
        1. Specify the operations (or procedures) used to produce or measure something
    B. Populations and Samples
        1. A population is the entire group of individuals who share some characteristic (p. 41)
        2. Samples comprise a subset of the population (p. 41, Table 2.1)
            a. A convenience sample is one selected because it was available at the time (p. 41)
            b. Should be representative and random (p. 41)
            c. Cross-cultural studies based on samples from at least two different cultures pose special sampling problems (p. 41)
    C. Eliminate the influence of expectations and demand characteristics by ensuring that both the observers and the participants are unaware or "blind" in the study (pp. 42-43, Fig. 2.5, Table 2.2)

III. Observational research designs do not show cause and effect relationships (p. 44, Fig. 2.6)
    A. Naturalistic observation involves careful observation under natural conditions (p. 44)
    B. Case histories involve detailed studies of an individual (p. 44)
    C. Surveys involve giving questionnaires to samples of individuals (pp. 44-45)
        1. It is important to get a random and representative sample (p. 41)
        2. People may express opinions even if they know little about a topic (p. 45)
        3. Results depend upon how a question is asked (pp. 45-46)
        4. A survey may intentionally bias the questions to get a desired answer (p. 46, Fig. 2.7)
    D. A correlational study examines the relationship between two variables, without controlling them (pp. 46-47)
        1. Strength of a relationship is measured using a statistic called a correlation coefficient. Coefficients range from -1 to +1 (p. 47, Fig. 2.8)
        2. Correlations observed in everyday life may be illusory (p. 48)
            a. An example of an illusory correlation is the belief that a full moon influences behavior (p. 48)
        3. Correlation does not imply that one variable causes the other (pp. 48-49, Fig. 2.9)
            a. For example, although one study found a correlation between hours slept each night and the likelihood of dying soon, it is unlikely that they are causally related (p. 49)

IV. Experiments involve the manipulation of variables (p. 49)
    A. Independent variables are manipulated and dependent variables are measures of behavior (p. 50)
        1. Only an experiment allows for a causal statement between the effect of the independent variable and the dependent variable (p. 50, Fig. 2.11)
    B. Experimental groups receive the treatment and control groups do not (p. 50, Fig. 2.12)
        1. Participants are randomly assigned to groups (p. 50)
    C. Examples of experiments investigating the effects of televised violence on aggressive behavior
        1. Zillman and Weaver (1999) – Viewing violence influences behavior
            a. College age participants were randomly assigned to watch four consecutive nights of violent films (pp. 51- 52)
            b. Participants who viewed four nights of violent films gave lower ratings than those who did not view the films (p. 52)
        2. Huesmann, Moise-Titus, Podolski, & Enron (2003) – Children viewing violent programs will become more violent over time (p. 52)

      a. The frequency with which 500 children viewed violent television programs was recorded (p. 52)

      b. Fifteen to eighteen years later, a correlation of +.2 between the frequency of viewing violent programs as a child and adult aggressive behavior was found (p. 52)

V. Some experiments raise ethical issues (pp. 52-54)
    A. Participants in research should give informed consent (p. 53)
    B. Research with nonhuman animals raises special ethical issues (pp. 53-54, Fig. 2.13)

The message: *Our understanding of complex human behavior has been increased by sound research although we may never have absolute proof (p. 54)*

Module 2.3 Measuring and Analyzing Results

VI. Descriptive statistics are mathematical summaries of results (pp. 56-58, Fig. 2.14)
    A. There are several measures of the central score (pp. 56-57, Fig. 2.16)
      1. Mean is the arithmetic average (p. 56)
      2. Median is the middle score in a set of ordered scores (p. 56)
      3. Mode is the most common score (p. 56, Fig. 2.15)
    B. Measures of variation refer to the spread of the scores (p. 58)
      1. Range is the difference between the highest and lowest scores (p. 58)
      2. Standard deviation measures the "average" distance of scores from the mean (p. 58, Figs. 2.17-2.18)

VII. Inferential statistics allow inferences about populations from small samples (pp. 59-60, Fig. 2.19)
    A. If a result is statistically significant, it probably did not occur by chance (p. 60)
      1. p values indicate how often results would occur by chance (p. 60)
      2. The lower the p value, the more convincing the results (p. 60)
      3. Influenced by differences between groups, sample size, and amount of variation (p. 60, Fig. 2.20)

The message: *Psychologists need statistics because they often measure small, variable effects. (p. 60)*

RELATED WEBSITES AND ACTIVITIES

Visit http://psychology.wadsworth.com/kalat_intro7e/ for online quizzing, glossary flashcards, crossword puzzles, annotated web links, and more.

LECTURE MATERIAL

Information from the text is only half of the picture. Don't forget to review your lecture material. Process each topic meaningfully. Most importantly, be sure that you understand the material in each lecture-if you don't, ask your instructor or teaching assistant.

STUDY TIP # 2: If you wordprocess your notes there are many different word processing functions you can use to enhance your notes. For example, hyperlinkbolding, underlining, double underlining, CAPITALIZING, changing font size, highlighting, and changing font color are a few of the tools you might find beneficial in helping you understand the information. Additionally, most programs allow you to easily (if not automatically) add outlines, comments, and live hyperlinks to interesting sites, pictures, graphics, audio and/or video files.

**TIP: Associate the lecture material with the information from the text, with things that you already know, with your personal experiences, or with real-life applications. Type or neatly re-write your notes. Make sure they are detailed and organized. Make comments on your notes. Then write questions to cover each concept.

CHAPTER MODULE ASSESSMENTS

Module 2.1 Thinking Critically and Evaluating Evidence
Answer these questions soon after reading the **Module 2.1: Thinking Critically and Evaluating Evidence**. There are several formats to the assessments. Answers to all questions appear on pp. 31-32.

Fill in the Blank
Provide a term(s) which best completes the statement below. Answers appear on p. 31.

1. A _____ is a comprehensive explanation of observable events that is usually supported by research.

2. An obligation to present evidence in support of one's claim is known as _____.

3. Scientists prefer a theory that explains results using the simplest assumptions. Thus, a theory that horses, dogs or other lower animals can perform mathematics would not possess the principle of _____.

4. A scientific experiment is _____ if most researchers following the same procedures gets approximately the same results.

5. _____ combines the results of many studies and analyzes them as though they were all one very large study.

Short Answer
The following questions require a short written answer (3-7 sentences). Answers appear on p. 31.

1. Describe two factors that would help you decide whether a theory is a good one.

2. Suppose you correctly anticipate what your friend will say. Explain why coincidence and subtle cues are more parsimonious explanations than is extrasensory perception.

3. Explain why anecdotes do not provide very strong scientific evidence.

Multiple Choice
Circle the best answer below. Check your answers on p. 32. If your answer was incorrect, try to write why it was incorrect. Check your reasons on p. 32.

1. Which of the following is not an appropriate order for steps involved in gathering and evaluating evidence?
   a. gather the data, then make up a hypothesis
   b. make up a hypothesis, then devise an appropriate method
   c. interpret the results, then try to replicate them
   d. gather the data, then think of alternative explanations

2. If a result is replicable, it:
   a. may be found by a few investigators, but many investigators cannot get the same results
   b. is not falsifiable
   c. is interpreted so that everyone agrees with the interpretation
   d. can be found by anyone who repeats the same procedures
   e. is a small effect that can only be found in a meta-analysis

3. What are the criteria for good scientific theories?
   a. predict new discoveries and are vague
   b. not falsifiable, but parsimonious
   c. are stated so that all types of evidence would fit
   d. make accurate predictions and are parsimonious
   e. change a few simple facts into complex ones and fit known facts

4. Clever Hans was actually:
   a. able to add and subtract but not multiply or divide
   b. able to do simple arithmetic of all types and was also able to identify musical notes
   c. able to respond to subtle cues given by the examiner
   d. better at answering questions when the examiner was out of sight

5. Anecdotes are not good scientific evidence for ESP because they:
   a. usually involve prediction before the event
   b. show that accurate predictions could not be coincidental
   c. produce accurate predictions when the predictions were very specific and precise
   d. usually involve selective memory; people remember when predictions come true, but not when they do not

True/False
Select the best answer by circling *T for True* or *F for False*. Check your answers on p. 32.

1. **T or F** A result is replicated only if exactly the same result is obtained.

2. **T or F** Inductive reasoning occurs when we infer a general principle from specific observations.

3. **T or F** Freud's theory that all dreams are motivated by wish fulfillment is falsifiable since it is possible to collect evidence that does not support the theory.

4. **T or F** Anecdotes, or people's reports of isolated events, are reliable sources of scientific evidence.

Module 2.2 Conducting Psychological Research
Answer these questions soon after reading the **Module 2.2: Conducting Psychological Research**. There are several formats to the assessments. Answers to all questions appear on pp. 33-35.

Fill in the Blank
Provide a term(s) which best completes the statement below. Answers appear on p. 33.

1. A(n) _____ is a study in which the investigator manipulates at least one variable while measuring at least one other variable.

2. The variable that an experimenter changes or controls (e.g., the amount of television watched) is known as the _____ variable.

3. In a(n) _____ study, both the participant and the observer are unaware of which participants are receiving the experimental condition (i.e., treatment).

4. A(n) _____ is a thorough description of an unusual individual that often relies on naturalistic observation.

Short Answer
The following questions require a short written answer (3-7 sentences). Answers appear on pp. 33-34.

1. Explain how a survey differs from a case history.

2. A researcher found that students who enrolled in a study skills class improved their GPAs more the next term than students who did not enroll. He concluded that GPAs increased because of the study skills class. What is wrong with this conclusion?

3. Describe how you would do a good experiment to see whether study skills classes help students. Indicate the independent and dependent variables.

4. Explain how a correlational study differs from an experiment both in terms of procedures and in terms of the types of conclusions that can be drawn.

5. For the studies on televised violence and aggression in the "What's the Evidence?" section, explain why it is unlikely that the boys who watched the violent shows were more aggressive to begin with than the boys who watched the nonviolent shows.

6. Explain how demand characteristics might play a role in an experiment to test two types of therapy and how you might try to minimize them.

7. Explain what is meant by informed consent in experimental participation.

Multiple Choice
Circle the best answer below. Check your answers on pp. 34-35. If your answer was incorrect, try to write why it was incorrect. Check your reasons on pp. 34-35.

1. Which of the following is the best operational definition of aggression?
   a. the number of times one person strikes another person during a 30-minute period
   b. how much physical force and verbal abuse is contained in a 30-minute period
   c. how much violence there is
   d. assaultive, offensive, and combative behavior

2. A researcher conducted a survey of all the customers at an expensive restaurant because she knows the owner and was able to get permission to do her survey there. She has
   a. selected a representative sample of the entire population
   b. used a random sample of the entire population
   c. conducted a cross-cultural study
   d. conducted single-blind study
   e. used a convenience sample

3. A news columnist asked readers to write in and indicate the importance of sex in their marriages. The responses were tallied and published. The columnist conducted:
   a. a correlational study
   b. an experiment
   c. a case history
   d. a survey

4. A researcher found that grade-point averages of college students are related to their family incomes. High GPAs generally go with higher incomes and low GPAs go with lower incomes. This study is:
   a. an example of an illusory correlation
   b. an experiment
   c. a correlational study
   d. a double-blind study

5. Generally, the weight of clothing that people wear goes down as the outdoor temperature goes up. This relationship would produce a:
   a. negative correlation
   b. zero correlation
   c. very high positive correlation
   d. very low positive correlation

Questions 6 to 9 refer to the following:

An experiment was conducted to determine whether a new approach to psychotherapy (interactive scream therapy) is effective in helping couples with marital problems. Couples who came to a clinic were randomly assigned to two groups-one group was given the new interactive scream therapy for 6 months and the other was placed on a waiting list and given no treatment. After 6 months, couples in both groups rated their marital happiness and therapists rated the adjustment of each couple.

6. What is the dependent variable?
   a. the therapy program
   b. the couples
   c. the ratings
   d. the clinic

7. What is the term for the group who received the therapy program?
   a. the experimental group
   b. the dependent variable
   c. the independent variable
   d. the control group

8. Why did the experimenter use random assignment?
   a. to be sure that the participants in the experiment were represented in the same proportions as participants in the population
   b. to reduce the possibility that the two groups differed in the beginning
   c. to avoid demand characteristics
   d. to ensure informed consent

9. Instead of using random assignment, another researcher obtained ratings from couples who had signed up for and completed the new therapy and those who did not sign up. She found better adjustment in the therapy group. What type would the study be and what conclusion could be made?
   a. experiment; the improvement is caused by the therapy
   b. correlation; interactive scream therapy "cures" marital problems
   c. experiment; there is a relationship between signing up for this therapy and adjustment
   d. correlation; there is a relationship between signing up for this therapy and adjustment

10. Which of the following would be unethical in conducting research?
   a. an experiment uses mild shock; participants were informed about the shock and agreed to participate
   b. an experiment involves eating disgusting things (such as cockroaches), but participants are told they are eating shrimp
   c. an experiment uses small doses of marijuana that have been approved by the Human Subjects Committee
   d. an experiment in which behavior is manipulated

True/False
Select the best answer by circling *T for True* or *F for False*. Check your answers on p. 35.

1. **T or F** The independent variable is the variable measured in the experiment.

2. **T or F** Representative samples attempt to have the same distribution of characteristics (e.g., gender, ethnicity, age) as found in the population.

3. **T or F** Placebos are used in experiments so that participants do not know if they are in the treatment or control group.

4. **T or F** A correlation of +0.5 is stronger than a correlation of -0.7.

Module 2.3 Measuring and Analyzing Results
Answer these questions soon after reading the **Module 2.3: Measuring and Analyzing Results**. There are several formats to the assessments. Answers to all questions appear on pp. 35-36.

Fill in the Blank
Provide a term(s) which best completes the statement below. Answers appear on p. 35.

1. If a random process would have a very low probability—generally less than 5%--of producing results as extreme as those found in some study, we say that the study's results were _____ significant.

2. The _____ is a measure of the amount of variation among scores in a distribution.

3. The _____ is the sum of all the scores in a group divided by the total number of scores.

4. For the set of scores containing 1, 2, 3, 46, and 999, the central score of 3 is known as the _____ of the distribution.

5. A symmetrical frequency of scores clustered around the mean is known as _____.

Short Answer

The following questions require a short written answer (3-7 sentences). Answers appear on p. 36.

1. Describe how you would find the means in the study skills experiment you designed and explain what a statistically significant difference at $p < .05$ would mean.

2. Using Figure 2.16 (Monthly salaries of employees at Company X), discuss why the mean and median are different. Which one represents the salaries more accurately?

Multiple Choice

Circle the best answer below. Check your answers on p. 36. If your answer was incorrect, try to write why it was incorrect. Check your reasons on p. 36.

1. A group of scores is 5, 6, 4, 8, 1. What is the median?
   a. 4
   b. 4.8
   c. 8
   d. 5

2. The researcher finds a difference between a therapy group and a control group that is statistically significant at $p < .01$. This means:
   a. the difference would occur by chance more than 1% of the time
   b. the probability that the difference was due to therapy is 1/100
   c. the explanation that therapy helped is parsimonious
   d. the difference would occur by chance less than 1% of the time

True/False

Select the best answer by circling *T for True* or *F for False*. Check your answers on p. 36.

1. **T or F** The standard deviation is a central score.

2. **T or F** A bimodal distribution is one in which the mean, median, and mode are the same value.

3. **T or F** The range is a measure of variability.

FINAL COMPREHESIVE CHAPTER ASSESSEMENT TEST

Check your answers on p. 36.

1. Prof. R tried to repeat an experiment that he read about in a scientific journal using exactly the same procedures as the original experiment. His results were different. Therefore, the original experiment was not:
   a. double-blind
   b. parsimonious
   c. statistically significant
   d. replicable

2. You suggest a theory and your instructor says it is not parsimonious. She means that it:
   a. does not make sense
   b. would not lead to replicable experiments
   c. would not lead to statistically significant differences
   d. would lead to experiments with demand characteristics
   e. does not make simple scientific assumptions

3. How did Clever Hans solve arithmetic problems?
   a. with ESP
   b. by taking advantage of coincidence
   c. by watching the examiner for subtle cues
   d. by using his native abilities to do arithmetic

4. In one experiment, people who said they had ESP were tested over several days. Sometimes they performed above chance and sometimes below chance. The researcher concluded that ESP depends on mood-it can be either positive (above chance) or negative (below chance). What is wrong with the explanation?
   a. it is not parsimonious-performance will vary around chance
   b. it is too parsimonious-some factor other than ESP must be operating
   c. it is replicable-people should not vary around chance
   d. there are too many demand characteristics that force performance below chance
   e. differential attrition occurred, so chance performance dropped

5. Advertisers often use testimonials in which a single person tells how a product helped. Why are such reports not good evidence?
   a. they are replicable
   b. they involve objective observation
   c. they involve experimental-control group designs
   d. they ignore the cases where the product did not help
   e. improvement could not occur by coincidence

6. Experiments with ESP have:
   a. had a history of flawed procedures and nonreplicable results
   b. produced positive results that are easily replicated
   c. proved that ESP occurs for people who can read brain waves
   d. shown that most professional psychics have ESP

7. Sometimes an inert pill is given to experimental participants, but they are told that the pill is effective. This pill is called a:
   a. placebo
   b. dependent variable
   c. double blind
   d. mode

8. A random sample involves selecting:
   a. only those people who volunteer
   b. people so that the percentages in the sample match the percentages in the population
   c. people from one specific culture
   d. so that every individual has an equal chance of being chosen
   e. all the studies on a topic for a meta-analysis

9. It has been found that children who have encyclopedias in their homes get better grades in school than children without encyclopedias. Can you conclude that using an encyclopedia makes children do better in school?
   a. yes, this is an experimental study and encyclopedias are the independent variable
   b. yes, this is a correlational study and the correlation is a strong positive one
   c. no, this is a correlational study; something other than encyclopedias might help grades
   d. no, this is an experiment but there is no control group
   e. no, this is a survey and experimenter bias might affect the conclusion

10. If there is a high correlation between parents' use of physical punishment and children's aggressiveness, then we can conclude:
    a. physical punishment causes aggression
    b. aggressive children cause parents to use physical punishment
    c. a third factor in the family causes both
    d. both a and b must be true
    e. nothing can be said about causality

11. If a correlation between variables A and B is -1, then:
    a. there is no relationship
    b. A causes B
    c. increases in A are perfectly associated with decreases in B
    d. increases in A are perfectly associated with increases in B

12. A study was conducted to test a new hay fever drug. Patients were randomly assigned to experimental and control groups. For 6 weeks, experimental patients took the drug daily and control patients took nothing. Each patient recorded hay fever attacks. The drug users had fewer and less severe attacks. What is wrong with this study?
    a. the groups probably were not equal in the beginning
    b. demand characteristics may have caused the effect
    c. the experiment lacks a dependent variable
    d. random assignment was not used
    e. informed consent was not obtained

13. Which of the following would best improve the design in Question 12?
    a. use a placebo rather than a "nothing" group
    b. include an independent variable
    c. use more participants to increase selective attrition
    d. include a dependent variable
    e. avoid the use of random assignment

14. An experiment was conducted to test the effect of rewards on learning. One group of subjects was paid 10 cents for every word they memorized and the other group was not paid. Number of words memorized was measured. Which of the following is true?
    a. number of words memorized is the dependent variable
    b. payment or not is the dependent variable
    c. random assignment should ensure that the groups differ in the beginning
    d. number of words memorized is the independent variable
    e. the control group is the one that is paid

15. A good question for deciding whether an experiment is ethical or not is:
    a. would subjects have agreed to participate if they had known what was going to happen?
    b. will the subjects experience any discomfort?
    c. is there any manipulation of behavior involved?
    d. will any subjects agree to participate?
    e. would any subject withdraw from the experiment?

16. Participants in an experiment are often kept "blind" about the condition to which they have been assigned. This will help prevent:
    a. surveyor bias
    b. an illusory correlation
    c. random assignment
    d. demand characteristics
    e. informed consent

17. A researcher found that subjects who were paid for memorizing words remembered more than subjects who were not paid, $p < .01$. This means:
    a. the reward group recalled 1% more than the nonreward group
    b. the results were not statistically significant
    c. the results are not replicable
    d. the results may have occurred because of an illusory correlation
    e. a difference that large would occur less than 1% of the time by chance alone

18. A class of seven students received the following grades on a test: 65, 78, 90, 89, 64, 78, 60.
    Which is true?
    a. the mode is 90
    b. the mean is 63
    c. the median is 89
    d. the mode is 89
    e. the median is 78

ANSWERS AND EXPLANATIONS FOR CHAPTER MODULE ASSESSMENTS

Answers to the Fill in the Blank Questions – Module 2.1

1. theory (p. 29)

2. burden of proof (p. 32)

3. parsimony (p. 34)

4. replicable (p. 33)

5. Meta-analysis (p. 34)

Answers to the Short Answer Questions – Module 2.1

1. Theories should make specific predictions that can be tested in experiments that are replicable. In other words, a theory should be falsifiable. Theories should be parsimonious so that their explanations use generally accepted scientific principles. (p. 34)

2. Scientists do not know how humans might receive "extrasensory" stimuli. Because there is no accepted explanation for this, it is not parsimonious. We do know that people in the same situation will have similar thoughts with some probability and that people and animals can read nonverbal cues in people. (pp. 36-37)

3. Anecdotes rely on memory, which may not be accurate; the observer may exaggerate; coincidence may be the correct explanation; people generally remember predictions only when they came true. (pp. 36-37)

Answers to the Multiple Choice Questions – Module 2.1

1.   a.   Correct! (pp. 32-33)
   b.   Incorrect. The question asked for orders that are not appropriate; each of these is appropriate
   c.   Incorrect. The question asked for orders that are not appropriate; each of these is appropriate
   d.   Incorrect. The question asked for orders that are not appropriate; each of these is appropriate

2.   a.   Incorrect. This would be considered replicated because a few investigators found it, but not replicable because most did not
   b.   Incorrect. Refers to theories, not results; theories are falsifiable if some set of observations would disconfirm them
   c.   Incorrect. Everyone may not agree with the interpretation, even though they can replicate the results
   d.   Correct! (p. 33)
   e.   Incorrect. A replicable result can be seen in other single experiments; meta-analysis combines many studies to look for small effects

3.   a.   Incorrect. Theories should be precise, not vague
   b.   Incorrect. They should be falsifiable
   c.   Incorrect. Should be able to imagine evidence that would falsify the theory
   d.   Correct! (p. 34)
   e.   Incorrect. Parsimony suggests that simple is better; shouldn't make simple things complex

4.   a.   Incorrect. He probably wasn't doing any arithmetic; c is more parsimonious
   b.   Incorrect. He probably couldn't do either; c is more parsimonious
   c.   Correct! (pp. 35-36)
   d.   Incorrect. The examiner needed to be in the horse's sight

5.   a.   Incorrect. Specific predictions are not usually made
   b.   Incorrect. Coincidence can explain many apparently accurate predictions
   c.   Incorrect. Predictions are usually not specific or precise
   d.   Correct! (p. 36)

Answers to the True/False Questions – Module 2.1

1. **False**: A researcher only needs to obtain a similar pattern of results not the exact same results. (p. 33)

2. **True**: See definition on p. 31. (p. 31)

3. **False**: Freud argued that when pleasant dreams occurred the "censor" had worked. Whereas, when unpleasant dreams occurred the "censor" had failed. See Domhoff (2003). (p. 32)

4. **False**: Although individuals' anecdotes can seem to provide reliable data, more often than not, these are unreliable and the result of coincidence or ambiguities in reports that allow us to "find" coincidences. (pp. 36-37)

Answers to the Fill in the Blank Questions – Module 2.2

1. experiment (p. 49)

2. independent (p. 49)

3. double blind (pp. 42-43)

4. case history (p. 44)

Answers to the Short Answer Questions – Module 2.2

1. A survey involves asking questions of a lot of people; a case history involves a much more detailed study of one person. The survey should use a random sample, so that everyone in the population of interest has an equal chance of being selected. A case study selects a specific person because of some interesting characteristic. (pp. 45-46)

2. The researcher conducted a correlational study. Students who signed up for the study skills class may differ from those who did not. The increase in GPA might have been due to something other than the class; perhaps those students were more motivated to improve and would have improved without the study skills class. (pp. 46-47)

3. Take a large group of students who are having difficulty in college. Randomly assign half of them to the study skills class. Look at the grades of both groups before the study skills class and look after the study skills class. The experimental group (who took the study skills class) should show a larger increase in grades than the control group (who did not take the class). The independent variable is whether the study skills class was taken or not; the dependent variable is the students' grades. (p. 50)

4. In an experiment, the researcher randomly assigns participants to specific groups. The groups should be equal in the beginning because of the random assignment. Any difference in the end should be due to the independent variable. The researcher has control over who gets which treatment. In a correlational study, the researcher compares existing groups, which may differ in more ways than the one in which the researcher is interested. Differences might be due to any of these original differences. The researcher does not control who gets which treatment. (pp. 46-50)

5. The researcher used random assignment. That means that the boys were placed in the violent and non-violent groups just by chance. The degree of violence of the boys in the two groups should have been about equal at the start of the experiment. The violent group made more aggressive acts because they watched the violent film because otherwise they were equated in all respects to the non-violent group due to the random assignment to groups. (pp. 51-52)

6. People might improve simply because they expect the therapy to work and not because the therapy itself is effective. Some sort of "placebo" therapy could be used in a control group. Participants would be led to expect that it would help, but actually it would be ineffective. If the therapists rating improvement don't know who got which therapy, the experiment would be double blind. If the participants know whether they're getting therapy or not, but the raters don't, it's a single-blind experiment. (pp. 42-43)

7. Participants should know what will happen in the experiment before they participate. In addition, they must be given the right to withdraw if they do not wish to participate once they know what will happen. (p. 53)

Answers to the Multiple Choice Questions – Module 2.2

1. a. Correct! (pp. 40-41)
    b. Incorrect. How would physical force and verbal abuse be measured?
    c. Incorrect. How is violence measured?
    d. Incorrect. What is meant by assaultive, offensive, combative?

2. a. Incorrect. It may be representative of people who eat in expensive restaurants, but not of the population
    b. Incorrect. Everyone in the population didn't have an equal chance of being selected, so it is not random
    c. Incorrect. Refers to comparing people from different societies
    d. Incorrect. Not used for surveys; refers to a situation in which either the subject or experimenter doesn't know the participant's group
    e. Correct! (p. 41)

3. a. Incorrect. Specific relationships were not studied
    b. Incorrect. No independent variable was manipulated
    c. Incorrect. Not an in-depth study of an individual
    d. Correct! (pp. 44-45)

4. a. Incorrect. The correlation is not illusory; it has been objectively observed
    b. Incorrect. A relationship was noted, but no variables were controlled or manipulated by the researcher
    c. Correct! (pp. 46-47)
    d. Incorrect. We don't know whether the experimenter knew which participants were from high- and low-income families; the participants probably knew

5. a. Correct! (p. 47, Fig. 2.8)
    b. Incorrect. The variables are related; correlation cannot be zero
    c. Incorrect. The variables do not increase together; one goes up and the other goes down
    d. Incorrect. The relationship is pretty strong so the correlation should be high; see c for why it is not positive

6. a. Incorrect. The researcher controls the therapy program (gives it to some couples, not others), so it is the independent variable
    b. Incorrect. The couples are the subjects or participants
    c. Correct! (p. 50)
    d. Incorrect. The clinic is the site of the study, not a variable

7. a. Correct! (p. 50)
    b. Incorrect. Dependent variable is the measure of behavior, not a group
    c. Incorrect. The therapy group is one level of the independent variable, not the independent variable itself
    d. Incorrect. Control group is the one that is not treated, i.e., the no-therapy group

8.   a.   Incorrect. This is a representative sample; random assignment refers to placing the sample into groups
       b.   Correct! (p. 50)
       c.   Incorrect. Demand characteristics could still be a problem if participants know they're supposed to improve
       d.   Incorrect. Informed consent doesn't have to do with assignment to groups; it means that the participants knew what was required of them in the experiment and they agreed to do it

9.   a.   Incorrect. Not an experiment because who got the therapy was not controlled by the experimenter; people who sign up for therapy may be different from people who don't
       b.   Incorrect. Correlational, but you cannot be sure that therapy is the only difference between the groups; the group who signed up may already be better adjusted or they may be more motivated
       c.   Incorrect. Not an experiment because the groups already existed; experimenter did not randomly assign couples to therapy
       d.   Correct! (pp. 46-49)

10.   a.   Incorrect. Participants knew they would be shocked and they agreed to participate; informed consent was obtained
       b.   Correct! (p. 53)
       c.   Incorrect. The Human Subjects Committee judged that the procedures were ethical
       d.   Incorrect. By definition, experiments manipulate behavior, but such manipulation is usually short-lived

Answers to the True/False Questions – Module 2.2

1. **False**: The variable measured is the dependent variable. (p. 50)

2. **True**: Characteristics of a representative sample are the same as the population from which the sample was drawn. (p. 41)

3. **True**: A placebo is a pill with no known pharmacological effects. Participants are given a placebo to reduce the chance that their expectations will influence their behavior. (p. 43)

4. **False**: The closer a correlation is to +1 or -1 the stronger the correlation. The + or – sign only indicates the direction of the correlation. (p. 47)

Answers to the Fill in the Blank Questions – Module 2.3

1. statistically significant (p. 60)

2. standard deviation (p. 58)

3. mean (p. 56)

4. median (p. 56)

5. normal distribution/normal curve (p. 59, Fig. 2.18)

Answers to the Short Answer Questions – Module 2.3

1. Add all the grade point averages (GPAs) of the students in a group and then divide by the number of students in that group. Do this for junior-year grades of the group that had the study skills class and for the group that did not. A significant difference at the .05 level would mean that the observed difference in grades between the groups would occur by chance less than 5% of the time. (pp. 56, 60)

2. The mean salary is $5,700 and the median salary is $3,000. The mean is greater than the mean because of the few extremely high salaries. Since most of the employees only earn around $2000-$5000 dollars, the median salary would be more accurate measure of centrality. (p. 56)

Answers to the Multiple Choice Questions – Module 2.3

1. a. Incorrect. Scores must be rank ordered first, then the middle score is the median
    b. Incorrect. This is the average or mean
    c. Incorrect. Highest score or top of the range
    d. Correct! (p. 54)

2. a. Incorrect. < means less than 1%--it's a rare event
    b. Incorrect. Probability that difference is due to chance is less than 1/100
    c. Incorrect. Statistical significance is unrelated to parsimony; a difference could be significant and the explanation still might not be the simplest
    d. Correct! (p. 60)

Answers to the True/False Questions – Module 2.3

1. **False**: Standard deviation is a measure of variability. (p. 58)

2. **False**: A bimodal distribution is one with <u>two</u> common scores. (p. 56, Fig. 2.15)

3. **True**: Although not frequently used the range is one measure of variability. (p. 58)

Answers to Final Comprehensive Assessment

1. d (p. 33)
2. e (p. 34)
3. c (pp. 35-36)
4. a (pp. 34, 36-37)
5. d (p. 33)
6. a (p. 38)
7. a (p. 43)
8. d (p. 41)
9. c (pp. 46-49)
10. e (pp. 48-49)
11. c (p. 47)
12. b (pp. 42-43)
13. a (p. 43)
14. a (p. 50)
15. a (p. 53)
16. d (pp. 42-43)
17. e (p. 60)
18. e (p. 56)

CHAPTER 3

BIOLOGICAL PSYCHOLOGY

CHAPTER OVERVIEW INFORMATION

LEARNING OBJECTIVES

By the end of Chapter 3 you should

- ✓ Be acquainted with biological functions at the level of the neuron.
- ✓ Be knowledgeable regarding the components of the nervous system
- ✓ Be knowledgeable about the divisions of the nervous system and the functions of the components of the brain

CHAPTER 3 OUTLINE

Chapter 3 reintroduces the philosophical themes that were initially explored in Chapter 1 namely Mind/Body and Nature/Nurture. However, information in this chapter provides a less philosophical discussion of these themes and starts to address the facts surrounding this information. Chapter 3 examines how biological systems and processes influence behavior and experience. The two biological systems that are explored are Neural and Nervous system.

Chapter 3 is presented below in outline format to assist you in understanding the information presented in the chapter. More detailed information on any topic can be found using the page references to the right of the topic.

Module 3.1 Neurons and Behvior
I. The nervous system is composed of neurons and glia (p. 69, Fig 3.1)
    A. A neuron consists of a cell body, dendrites, and an axon (pp. 69-70, Figs. 3.2-3.3)
    B. Nerve impulses are called action potentials (p. 70, Fig 3.3)
        1. Inflow of sodium ions makes inside of axon positive (pp. 70-72, Figs. 3.4-3.6)
    C. Gaps between neurons are called synapses (pp. 72-74, Fig. 3.7)
        1. Neurotransmitters are released from presynaptic endings (pp. 73-74, Figs. 3.8-3.9)
            a. Neurotransmitters from one animal can affect another animal (p. 75, Fig. 3.10)
    D. Different neurotransmitters have different effects on behavior (pp. 75-77)
        1. Parkinson's disease occurs because neurons producing dopamine die (p. 76, Fig. 3.11)

The message: *Behavior is not determined by a single neuron but by patterns of activity shown by many nerve cells. (p. 77)*

Module 3.2 The Nervous System an Behvior
II. Major Divisions of the Nervous System
    A. Neurons are organized into the central nervous and peripheral nervous systems (p. 78, Fig. 3.12)
        1. The central nervous system includes the brain and the spinal cord (p. 78, Fig. 3.12)
            a. Central nervous system starts as three lumps (hind, mid, and forebrains) (pp. 78-79, Fig. 3.13)
        2. The peripheral nervous system includes the somatic and autonomic nervous systems and is bundles of axons between the spinal cord and the rest of the body (p. 78, Fig. 3.12).

        a.   The somatic nervous system communicates with the skin and muscles (p. 78, Fig. 3.12).

        b.   The autonomic nervous system controls the heart, stomach and other organs. (p. 78, Fig. 3.12)

B. The Forebrain and Cerebral Cortex

    1. Cortex consists of left and right hemisphere (p. 79, top of Fig. 3.15)

        a.   Cortical hemispheres are made of cell bodies, gray matter (p. 79, Fig. 3.16)

        b.   Axons covered with white insulation, called myelin, lie beneath the cortex (p. 79, Fig. 3.16)

    2. Cerebral cortex consists of four lobes (pp. 79-82, Fig. 3.17)

        a.   Occipital lobe is specialized for vision (p. 79)

           i.   Damage to different areas of the visual cortex result in different deficits (p. 79)

        b.   Parietal lobe is specialized for body senses (pp. 79-80)

           i.   Primary somatosensory cortex senses touch in different body areas (pp. 79-80, Fig. 3.18a)

          ii.   Damage to the parietal lobe can lead to impaired sensation or inattention (p. 80)

        c.   Temporal lobes are involved in hearing (p. 80, Fig. 3.19)

           i.   Damage to temporal lobe results in inability to recognize complex patterns and sounds (p. 80)

        d.   Frontal lobes have several different functions (p. 81)

           i.   Primary motor cortex controls movement on opposite side of body (pp. 81-82, Fig. 3.18b)

          ii.   Prefrontal cortex is critical for keeping track of memories and planning actions based on them (p. 82)

C. How the Cerebral Cortex Communicates with the Body

    1. Spinal cord connects the peripheral nervous system and the rest of the body (pp. 82-83, Fig. 3.20)

    2. Thalamus relays sensory information (except olfactory) to the cerebral cortex (p. 82, Fig. 3.19)

    3. Hindbrain consists of the medulla, pons, and cerebellum (p. 83, Fig. 3.14)

        a.   Medulla and pons receive sensory input and control life-preserving functions (p. 82)

           i. The reticular formation serves an arousal function (p. 82)

        b.   Cerebellum is important in movement and timing (p. 83)

D. The Autonomic Nervous System and the Endocrine System (p. 83)

    1. Sympathetic and parasympathetic nervous systems comprise autonomic nervous system (p. 83, Fig 3.21)

        a.   Sympathetic nervous system readies body for fight or flight activities (p. 83)

        b.   Parasympathetic nervous system promotes bodily activities during rest (p. 83)

    2. Endocrine system produces hormones that are similar to neurotransmitters (p. 83, Fig 3.22)

III. Measuring Brain Activity

  A. Electroencephalographs (EEG) measure brain electrical activity (p. 83, Fig 3.23)

  B. Magnetoencephalographs (MEG) measure brain magnetic changes (p. 83)

  C. Positron-emission tomography (PET) measures brain activity via injected radioactive compounds (p. 84, Fig 3.24)

  D. Functional magnetic resonance imaging (fMRI) measures brain activity by measuring the amounts of hemoglobin with and without oxygen. (p. 84, Fig 3.25)

IV. Effects of Experience on Brain Structure
   A. Brain structure (e.g., brain volume, dendritic changes and synaptical renewal) tends to change with age, medical conditions, and diseases like Alzheimer's. (p. 85)
   B. Studying to exercise one's brain only has effects in the area studied (p. 85)
   C. Practicing certain skills does seem to modify different brain structures (pp. 85-86)
   D. Physical exercise and mental activity are related to greater dendritic branching (p. 86)

V. The Binding Problem
   A. Parietal lobe plays role in understanding how separate brain areas combine to produce a unified perceptions (p. 87)
   B. Binding takes longer as complexity of the stimulus increases (p. 87)

VI. The Corpus Callosum and the Split-Brain Phenomenon
   A. Split-brain operations involve cutting a set of axons connecting the cerebral cortex of the left and right hemispheres known as the corpus callosum (p. 87, Fig. 3.26)
      1. Helps epilepsy by stopping spread of seizures (pp. 87-88)
      2. Fibers from each retina still go to each hemisphere (p. 88, Fig. 3.27)
         a. Half of the optic nerves cross over to the other side of the brain (p. 88)
      3. Cutting the corpus callosum creates two separate hemispheres (pp. 88-89)
         a. Information presented to the right visual field (left hemisphere) can be named, but information presented to the left visual field cannot (pp. 89-90, Fig. 3.28)
   B. The Left and Right Hemispheres
      1. There are many misconceptions about the brain (p. 90)
      2. Although the right and left hemispheres are specialized, all tasks rely on both hemispheres (p. 90)
      3. No evidence to support the misconception of right or left-brained people (p. 90)

The message: *Many specialized brain areas work together to produce behavior and conscious experience. (p. 90)*

RELATED WEBSITES AND ACTIVITIES
Visit http://psychology.wadsworth.com/kalat_intro7e/ for online quizzing, glossary flashcards, crossword puzzles, annotated web links, and more.

LECTURE MATERIAL
Information from the text is only half of the picture. Don't forget to review your lecture material. Process each topic meaningfully. Most importantly, be sure that you understand the material in each lecture-if you don't, ask your instructor or teaching assistant.

STUDY TIP # 3: Review your outline prior to the lecture over the material. Convert your outline to electronic form, print it out, take it to lecture, and take notes directly in your outline. Later you can then enter your class notes into your electronic outline.

TIP: Associate the lecture material with the information from the text, with things that you already know, with your personal experiences, or with real-life applications. Type or neatly re-write your notes. Make sure they are detailed and organized. Make comments on your notes. Then write questions to cover each concept.

Module 3.1 Neurons and Behaviors
Answer these questions soon after reading the **Module 3.1: Neurons and Behaviors**. There are several formats to the assessments. Answers to all questions appear on pp. 49-51.

Fill in the Blank
Provide a term(s) which best completes the statement below. Answers appear on p. 49.

1. Chemicals that are released from nerve cells and can activate receptors of other neurons are called _____.

2. Axons on nerve cells transmit information along the surface through a combination of electrical and chemical processes called the _____.

3. The space between neurons across which neurotransmitters are released is known as the _____.

4. The brain contains neurons and _____ cells which support neurons by insulating them and removing waste.

5. _____ neurons transmit impulses from the central nervous system to the muscles and glands.

6. The _____ are widely branching structures that receive transmissions from other neurons.

Short Answer
The following questions require a short written answer (3-7 sentences). Answers appear on pp. 49-50.

1. What are the main symptoms of Parkinson's disease and what is the common treatment?

2. Describe how nerve impulses travel through neurons and describe what happens when an impulse reaches the end of a neuron.

3. After the message has been terminated the receptor molecule is in the synaptic cleft. Where does it go following termination?

4. What is ADD and how it is treated?

5. List the three parts of a neuron and describe characteristics about each.

6. Explain how anesthetic drugs like Novocain work.

Multiple Choice
Circle the best answer below. Check your answers on p. 50. If your answer was incorrect, try to write why it was incorrect. Check your reasons on p. 50.

1. Which of the following is true?
   a. neurons are larger and more numerous than glia cells
   b. each neuron physically touches at least one other neuron
   c. neurons are all similar in shape and size
   d. neurons consist of a cell body, dendrites, and an axon
   e. neurons decrease dendritic branching with enriched experience

2. The action potential:
   a. occurs when positive sodium ions enter an axon
   b. becomes weaker as it travels down an axon
   c. can be speeded up by anesthetic drugs
   d. occurs when potassium enters the axon

3. What happens at the synapse between neurons?
   a. synaptic vesicles are released from postsynaptic endings
   b. presynaptic endings are destroyed by action potentials
   c. neurotransmitters are released from terminal buttons
   d. neurotransmitters excite the next neuron

4. Parkinson's disease:
   a. involves muscle twitches and hallucinations
   b. results from the death of axons that use dopamine
   c. can be helped by having the patient take dopamine
   d. results from a deficit in MPTP

5. Axons convey information by a special combination of electrical and chemical processes called a(n) _____.
   a. resting potential
   b. action potential
   c. synapses
   d. terminal button

True/False
Select the best answer by circling *T for True* or *F for False*. Check your answers on pp. 50-51.

1. **T or F** The motor neurons carry information about touch, pain, and other senses from the periphery of the body to the spinal cord.

2. **T or F** The brain processes information via billions of neurons or nerve cells.

3. **T or F** Inhibition is the absence of excitation.

4. **T or F** Glia cells help support the neurons and remove waste.

5. **T or F** The part of the neuron that receives information from other neurons is the axon.

6. **T or F** Parkinson's disease is results from gradual decay of one pathway of axons that release the neurotransmitter dopamine.

Module 3.2 The Nervous System and Behavior
Answer these questions soon after reading the **Module 3.2: The Nervous System and Behavior**. There are several formats to the assessments. Answers to all questions appear on pp. 51-53.

Fill in the Blank
Provide a term(s) which best completes the statement below. Answers appear on p. 51.

1. The central nervous system consists of the _____ and _____.

2. The main processing area of the brain for hearing is the _____ lobe.

3. The set of axons that connects the left and right hemispheres of the brain is the _____.

4. The _____ system is a set of glands that produce hormones and release them into the blood.

5. The outer covering of the forebrain is known as the _____.

6. How separate brain areas combine to produce a unified perception of experience is referred to as the _____.

7. The autonomic nervous system consists of the _____ nervous system, which controls the flight-or-fight response, and the _____ nervous system that promotes activities of the body that take place during rest.

8. _____ is a condition in which neurons somewhere in the brain emit abnormal rhythmic, spontaneous impulses.

9. A _____ is a rapid, automatic response to a stimulus.

10. The _____ lobe is the rear portion of each cerebral hemisphere, critical for vision.

11. The _____ is the structure adjacent to the medulla that receives sensory input from the head and controls many muscles in the head.

Short Answer
The following questions require a short written answer (3-7 sentences). Answers appear on pp. 51-52.

1. Describe the autonomic nervous system. How is it similar to the endocrine system?

2. Name the four lobes of the cerebral cortex and describe the function of each.

3. Describe an example of how experience changes brain structure.

4. How does a split-brain operation help epilepsy, and what are the major consequences of such an operation?

5. Describe the path of the nerve fibers from each eye to the two hemispheres of the brain.

6. Describe a PET and fMRI scans.

7. Name the three structures of the hindbrain and describe their functions.

Multiple Choice

Circle the best answer below. Check your answers on pp. 52-53. If your answer was incorrect, try to write why it was incorrect. Check your reasons on pp. 52-53.

1. John is about to give a speech and his heart is racing, he is breathing rapidly, and he has "butterflies in his stomach." What part of his nervous system is controlling this reaction?
   a. parasympathetic nervous system
   b. spinal cord
   c. endocrine system
   d. sympathetic nervous system
   e. sensory nerves

2. A person has damage to the hindbrain. Which of the following would be **LEAST** likely?
   a. the person may have difficulty with memory because of damage to the hippocampus
   b. the person may have difficulty walking a straight line because of cerebellum damage
   c. the person may not show much arousal because of damage to the reticular formation
   d. the person may die because of damage to the medulla and pons

3. The primary somatosensory cortex is:
   a. located in the frontal lobe
   b. the receiving area for touch from the same side of the body
   c. located in the parietal lobe
   d. located behind the cerebral cortex

4. How does cutting the corpus callosum control the seizures of epilepsy?
   a. it removes the part of the brain that is damaged
   b. it prevents seizures from spreading to the other hemisphere
   c. it prevents visual input from reaching the brain
   d. it prevents axons from the retina from crossing at the optic chiasm

5. If a person with a split-brain operation closes her right eye and looks at a picture as long as she wants with her left eye, where does the picture end up in her brain?
   a. in her right hemisphere because the axons from the retina cross at the optic chiasm
   b. in her left hemisphere because the axons from the retina go straight back at the optic chiasm
   c. both hemispheres-axons from the left side of the eye go to left hemisphere; axons from the right side of the eye go to right hemisphere
   d. both hemispheres-axons from the right side of the eye go to left hemisphere; axons from the left side of the eye go to right hemisphere

6. _____ is a condition in which neurons somewhere in the brain emit abnormal rhythmic, spontaneous impulses.
   a. Attention deficit disorder
   b. Epilepsy
   c. Parkinson's disease
   d. Corpus callosum

7. Which brain scanning technique is performed using radioactive chemicals?
   a. CAT scan
   b. PET scan
   c. fMRI
   d. EEG

8. Which of the following actions does NOT describe a function of the sympathetic nervous system system?
   a. pulse quickens
   b. sweat increases
   c. pupils constrict
   d. epinephrine secreted

True/False
Select the best answer by circling *T for True* or *F for False*. Check your answers on p. 43.

1. **T or F** The endocrine system is not part of the nervous system.

2. **T or F** The central nervous system is the primary system that controls internal organ functioning such as heart rate.

3. **T or F** The medulla is located within the temporal lobe and is responsible for our recognition of fear and anxiety.

4. **T or F** In humans, information from the left visual field strikes the left half of both retinas and is processed in the left hemisphere of the brain.

5. **T or F** We primarily use the left hemisphere of the brain for language and the right hemisphere for spatial tasks.

6. **T or F** A positron-emission tomography (PET) passes x-rays through the head of someone who has a dye in the blood to increase contrast between fluids and brain cells.

FINAL COMPREHENSIVE CHAPTER ASSESSMENT TEST

Check your answers on p. 54.

1. Which of the following is the correct order of how information is processed in a neuron?
   a. Dendrite, axon, cell body
   b. Dendrite, cell body, axon
   c. Axon, cell body, dendrite
   d. Axon, dendrite, cell body

2. According to Figure 3.1, what is the estimated number of neurons in an adult?
   a. less 50 billion
   b. 85 million
   c. 100 billion
   d. 100 million

3. Which of the following accurately describes a characteristic of neurotransmitters?
   a. The brain only produces one type of neurotransmitter
   b. One or more neurotransmitters reside in a neuron
   c. Neurotransmitters can be emitted outside of the brain to affect others
   d. None of the above

4. Which of the following is true regarding glia cells?
   a. They are larger than neurons
   b. They are supported by the neurons
   c. They produce action potentials
   d. They are smaller than neurons

5. Action potentials:
   a. occur when potassium ions enter the axon of a neuron
   b. make the inside of an axon negative relative to the outside
   c. become weaker as they travel down an axon
   d. generally travel away from the cell body
   e. can be increased in strength with anesthetic drugs

6. How does one neuron send its signal to another neuron?
   a. its terminal button touches the next neuron
   b. the two axons touch so that the action potential is passed from one to the next neuron
   c. the positively charged ions from one neuron stimulate the axon of the next
   d. the postsynaptic neuron receives stimulation directly from the dendrites of the presynaptic neuron
   e. it releases a chemical that attaches to a receptor on the next neuron

7. Loewi collected fluid around the heart after stimulating axons that slowed down the heart and then transferred the fluid to the heart of a second animal. What happened?
   a. nothing; fluid from one animal had no effect on another animal
   b. the second animal's heart sped up; that is, the fluid produced the opposite effect on the second animal
   c. neurotransmitters contained in the fluid stimulated the second animal's heart to slow
   d. myelin contained in the fluid stimulated the second animal's heart to slow
   e. axons contained in the fluid stimulated the second animal's heart to slow

8. Parkinson's disease can be helped by:
   a. taking pills that contain dopamine
   b. taking pills that contain MPTP
   c. injections of epinephrine
   d. injections of serotonin
   e. taking pills that contain L-DOPA

9. The sympathetic nervous system:
   a. lies at the very top and very bottom of the spinal cord
   b. controls the peripheral nerves that communicate with the skin and muscles
   c. transmits impulses from the central nervous system to the muscles and glands
   d. increases heart rate and breathing rate
   e. increases digestive activities

10. Hormones differ from neurotransmitters in that hormones:
    a. affect only the cells close to where they are released; neurotransmitters are diffused throughout the body
    b. are released into the blood stream; neurotransmitters are released adjacent to the cell they are to excite or inhibit
    c. have only short-lived influence; neurotransmitters can have long-term influences
    d. have no effect on behavior; neurotransmitters can have large behavioral effects

11. Damage to which of the following is most likely to be fatal?
    a. cerebellum
    b. spinal cord
    c. medulla
    d. midbrain
    e. limbic system

12. What is concluded in your text about the relationship between brain and mind?
    a. they are inseparable; if a part of the brain is lost, that part of behavior and experience is lost
    b. "mind" is the central area where all sensations are funneled and organized
    c. the loss of any one specific part of brain will cause total disorganization of "mind"
    d. loss of large parts of the brain has little effect on "mind"; they seem to be separate

13. The primary somatosensory cortex is:
    a. in the temporal lobe
    b. the part of the brain that controls fine motor movement
    c. organized with a larger area devoted to more sensitive parts of the body
    d. in the occipital lobe
    e. contributes primarily to the organization and planning of movements

14. Damage to which of the following areas is likely to result in blindness even if there is no problem with the person's eyes or with the nerves going to this area?
    a. occipital cortex
    b. temporal lobe
    c. parietal lobe
    d. frontal lobe

15. A person who has epilepsy has a split-brain operation. Which of the following is true?
    a. the person's corpus callosum has been cut
    b. seizures will increase
    c. seizures will occur more often than before the operation, but they will be less severe
    d. the fibers from each retina will only go to one hemisphere
    e. the person's optic chiasm has been cut

16. A right-handed split-brain patient sees the word cupcake presented very briefly such that cup is in the left visual field and cake is in the right visual field. Which of the following will occur?
    a. she will say that she saw the word "cup"
    b. she will pick out a cup with her left hand
    c. she will say that she saw the word "cupcake"
    d. she will pick out a cake with her left hand
    e. both a and d

17. In Question 17, the word "cup" will fall on the:
    a. right side of both retinas and go to the left hemisphere
    b. left retina only and go to the right hemisphere
    c. left side of both retinas and go to the left hemisphere
    d. right side of both retinas and go to the right hemisphere
    e. right side of the left eye and left side of the right eye and go to both hemispheres

18. The idea that some people are right-brained and some people are left-brained:
    a. is correct; some people use their left hemisphere for all tasks and some use their right
    b. is wrong because most people only use 10% of their brains and that 10% is almost always in the left hemisphere
    c. is correct and based on the fact that small neurons are constantly maturing so that only 10% of the neurons in only one hemisphere are mature at any given time is wrong; all people are left-brained; the right hemisphere is virtually useless
    d. is wrong because all tasks involve both hemispheres to some extent

ANSWERS AND EXPLANATIONS FOR CHAPTER MODULE ASSESSMENTS

Answers to the Fill in the Blank Questions – Module 3.1

1. neurotrasmitters (pp. 73-74)

2. action potential (pp. 70-72)

3. synapse (pp. 72-74)

4. glia (p. 69)

5. Motor (p. 69)

6. dendrites (pp. 69-70)

Answers to the Short Answer Questions – Module 3.1

1. The main symptoms are difficulty in initiating voluntary movement, slowness of movement, tremors, rigidity, and depressed mood. One common treatment is the drug L-dopa, which enters the brain, where neurons convert it into dopamine. (p. 76)

2. Nerve impulses travel through the axons of neurons. The impulse is a positive charge inside an axon that occurs because sodium ions rush in. The impulse continues from the cell body end of the axon to the presynaptic ending, where the impulse causes neurotransmitters to be released into the synapse. (pp. 70-74, Figs. 3.3-3.6)

3. There are several different options for the receptor molecule in that it may become reabsorbed through something we call reuptake (reabsorbed through axon which it was released); it may be excreted through urine and blood, diffused away, metabolized, or it may re-excite and attach to the postsynaptic receptor (p. 74)

4. Attention Deficit Disorder (ADD) is a condition characterized by impulsive behavior and a short attention span. Although the drugs that treat the disorder seem to explain the biological problem with ADD, other research has shown that these explanations don't always add up; therefore, the cause of ADD is not quite clear. Amphetamine and methylphenidate are drugs that are used to reduce the affects of ADD. They work by preventing presynaptic neurons from reabsorbing serotonin and dopamine, which are neurotransmitters. In addition, Amphetamine speeds up the release of dopamine; this promotes higher levels of activity. Therefore, these two drugs keep serotonin and dopamine activating synaptic receptors for a longer period of time. The end result is an improvement in attention span. (pp. 76-77)

5. The cell body contains the nucleus of the cell. The dendrites are widely branching structures that receive transmissions from other neurons. The axon is a single, long, thin, straight fiber with branches near its tip. The axon sends the information while the dendrites receive the information. Some axons are covered by a myelin sheath which makes an impulse transmission occur more rapidly. Basically, neurons work like a network; dendrites and axons of various cell bodies connect, sending excitatory impulses from one cell to another. Also, dendrites and axons usually growing new branches and "shedding" old branches. (pp. 69-70)

6. Anesthetic drugs work by blocking the sodium gates of your neurons, thereby halting the action potential and silencing the message of "Pain!" that is being sent to your brain. (p. 72)

Answers to the Multiple Choice Questions – Module 3.1

1.   a.   Incorrect. Glia cells are more numerous
    b.   Incorrect. Neurons do not actually touch each other
    c.   Incorrect. Neurons differ in shape, depending on how many sources of information they have and where their impulses travel
    d.   Correct! (pp. 69-75)
    e.   Incorrect. Studies with rats show that enriched environments result in an increase in dendritic branching

2.   a.   Correct! (pp. 70-72)
    b.   Incorrect. The impulse remains at the same intensity
    c.   Incorrect. Anesthetics prevent action potentials
    d.   Incorrect. Potassium ions leave the axon as sodium enters

3.   a.   Incorrect. Released from presynaptic endings
    b.   Incorrect. Endings are part of structure; not destroyed
    c.   Correct! (pp. 73-74)
    d.   Incorrect. Postsynaptic neurons may be either excited or inhibited

4.   a.   Incorrect. Movement problems and depression, not hallucinations
    b.   Correct! (p. 76)
    c.   Incorrect. Dopamine does not cross blood-brain barrier, must use L-DOPA
    d.   Incorrect. A chemical that causes symptoms similar to

5.   a.   Incorrect. When not stimulated, the axon's membrane has a resting potential.
    b.   Correct! (p. 70)
    c.   Incorrect. A synapse is the specialized junction between one neuron and another
    d.   Incorrect. A typical axon has several branches, each ending with a little bulge called a presynaptic ending or terminal button.

Answers to the True/False Questions – Module 3.1

1. **False**: Sensory neurons carry information about touch, pain, and other senses from the periphery of the body to the spinal cord. Motor neurons transmit impulses from the central nervous system to the muscles and glands. (p. 69)

2. **True**: Many of the neurons in the human nervous system are extremely small. (p.69)

3. **False**: Inhibition is like stepping on a brake, it prevents certain messages. (p. 73)

4. **True**: The nervous system contains both neurons and glia cells. (p. 69)

5. **False**: Neurons receive information from other neurons via the dendrites. (pp. 69-70)

6. **True**: Parkinson's disease is the result of a decrease in dopamine. (p. 76)

Answers to the Fill in the Blank Questions – Module 3.2

1. brain; and spinal cord (p. 78)

2. temporal (p. 80)

3. corpus callosum (p. 87)

4. endocrine (p. 83)

5. cerebral cortex (pp. 79-82)

6. binding problem (p. 87)

7. sympathetic; parasympathetic (p. 83)

8. Epilepsy (p. 87)

9. reflex (p. 82)

10. occipital (p. 79)

11. pons (p. 83)

Answers to the Short Answer Questions – Module 3.2

1. The autonomic nervous system lies just outside the spinal cord and it consists of two parts: sympathetic and parasympathetic. The sympathetic nervous system prepares the body to "fight or flight" by increasing heart and breathing rates and decreasing digestive processes. The parasympathetic nervous system does just the opposite; it decreases heart and breathing rates and increases digestion. The endocrine system consists of glands that secrete hormones that can function like neurotransmitters. (p. 83)

2. Occipital: Vision, although specific areas contribute to different aspects of visual coding, including motion, shape, and color. Parietal: Body senses, including touch, pain, temperature, and awareness of body part location. Primary somatosensory cortex is here. Temporal: Hearing, emotional behavior, language comprehension. Frontal: Primary motor cortex controls fine movement; prefrontal area contributes to organization and planning of movements; left frontal lobe involved in language production. (pp. 79-82, Fig. 3.17)

3. Any of these examples would work: (a) Profession musicians have a larger auditory cortex as well as some other brain areas. (b) Larger posterior hippocampus areas, important for spatial memory, are found in London taxi drivers. (c) Physical activity benefits brain size in old age. (p. 86)

4. The corpus callosum is cut to severe the connections between right and left cerebral hemispheres. This prevents seizures from spreading between the hemispheres. Split-brain patients generally exhibit normal behavior, but if information is presented very briefly to one visual field that information is only processed in the opposite hemisphere. If processed in the right hemisphere the patient will not be able name the object. However, if processed in the left hemisphere the patient will be to name the object. (pp. 87-90)

5. Information presented to each visual field gets into both eyes. For example, information in the left visual field goes onto the right side of each retina. The optic fibers on the nose side (right) of the left eye cross to the right hemisphere, and the fibers on the temple side (right) of the right eye go back to the right hemisphere. Hence, information from the left visual field goes to the right hemisphere and information from the right visual field goes to the left hemisphere. (If this is unclear, review pp. 89-90 and Figs. 3.27-3.28)

6. Positron-emission tomography (PET) provides a high-resolution image of brain activity by recording radioactivity emitted from injected chemicals. Functional magnetic resonance imaging (fMRI) uses magnetic detectors outside the head to measure the amounts of hemoglobin with and without oxygen in different parts of the brain. (pp. 84)

7. The medulla is an elaboration of the spinal cord and controls many muscles in the head and several life-preserving functions, such as breathing. The pons is adjacent to the medulla that receives sensory input from the head and controls many muscles in the head. The cerebellum controls movement, especially complex, rapid motor skills and behaviors that require precise timing. (p. 82)

Answers to the Multiple Choice Questions – Module 3.2

1. a. Incorrect. Has the opposite reactions; "calms" body down
    b. Incorrect. Part of nervous system that controls internal organs lies just outside of spinal cord
    c. Incorrect. Not part of nervous system; secretes hormones
    d. Correct! (p. 83)
    e. Incorrect. Carry sensory information to spinal cord

2. a. Correct! (p. 83)
    b. Incorrect. This is a function of hindbrain, so it is likely
    c. Incorrect. This is a function of hindbrain, so it is likely
    d. Incorrect. This is a function of hindbrain, so it is likely

3. a. Incorrect. It is in parietal lobe
    b. Incorrect. From the opposite side of body
    c. Correct! (pp. 79-80)
    d. Incorrect. It is part of cerebral cortex

4. a. Incorrect. Connection between hemispheres, not site of damage, is cut
    b. Correct! (pp. 87-88)
    c. Incorrect. Visual input still goes to one hemisphere, but not to both
    d. Incorrect. Optic chiasm is not interfered with in split brain

5. a. Incorrect. Only axons from the right half of the left eye cross to the right hemisphere
    b. Incorrect. Only axons from the left half of the left eye go straight back to the left hemisphere
    c. Correct! (p. 88)
    d. Incorrect. Reversed-axons from the right side of an eye go to the right

6. a. Incorrect. A condition marked by impulsive behavior and short attention span
    b. Correct! (p. 87)
    c. Incorrect. A condition cause by a gradual decay of one pathway of axons that release dopamine
    d. Incorrect. A set of axons connection the two hemispheres of the brain

7. a. Incorrect. X-rays generate a computerized image
    b. Correct! (p. 84)
    c. Incorrect. Use magnetic detectors outside of head
    d. Incorrect. A system that uses electrodes placed on a person's scalp to show

8. a. Incorrect. This is a function of the sympathetic nervous system. It is the parasympathetic system constricts the pupils because this system conserves energy
    b. Incorrect. This is a function of the sympathetic nervous system. It is the parasympathetic system constricts the pupils because this system conserves energy
    c. Correct! (p. 83)
    d. Incorrect. This is a function of the sympathetic nervous system. It is the parasympathetic system constricts the pupils because this system conserves energy

Answers to the True False Questions – Module 3.2

1. **True**: Although it is closely related to the nervous system, it is not actually a part of it. (p. 83)

2. **False**: The autonomic nervous system controls internal organ functioning. (p. 83)

3. **False**: It is the amygdala that is responsible for these functions. The medulla is located in the hindbrain and receives sensory input from the head and sends impulses for motor control of the head. (p. 80)

4. **False**: The information from the left visual field strikes the right half of both retinas and is sent to the right hemisphere of the brain. (p. 88)

5. **True**: For most people the left hemisphere of the brain is specialized for language and the right is specialized for emotional perception and visual-spatial tasks. (p. 90)

6. **False**: A positron-emission tomography provides a high-resolution image of brain activity by recording radioactivity emitted from injected chemicals. (p. 84)

Answers to Final Comprehensive Assessment

1. b (pp. 69-70)
2. b (p. 69, Fig. 3.1)
3. b (pp. 73-75)
4. d (p. 69)
5. d (pp. 70-72)
6. e (pp. 73-74)
7. c (p. 75)
8. e (p. 76)
9. d (p. 83)
10. b (p. 83)
11. c (p. 82)
12. a (p. 78)
13. c (pp. 79-80)
14. a (p. 79)
15. a (p. 87)
16. b (pp. 88-90)
17. d (pp. 88-90)
18. e (p. 99)

CHAPTER 4

SENSATION AND PERCEPTION

CHAPTER OVERVIEW INFORMATION

LEARNING OBJECTIVES

By the end of Chapter 4 you should

- ✓ Be acquainted with the principles of the anatomy and function of the eye and the theories of color vision
- ✓ Be knowledgeable about the components and functioning of the other senses
- ✓ Be knowledgeable about the processes of perception and how it is influenced by biological and other factors

CHAPTER 4 OUTLINE

Chapter 4 examines how our senses work and how we understand the information that comes to us via our senses. The processes above really describe the difference between sensation (how the senses work) and perception (understanding the information acquired).

Chapter 4 is presented below in outline format to assist you in understanding the information presented in the chapter. More detailed information on any topic can be found using the page references to the right of the topic.

Module 4.1 Vision

I. The Detection of Light
    A. Vision involves reception of radiated energy (p. 96, Fig. 4.1)
    B. Receptors are specialized cells that convert energy (p. 97)
    C. Structure of the Eye
        1. Light passes through the cornea, pupil, and lens onto the fovea (pp. 98-99, Figs. 4.2-4.3)
    D. Some Common Disorders of Vision
        1. Elongated eyeballs cause nearsightedness; flattened eyeballs cause farsightedness (p. 99, Figs. 4.5 a-b)
        2. Glaucoma is increased pressure in the eyeball which can damage the optic nerve (p. 99)
        3. The lens becomes cloudy with cataracts (p. 99)
    E. The Visual Receptors
        1. Rod and cone receptors are located on the retina (p. 99, Table 4.1, Fig. 4.6)
        2. Rods are sensitive in dim light (pp. 99-101, Fig. 4.7)
        3. Cones are sensitive to color and give detailed vision (pp. 99-101, Table 4.1)
            a. Fovea consists of cones (p. 100)
    F. Dark adaptation
        1. Occurs for both rods and cones (pp. 101-102, Fig. 4.8a-b)
    G. The Visual Pathway
        1. Neural impulses travel through the bipolar cells, ganglion cells, and optic nerve to the brain (p. 102)
        2. There are multiple blind spots but the largest one is where the optic nerve leaves the retina (pp. 102-103, Figs. 4.9-4.10)
        3. Binocular rivalry happens when left- and right-eye images conflict (p. 104, Fig. 4.11)

4. Devices now available to translate image in a message sent to visual cortex (p. 104, Fig. 4.12)

II. Color Vision
   A. Color vision depends on cones (p. 104)
   B. The Trichromatic Theory- three types of cones used to explain color vision (pp. 104-105, Figs. 4.13-4.14)
   C. The Opponent Process Theory- three two-color systems used to explain color vision (pp. 105-106, Fig. 4.15)
      1. Can explain negative afterimages (p. 106)
   D. Retinex Theory -- retina and cortex interact to determine color vision (pp. 106-108)
      1. Can explain color constancy (pp. 106-108, Fig. 4.16a-d)
   E. Color Vision Deficiency
      1. Color blindness occurs because of a deficiency in the cones (pp. 108-109, Figs. 4.17-4.18)
   F. Color Vision, Color Words, and Culture
      1. Different cultures have different names for colors which may be influenced by physical changes in the lens or literacy rates. (pp. 109-110, Fig. 4.19)

The message: Vision is a construction, not a copy, of the outside world (p. 110)

Module 4.2 The Nonvisual Senses

III. Hearing
   A. In hearing, sound waves are translated into neural impulses (p. 112)
   B. Sound waves are detected via the following path: is eardrum, three tiny bones, cochlear fluid, basilar membrane, hair cells which are the receptors (pp. 112-113, Fig. 4.21)
      1. Loudness is a perception related to amplitude of sound waves (p. 112, Fig. 4.20)
      2. Pitch is a perception related to frequency of sound waves, (pp. 114-115, Figs. 4.20 and 4.22)
      3. Conduction deafness occurs when sound waves aren't properly transmitted to the cochlea (p. 113)
      4. Nerve deafness occurs because of damage to the cochlea, hair cells, or auditory nerve (p. 113)
   C. Pitch Perception
      1. Pitch perception depends on three mechanisms (p. 114, Fig. 4.22)
         a. Neurons fire in synchrony for low frequencies (frequency principle) (p. 114)
         b. Groups of neurons fire in synchrony for middle frequencies (volley principle) (p. 114)
         c. Different parts of basilar membrane vibrate for high frequencies (place principle) (p. 114)
   D. Localization of Sounds
      1. Sound is localized by differences in loudness and time of arrival at the two ears (p. 115, Fig. 4.23)

IV. The Vestibular Sense
   A. Receptors for vestibular senses are in inner ear (pp. 115-116, Fig. 4.24)
      1. Semicircular canals detect acceleration (p. 116)
      2. Otolith organs detect tilt of the head (p. 116)

V. The Cutaneous Senses
    A. The cutaneous senses depend upon receptors in the skin and internal organs (pp. 116-117, Fig. 4.25)
        1. Receptors allow perceptions of pain, pressure, temperature, itching and tickling (pp. 116-117)
    B. Pain
        1. Pain is a mixture of sensation and emotion (p. 117)
            a. Gate theory of pain suggests that pain message pass through a gate which can be open or closed (pp. 117-118, Fig. 4.26)
            b. Pain can be decreased by the release of endorphins which block release of Substance P (p. 118, Fig. 4.27)
            c. Capsaicin causes a burning sensation followed by a reduction in pain (p. 119)
    C. Phantom Limbs
        1. A sensation of an amputated body part continues (pp. 119-120)
            a. Somatosensory cortex areas for amputated body part receives activation from other areas (p. 120, Fig. 4.28)

VI. Chemical receptors are responsible for taste and smell (pp. 121-123)
    A. Taste receptors are taste buds on the tongue (p. 121, Fig. 4.29)
        1. The primary tastes are sweet, sour, salty, and bitter. Now evidence for MSG (p. 121)
            a. Individual differences affected by genetics, age, gender, and pregnancy (p. 121)
        2. Olfactory (smell) receptors are on mucous membranes at rear of nose (p. 121, Fig. 4.31)
            a. The nose has at least 100 different receptors. (pp. 122-123, Fig. 4.30)
            b. Animals identify each other by pheromones chemicals the animal releases (p. 123)

The message: Senses are adapted to provide information about what is most important to a species. (p. 123)

Module 4.3 The Interpretation of Sensory Information

VII. Perception of Minimal Stimuli
    A. The perceived world is created from the real world (p. 125)
    B. Sensory Thresholds and Signal Detection
        1. An absolute threshold is the minimum intensity that a person can detect half the time (pp. 125-126, Fig. 4.33)
            a. Sensory adaptation can change the threshold (p. 126)
        2. Observers' willingness to make false alarms can affect threshold (p. 126, Fig. 4.34)
            a. This is studied in signal-detection theory (pp. 126-127, Fig. 4.35)
    C. Subliminal Perception
        1. Subliminal perception occurs below the conscious threshold (p. 127)
    D. What Subliminal Perception Cannot Do
        1. Subliminal messages don't do many things they are claimed to do (p. 127)
            a. They do not cause people to buy things (p. 127)
            b. Backward messages are not understood (p. 127)
            c. Subliminal audiotapes do not cause behavioral changes (p. 127)
    E. What Subliminal Perception Can Do
        1. There is some evidence that stimuli that aren't conscious are processed (pp. 127-128)
            a. Subliminal messages may cause weak and short-lived changes (p. 128)

VIII. Perception and the Recognition of Patterns
    A. Perceived brightness depends on context (pp. 128-129, Figs. 4.36-4.37)
    B. Face recognition depends on both specific feature and how they fit together into an overall pattern (p. 129, Figs. 4.38-4.39)
    C. The Feature-Detector Approach
        1. Feature detectors break patterns into simple components (pp. 129-130)
            a. Cells that detect specific features have been found in animals (pp. 130-131, Fig. 4.40)
            b. Fatigued feature-detector cells produce illusions (pp. 131-132, Fig. 4.41)
        2. Do Feature Detectors Explain Perception?
            a. More complex identification depends on context (p. 132, Figs. 4.42a-b)
    D. Gestalt Psychology
        1. Suggested that we actively construct overall patterns (p. 133, Fig. 4.43)
            a. Reversible figures are evidence for active organization (p. 133, Figs. 4.44 and 4.45)
            b. The Gestalt principles of proximity, similarity, continuation, closure, and good figure help to explain the organization of stimuli (pp. 134-135, Figs. 4.46-4.47)
        2. Gestalt Principles in Hearing
            a. Principles of perceptual organization apply to hearing (pp. 135-136)
    E. Feature Detectors and Gestalt Psychology
        1. Both are important for perception (p. 136, Figs. 4.48-4.49)

IX. Perception of Movement and Depth
    A. Distance and movement are interpretations of changes on the retina (p. 136)
        1. Objects are perceived as constant in size and shape (p. 136, Fig. 4.50)
    B. Perception of Movement
        1. Movement of an object doesn't occur when the eyes move (pp. 136-137)
            a. Induced movement occurs when the background moves and the object is stationary (p. 137)
            b. Stroboscopic movement occurs when stationary images are presented (p. 137, Figs. 4.51-4.52)
    C. Depth Perception
        1. Several cues are used to perceive distance (p. 138)
            a. Retinal disparity occurs because the two retinas receive different images (p. 138)
            b. The eyes must converge more to focus on close objects (p. 138, Fig. 4.53)
            c. Monocular cues involve only one eye (pp. 138-139)
                i. Object size, linear perspective, detail, interposition, texture gradients, and shadows can be used to judge distance in pictures (p. 139, Fig. 4.54)
                ii. Motion parallax involves relative movement and requires real scenes (p. 140)

X. Optical Illusions
    A. Illusions occur because of misinterpretations (pp. 140-141, Fig. 4.56)
    B. The Relationship Between Depth Perception and Size Perception
        1. Sometimes changes in distance are interpreted as size changes (pp. 140-141, Figs. 4.57-4.59)
        2. Interpreting two-dimensional drawings as three-dimensional can cause depth perception errors (p. 141, Figs. 4.60-4.61)

C. Further Evidence Linking Illusions to Depth Perception
    1. Brain constructs perceptions to match possible reality (pp. 141-142, Figs. 4.62-4.63)
D. The Moon Illusion
    1. The moon looks much larger on the horizon than high in the sky (pp. 142-144, Fig. 4.64)
        a. There are several theories of the moon illusion, but none explains completely (pp. 142-144)

The message: *Perception depend on our experience and knowledge to build up an interpretation of sensory information. (p. 144)*

RELATED WEBSITES AND ACTIVITIES

Visit http://psychology.wadsworth.com/kalat_intro7e/ for online quizzing, glossary flashcards, crossword puzzles, annotated web links, and more.

LECTURE MATERIAL

Information from the text is only half of the picture. Don't forget to review your lecture material. Process each topic meaningfully. Most importantly, be sure that you understand the material in each lecture-if you don't, ask your instructor or teaching assistant.

STUDY TIP # 4: Try to study in a place that is quiet, distraction free, well illuminated and has a desk/table large enough so you can spread out your materials. One way to make a relatively quiet place more quiet is to wear earplugs while studying. This reduces most ambient noises. Also, turn off your TV, radio, cell phone, etc. Ambient noises such as these attract your attention and decrease your effectiveness.

TIP: Associate the lecture material with the information from the text, with things that you already know, with your personal experiences, or with real-life applications. Type or neatly re-write your notes. Make sure they are detailed and organized. Make comments on your notes. Then write questions to cover each concept.

CHAPTER MODULE ASSESSMENTS

Module 4.1 Vision
Answer these questions soon after reading the **Module 4.1: Vision**. There are several formats to the assessments. Answers to all questions appear on pp. 72-73.

Fill in the Blank
Provide a term(s) which best completes the statement below. Answers appear on p. 72.

1. The _____ is an adjustable opening in the eye through which light enters.

2. The gradual improvement in the ability to see in dim light is called _____.

3. The tendency of an object to appear nearly the same color under a variety of lighting conditions is called _____.

4. According to the _____ theory of color vision, we perceive color in terms of a system of paired opposites such as red versus green.

5. As people age they gradually develop _____ or decreased flexibility of the lens and an inability to focus on nearby objects.

6. The _____ is the area in the eye where the optic nerve exits the retina leaving no room for receptors.

Short Answer

The following questions require a short written answer (3-7 sentences). Answers appear on p. 72.

1. What is the function of receptors? How are they involved in the relationship between the external and internal worlds?

2. Describe three differences between rods and cones other than their shapes.

3. Contrast the Young-Helmholtz, opponent-process, and retinex theories of color perception.

4. Explain what occurs in the cones when people are color-blind.

5. Name and describe the two visual receptor cells located in the retina.

Multiple Choice
Circle the best answer below. Check your answers on p. 73. If your answer was incorrect, try to write why it was incorrect. Check your reasons on p. 73.

1. The nervous system:
   a. builds a copy of the external stimulus in the brain
   b. registers the exact intensity and direction of every stimulus
   c. uses receptors to interpret information and to extract meaning
   d. translates external stimuli into internal representations

2. Professor Frodul is myopic. He:
   a. is farsighted
   b. has an eyeball that is flattened
   c. has a cornea that is too round
   d. has a faulty optic nerve
   e. has an eyeball that is elongated

3. John is a night watchman. He thinks he hears someone outside in the dim light. In order to see this as clearly as possible, he should:
   a. look slightly to the side of the fovea so rods will be stimulated
   b. look through his widened pupil so cones will be stimulated
   c. make the image fall on his fovea so cones will be stimulated
   d. be sure that the entire electromagnetic spectrum falls on his retina
   e. try to get the image into his blind spot so that his cornea will be clear

4. Dark adaptation takes much longer if you stare at a faint light while another light flashes in the periphery of your vision than if you just stare at the first light. Why?
   a. having the two lights stimulates more cones
   b. the second light stimulates cones, which take longer to adapt
   c. the second light stimulates rods, which take longer to adapt
   d. having two lights stimulates the ganglion cells as well as the bipolar cells
   e. the second light moves the stimulation from the first light from the blind spot

5. According to the opponent-process theory, we see green when:
   a. the medium wavelength cone is more active than the other two
   b. the cortex synthesizes a color from active areas of the retina
   c. particular ganglion cells are inhibited and others are excited
   d. we have a negative afterimage of a yellow light

True/False
Select the best answer by circling *T for True* or *F for False*. Check your answers on p. 73.

1. **T or F** Glaucoma is a disorder in which the lens becomes cloudy.

2. **T or F** Rods are receptors adapted for color vision, daytime vision, and detailed vision.

3. **T or F** When a person enters a dark room their eyes adjust to the changes in light so that in time the person can see better.

4. **T or F** A person with hyperopia, or farsightedness, has difficulty focusing on far away objects.

5. **T or F** The proportion of rods is highest toward the center of the retina.

Module 4.2 The Nonvisual Senses
Answer these questions soon after reading the **Module 4.2: The Nonvisual Senses**. There are several formats to the assessments. Answers to all questions appear on pp. 73-76.

Fill in the Blank
Provide a term(s) which best completes the statement below. Answers appear on pp. 73-74.

1. _____ are neurotransmitters that are similar to morphine weaken pain sensations.

2. A _____ is the continuing sensation of an amputated body part.

3. _____ results when the bones connected to the eardrum fail to transmit sound waves properly to the cochlea.

4. _____ are chemicals that are released into the environment by nearly all nonhuman mammals for sexual communication.

5. The _____ is the snail-shaped, fluid filled structure that contains the receptors for hearing.

Short Answer
The following questions require a short written answer (3-7 sentences). Answers appear on p. 74.

1. Explain how pitch is perceived for sounds of different frequencies.

2. According to the gate theory of pain, why do reports of pain differ so much, even when the physical damage is similar?

3. Why are people generally less sensitive to low concentrations of bitter substances than other tastes?

4. What is the vestibular sense?

5. Describe the phenomenon known as the "phantom limb".

Multiple Choice
Circle the best answer below. Check your answers on pp. 74-75. If your answer was incorrect, try to write why it was incorrect. Check your reasons on pp. 74-75.

1. Which of the following is the correct path of sound waves to the receptors for hearing?
   a. eardrum, cochlea, three tiny bones, hair cells, basilar membrane
   b. eardrum, three tiny bones, cochlear fluid, basilar membrane, hair cells
   c. three tiny bones, cochlear fluid, basilar membrane, eardrum, hair cells
   d. three tiny bones, basilar membrane, hair cells, eardrum, cochlear fluid

2. How does the human ear encode a tone of 10,000 hertz?
   a. the basilar membrane vibrates in synchrony; hair cells send impulses at that frequency
   b. the basilar membrane vibrates in synchrony with it, and groups of hair cells volley impulses in synchrony with the tone
   c. by the difference in time and loudness at the two ears
   d. the basilar membrane vibrates maximally at a specific location; those hair cells send impulses

3. If you have damage to your semicircular canals:
   a. you may have trouble with balance
   b. your vestibular sense would be poor
   c. your free nerve endings would not send impulses
   d. both b and c
   e. both a and b

4. Jalapeño peppers cause somewhat painful sensations because they result in the release of:
   a. endorphins
   b. capsaicin
   c. sodium lauryl sulfate
   d. substance P
   e. pheromones

5. The olfactory sense in humans:
   a. is very poor because the receptors are not sensitive
   b. is particularly important because of the role played by pheromones
   c. results from receptors that are called taste buds
   d. is limited to only four tastes: sweet, sour, bitter, and salty
   e. is stimulated by gaseous molecules that we inhale

6. Pheromones act primarily on the _____, a set of receptors near, but separate from, the standard olfactory receptors.
   a. taste buds
   b. vomeronasal organ
   c. both a and b
   d. none of the above

7. In which case would all of the hair cells in the cochlea be excited equally?
   a. When the tone is less than about 100Hz
   b. When the tone ranges from 100 to 4000Hz
   c. When the tone is beyond 4000Hz
   d. They are always excited equally

True/False
Select the best answer by circling *T for True* or *F for False*. Check your answers on pp. 75-76.

1. **T or F** Endorphins are released only in painful situations.

2. **T or F** Pitch is a perception that depends on the amplitude of sound waves.

3. **T or F** Collectively, sensations such as warmth, cold, pain, vibration, and movement across the skin are known as the cutaneous senses.

4. **T or F** Some cases of nerve deafness can be treated with surgery.

5. **T or F** The volley principle tells us the direction of tilt, the amount of acceleration, and the position of the head with respect to gravity.

6. **T or F** The vestibular sense provides information regarding acceleration of the head and the position of the head with respect to gravity.

7. **T or F** Following surgery to remove a limb a patient may still sense the amputated body part. The phantom limb is a continuing sensation of a body part.

8. **T or F** The place principle is the identification of pitch by determining which auditory neurons, coming from which part of the basilar membrane, are most active.

9. **T or F** Nearly all nonhuman mammals rely on pheromones for sexual communications.

10. **T or F** The sensation of pain by the nervous system is due to a release of endorphins.

Module 4.3 The Interpretation of Sensory Information

Answer these questions soon after reading the **Module 4.3: The Interpretation of Sensory Information**. There are several formats to the assessments. Answers to all questions appear on pp. 76-78.

Fill in the Blank

Provide a term(s) which best completes the statement below. Answers appear on p. 76.

1. _____ is our interpretation of sensory information.

2. Our perception of distance, or _____ perception, allows us to experience the world in three dimensions.

3. A _____ is the intensity at which a given individual can detect a sensory stimulus 50% of the time.

4. _____ psychology is a field of study that focuses on our ability to perceive overall patterns.

5. _____ theory is the study of people's tendencies to make hits, correct rejections, misses, and false alarms.

6. The _____ is the apparent difference between the size of the moon at the horizon and its size when viewed higher in the sky.

7. _____ cues enable a person to judge depth and distance effectively with just one eye.

Short Answer

The following questions require a short written answer (3-7 sentences). Answers appear on pp. 76-77.

1. How does the signal-detection approach to detection differ from the threshold approach?

2. What are the problems in studying subliminal perception? What does modern research suggest about the possibility of subliminal perception?

3. Contrast the feature-detector and Gestalt approaches to perception.

4. Explain how Gestalt principles apply to hearing.

5. Assume that you have a negative afterimage of the U.S. flag. Describe what would happen if you looked at a white screen that is very close to you and then at one that is very far away. Use this example to explain how size and distance are related.

Multiple Choice
Circle the best answer below. Check your answers on pp. 77-78. If your answer was incorrect, try to write why it was incorrect. Check your reasons on pp. 77-78.

1. An observer might often detect stimuli that are below the absolute threshold because:
   a. dark adaptation has occurred, lowering the threshold
   b. thresholds are defined as 50% detection, so observers will detect below-threshold stimuli half the time
   c. observers set a stringent criterion and make few false alarms
   d. evidence for subliminal perception can be found easily and such perception has been shown to have long-lasting influences on behavior

2. The feature-detector approach differs from the Gestalt approach because the feature-detector approach:
   a. suggests that we break stimuli down into components; the Gestalt approach argues that we perceive "wholes"
   b. relies on the measurement of thresholds; the Gestalt approach emphasizes optical illusions
   c. points out the importance of visual constancies; the Gestalt approach emphasizes reversible figures
   d. argues that aftereffects should not be found after fatiguing specific feature detectors; Gestalt approach argues that they should

3. Many computer printers produce letters that consist of unconnected small dots. Yet we see the patterns as complete letters. Which Gestalt principle is operating here?
   a. separation of figure and ground
   b. similarity
   c. closure
   d. reversible figure
   e. proximity

4. When a rectangular door is slightly open, it projects a trapezoidal image on the retina, yet you see it as rectangular. Why?
   a. size constancy makes it appear the same
   b. visual constancies cause you to interpret changes on the retina as actual changes in the size and shapes of objects
   c. shape constancy tells you that it has changed position, not shape
   d. convergence tells you that its shape has not changed
   e. because a door is a door even if it's ajar

5. Which depth cue could not be used by a person with one eye?
   a. size
   b. closer objects overlap farther objects
   c. amount of detail in objects
   d. convergence
   e. motion parallax

6. Jack, who is standing perfectly still, says that there is some wind because the leaves on the trees are moving; Jill, who is riding up the hill, says "No, the leaves aren't moving." How can this discrepancy be explained?
   a. Jill's vestibular system tells her that she is moving
   b. induced movement tells Jack that the leaves are moving
   c. Jack is having an illusion similar to the Mueller-Lyer illusion
   d. the background is stationary to Jill

7. The moon illusion:
   a. is not an illusion at all; the moon is larger when it is close to the horizon
   b. occurs because light rays bend differently near the horizon
   c. occurs because we interpret the horizon as being farther away than the overhead sky
   d. occurs because we are likely to compare the moon's size with objects at the horizon
   e. both c and d may be partly correct, but the moon illusion is difficult to explain

8. The tendency to perceive objects as keeping their shape, size, and color, even though what actually strikes the retina changes is known as
   a. induced movement
   b. stroboscopic movement
   c. visual constancy
   d. proximity

True/False
Select the best answer by circling *T for True* or *F for False*. Check your answers on p. 78.

1. **T or F** Monocular cues depend on the action of both eyes.

2. **T or F** One form of induced movement occurs as the result of the rapid succession of stationary images.

3. **T or F** There is not a sharp dividing line between sensory stimuli that can be perceived and sensory stimuli that can not be perceived.

4. **T or F** Motion parallax is the principle that the faster an object passes by, the closer it must be.

5. **T or F** Convergence is a binocular cue used to estimate the distance of an object.

FINAL COMPREHENSIVE CHAPTER ASSESSMENT TEST

Check your answers on p. 79.

1. What is the relationship between what we sense and what is really there?
    a. there is a perfect relationship between external events and our internal representations
    b. models of external stimuli are created in the brain
    c. they are physically identical
    d. external stimuli are translated into a neural "language"
    e. for vision, internal copies are made but for other senses that are nonspatial, other types of representations are formed

2. When a person is farsighted:
    a. the lens does not become thin and flat as it should for distant objects
    b. he or she has myopia
    c. the eyeball is elongated
    d. the eyeball is flattened
    e. both b and c

3. Why can you see fine detail better if you look straight at an object than if you look out of the corner of your eye?
    a. the object falls on the fovea, where there are many rods
    b. the object falls on the periphery, where there are many cones
    c. the object falls on rods, many of which send impulses to the same ganglion cell
    d. the object falls in the blind spot, where detailed vision is good
    e. the object falls on the fovea, where there are many cones

4. Why does everyone have a blind spot in each eye?
    a. there are no rods or cones where the optic nerve leaves the retina
    b. there are no cones on the periphery of the retina
    c. the retina is organized with rods and cones at the front and ganglion cells at the rear
    d. the fovea contains no rods
    e. the rods on the far periphery contain no photopigments

5. Which of the following best supports retinex theory?
    a. negative afterimages occur in the opposite color
    b. people are usually red-green color-blind
    c. different cones show different levels of responding to different colors
    d. three different colors of light can be mixed to make all other colors
    e. the apparent color of an object depends upon the colors of the objects around it

6. Colorblind people:
   a. usually cannot distinguish any colors
   b. see green objects as red
   c. most often have trouble distinguishing yellow from blue
   d. most often have trouble distinguishing red from green
   e. do not have any photopigments in their cones

7. What happens to the basilar membrane when a low tone (below 100 Hz) is sensed?
   a. a very small area of it vibrates; the rest is relatively stationary
   b. it vibrates in synchrony with the sound waves
   c. it volleys in synchrony with the sound waves
   d. the left basilar membrane responds faster than the right one
   e. it will respond to more reflected sounds than with a higher tone

8. When a sound comes from directly overhead, it is difficult to localize because:
   a. it reaches one ear earlier than the other
   b. the basilar membrane is unable to respond to such a sound
   c. it sounds louder in one ear than the other
   d. it reflects off objects too much
   e. it reaches the two ears at the same time and with the same intensity

9. Why is it easier to read when your head is moving than when the page is moving?
   a. the vestibular system keeps your eyes focused when your head moves but not when the book moves
   b. the basilar membrane vibrates when your head moves, but not when the book moves
   c. the somatosensory system keeps your eyes focused when your head moves but not when the book moves
   d. the gate in the spinal cord prevents stimulation to the brain when your eyes move, but the signal gets through the gate when the book moves
   e. capsaicin is released when the head moves; this causes the release of substance P, which keeps the eyes focused when the head moves

10. Endorphins are:
    a. drugs made from the opium poppy that are similar to morphine
    b. neurotransmitters that cause the release of substance P and decrease pain
    c. used to decrease the sensitivity of the olfactory system
    d. neurotransmitters that occur naturally and are similar to morphine
    e. naturally occurring substances that cause the release of capsaicin in the body

11. The five types of taste buds are:
    a. each located in a different part of the tongue
    b. important for sensing the location of the substance on the tongue
    c. interrelated, so that if one of them is affected by some chemical, all are affected
    d. located almost exclusively along the sides of the tongue
    e. unrelated to heat and cold so that changing the temperature does nothing to the taste

12. Pheromones:
    a. are used by animals to recognize one another
    b. are very important in human sexual behavior
    c. do not exist in humans
    d. are neurotransmitters that help to reduce pain
    e. cannot be detected by the human olfactory system

13. Which of the following claims about subliminal perception is true?
    a. people choose a picture that was presented subliminally more often than one that wasn't presented
    b. subliminal messages presented backward in songs can make people believe in the devil
    c. subliminal messages in movies influence people to buy snacks
    d. subliminal tapes can make people change their behavior; they are especially effective for increasing self-esteem

14. Which of the following supports the feature-detector model of pattern recognition?
    a. Hubel and Wiesel found that some brain cells responded only to angles
    b. some figures are reversible so that the background becomes the object
    c. things which are close together tend to be grouped into a unit
    d. we tend to "hear" missing syllables in speech
    e. stimuli are identified in context such that additional stimuli can either help or hurt identification

15. Gestalt psychologists:
    a. try to break stimuli into their basic components
    b. believe that perceptions depend on overall configurations
    c. argue that perception is simply the passive reception of energy
    d. emphasize the study of feature detectors
    e. believe in the theories of their founder, B. F. Gestalt

16. Why are you more likely to see the item below as columns of Ks rather than rows of Ks?

```
K   K   K   K   K
K   K   K   K   K
K   K   K   K   K
K   K   K   K   K
```

    a. figure-ground principle
    b. closure
    c. proximity
    d. continuity
    e. similarity

17. Which of the following is not a cue for distance?
    a. convergence of the two eyes
    b. different views seen by the two eyes
    c. haziness of objects
    d. curvature of the cornea when focusing
    e. size of objects

18. As the $100 bill that you just won blows away from you in the wind, you do not perceive it as becoming smaller. Why?
    a. you have size constancy
    b. you are not responding to visual constancies
    c. your eyes compensate by converging more and more to focus
    d. your lens is unable to change fast enough to notice the size change
    e. you assume that objects in the distance are moving closer

19. The Mueller-Lyer illusion is:
    a. seeing the moon as larger when it is closer to the horizon than when it is high in the sky
    b. seeing lines as longer when arrowheads point inward than when they point outward
    c. stronger for people who live in cities and more technological societies than for people from more rural cultures
    d. only experienced by people who have lots of experience with drawings of objects
    e. larger for adults than for children

20. Which statistic most accurately describes the prevalence of color blindness.
    a. more than 20% of males are color blind
    b. more than 20% of females are color blind
    c. about 8% of males are color blind
    d. about 8% of females are color blind

Answers to the Fill in the Blank Questions – Module 4.1

1. pupil (p. 98)

2. dark adaptation (pp. 101-102)

3. color constancy (p. 107)

4. opponent-process (pp. 105-106)

5. presbyopia (p. 99)

6. blind spot (p. 102)

Answers to the Short Answer Questions – Module 4.1

1. Receptors convert physical energy into nerve impulses, or stimuli in the external world into internal stimuli. The internal experience is lawfully related to the external stimuli, but they are not perfectly related. (pp. 97-98)

2. Rods are sensitive in dim light; cones are sensitive only in bright light. Rods are color-blind; cones respond to color. Cones are concentrated on the fovea at the center of the retina; rods are on the periphery. (pp. 99-101, Table 4.1)

3. Young-Helmholtz theory holds that there are three types of cones that respond maximally to different colors. Opponent-process theory holds that higher-level cells are excited (speeded up) to one color and inhibited (slowed down) to another. Retinex theory stresses interpretation of color by the cortex. (pp. 104-108)

4. Usually, there is an abnormality in either the red or green cones (although other types of colorblindness also occur). If the problem is in the green cones (medium-wavelength) it is called deuteranopia; if it is in the red cones (long-wavelength) it is called protanopia. The abnormal cones don't respond properly to the green or red light, so the person has difficulty discriminating red from green. (pp. 108-109)

5. The two receptor cells are cones and rods. Cones are receptor cells adapted for color vision, daytime vision, and detailed vision. The human eye contains about 6 million cones. The rods are receptor cells adapted for vision in dim light. The human eye contains about 120 million rods. (pp. 99-101)

Answers to the Multiple Choice Questions – Module 4.1

1. a. Incorrect. The internal representation may not resemble the external stimulus in any way
   b. Incorrect. Internal representations are related to external stimuli, but they aren't the same
   c. Incorrect. This is perception; receptors are responsible for sensation
   d. Correct! (p. 97)

2. a. Incorrect. Myopic means nearsighted; presbyopia means farsighted
   b. Incorrect. This occurs in farsightedness
   c. Incorrect. Cornea shape is unrelated to nearsightedness
   d. Incorrect. Optic nerve goes from ganglion cells to brain
   e. Correct! (p. 99)

3. a. Correct! (p. 100)
   b. Incorrect. Cones cannot see well in dim light; a widened pupil makes it more likely that rods will be stimulated
   c. Incorrect. Cones cannot respond in dim light
   d. Incorrect. The entire spectrum is not visible, only part of it
   e. Incorrect. Blind spot is where axons leave retina; nothing can be seen there

4. a. Incorrect. Second light would only stimulate rods
   b. Incorrect. Rods take longer to adapt than cones
   c. Correct! (pp. 99-101)
   d. Incorrect. Both lights would stimulate both types of cells
   e. Incorrect. Nothing can be seen in the blind spot; a second light wouldn't affect where the first one falls

5. a. Incorrect. Young-Helmholtz theory (emphasis on cones)
   b. Incorrect. Retinex theory (emphasis on cortex)
   c. Correct! (p. 106)
   d. Incorrect. Blue would produce a yellow afterimage

Answers to the True/False Questions – Module 4.1

1. **False**: Glaucoma is a condition characterized by increased pressure within the eye. A cataract is a disorder in which the lens becomes cloudy. (p. 99)

2. **False**: Rods are receptors adapted for vision in dim light. (p. 100)

3. **True**: Dark adaptation is the gradual adjustment of vision that one experience when entering a dark or very dimly lit area. (p. 101)

4. **False**: Hyperopia results in a difficulty of focusing on close objects. Myopia, or nearsighteness, results in a difficulty of focusing on far away objects. (p. 99)

5. **False**: Proportion of cones is highest in the fovea or center of the retina. Cones are what allow us to see detail and in color while rods are used more in night vision. (p. 100)

Answers to the Fill in the Blank Questions – Module 4.2

1. Endorphins (p. 118)

2. phantom limb (p. 119)

3. Conduction deafness (p. 113)

4. Pheromones (p. 123)

5. cochlea (pp. 112- 113)

Answers to the Short Answer Questions – Module 4.2

1. For low sounds (under 100 Hz), the basilar membrane vibrates in synchrony with the sound and nerve impulses are sent in synchrony. Middle sounds (100-5000 Hz) are coded in a similar manner, except that individual hair cells cannot send impulses that fast, so groups of cells volley and, as a group, send impulses that are in synchrony with the sound. High sounds (over 5000 Hz) cause maximum vibration at certain places on the basilar membrane, and only those hair cells send impulses to the brain. (pp. 114-115, Fig. 4.22)

2. According to the gate theory, pain messages pass through a gate in the spinal cord. The brain can send messages to the spinal cord to open the gate and let the pain impulses through or to close the gate and block the pain. Although some of the details of this gate theory are wrong, the basic idea that the brain facilitates or inhibits the transmission of pain messages is correct. Distraction may help to close the gate, or distraction may cause the release of endorphins, which are natural painkillers that work in the brain. (pp. 117-118)

3. We have about 40 to 80 kinds of bitter receptors, but not many of each of those types. So a weak concentration will not excite many bitter receptors. (pp. 121-122)

4. A structure in the inner ear on each side of the head called a vestibule that tells us the direction of tilt and amount of acceleration of the head and the position of the head with respect to gravity. It plays a key role in posture and balance. (p. 115)

5. A phantom limb is a continuing sensation of an amputated body part. For example, someone might report occasional feelings of touch, tingling, or pain from an amputated hand, arm, leg, foot, or any other amputated part. The phantom sensation might last only days or weeks after the amputation, but it sometimes lasts years or even a lifetime. (p. 119)

Answers to the Multiple Choice Questions – Module 4.2

1. a. Incorrect. Three tiny bones are between eardrum and cochlea
   b. Correct! (pp. 112-113)
   c. Incorrect. Eardrum comes before three tiny bones
   d. Incorrect. Eardrum comes first, cochlear fluid before basilar membrane

2. a. Incorrect. For low tones, below 100 hertz
   b. Incorrect. For medium tones, 100-5000 hertz
   c. Incorrect. This is how sound is localized
   d. Correct! (p. 114)

3. a. Incorrect, but your vestibular sense would also be poor.
    b. Incorrect, but you may also have trouble with balance.
    c. Incorrect. Free nerve endings are receptors for pain and temperature, not vestibular sense
    d. Incorrect. Your vestibular sense would be poor, but your free nerve endings would send impulses
    e. Correct! (p. 116)

4. a. Incorrect. Neurotransmitters that inhibit the release of substance P
    b. Incorrect. This is the chemical in the jalapeños that causes the release of substance P
    c. Incorrect. A chemical that weakens the response to sweet tastes
    d. Correct! (p. 118)
    e. Incorrect. Odorous chemicals released by mammals

5. a. Incorrect. Each receptor is sensitive; we just don't have as many as other animals
    b. Incorrect. Less important for humans than other animals
    c. Incorrect. Taste buds are for taste, not smell
    d. Incorrect. Olfactory means smell, not taste
    e. Correct! (p. 121)

6. a. Incorrect. Taste buds are where our taste receptors are located
    b. Correct! (p. 123)
    c. Incorrect. Pheromones act primarily on the vomeronasal organ only
    d. Incorrect. The Vomeronasal Organ is correct

7. a. Correct! (p. 114)
    b. Incorrect. At this range, the volley principle is in effect: at least a few hair cells are excited, and groups of them respond to each vibration by producing an action potential
    c. Incorrect. The highest frequency sounds vibrate hair cells only near the stirrup end of the basilar membrane, according to the place principle
    d. Incorrect. At each point along the cochlea, hair cells are tuned resonators that vibrate only for sound waves of a particular frequency, thus, they will not always be excited equally

Answers to the True/False Questions – Module 4.2

1. **False**: Endorphins are released in painful situations AND pleasant experiences, which explains why a pleasant view helps to ease post surgical pain. (p. 118)

2. **False**: Pitch is a perception closely related to the wave's frequency not amplitude. A high frequency sound is perceived as high pitched whereas a low frequency sound is perceived as low pitched. (p. 114)

3. **True**: All of the cutaneous senses rely on receptors in the skin or internal organs. (p. 116)

4. **False**: Surgery cannot correct nerve deafness, which results from damage to the cochlea, hair cells or auditory nerve. (p. 115)

5. **False**: The volley principle applies to how we perceive mid-level frequency sounds. Each sound wave excites some hair cells, and at mid-level frequencies, groups of hair cells volley their response since each individual hair cell could not individual respond at the required rate (p. 114)

6. **True**: The vestibular sense is comprised of the semicircular canals and the otolith organs located within the inner ear. (pp. 115-116)

7. **True**: Otherwise known as the phantom limb phenomenon, some patients continue to sense the amputated body part. (p. 119)

8. **True**: Neurons on different parts of the basilar membrane will become active based on different high frequency sounds. (p. 114)

9. **True**: Pheromones are chemicals animals emit to communicate with others. For example, a female dog that is in her fertile state will emit pheromones to attract nearby males. (p. 123)

10. **False**: Pain stimuli cause the release of Substance P; endorphins inhibit the release of Substance P. (p. 118)

Answers to the Fill in the Blank Questions – Module 4.3

1. Perception (p. 125)

2. depth (p. 138)

3. sensory threshold (p. 125)

4. Gestalt (p. 133)

5. Signal-detection (p. 126)

6. moon illusion (p. 142)

7. monocular (pp. 138-139)

Answers to the Short Answer Questions – Module 4.3

1. Thresholds are found by determining the lowest-intensity stimulus that can be detected half of the time. Thresholds will vary depending upon other factors, such as degree of dark adaptation. Using signal-detection theory, both the ability to detect a stimulus and the observer's criterion are taken into account. An observer may detect more stimuli under some conditions, but if she also makes a lot of false alarms (detecting the stimulus when it isn't present), detection isn't any better; the criterion is simply less stringent (strict). (pp. 125-127)

2. One problem is identifying whether stimuli are really subliminal (below threshold) because subjects may or may not report seeing or hearing them, depending upon how cautious they are about their responses. There is evidence that the nervous system processes stimuli even though we are unaware of them, but these effects don't last very long. These can influence our perception of other stimuli, but there is no evidence that subliminal messages influence buying behavior or have any effect on breaking bad habits. (pp. 127-128)

3. The feature-detector approach argues that people break stimuli down into components, such as lines and angles. The brain then analyzes the components to decide what a stimulus is. The Gestalt approach argues that we take in whole stimuli rather than breaking them into components. (pp. 129-136)

4. There are reversible figures in sound as well as in vision. For example, a clock can sound like "tick, tock, tick, tock" or "tock, tick, tock, tick." People also lock onto one interpretation of a sound and cannot hear the other one. If they organize the words in a sentence in one way, they may organize the words in the next sentence in the same way until they discover that the organization doesn't make sense. (pp. 135-136)

5. The negative afterimage has a certain size on your retina. If you look at a white piece of paper near your eyes, you will see a small image. If you look at a piece of paper far away, you will see a large image. In the far case, you assume that the actual size must be quite large for the afterimage to be that big on your retina and that far away. In the close case, you assume that the actual size is small because the distance is close. (pp. 140-141)

Answers to the Multiple Choice Questions – Module 4.3

1.　a.　Incorrect. The absolute threshold is measured when dark adaptation is complete; it's the lowest measurable threshold
　　b.　Correct! (p. 125)
　　c.　Incorrect. A stringent criterion would result in more misses and fewer false alarms
　　d.　Incorrect. Evidence for subliminal perception is not always found and, when it is, it is short-lived

2.　a.　Correct! (pp. 129-136)
　　b.　Incorrect. Feature detection emphasizes components, but not necessarily thresholds; Gestalt relies on more than illusions
　　c.　Incorrect. Visual constancies not particularly relevant to features; reversible figures are one demonstration
　　d.　Incorrect. Such fatigue is evidence for feature detectors

3.　a.　Incorrect. Involves picking out object from background
　　b.　Incorrect. Tendency to see similar things as going together
　　c.　Correct! (p. 134)
　　d.　Incorrect. Tendency to see parts as either figure or ground
　　e.　Incorrect. Tendency to see things that are close as going together

4.　a.　Incorrect. Shape is emphasized here, not size
　　b.　Incorrect. We do not interpret changes as actual changes in objects
　　c.　Correct! (pp. 136-137, Fig. 4.50)
　　d.　Incorrect. Convergence is a cue to distance
　　e.　Incorrect. A bad joke, but that's what shape constancy suggests

5. a. Incorrect. Can be seen with one eye
   b. Incorrect. Can be seen with one eye
   c. Incorrect. Can be seen with one eye
   d. Correct! (p. 138)
   e. Incorrect. Differential movement across retina can be seen with one eye, although not in a picture

6. a. Correct! (p. 136)
   b. Incorrect. Occurs when background moves and object doesn't; object is moving here
   c. Incorrect. Seeing lines with outward arrowheads as longer than lines with inward arrow heads; not relevant here
   d. Incorrect. Background would be moving to Jill since she is moving

7. a. Incorrect. Moon is same size
   b. Incorrect. It is a psychological, not a physical effect
   c. Incorrect. This one is possibly correct, but try again.
   d. Incorrect. This one is possibly correct, but try again.
   e. Correct! (pp. 142-144)

8. a. Incorrect. Induced movement is when we incorrectly perceive an object as moving against a stationary background
   b. Incorrect. Stroboscopic movement is an illusion of movement create by a rapid successions of stationary images
   c. Correct! (p. 136)
   d. Incorrect. Proximity is the tendency to perceive objects that are close together as belonging to a group

Answers to the True/False Questions – Module 4.3

1. **False**: Binocular cues depend on the action of both eyes. Monocular cues enable a person to judge depth and distance effectively with one eye. (pp. 138-140)

2. **False**: Induced movement is when we incorrectly perceive the object as moving against a stationary background. (p. 137)

3. **True**: Since the sensory threshold is the point at which 50% of the stimuli are detected, that means there are stimuli that are detected below and above 50%. It is not an all or nothing proposition. (pp. 125-126)

4. **True**: This is one of the monocular cues used to judge the distance of an object from the viewer. (p. 139)

5. **True**: Convergence of the eyes, or how much the eyes turn in, provides a cue as to the distance of an object. The more the eyes turn in, the closer the object. (p. 138)

Answers to Final Comprehensive Assessment

1. d (p. 97)
2. d (p. 99)
3. e (p. 100)
4. a (pp. 102-103)
5. e (pp. 106-108)
6. d (pp. 108-109)
7. b (p. 114)
8. e (p. 115)
9. a (pp. 115-116)
10. d (p. 118)
11. d (p. 121, Fig. 4.29)
12. a (p. 123)
13. a (pp. 127-128)
14. a (pp. 130-131)
15. b (p. 133)
16. c (p. 134)
17. d (pp. 138-139)
18. a (p. 136)
19. c (pp. 140-141)
20. c (pp. 108-109)

CHAPTER 5

STATES OF CONSCIOUSNESS

CHAPTER OVERVIEW INFORMATION

LEARNING OBJECTIVES

By the end of Chapter 5 you should

- ✓ Understand the processes of sleep and the role that sleep and dreaming play in mental functioning
- ✓ Have an increased understanding of what hypnosis is and its valid uses
- ✓ Have knowledge of the classes of drugs and the problems of drug abuse and dependence

CHAPTER 5 OUTLINE

Chapter 5 explores the unique experiences and behaviors that result from different states of consciousness. Sleep and Dreams, Hypnosis, and Drugs and their Effects are the three states discussed. Sleeping consumes a significant portion (25-33%) of a person's life. Effects of hypnosis are explored in an attempt to determine what the scientific evidence suggests about what hynosis can and cannot do. The different effects of drugs on behavior and experience is also presented.

Chapter 5 is presented below in outline format to assist you in understanding the information presented in the chapter. More detailed information on any topic can be found using the page references to the right of the topic.

Module 5.1 Sleep and Dreams

I. Sleep and Dreams
    A. Rhythms of activity and inactivity are called circadian rhythms (p. 153, Fig. 5.1)

II. Our Circadian Rhythms
    A. Morning People and Evening People
        1. Some people are morning people and some are evening people (p. 154, Fig. 5.1)
        2. Older people mostly morning people. Younger people most evening people (p. 154, Fig. 5.2)
    B. Shifting Sleep Schedules
        1. West-shift (going to bed later) is easier than east-shift (going to bed earlier) (pp. 155-156, Figs. 5.3-5.4)
        2. Jet lag is a period of discomfort and inefficiency due to internal clock being out of phase (p. 155)
    C. Brain Mechanisms of Circadian Rhythms
        a. The superchiasmic nucleus controls the circadian rhythms (p. 156, Fig. 5.5)
            i. It regulates the secretion of melatonin (p. 156)

III. Why We Sleep
    A. Sleep must serve some function (p. 156)
    B. The Repair and Restore Theory
        1. The purpose of sleep is to enable the body to recover from exertions of the day (pp. 156-157)

2. There are several weaknesses in this theory (pp. 156-157)
    a. People don't need much more sleep after a day of extreme activity (p. 156)
    b. Some people get by with very little sleep (p. 156)
    c. People who go intentionally without sleep don't need much to be recovered (p. 157, Fig. 5.6)
C. The Evolutionary, or Energy-Conservation, Theory
    1. Evolutionary or Energy Conservation theory suggests that sleep protects from danger (pp. 157-158, Fig. 5.7)
    a. Species vary in how much they sleep, but all sleep some (pp. 157-158, Fig. 5.8)

IV. Stages of Sleep
A. REM (Rapid Eye Movement) or Paradoxical sleep is observed when the eyes and brain are active but the major muscles are relaxed (pp. 158-159)
B. Sleep Cycles During the Night
    1. Stages determined by EEG activity (p. 159, Figs. 5.9-5.10)
    2. Sleep cycles through four stages (p. 159)
    3. Stages are 1-NREM, 2, 3, 4, 3, 2, 1-REM (p. 159, Fig. 5.11)
    4. A cycle through the stages takes 90-100 minutes (p. 159)
C. Sleep Stages and Dreaming
    1. Dreaming occurs during REM sleep (p. 159)
D. The Functions of REM Sleep
    1. Deprivation of REM sleep leads to anxiety, irritability, and impaired concentration (p. 160)
    2. Infants have more REM sleep than older children or adults (p. 161, Fig. 5.12)
    3. REM sleep may improve memory storage and new learning may prompt extra REM sleep (p. 162)

V. Abnormalities of Sleep
A. Insomnia
    1. Insomnia means lack of sleep resulting in a feeling of not being well rested (p. 162)
    a. Research suggests that most people suffering from insomnia also have other medical or psychological (e.g., depression or anxiety) conditions (p. 162)
B. Sleep Apnea
    1. People with sleep apnea awaken because they cannot breathe while asleep (pp. 162-163)
C. Narcolepsy
    1. People with narcolepsy fall asleep during the day (p. 163)
    2. Only 1 in 5,000 people have this condition (p. 163)
D. Sleep Talking, Sleepwalking, Nightmares, and Night Terrors
    1. Sleep talking, sleepwalking, nightmares, and night terrors are fairly common (p. 163)
    a. Sleep talking is common and usually occurs in Stage 2 sleep (p. 163)
    b. Sleepwalking usually occurs in children during stage 4 (p. 163)
        i. Waking sleepwalkers poses no problems (p. 163)
    c. Nightmares are unpleasant dreams (p. 163)
    d. Night terrors are accompanied by extreme panic (p. 163)
        i. These are more common in children and occur in Stages 3 and 4 (p. 163)
E. Leg Movements While Trying to Sleep
    1. Periodic limb movement disorder or restless leg syndrome can cause poor sleep (p. 163)
F. Hypersomnia
    1. Hypersomnia is excessive but unrefreshing sleep (p. 164)

G. If You Have Trouble Sleeping
   1. Associate bed with sleeping, establish a regular sleep schedule, avoid stimulants in evening, avoid us of alcohol, make bedroom quiet, and exercise daily (p. 164)

VI. The Content of Our Dreams
   A. The content of dreams is usually related to recent thoughts and concerns (p. 164)
   B. Freud's Approach
      1. Examine manifest and latent contents of dreams to understand (p. 164)
      2. No way to test interpretations (pp. 164-165)
   C. The Activation-Synthesis Theory
      1. The activation-synthesis theory suggests that the brain is active during sleep and that the brain tries to make sense of these relatively haphazard activity (p. 165)
   D. The Neurorcognitive Theory
      1. Proposes dreams as thinking that occurs under certain circumstances (p. 166, Table 5.1)
      2. Blind people who could see at one time have visual dreams; those who have never seen or who have damage to the visual cortex don't have visual dreams (p. 167)

The message *The brain is active even when sleeping (p. 168)*

Module 5.2 Hypnosis

VII. Ways of Inducing Hypnosis
   A. Hypnosis is a state of increased suggestibility (p. 169)
   B. It can be induced in several different ways (pp. 169-170)
      1. The first step is agreeing to try it (p. 170)

VIII. The Uses and Limitations of Hypnosis
   A. What Hypnosis Can do
      1. Hypnosis can do a number of things (pp. 170-171)
         a. The distress of pain can be reduced (p. 171, Fig. 5.13)
         b. Posthypnotic suggestions can help people to change their habits (p. 171)
   B. Distortions of Perception Under Hypnosis
      1. Hypnosis can result in distortions of perception or hallucinations (p. 171)
         a. People may claim that they do not hear or see stimuli, but those stimuli can still influence behavior (p. 171, Fig 5.14)
   C. What Hypnosis Cannot Do
      1. Hypnosis cannot do other things that are claimed (pp. 175-176, Fig. 5.15)
         a. Hypnotized people "remember" actual facts, but they mix in fantasies (p. 173, Fig 5.16)
         b. Hypnotized people do not relive childhood (p. 173)
         c. Hypnosis doesn't lead to recall from previous lives or periods earlier in life (p. 173, Fig. 5.17)
         d. People under hypnosis may do strange (and dangerous) things, but so do people who are pretending to be hypnotized (pp. 174-175)
   D. Is Hypnosis an Altered State of Consciousness
      1. How Well Can a Nonhypnotized Person Pretend to Be Hypnotized
         a. Hypnotized people and people pretending to be hypnotized show some different behavior (but there are lots of similarities too) (pp. 175-176)
            i. Hypnotized people are puzzled by seeing double realities; pretenders don't report seeing double realities (p. 175)

IX. Meditation: In Some Ways Like Hypnosis
  A. Meditation is another method of inducing a calm, relaxed state (p. 175)

The message: *Hypnosis enables people to relax and follow suggestions more than they usually do. (p. 176)*

Module 5.3 Drugs and Their Effects

X. A survey of Abused Drugs and Their Effects
  A. Most abused drugs increase activity at dopamine synapses (p. 178, Figs. 5.18, Table 5.3)
  B. Stimulants
    1. Stimulants heighten alertness and increase activity (p. 179)
       a. Cocaine increases heart rate but it decreases brain activity (p. 180)
          i. Crack is cocaine that can be smoked (p. 180)
          ii. Crack is very habit-forming because it enters the brain very rapidly (p. 180)
       b. Caffeine can result in dependency (p. 180)
       c. Nicotine increases heart rate and blood pressure, but decreases breathing rate (p. 180)
  C. Depressants
    1. Primary effect is to decrease arousal (p. 180)
       a. Alcohol acts as a relaxant (p. 181, Fig. 5.19)
          i. Excessive use damages the liver, aggravates medical conditions, and impairs memory and motor control (p. 181)
       b. Tranquilizers help people to relax and fall asleep (p. 181)
          i. Benzodiazepines facilitate the neurotransmitter GABA (p. 181)
  D. Narcotics
    1. Produce drowsiness, insensitivity to pain and decreased responsiveness (p. 181)
    2. Opiates bind to synapses that use endorphins which are naturally occurring brain chemicals (pp. 181-182)
       a. Morphine is used as a pain killer in controlled doses (p. 182)
  E. Marijuana intensifies sensory experiences (pp. 182-183)
    1. Some memory problems when being used. Memory ability recovered after stopped (p. 182)
    2. Medicinal properties used to reduce nausea, suppress tremors, reduce eye pressure (p. 182)
    3. THC, the active ingredient, attaches to receptors mostly in the hippocampus (p. 182)
  F. Hallucinogens
    1. Hallucinogens induce sensory distortions (p. 183, Fig 5.20)
       a. Most naturally occurring, but some are manufactured including MDMA (p. 183)

XI. Chronic Drug Effects
  A. Drug Withdrawal
    1. Withdrawal symptoms occur when habitual use ceases (p. 184)
       a. Specific effects depend upon the drug (p. 184)
          i. Physical dependence occurs when people use the drug to reduce withdrawal effects (p. 184)
          ii. Psychological dependence is a strong desire to use the drug but no physical withdrawal symptoms (p. 184)

B. Drug Tolerance
   1. Drug tolerance means that more and more drug is required to get the same effects (p. 184)
      a. Tolerance may result from both automatic chemical changes and psychological effects (p. 184)

The message: *Almost all drugs impair the brain's functioning in some way. (p. 185)*

RELATED WEBSITES AND ACTIVITIES

Visit http://psychology.wadsworth.com/kalat_intro7e/ for online quizzing, glossary flashcards, crossword puzzles, annotated web links, and more.

LECTURE MATERIAL

Information from the text is only half of the picture. Don't forget to review your lecture material. Process each topic meaningfully. Most importantly, be sure that you understand the material in each lecture-if you don't, ask your instructor or teaching assistant.

STUDY TIP # 5: Re-write/type your notes as soon after the lecture as possible. Doing so will reinforce the learning that has occurred and will allow you to develop questions to ask your professor the next time you meet.

TIP: Associate the lecture material with the information from the text, with things that you already know, with your personal experiences, or with real-life applications. Type or neatly re-write your notes. Make sure they are detailed and organized. Make comments on your notes. Then write questions to cover each concept.

CHAPTER MODULE ASSESSMENTS

> **Module 5.1 Sleep and Dreams**
> Answer these questions soon after reading the **Module 5.1: Sleep and Dreams**. There are several formats to the assessments. Answers to all questions appear on pp. 96-99.

Fill in the Blank
Provide a term(s) which best completes the statement below. Answers appear on p. 96.

1. According to the _____ theory, the purpose of sleep is to enable the body to recover from the exertions of the day.

2. People are more likely to report dreams during the paradoxical, or _____ stage of sleep, during which the sleeper's eyes move rapidly back and forth under their closed.

3. The _____ theory suggests that dreams are the brain's attempt to make sense of random sensory experiences and activities that occur during sleep.

4. _____ literally means "lack of sleep" and indicates that a person does not feel well rested.

5. Freud believed that all dreams had a manifest, or surface content, and a hidden, symbolic or _____ content.

6. The_____ theory treats dreams as just another example of thinking that occurs under special conditions.

7. People who fail to breathe for a minute or longer and wake up gasping for breath suffer from _____.

8. Each species generates a _____ rhythm, or rhythm of activity and inactivity that lasts about 24 hours.

9. _____ is a medical condition where people suddenly and unexpectedly fall asleep during the middle of the day.

Short Answer
The following questions require a short written answer (3-7 sentences). Answers appear on pp. 96-97.

1. Describe evidence that supports the idea that humans have built-in mechanisms that produce a 24-hour wake-sleep cycle.

2. Briefly describe the repair and restoration theory of sleep. Discuss two weaknesses of the theory.

3. Explain the evolutionary view of sleep.

4. Describe the stages of sleep including the EEG activity that accompanies them. Discuss two characteristics of REM sleep.

5. What are the effects of REM sleep deprivation?

6. What is narcolepsy? How does it differ from insomnia?

7. Discuss sleep talking, sleepwalking, and night terrors.

Multiple Choice
Circle the best answer below. Check your answers on pp. 97-98. If your answer was incorrect, try to write why it was incorrect. Check your reasons on pp. 97-98.

1. Which of the following provides evidence that our 24-hour sleep-waking cycle is the result of a built-in mechanism?
   a. some people sleep only 5-6 hours a night; others sleep 7-8 hours
   b. only a little more sleep is needed after a day of exertion than after a day of little activity
   c. people who live in an environment in which everything is constant still go to sleep and wake at about the same time each day
   d. prisoners who are forced to stay awake for long periods of time develop severe health problems

2. Jet lag occurs whenever you change time zones quickly. Which type of trip will result in the most difficult adjustment?
   a. Flying from Los Angeles to New York
   b. Flying for 1 1/2 hours but staying in the same time zone
   c. Flying from New York to Chicago
   d. Flying from New York to Los Angeles

3. Which of the following is evidence for the repair and restoration theory of sleep?
   a. the body increases its rate of cell division during sleep
   b. species that are less likely to be attacked sleep longer
   c. people can survive without sleep for 10 or 11 days
   d. people need only a little more sleep following a day of extreme activity than following a day of inactivity
   e. some people have hypersomnia

4. The evolutionary theory of sleep predicts which type of animal should sleep the least? One that is:
   a. unlikely to be attacked by other animals
   b. sleeping in a familiar environment
   c. able to complete its eating in a short time
   d. likely to be attacked by other animals

5. The high-school student who stayed awake for several days:
   a. was near death by the time he slept
   b. slept for many days when he finally went to sleep
   c. didn't fully recover until he had several nights of normal sleep
   d. slept longer than usual when he did go to sleep, but was fully refreshed upon awakening

6. REM sleep is also called paradoxical sleep because:
   a. the brain is very active, but heart rate, breathing rate, and temperature fluctuate greatly and the muscles are relaxed
   b. the brain is relatively inactive and the heart rate is very low
   c. the large muscles are very active but the temperature is very low
   d. the large muscles are relaxed and heart rate is low
   e. dreams occur here yet the times are much shorter than the perceived length of dreams

7. Electroencephalograph (EEG) waves:
   a. are similar when a person is in stage 4 sleep and awake
   b. become shorter and choppier as a person moves from stage 1 to stage 4 sleep
   c. become larger as a person goes into deeper sleep because a larger proportion of the active neurons are active at the same time
   d. are the largest when a person is very awake because the brain is most active

8. Which of the following is the proper order of sleep stages in a cycle?
   a. (NREM), 2, 3, 4, 1 (REM), 2, 3, 4
   b. (REM), 2, 3, 4, 1 (REM), 2, 3, 4
   c. (REM), 2, 3, 4, 3, 2, 1 (REM)
   d. (NREM), 2, 3, 4, 3, 2, 1 (REM)

9. Dreams:
   a. only occur in REM sleep
   b. may occur in NREM sleep but they are less vivid and visual than in REM sleep
   c. are almost always in color
   d. may occur in REM sleep but they are less vivid and visual than in NREM sleep
   e. never occur in blind people

10. People who have been selectively deprived of REM sleep:
    a. have difficulty waking up in the morning and falling asleep at night
    b. become very depressed
    c. often show REM rebound
    d. develop narcolepsy

11. Which of the following is not true?
    a. Dreams last about as long as REM sleep does
    b. Sleep talking occurs only during REM sleep
    c. People who have the same dream over and over report more anxiety, depression, and stress than do other people
    d. Night terrors are common among young children and usually occur during stages 3 and 4
    e. Restless leg syndrome is a common cause of poor sleep in people over 50

True/False
Select the best answer by circling *T for True* or *F for False*. Check your answers on pp. 98-99.

1. **T or F** You should never awaken a sleepwalker.

2. **T or F** Sleep apnea is a condition in which a person has problems with nightmares, which causes them not to sleep.

3. **T or F** A person traveling from west to east is likely to experience greater jet lag than a person traveling from east to west.

4. **T or F** It is likely that as you approach your 60s that you are more likely to become a "morning person".

5. **T or F** Sleep allows us to recover from the exertions of the day is a statement consistent with the repair and restore theory of why we sleep.

6. **T or F** Someone in REM sleep is likely to be moving around while sleeping.

7. **T or F** Chris only sleeps 3-4 hours a night but always feels well rested in the morning. Chris suffers from insomnia.

8. **T or F** Researchers can use an EEG to determine the stage of sleep a person is experiencing.

Module 5.2 Hypnosis
Answer these questions soon after reading the **Module 5.2: Hypnosis**. There are several formats to the assessments. Answers to all questions appear on pp. 99-100.

Fill in the Blank
Provide a term(s) which best completes the statement below. Answers appear on p. 99.

1. _____ is a condition of increased suggestibility that occurs in the context of a special relationship.

2. A suggestion to do or experience something particular after coming out of hypnosis is a _____.

3. Sometimes hypnotized people will report seeing, hearing or feeling things that are not physically present. These are known as _____.

4. _____ is similar to hypnosis in that a calm, relaxed state is achieved through the use of special techniques.

Short Answer
The following questions require a short written answer (3-7 sentences). Answers appear on p. 99.

1. Describe the modern view of hypnosis. How does it differ from Mesmer's view?

2. Describe how people imitating hypnosis are similar to and different from people who are actually hypnotized.

Multiple Choice
Circle the best answer below. Check your answers on pp. 99-100. If your answer was incorrect, try to write why it was incorrect. Check your reasons on pp. 99-100.

1. The state of hypnosis is best described as a:
   a. condition of heightened suggestibility
   b. trance state that is similar to sleep
   c. power emanating from the hypnotist's body
   d. state in which the mind and body become separated

2. A well-established effect of hypnosis on perception is:
   a. the elimination of certain illusions as a result of suggestion
   b. the ability to become deaf
   c. a reduction in the distress of pain
   d. a large reduction in the intensity of pain

3. There are many myths about hypnosis. Which of the following is actually true?
   a. People can remember things very accurately that they cannot remember without hypnosis
   b. Hypnotized people can become stiff as a board
   c. People under hypnosis will do strange things that nonhypnotized people would never do
   d. Posthypnotic suggestions cause long-term behavior change
   e. Hypnotized people can remember most events from childhood

4. Hypnosis is effective in
   a. helping people relive previous lives
   b. reducing the stress associated with pain
   c. helping people know about their future
   d. none of the above

True/False
Select the best answer by circling *T for True* or *F for False*. Check your answers on p. 100.

1. **T or F** Hypnosis is an altered state of consciousness, which results in an increased susceptibility to suggestion.

2. **T or F** Mesmer was the first person to use hypnosis when treating medical conditions.

3. **T or F** Only hypnotized people will engage in strange and dangerous behaviors.

4. **T or F** Results regarding the efficacy of a post hypnotic suggestion are mixed.

5. **T or F** Meditation can result in decreases in physiological arousal, as measured by heart rate, breathing rate, blood pressure, and EEG patterns.

Module 5.3 Drugs and Their Effects

Answer these questions soon after reading the **Module 5.3: Drugs and Their Effects**. There are several formats to the assessments. Answers to all questions appear on pp. 100-102.

Fill in the Blank
Provide a term(s) which best completes the statement below. Answers appear on p. 100.

1. Drugs that induce sensory distortions are known as _____.

2. Narcotic drugs such as _____ decrease pain by stimulating endorphin synapses in the brain.

3. A person suffers from drug _____ when they take a drug repeatedly and its effects grow weaker and weaker unless they increase the dose.

4. _____ drugs boost energy, heighten alertness, increase active, and produce a pleasant feeling.

5. The brain produces several chemicals called _____ that bind to opiate receptors and inhibit chronic pain.

6. Depressant drugs like alcohol and _____ produce relaxation by facilitating the effects of GABA, an inhibitory neurotransmitter.

Short Answer
The following questions require a short written answer (3-7 sentences). Answers appear on p. 101.

1. Explain how crack differs from cocaine both in terms of the substance itself and in terms of its effects.

2. Explain how drug withdrawal symptoms might work to keep someone using the drug.

Multiple Choice
Circle the best answer below. Check your answers on p. 101. If your answer was incorrect, try to write why it was incorrect. Check your reasons on p. 101.

1. Which drugs boost energy, heighten alertness, and increase activity?
   a. hallucinogens
   b. alcoholic beverages
   c. barbiturates
   d. stimulants
   e. opiates

2. Research has shown that the relationship between brain receptors and THC is that THC:
   a. attaches to specialized receptors, found mostly in the hippocampus
   b. doesn't attach to receptors but modifies neuronal membranes
   c. may attach to a few receptors but those are rare in the brain
   d. attaches to the same receptors as endorphins do

3. In rats, it has been shown that the coordination of rats after 24 injections of alcohol is better at the end if they have been tested after each injection. This shows that:
   a. alcohol is not addictive
   b. alcohol produces strong withdrawal symptoms
   c. tolerance results from more than simple repeated exposures to the drug
   d. drug tolerance depends on purely automatic chemical changes

4. Which of the following is NOT supported regarding the use of marijuana?
   a. decreased memory functioning
   b. has medicinal uses
   c. increases ability to keep track of time
   d. decrease the release of both excitatory and inhibitory neurotransmitters

5. Which of the following drugs produces stimulant effects at low doses and hallucinogenic effects at higher doses?
   a. MDMA or ecstasy
   b. alcohol
   c. caffeine
   d. valium

True/False
Select the best answer by circling *T for True* or *F for False*. Check your answers on pp. 101-102.

1. **T or F** Two common types of depressants are alcohol and tranquilizers.

2. **T or F** Physical dependence on a drug is a strong repetitive desire for something without any accompanying physical symptoms of withdrawal.

3. **T or F** Drug tolerance is observed when a person needs more of a drug to obtain the same effects.

4. **T or F** The effect of morphine is similar to that observed with the release of endorphins.

FINAL COMPREHENSIVE CHAPTER ASSESSMENT TEST

Check your answers on p. 102.

1. What happened to the sleep cycles of the people who spent a few weeks in Mammoth Cave?
   a. they spontaneously adapted to a 28-hour day
   b. they slept for about 4 hours and stayed awake for about 4 hours
   c. they could not keep a set cycle; sleeping and waking times varied greatly from day to day
   d. they kept a 24-hour cycle, waking up and going to sleep at about the same time each day
   e. they were sleepy in the morning, but not at night

2. Sleep deprivation for a period of several days results in:
   a. dizziness, slurred speech, and hallucinations in everyone
   b. a loss of skill, such as that needed to play arcade games
   c. the need to sleep for 24 hours or more before recovery can occur
   d. minimal effects in some people who have control of the situation
   e. a total loss of ability to concentrate; even the simplest tasks cannot be completed

3. Which of the following is consistent with the repair and restoration theory of sleep?
   a. some people need much less sleep than other people
   b. only a little more sleep is needed after a day of exertion than after a day of inactivity
   c. people who stay awake are sleepier at night than in the morning
   d. people can go for 10 or more days without sleep
   e. the body increases the rate of cell division and new protein production during sleep

4. According to the evolutionary theory of sleep, some animals sleep more than others because they:
   a. are more active
   b. must expend more energy to kill their prey
   c. eat such low-calorie food that they must rest often
   d. are less vulnerable to attack
   e. have higher metabolic rates

5. Why is it better to shift work schedules from an eight-to-four shift to a four-to-midnight shift than the other way around?
   a. the body is better able to repair and restore when sleep occurs later than earlier
   b. it is like flying east--going toward the sunrise makes it easier to fall asleep than going away from it
   c. the direction of the shift is irrelevant as long as the lights are kept dim for the night shift
   d. it is like flying west--it is easier to go to bed later than usual
   e. this type of shift makes you feel safer in your bedroom, so you sleep better

6. Sam Snore volunteered for a psychology experiment in which he slept for two nights in the laboratory. On the first night, he was awakened every time he entered REM sleep. The result was that he had almost no REM sleep during that night. His EEG on the next night would show:
   a. more stage 4 sleep than usual
   b. more stage 2 sleep than usual
   c. less REM sleep than usual
   d. less stage 4 sleep than usual
   e. more REM sleep than usual

7. Bob seems to be deeply asleep, yet his brain waves resemble those of an alert, waking state. Bob is now in _____ sleep and just before this he was in _____.
   a. REM; a drowsy, awake state
   b. REM; stage 1 sleep
   c. Stage 4; stage 2 sleep
   d. Stage 2; stage 1 sleep
   e. paradoxical; stage 4 sleep

8. REM sleep:
   a. may play some role in memory storage
   b. lasts longer during the first than during the second half of the night
   c. is the time when sleepwalking is most likely to occur
   d. is the only stage in which dreams occur at night
   e. is absolutely necessary; even a few nights of deprivation can cause death

9. The content of dreams is influenced by:
   a. experiences of the past day
   b. stimuli being experienced during sleep
   c. spontaneous brain activity
   d. all of the above

10. Why is it impossible for sleepwalking to occur during REM sleep?
    a. the postural muscles are so relaxed that they would not support a person
    b. the heart rate is so slow that there would not be enough blood flowing to the large muscles
    c. the part of the brain that is responsible for movement becomes inactive
    d. the EEG shows too much spontaneous activity for specific muscles to be stimulated
    e. the eye movements use so much energy that there is little left for coordinated movement

11. Which of the following is false?
    a. night terrors usually occur during Stage 3 or Stage 4 sleep
    b. most people talk in their sleep, at least some of the time
    c. the activation-synthesis theory of dreams suggests that the brain is actively organizing sensory information during dreams
    d. sleepwalking occurs in adults more often than in children
    e. dream content is often related to the day's activities

12. Narcolepsy involves:
    a. a failure to breathe while sleeping that may results in awakening many times each night
    b. very unpleasant dreams that keep children awake
    c. prolonged creepy-crawly sensations in the legs
    d. frequent awakenings during the night
    e. sudden attacks of extreme sleepiness during the day

13. Mesmer's animal magnetism:
    a. worked because magnets redirected patients' flow of blood
    b. made physicians and scientists associate hypnosis with eccentrics
    c. was based on the idea that hypnosis is a state of enhanced suggestibility
    d. induced hypnotic trances, which redistributed brain activity
    e. worked with actual magnets, but not without them

14. Scientific studies have most strongly supported the contention that hypnosis can:
    a. reduce the distress of pain, although it reduces the intensity of pain only slightly
    b. make people totally deaf
    c. eliminate illusions if the hypnotist says to ignore the contextual stimuli
    d. give you physical strength that you would not have otherwise
    e. make you do things that you would never do otherwise

15. Hypnosis has been used to help people remember things. These memories:
    a. are extremely accurate
    b. often include things that the hypnotized person has made up
    c. are quite accurate under hypnosis, but become mixed with fantasy when the person comes out of hypnosis
    d. are very accurate if they involve the person's childhood; otherwise they are not accurate

16. Which of the following is true of people who are actually hypnotized as compared with people who are pretending?
    a. pretenders cannot tolerate pain without flinching
    b. when asked to sit down, pretenders look for a chair first; hypnotized people do not
    c. when told to experience anger, hypnotized people show physiological reactions, pretenders do not
    d. hypnotized people will imagine seeing someone sitting in a chair and also see the entire chair; pretenders do not report seeing the chair
    e. pretenders will report seeing a single individual in two places; hypnotized people will not report seeing the same person in two places

17. Marijuana:
    a. is chemically similar to crack
    b. causes sexual debauchery
    c. facilitates transmission at synapses using GABA
    d. can help relieve glaucoma
    e. is gone from the body within 3 hours after use

18. Cocaine:
    a. increases heart rate, but decreases overall brain activity
    b. has no anesthetic properties
    c. has less of an effect after it is treated with ether
    d. is called a designer drug because people from high society use it
    e. is not addictive

19. Symptoms of withdrawal from opiate drugs include:
    a. sweating, sleeplessness, and possibly hallucinations and seizures
    b. nervousness and sleeplessness
    c. anxiety and heightened sensitivity to pain
    d. only mild withdrawal symptoms or no withdrawal symptoms occur

20. How are drug withdrawal and drug tolerance related?
    a. both are purely physiological effects
    b. both are purely psychological effects
    c. together they lead to decreased use of a drug
    d. increased tolerance makes a drug less effective so users may take more of the drug to fight withdrawal effects
    e. increased tolerance makes a drug more effective, so less of the drug is needed to eliminate withdrawal effects

ANSWERS AND EXPLANATIONS FOR CHAPTER MODULE ASSESSMENTS

Answers to the Fill in the Blank Questions – Module 5.1

1. repair and restoration (p. 156)

2. REM (p. 158)

3. activation-synthesis (p. 165)

4. Insomnia (p. 162)

5. latent (p. 164)

6. neurocognitive (p. 166)

7. sleep apnea (pp. 162-163)

8. circadian (p. 153)

9. Narcolepsy (p. 163)

Answers to the Short Answer Questions – Module 5.1

1. Two people spent several weeks in a cave in which the temperature was constant and they controlled their own lighting. They tended to go to sleep and awaken at their usual times even though there were no cues in the environment. (pp. 153-154)

2. The body needs sleep in order to repair and restore itself from the day's exertions. Cell division and the rate at which the body produces new proteins increase. One weakness is that we do not seem to need more sleep after a day of extreme activity than after a day of inactivity. Another weakness is that people vary greatly in the amount of sleep that they need. (pp. 156-157)

3. Sleep may have a restorative function, but it also occurs at a time when the animal is likely to be inefficient. How often and how long an animal sleeps depends upon whether it is a predator and can afford lots of sleep or a prey and can afford little sleep. It also depends upon whether meals are short or whether the animal must eat constantly. (p. 156)

4. Stage 1 (NREM) - stage 2 - stage 3 - stage 4 - stage 3 - stage 2 - stage 1 (REM). The cycle takes about 90 min. Brain waves go from short, choppy waves to long, slow waves at stage 4. During REM sleep, the person's EEG shows short, choppy waves; postural muscles are relaxed; and the person is hard to awaken. (p. 159, Fig. 5.10)

5. People who are deprived of REM show anxiety, irritability, and difficulty in concentrating. When participants are allowed to sleep undisturbed, REM rebound occurs; they spend more time in REM than usual. Because REM sleep facilitates memory storage, deprivation of REM sleep may also slow down learning, at least in animal studies. (p. 160)

6. Narcolepsy is a condition in which people fall asleep, often going into REM sleep, in the middle of the day. This is the opposite of insomnia. The person with insomnia cannot fall asleep at night; the person with narcolepsy falls asleep during the day. (p. 163)

7. Most people talk in their sleep sometimes. It occurs both during REM and NREM sleep and is not abnormal. Children are more likely to sleepwalk than adults. It occurs during stage 4 sleep because the muscles are too relaxed during REM sleep. Night terrors are fairly common in young children. The child usually awakens in an extreme state of panic and has a very high heart rate. These occur in sleep stages 3 and 4. (p. 163)

Answers to the Multiple Choice Questions – Module 5.1

1. a. Incorrect. They still may have a 24-hour cycle
    b. Incorrect. Problem for repair-restoration theory but not evidence for cycles
    c. Correct! (pp. 153-154)
    d. Incorrect. But those who stay awake on their own usually don't; not evidence for 24-hour cycles

2. a. Correct! (p. 155)
    b. Incorrect. This should not cause jet lag because time doesn't change
    c. Incorrect. Going west is not as bad as going east; it's easier to go to bed later than earlier
    Incorrect. Going west is not as bad as going east; it's easier to go to bed later than earlier

3. a. Correct! (pp. 156-157)
    b. Incorrect. Evidence for evolutionary theory
    c. Incorrect. Weakness of repair-restoration theory
    d. Incorrect. Weakness of repair-restoration theory
    e. Incorrect. Weakness of repair-restoration theory

4. a. Incorrect. An animal that is a predator will sleep a lot
    b. Incorrect. Should increase sleeping; no need to fear attack
    c. Incorrect. Can sleep a lot because eating takes little time
    d. Correct! (pp. 157-158)

5. a. Incorrect. Consequences are not that serious
    b. Incorrect. Sleep only a few more hours than normal
    c. Incorrect. Usually recover after one night's sleep
    d. Correct! (p. 157)

6. a. Correct! (pp. 158-159)
    b. Incorrect. Brain is active; heart rate fluctuates
    c. Incorrect. Large muscles are very relaxed; temperature and heart rate fluctuate
    d. Incorrect. Large muscles are very relaxed; temperature and heart rate fluctuate
    e. Incorrect. Subjective time for dreams is about the same as REM periods

7. a. Incorrect. Stage 4 waves are much larger and slower
   b. Incorrect. They become longer and less choppy with sleep
   c. Correct! (p. 159)
   d. Incorrect. When the brain is active, neurons are out of synchrony and they cancel each other

8. a. Incorrect. Goes from 4 to 3, not to 1
   b. Incorrect. Goes from 4 to 3, not to 1
   c. Incorrect. The first stage is 1, NREM; REM later replaces Stage 1
   d. Correct! (p. 159)

9. a. Incorrect. Some dreaming occurs in NREM sleep
   b. Correct! (p. 159)
   c. Incorrect. Maybe, but people report color only about half the time
   d. Incorrect. NREM dreams are less vivid and visual
   e. Incorrect. Visual dreams occur in people who had vision and lost it; people who never had vision dream about touch

10. a. Incorrect. Characteristics of jet lag
    b. Incorrect. This can improve mood in depressed people
    c. Correct! (pp. 160-161)
    d. Incorrect. They show more REM the next night; they don't fall asleep suddenly during the day

11. a. Incorrect. This is a correct statement, so it is not a correct answer to the question which asked you to select the statement that was not true
    b. Correct! (p. 163)
    c. Incorrect. This is a correct statement, so it is not a correct answer to the question which asked you to select the statement that was not true
    d. Incorrect. This is a correct statement, so it is not a correct answer to the question which asked you to select the statement that was not true
    e. Incorrect. This is a correct statement, so it is not a correct answer to the question which asked you to select the statement that was not true

Answers to the True/False Questions – Module 5.1

1. **False**: Sleep research reports that waking a sleepwalker is neither dangerous nor harmful but the person is often disoriented. (p. 163)

2. **False**: Sleep apnea is a condition causing a person to have trouble breathing while sleeping. (pp. 162-163)

3. **True**: Research shows people experience more discomfort and inefficiency due to traveling east than west. (p. 155)

4. **True**: Morning people are those that awaken easily, are full of energy, and do their best work before noon. Most people in their 60s or older are morning people. (p. 158)

5. **True**: The repair and restore theory suggest that sleep allows us to recover from our daily exertions. (pp. 156-157)

6. **False**: During REM, or Rapid Eye Movement sleep, the brain is very active but the major muscles are not. (pp. 158-159)

7. **False**: Although Chris is not getting what is considered a normal amount of sleep, she still feels well rested and therefore is not suffering from insomnia. (p. 162)

8. **True**: Examining the results of an EEG can be used to determine which stage of sleep the person is in. (p. 159)

Answers to the Fill in the Blanks Questions – Module 5.2

1. Hypnosis (p. 169)

2. post hypnotic suggestion (p. 171)

3. hallucinations (p. 171)

4. Meditation (p. 176)

Answers to the Short Answer Questions – Module 5.2

1. Hypnosis is considered to be a state of heightened suggestibility. People who are hypnotizable are likely to do what the hypnotist tells them without question. In terms of ability to move about and to respond to stimuli, it is more like waking than sleeping. Mesmer thought that the powers were within him, the hypnotist. In fact, hypnotizability seems to be due more to the participant's willingness to accept suggestions than to the hypnotist. (pp. 169-170)

2. People who are imitating hypnosis will tolerate pain without flinching, recall old memories, make their bodies stiff as a board and lie between two chairs, and show physiological changes when told to experience an emotion. However, they are not as inconsistent as actually hypnotized people who will report seeing a person sitting in a chair and also report seeing the entire chair. Real hypnotized people report seeing two images of the same person, but pretenders do not. (pp. 175-176)

Answers to the Multiple Choice Questions – Module 5.2

1. a. Correct! (p. 169)
    b. Incorrect. In terms of ability to move about and respond to stimuli, hypnosis is more like waking
    c. Incorrect. Being a hypnotist requires no unusual personality traits
    d. Incorrect. People just become more suggestible under hypnosis

2. a. Incorrect. Illusions still occur, even when their cause is supposedly not perceived
    b. Incorrect. The behavior of hypnotized people suggests that they still hear, even when they say they don't
    c. Correct! (p. 171)
    d. Incorrect. The intensity of pain is changed only a little

3. a. Incorrect. Many memories that come out under hypnosis are wrong
    b. Correct! (pp. 170-172, Fig. 5.15)
    c. Incorrect. Nonhypnotized "pretenders" do strange things too
    d. Incorrect. Usually change is short-lived, but if there is long-term change, it's probably due to the person's resolve and not the hypnotic suggestion
    e. Incorrect. Many such "memories" are not accurate

4. a. Incorrect. Although people may believe and act as if they are reliving a previous life there is unlikely to be a method to verify it
    b. Correct! (p. 171)
    c. Incorrect. No evidence exists to suggest hypnotized people can learn about future events
    d. Incorrect. Since b is the correct answer, this answer of "none of the above" is not correct

Answers to the True/False Questions – Module 5.2

1. **True**: Under hypnosis people become more suggestible than usual (p. 169)

2. **True**: Mesmer believed passing a magnet back and forth across the patient's body to redirect the flow of blood, nerve activity, and certain undefined "fluids" would make the feel better. (p. 169)

3. **False**: Research suggests that non-hypnotized people will also engage in strange and dangerous behaviors. (p. 175)

4. **True**: Results suggest small and weak effects of the post hypnotic suggestion as compared to a placebo condition. (p. 171)

5. **True**: Meditation does seem to put the body into a relaxed state. However, this does not mean that there are any spiritual effects. (p. 176)

Answers to the Fill in the Blank Questions – Module 5.3

1. hallucinogens (p. 183)

2. morphine (p. 182)

3. tolerance (p. 184)

4. Stimulants (p. 179)

5. endorphins (pp. 181-182)

6. benzodiazepines (p. 181)

Answers to the Short Answer Questions – Module 5.3

1. Cocaine can be sniffed or injected, but not smoked. In order to smoke it, the drug must have the hydrochloride removed, turning it into "freebase" cocaine, commonly called crack. Crack enters the brain more rapidly than cocaine, so it is more likely to be addictive. It is also more likely to lead to mental confusion, heart attacks, lung disease, and neglect of daily activities. (p. 180)

2. Drugs usually provide the stimulus for pleasant emotional states. As drugs wear off, however, the user moves into the opposite state. Because drugs produce tolerance effects, initial highs grow weaker and weaker with use. Finally, users may need to take the drugs to avoid the negative, opposite states produced as the effects of drugs wear off. (p. 184)

Answers to the Multiple Choice Questions – Module 5.3

1. a. Incorrect. Causes hallucinations and sensory distortions actually a relaxant
   b. Incorrect. May appear to stimulate because it inhibits some brain areas
   c. Incorrect. Results in sleep, a sedative
   d. Correct! (p. 179)
   e. Incorrect. Analgesics; these reduce pain

2. a. Correct! (p. 182)
   b. Incorrect. Scientists used to think this, but specific receptors have been found
   c. Incorrect. THC receptors may be among the most numerous in the brain
   d. Incorrect. Opiates do this; anandamide is the neurotransmitter that binds to the same receptors as THC

3. a. Incorrect. Alcohol is an addictive drug
   b. Incorrect. Alcohol does produce withdrawal symptoms, but this drug tolerance example doesn't show this
   c. Correct! (p. 184)
   d. Incorrect. If tolerance was purely automatic, then practice would have no effect

4. a. Incorrect. Marijuana causes some memory problems
   b. Incorrect. Marijuana is used to treat conditions such as glaucoma and nausea
   c. Correct! (p. 182, Table 5.3)
   d. Incorrect. A chemical in marijuana blocks the release of both excitatory and inhibitory neurotransmitter

5. a. Correct! (p. 183)
   b. Incorrect. Alcohol is primarily a relaxant/depressant
   c. Incorrect. Caffeine is actually just a stimulant
   d. Incorrect. Valium is a tranquilizer

Answers to the True/False Questions – Module 5.3

1. **True**: Depressants are drugs that predominantly decrease arousal. (pp. 180-181)

2. **False**: Physical dependence occurs when someone feels compelled to use a drug to reduce unpleasant withdrawal symptoms. (p. 184)

3. **True**: Tolerance may result from both physiological and psychological changes. Thus more of a drug in needed to produce the same effects. (p. 184)

4. **True**: Morphine seems to bind to a set of neurotransmitter receptors like endorphins. (p. 182)

Answers to Final Comprehensive Assessment

1. d (pp. 153-154)
2. d (p. 154)
3. e (p. 156)
4. d (pp. 157-158)
5. d (pp. 155-156)
6. e (p. 161)
7. b (p. 159)
8. a (p. 162)
9. d (p. 164)
10. a (pp. 158-159)
11. d (p. 163)
12. e (p. 163)
13. b (p. 169)
14. a (p. 171)
15. b (p. 173)
16. d (pp. 175-176)
17. d (p. 182)
18. a (p. 180)
19. c (p. 182)
20. d (p. 184)

CHAPTER 6

LEARNING

CHAPTER OVERVIEW INFORMATION

LEARNING OBJECTIVES

By the end of Chapter 6 you should

- ✓ Be familiar with the basic principles of behaviorism
- ✓ Be familiar with and recognize the processes of classical conditioning
- ✓ Understand the principles and applications of operant conditioning
- ✓ Be familiar with social and other kinds of learning

CHAPTER 6 OUTLINE

Learning. We all do it but what does it mean to learn? Most of us think of learning when we think about the learning that occurs in a classroom. But do we really know what happens when someone learns? The ambiguous answer to this question is maybe!

In Chapter 6, behaviorism and three types of learning (Classical, Operant and Other) are explored. However, learning is not called learning in Chapter 6 instead learning is relabeled conditioning. As you read and process the information in this chapter whenever you encounter the term conditioning you may find it helpful to substitute in learning.

Chapter 6 is presented below in outline format to assist you in understanding the information presented in the chapter. More detailed information on any topic can be found using the page references to the right of the topic.

Module 6.1 Behaviorism

I. Behaviorists study measurable, observable behaviors (p. 191)
    A. Radical and methodological behaviorists differ in the degree to which they believe that mental processes exist and can be inferred (p. 191)

II. The Rise of Behaviorism
    A. Early behaviorists explained behavior in terms of stimulus-response connections (p. 192)

III. The Assumptions of Behaviorism (p. 193)
    A. Determinism - all behavior is caused (determinism) (p. 193)
    B. The Ineffectiveness of Mental Explanations
        1. Mental explanations do not explain causes of behavior (p. 193)
    C. The Power of the Environment to Mold Behavior
        1. Behavior is molded by the environment (p. 193)

The message: Behaviorists believe that your behaviors are caused by your present and past environments. (p. 194)

Module 6.2 Classical Conditioning

IV. Pavlov and Classical Conditioning
    A. Pavlov first described classical conditioning (pp. 195-197)
    B. Pavlov's Procedures
        1. Unconditioned stimuli (UCS) produce unconditioned responses (UCR) (p. 196, Figs. 6.2-6.3)
            a. A neutral stimulus (CS) paired with the UCS causes a similar response (CR) (p. 196, Figs. 6.2-6.3)
    C. More Examples of Classical Conditioning
        1. Conditioning of an eye blink through pairing of a tone (CS) and air puff to the eye (US) (p. 197, Fig. 6.5)
        2. Condition of waking up to a neutral sound (CS) paired with an alarm from an alarm clock (US) (p. 197)
    D. The Phenomena of Classical Conditioning
        1. Many phenomena are associated with conditioning (p. 198, Fig. 6.4)
            a. Acquisition occurs when the CR is strengthened following UCS and CS pairings (p. 198)
            b. Extinction occurs if the CS is presented often without the UCS (p. 198)
            c. Spontaneous recovery occurs when extinguished responses return temporarily after a delay (p. 199, Fig. 6.4)
            d. Stimulus generalization has occurred if CRs are made to stimuli that are similar to the CS (p. 199, Fig. 6.6)
            e. Discrimination has occurred if the animal responds to some stimuli but not others (pp. 199-200)

V. Drug Tolerance as an Explanation of Classical Conditioning
    A. Drug tolerance can be explained by classical conditioning (p. 201)
        1. Stimuli that precede the drug become CSs for a defense reaction by the body (p. 201)
        2. The drug has weaker effects because of this conditioned response (p. 201)

VI. Explanations of Classical Conditioning
    A. There are differing explanations of classical conditioning (pp. 201-204)
        1. Pavlov thought that presenting the CS and UCS at nearly the same time caused conditioning (p. 201, Fig. 6.8)
        2. CSs are reacted to as signals, not as if they were UCSs (p. 201)
        3. CS and UCS occurring close in time is not the entire explanation (pp. 201-203)
            a. Animals do not respond much to a CS when other CSs predict the UCS (p. 202, Fig. 6.9)
            b. Animals do not learn about a CS if the UCS often occurs without it (p. 202)
        4. A blocking effect occurs when a previously established association blocks a new one from being formed (p. 203, Fig. 6.10)
        5. Both contingency and timing are important (p. 203)

The message: *Classical conditioning creates signals that prepare us for what happens in our environment. (p. 204)*

Module 6.3 Operant Conditioning

VII. Thorndike and Operant Conditioning
    A. Thorndike first studied operant (instrumental) conditioning (pp. 206-207, Figs 6.11-6.12)
        1. Reinforcement increases the probability of a response (p. 207)
            a. The law of effect states that a response that is followed by favorable consequences will be more likely in the future (p. 207)
            b. Classical conditioning applies mostly to visceral responses; operant conditioning applies to skeletal responses, although the distinction sometimes breaks down (p. 207)

VIII. Reinforcement and Punishment
    A. A reinforcer increases the probability of a response (pp. 207-208)
        1. Premack principle states that more frequent responses can serve as reinforcers for less frequent responses (p. 208)
        2. Disequilibrium principle states that activities are reinforcing if we have spent less than our usual time on them (p. 208)
    B. Primary and Secondary Reinforcers
        1. A primary (unconditioned) reinforcer meet biological needs (p. 208)
        2. A secondary (conditioned) reinforcer has been associated with primary reinforcers (p. 209)
    C. Punishment
        1. Punishment decreases response frequency (p. 209, Table 6.1)
            a. Event that decreases behavior is added for punishment (p. 210, Table 6.1)
                i. Effective only if it is prompt and consistent (p. 209)
                ii. No causal relationship between spanking and likelihood of ill-behaved children (p. 209)
                iii. Also called passive avoidance learning (p. 210)
    D. Categories of Reinforcement and Punishment (p. 210, Table 6.1)
        1. Positive reinforcement is the presentation of an event to <u>increase</u> a behavior (p. 210)
        2. Negative reinforcement (avoidance or escape learning) is the removal of an unpleasant event to <u>increase</u> a behavior (p. 210)
        3. Punishment (passive avoidance learning) is the presentation of an event to <u>decrease</u> a behavior (p. 210)
        4. Negative punishment (omission training) removal of a pleasant event to <u>decrease</u> a behavior (p. 210)

IX. Additional Phenomena of Operant Conditioning
    A. Extinction, Generalization, Discrimination, and Discriminative Stimuli
        1. Extinction results in a weakening of a response after a period without reinforcement (p. 211)
        2. Generalization occurs when a response is more likely when a new a similar stimulus is presented (p. 211)
        3. Responding one way to one stimulus and another way to a different stimulus is known as discrimination (p. 211)
        4. A discriminative stimulus is one that indicates which response is appropriate (pp. 211-212)
    B. Why Are Certain Responses Learned More Easily Than Others
        1. Some responses are more easily learned than others (p. 212)
            a. Some stimuli and responses show belongingness (p. 212, Fig. 6.14)

X. B. F. Skinner and the Shaping of Responses
   A. B. F. Skinner first demonstrated shaping (pp. 212-213, Fig. 6.15)
   B. Shaping Behavior
      1. Shaping involves reinforcement of responses that become closer to the final response (p. 213)
   C. Chaining Behavior
      1. In chaining, each response is reinforced by an opportunity to perform the next response (pp. 213-214, Fig. 6.16)
   D. Schedules of Reinforcement
      1. Reinforcement does not follow every response when a schedule is used (p. 214, Table 6.3)
         a. Reinforcement is given after some set number of responses in fixed ratio (p. 215, Table 6.3)
         b. Reinforcement is given on the average after some number of responses in variable ratio (p. 215, Table 6.3)
         c. Reinforcement is given for the first response after some time period in fixed interval (p. 215 Table 6.3)
         d. Reinforcement is given on the average after some time period in variable interval (pp. 215-216, Table 6.3)
         e. Extinction takes longer following intermittent reinforcement than following continuous reinforcement (p. 216)

XI. Applications of Operant Conditioning
   A. Animal Training
      1. Animals are trained through shaping and reinforcement (p. 216)
   B. Persuasion
      1. Reinforcements can be used to persuade people (p. 217)
   C. Applied Behavior Analysis/Behavior Modification
      1. Applied Behavior Analysis can modify problem behaviors (p. 217)
   D. Breaking Bad Habits
      1. Bad habits can be broken with operant conditioning (pp. 217-218, Fig. 6.17)

The message: Survival depends on the sensitivity of our behavior to its consequences. (p. 218)

Module 6.4 Other Kinds of Learning

XII. Conditioned Taste Aversions
   A. Taste-aversion learning can occur in a single trial and with long delays between UCS and CS (pp. 220-222, Fig. 6.18)
      1. Some CSs work better than others; e.g., tastes condition more to illness than lights and noises (pp. 221-222, Fig. 6.19)

XIII. Birdsong Learning
   A. Song learning in birds differs from classical and operant conditioning (pp. 222-223)
      1. Birds learn to sing during an early sensitive period (p. 222)
      2. Birds learn to sing the songs of their own species (p. 222)
      3. Songs are learned by listening and perfected by practice (p. 222)

XIV. Social Learning
   A. Much learning occurs from observing others, according to social-learning theory (p. 223)
   B. Modeling an Imitation
      1. People model their behavior after others' behavior; they imitate (pp. 223-224, Fig. 6.20)
   C. Vicarious Reinforcement and Punishment
      1. Some behaviors occur or do not occur because similar behaviors in other people have been reinforced (vicarious reinforcement) or punished (vicarious punishment) (p. 224)
         a. Vicarious punishment doesn't work as well as vicarious reinforcement (pp. 224-225)
   D. Self-Efficacy in Social Learning
      1. Self-efficacy may be necessary for imitation (p. 225)
   E. Self-Reinforcement and Self-Punishment in Social Learning
      1. Much behavior is maintained through self-reinforcement (pp. 225-226)

The message: Many forms of learning influence your behavior. (p. 226)

RELATED WEBSITES AND ACTIVITIES

Visit http://psychology.wadsworth.com/kalat_intro7e/ for online quizzing, glossary flashcards, crossword puzzles, annotated web links, and more.

LECTURE MATERIAL

Information from the text is only half of the picture. Don't forget to review your lecture material. Process each topic meaningfully. Most importantly, be sure that you understand the material in each lecture-if you don't, ask your instructor or teaching assistant.

STUDY TIP # 6: Visit your professor/teaching assistant during their office hours and start these visit(s) early in the semester. During the course of a semester the professor/teaching assistant is there to help you. You have paid for their help, so seek them out if you need it.

TIP: Associate the lecture material with the information from the text, with things that you already know, with your personal experiences, or with real-life applications. Type or neatly re-write your notes. Make sure they are detailed and organized. Make comments on your notes. Then write questions to cover each concept.

CHAPTER MODULE ASSESSMENTS

Module 6.1 Behaviorism
Answer these questions soon after reading the **Module 6.1: Behaviorism**. There are several formats to the assessments. Answers to all questions appear on p. 120.

Fill in the Blank
Provide a term(s) which best completes the statement below. Answers appear on p. 120.

1. _____ believe that psychologists should study only _____ and _____ behaviors, not mental processes.

2. _____ behaviorists deny that hunger, fear, or any other internal, private event causes behavior.

3. _____ was one of the founders of behaviorism and believed that the environment controls practically all aspects of behavior.

4. The most influential radical behaviorist was _____.

Short Answer
The following questions require a short written answer (3-7 sentences). Answers appear on p. 120.

1. Describe the three assumptions of behaviorism.

2. Describe the difference between radical behaviorists and methodological behaviorists.

Multiple Choice
Circle the best answer below. Check your answers on p. 120. If your answer was incorrect, try to write why it was incorrect. Check your reasons on p. 120.

1. Which of the following is <u>not</u> a basic assumption of behaviorists?
   a. behavior should be explained by internal motivations
   b. behavior is molded by the environment
   c. explanations based on internal states are not useful
   d. determinism is the appropriate philosophy

2. _____ behaviorists study only events that they can measure and observe, but sometimes use these observations to make inferences about internal events such as hunger.
   a. Radical
   b. Social
   c. Methodological
   d. none of the above

True/False
Select the best answer by circling *T for True* or *F for False*. Check your answers on p. 120.

1. **T or F** Initially, behaviorists had people describe their own mental processes to understand behavior.

2. **T or F** B. F. Skinner was a Russian physiologist who had won a Nobel Prize in physiology for his research on digestion. He is well-known for his studies of classical conditioning.

3. **T or F** Most behaviorists would agree that, in some form, behavior is deterministic.

Fill in the Blank
Provide a term(s) which best completes the statement below. Answers appear on p. 121.

1. A(n) _____ reflex is an automatic connection between a stimulus such as food and a response such as salivation.

2. Stimulus _____ is the extension of a conditioned response from a training stimulus to a similar stimulus.

3. The Russian physiologist _____ first described the principles of classical conditioning.

4. The process that establishes or strengthens a conditioned response is known as _____.

5. A stimulus that indicates which response is appropriate or inappropriate is called _____.

6. _____ refers to a temporary return of an extinguished response after a delay.

7. _____ occurs when users of certain drugs experience progressively weaker effects after taking the drugs repeatedly.

Short Answer
The following questions require a short written answer (3-7 sentences). Answers appear on p. 121.

1. Describe how a person might come to feel frightened at a corner after having had an auto accident at that corner.

2. John's girlfriend is trying to get him to wink on command. She blows a puff of air into his eye and then says "Hi ya." After doing this many times, John still doesn't blink to "Hi ya." Explain why not.

3. Describe one example of evidence that classical conditioning is not simply the result of the CS and UCS occurring close in time.

Multiple Choice
Circle the best answer below. Check your answers on pp. 121-122. If your answer was incorrect, try to write why it was incorrect. Check your reasons on pp. 121-122.

1. Every time the toilet in a neighboring apartment is flushed, your shower becomes very hot and you jump back. Soon you learn to jump back at the sound of the flushing even before the water gets hot. Which of the following is correct?
   a. pulling back from a painful stimulus is a conditioned reflex
   b. the flushing sound is the UCS
   c. jumping back at the sound is the UCR
   d. the flushing sound is the CS
   e. jumping back from the hot water is the CR

2. Which of the following would produce the best classical conditioning?
   a. an unfamiliar sound presented 1 sec. before the UCS
   b. a familiar sound presented 1 sec. before the UCS
   c. presentation of the CS many times without the UCS
   d. presentation of the CS immediately after the UCS

3. A child named Albert learned to fear a rat because the sight of it was paired with a loud, frightening sound. Later the child also showed fear of his mother's fur coat. Why?
   a. there was no contingency between the noise and the rat
   b. he formed a discrimination for the situations when the UCS would and would not occur
   c. stimulus generalization occurred from the furry rat to the similar coat
   d. extinction probably caused him to associate the coat with the noise
   e. spontaneous recovery occurred following extinction of the fear

4. An individual always takes a drug injection in his small, cramped room. One reaction of his body to the drug is an increase in heart rate. The conditioned response in this case is likely to be:
   a. a decrease in heart rate
   b. an increase in heart rate
   c. things in the small, cramped room
   d. the injection of the drug itself
   e. the injection procedure

True/False
Select the best answer by circling *T for True* or *F for False*. Check your answers on p. 122.

1. **T or F** The process that establishes or strengthens a conditioned response is known as spontaneous recovery.

2. **T or F** Visceral responses, responses of the internal organs, applies primarily to operant conditioning.

3. **T or F** A blocking effect occurs when a previously established association blocks a new one from being formed

4. **T or F** An association between the US and UCS develops whenever they occur close in time.

5. **T or F** An animal is showing discrimination when a previously extinguished response returns temporarily.

Module 6.3 Operant Conditioning
Answer these questions soon after reading the **Module 6.3: Operant Conditioning**. There are several formats to the assessments. Answers to all questions appear on pp. 122-125.

Fill in the Blank
Provide a term(s) which best completes the statement below. Answers appear on p. 122.

1. Any event that decreases the probability of a response, such as administering a painful electric shock, is _____.

2. Rules or procedures for the delivery of reinforcement are known as _____ of reinforcement.

3. The _____ principle states that "The opportunity to engage in frequent behavior (such as talking with your friends) will be a reinforcer for any less-frequent behavior (such as studying).

4. Skinner developed a technique called _____ for establishing a new response by reinforcing successive approximations to it.

5. A _____ is any event that increases the future probability that a response will occur.

6. Instrumental or _____ conditioning is the process of changing behavior by following a response with a reinforcement.

7. If responses stop producing reinforcements _____ will occur.

8. The ability of a stimulus to encourage some responses and discourage others is known as _____.

Short Answer
The following questions require a short written answer (3-7 sentences). Answers appear on p. 123.

1. Design an operant conditioning program to get a dog to press a lever to turn on a light.

2. Explain how negative and positive reinforcement differ.

3. Describe Skinner's view of punishment and also describe the more current view.

4. Describe the four schedules of reinforcement and describe the effect of intermittent versus continuous reinforcement on extinction.

5. Explain how shaping could be used to get prisoners to say things publicly that they don't believe.

Multiple Choice

Circle the best answer below. Check your answers on pp. 123-124. If your answer was incorrect, try to write why it was incorrect. Check your reasons on pp. 123-124.

1. Thorndike's cats learned to escape the puzzle box because:
   a. positive reinforcement followed the correct response
   b. their learning curves showed a gradual increase
   c. visceral responses were changed by instrumental conditioning
   d. skeletal responses were changed by classical conditioning

2. How does extinction occur in <u>operant</u> conditioning?
   a. present the CS many times without the UCS
   b. present the CS many times without the UCS; then wait for a day and present the CS again
   c. withhold positive reinforcement following a correct response
   d. set up the situation so that the opportunity to make the next response is the reinforcement for each response

3. The lion in a circus stands up on a chair and from there jumps through a hoop that is on fire. No reinforcement is given until it goes to the center of the stage and stands on its hind legs. How was this animal trained?
   a. by shaping
   b. by reinforcing each successive approximation to the response
   c. by chaining the shaped responses
   d. by first giving positive reinforcement only when the entire sequence was correct
   e. a, b, and c

4. Many cars have loud, obnoxious buzzers that continue until the driver buckles the seat belt. Buckling the belt turns off the buzzer. This is an example of which type of operant conditioning?
   a. positive reinforcement
   b. negative punishment
   c. punishment
   d. negative reinforcement

5. What do psychologists currently believe about punishment?
   a. it is effective in the short run but not in the long run
   b. punishment can be effective if it is immediate and very severe
   c. punishment can be effective if it is immediate and predictable
   d. punishment is never effective and should be avoided at all costs
   e. punishment sometimes reduces the behavior because attention is reinforcing

6. Your father promises you your own credit card if you do well in your first year at college. The credit card is:
   a. a primary reinforcer
   b. valuable because you have been shaped to appreciate it
   c. a secondary reinforcer
   d. an example of fixed-ratio reinforcement

7. Jake, a fly fisherman, finds that he gets an average of five bites per 50 casts. If getting bites is reinforcing, he is:
   a. on a fixed-ratio schedule of reinforcement
   b. on a fixed-interval schedule of reinforcement
   c. in a negative reinforcement situation
   d. on a variable-ratio schedule of reinforcement
   e. on a continuous reinforcement schedule

8. Jake, from the question above, goes fishing with Bud who, in the past, has gotten a bite with every cast. They go to a river where there are no fish and they get no bites. How long will each continue to cast?
   a. Jake will continue longer than Bud because he had been on intermittent reinforcement
   b. Bud will continue longer than Jake because he had been on intermittent reinforcement
   c. both will continue the same time because they are in a punishment situation
   d. Bud will continue longer because he was on a variable-interval schedule before and that prolongs extinction

9. A girl with a developmental disability is being taught to comb her hair, to brush her teeth, and to be generally neat and clean every day. She receives tokens that can be traded for goods and privileges. At first, almost any attempt at neatness earns a token, but later she must do more to earn a token. The girl is:
   a. being reinforced by the Premack principle
   b. receiving negative punishment
   c. receiving primary reinforcers
   d. in an applied behavior analysis program
   e. being forced into disequilibrium by her behavior

True/False
Select the best answer by circling *T for True* or *F for False*. Check your answers on p. 125.

1. **T or F** Omission training occurs when the omission of the response leads to restoration of the usual privileges.

2. **T or F** Negative reinforcement is NOT a punishment; it is reinforcement by the REMOVAL or ABSENCE of something.

3. **T or F** In a variable ratio schedule of reinforcement, reinforcement is delivered after varying amounts of time.

4. **T or F** The disequilibrium principle can best be stated as: The opportunity to engage in frequent behavior (e.g., eating) will be reinforcing for any less-frequent behavior (e.g., lever pressing).

5. **T or F** Primary reinforcers become reinforcing because of their previous association with a secondary reinforcer.

6. **T or F** People have applied operant conditioning to animal training, persuasion, applied behavior analysis, and the breaking of bad habits.

Module 6.4 Other Kinds of Learning
Answer these questions soon after reading the **Module 6.4: Other Kinds of Learning**. There are several formats to the assessments. Answers to all questions appear on pp. 125-126.

Fill in the Blank
Provide a term(s) which best completes the statement below. Answers appear on p. 125.

1. The _____ is the view that people learn by observing and imitating the behavior of others and by imagining the consequences of their own behavior.

2. People imitate someone else's behavior only if they have a sense of _____, the perception that they themselves could perform the task successfully.

3. _____ reinforcement occurs when you imitate the behavior of someone who has been reinforced for that behavior.

Short Answer
The following questions require a short written answer (3-7 sentences). Answers appear on p. 125.

1. How does song learning in birds differ from classical and operant conditioning?

2. How would a social-learning theorist explain a child's learning to smoke cigarettes?

3. Describe the roles of self-efficacy and self-reinforcement in learning.

Multiple Choice
Circle the best answer below. Check your answers on p. 126. If your answer was incorrect, try to write why it was incorrect. Check your reasons on p. 126.

1. If you eat a new food and then get sick because of the flu, you might dislike that food and avoid it in the future. Which of the following is true?
   a. you would also avoid the type of plate upon which the food was served
   b. classical conditioning could not have occurred because the delay between the taste and illness would be too long
   c. a conditioned taste aversion was acquired; the association between taste and illness is easily learned
   d. a conditioned taste aversion developed with taste as the UCS for illness

2. John was able to stop smoking after seeing that his racquetball partner was able to play better and not become short of breath after he stopped. John:
   a. was able to stop because of his poor self-efficacy
   b. changed his behavior because of vicarious reinforcement
   c. began to change his behavior because of positive reinforcement
   d. changed his behavior because of vicarious punishment

3. If you have received vicarious reinforcement for a behavior, you are likely to be successful at executing the behavior if you:
   a. have poor self-efficacy
   b. have doubts about your ability but are willing to try anyway
   c. use appropriate self-reinforcement
   d. have high self-efficacy
   e. both c and d

True/False
Select the best answer by circling *T for True* or *F for False*. Check your answers on p. 126.

1. **T or F** One kind of learning that does occur reliably after a single trial is an association between eating something and getting sick which is termed conditioned taste aversion.

2. **T or F** Self-reinforcement and self-punishment are not effective tools for modifying one's behavior.

3. **T or F** Birds automatically learn how to sing their species' song without listening or practice.

FINAL COMPREHENSIVE CHAPTER ASSESSMENT TEST

Check your answers on p. 126.

1. Which of the following is <u>not</u> an assumption of behaviorism?
   a. examining people's thoughts provides valid data
   b. all behavior is caused
   c. mental explanations do not explain causes of behavior
   d. behavior is molded by the environment

2. Which of the following would most likely be a statement made by a radical behaviorist?
   a. learning is a change in an individual's response to a stimulus
   b. we can tell what people have learned by asking how well they think they know material
   c. having people describe thoughts and ideas is the only real way to observe learning
   d. behavior is often unpredictable because of free will
   e. both b and c

3. Our dog drools saliva whenever he hears the "doggy snacks" cupboard open. Which of the following is true?
   a. the sound of the cupboard is a UCS for salivating, which is the UCR
   b. the sound of the cupboard is the CS; the doggy snacks are the UCS
   c. salivating to the sound is the UCR; salivating to the snacks is the CR
   d. the snacks are the CS; salivating to the cupboard is the UCS
   e. the snacks are the UCS; salivating to the cupboard is the UCR

4. Which of the following is an example of spontaneous recovery?
   a. a dog hears a tone CS many times without the UCS
   b. a child who has learned to stop wetting the bed wakes up when he has stomach cramps as well as when he has a full bladder
   c. an alcoholic learns not to drink in the lab because he will become sick but learns that he can drink in the local bar
   d. a fear that was removed by presenting the object over and over without harm returns when the object hasn't been seen for weeks
   e. a dog salivates to the sound of any cupboard opening

5. Pavlov believed that the CS and UCS must be presented in close in time. What do psychologists believe today?
   a. timing is even more important than Pavlov thought
   b. CS must predict the coming UCS
   c. long delays between CS and UCS make all learning impossible
   d. Presenting the UCS before the CS produces even stronger conditioning than presenting the CS first
   e. extinction will only occur if the UCS is presented without the CS

6. Which of the following is an example of <u>operant</u> conditioning?
   a. a child fears the sight of dogs because she was once bitten by one
   b. a cancer patient feels sick when she sees the hospital where she receives a strong drug treatment
   c. a rabbit blinks its eyelid to a tone that has been paired with shock
   d. a chimpanzee pulls the lever on a slot machine to get banana chips

7. What procedure would you use to train your dog to go to the bedroom, pick up your slippers, carry them to your favorite chair, go to the door, get the newspaper, and bring it to you?
   a. shaping
   b. classical conditioning
   c. chaining
   d. both b and c
   e. both a and c

8. I have learned to open my umbrella in order to stop the rain from soaking me. What type of contingency led to this learning?
   a. positive reinforcement
   b. negative punishment
   c. punishment
   d. negative reinforcement
   e. omission training

9. Which of the following would increase the likelihood that punishment would be effective?
   a. make sure that there are no alternative ways of getting reinforcement
   b. make a child's punishment intense and with no explanation
   c. make a child's punishment quick and predictable
   d. give a child as little attention as possible, except when punishing him
   e. punish a behavior that is strongly motivated and give the animal no other way to satisfy the motivation

10. Dogs are frequently trained with verbal praise, such as "Good boy," as the reinforcer. What type is it?
    a. a primary reinforcer
    b. a negative reinforcer
    c. a punisher
    d. an instrumental reinforcer
    e. a secondary reinforcer

11. A study examining playground behavior of children found that by offering simple reinforcements for safe behavior, the frequency of dangerous behaviors could be decreased. These results are consistent with?
    a. behavior modification
    b. free will of the children
    c. self-reinforcement
    d. classical conditioning

12. The disequilibrium principle states that:
    a. any high-frequency behavior can be used to reinforce a low-frequency behavior
    b. any behavior that has been performed less often than usual can reinforce behavior
    c. rare behaviors can never be used to reinforce more frequent behaviors
    d. secondary reinforcers are more powerful than primary reinforcers
    e. individuals learn what leads to what rather than automatically increasing reinforced behaviors

13. Which of the following is an example of a variable-interval schedule?
    a. Bertha gets one chocolate-chip cookie for every 10 sit-ups she does
    b. A pigeon gets food the first time it pecks a key after 10 sec. have passed
    c. Freddie gets a dime each morning that he makes his bed
    d. A gambler wins on 3 out of 10 poker hands on the average
    e. A fisherman gets a bite once every 15 minutes on the average

14. Under a continuous schedule of reinforcement the animal is reinforced
    a. after a fixed number of responses
    b. after a fixed amount of time
    c. after a variable number of responses
    d. after a variable amount of time
    e. after every response

15. Rats that have been shocked while drinking sweetened water from a tube that produces loud noises and bright lights will later:
    a. avoid tubes with noises and lights
    b. avoid sweet-tasting water
    c. avoid both sweet-tasting water and tubes with noises and lights
    d. avoid all sweet-tasting substances
    e. completely stop eating and drinking

16. Which of the following could be used to support the argument that bird song learning is different from operant conditioning?
    a. adult songs are UCSs not reinforcers
    b. songs are learned just by listening with no obvious reinforcer
    c. songs are learned by classical conditioning
    d. songs are not learned until adulthood, but operant conditioning occurs in childhood
    e. birds learn to sing whatever songs they hear

17. According to social-learning theory:
    a. we learn because of unconditioned reinforcement
    b. we usually learn because we are classically conditioned by society
    c. much human learning occurs because of imitation
    d. operant conditioning is irrelevant for human learning
    e. society could be improved through operant conditioning

18. Vicarious punishment:
    a. works better than vicarious reinforcement
    b. involves actual physical consequences to the learner
    c. affects behavior less than vicarious reinforcement
    d. does not involve a model

19. Which of the following is **<u>not</u>** part of Azrin and Nunn's three step method to breaking bad habits?
    a. do something incompatible with the offending habit
    b. do nothing and wait to grow out of the bad habit
    c. become more aware of your bad habit
    d. provide your own reinforcements

20. Although it is clear that the gymnast was reinforced for her excellent tumbling routine, most people would not imitate her. Why?
    a. vicarious reinforcement did not occur
    b. vicarious punishment occurred
    c. self-reinforcement doesn't work for gymnastics
    d. self-efficacy would be low for most people
    e. the gymnast would not be a good model

ANSWERS AND EXPLANATIONS FOR CHAPTER MODULE ASSESSMENTS

Answers to the Fill in the Blank Questions – Module 6.1

1. Behaviorists; observable; measurable (p. 191)

2. Radical (p. 191)

3. John B. Watson (p. 194)

4. B. F. Skinner (pp. 191-192)

Answers to the Short Answer Questions – Module 6.1

1. All behavior has a cause that can be understood with scientific methods; 2) explanations based on internal causes and mental states are not useful; explanations should be based on external, observable events; 3) the environment molds behavior, and we are influenced by our surroundings. (p. 193)

2. Methodological behaviorists study only the events that they can measure and observe, but they sometimes use those observations to make inferences about internal events. Radical behaviorists deny that hunger, fear or any other internal, private event causes behavior. (pp. 191-192)

Answers to the Multiple Choice Questions – Module 6.1

1. a. Correct! The emphasis was on observable behavior, not on unobservable internal states (p. 193)
   b-d. Incorrect. These are basic assumptions of behaviorists

2. a. Incorrect. Radical behaviorists deny that hunger, fear, or any other internal, private event causes behavior
   b. Incorrect. Not mentioned in book
   c. Correct! (p. 191)
   d. Incorrect. Answer is c

Answers to the True/False Questions – Module 6.1

1. **False**: Structuralists had people describe their own mental processes. Behaviorists were interested in only studying observable behaviors. (p. 191)

2. **False**: Ivan Pavlov was this Russian physiologist. Skinner was a very influential American behaviorist. (p. 191)

3. **True**: One of the assumptions of behaviorism is that behavior is deterministic. (p. 193)

Answers to the Fill in the Blank Questions – Module 6.2

1. unconditioned (p. 196)

2. generalization (p. 199)

3. Pavlov (p. 195)

4. acquisition (p. 198)

5. discriminative stimulus (pp. 199-200)

6. Spontaneous recovery (p. 199)

7. Drug tolerance (p. 201)

Answers to the Short Answer Questions – Module 6.2

1. Classical conditioning could explain this. The fear at the sight of the corner is a conditioned response. Fear at the time of the accident is the unconditioned response to the unconditioned stimuli of loud noise and pain. The particular corner is the CS, but other corners may also produce fear through generalization. If only that corner produces fear, discrimination has occurred. (pp. 198-200)

2. For conditioning to occur, the CS ("Hi ya") needs to precede (predict) the UCS (puff of air). Simple contiguity is not enough; the UCS should be contingent upon the CS (the puff of air should only occur following the "Hi ya" stimulus). She should present the CS a second before the UCS and then John might wink on command. She would also get better results with a phrase John hears only in this context (p. 201)

3. If a CS has already been conditioned to a UCS, then a second, simultaneous, CS is not learned about because it is redundant and not informative. This is true even though it has occurs close in time to the UCS. Another piece of evidence is that conditioning does not occur when the UCS occurs alone frequently without the CS, even though presentations of the CS are always followed by the UCS. (pp. 201-202)

Answers to the Multiple Choice Questions – Module 6.2

1. a. Incorrect. Pulling back from a painful stimulus is an unconditioned reflex
   b. Incorrect. Flushing sound is CS; response to it is learned (conditioned)
   c. Incorrect. Jumping back from sound is CR; it is learned
   d. Correct! (p. 196)
   e. Incorrect. Jumping back from hot water is UCR; it is not learned

2. a. Correct! (p. 196)
   b. Incorrect. It is more difficult to learn CRs to familiar stimuli
   c. Incorrect. This will produce extinction if conditioning has already occurred; otherwise no learning will occur
   d. Incorrect. CS must precede the UCS for good conditioning

3. a. Incorrect. There was a contingency; the appearance of the rat predicted the noise
    b. Incorrect. No; he responded in the new situation rather than discriminating it and not responding
    c. Correct! (p. 199)
    d. Incorrect. Extinction refers to the reduction of CRs to a CS, not to responding to other stimuli
    e. Incorrect. The original fear was not extinguished; rat was not presented alone many times

4. a. Correct! (p. 201)
    b. Incorrect. Unconditioned response due to the drug itself; an opposite defense reaction is conditioned
    c. Incorrect. Would be part of the conditioned stimuli
    d. Incorrect. This is the unconditioned stimulus
    e. Incorrect. Part of the conditioned stimuli

Answers to the True/False Questions – Module 6.2

1. **False**: The process that establishes or strengthens a conditioned response is known as acquisition. (p. 198)

2. **False**: Visceral responses, responses of the internal organs, applies primarily to classical conditioning. Skeletal responses, movements of leg muscles, arm muscles, etc., applies primarily to operant conditioning. (p. 207)

3. **True**: Blocking precludes a second stimulus from being associated with a response. (p. 203, Fig. 6.10)

4. **False**: In addition to timing of the US and UCS, the contingency or predictability is also important. (pp. 201-203)

5. **False:** The animal is actually showing spontaneous recovery of the response. (p. 199)

Answers to the Fill in the Blank Questions – Module 6.3

1. punishment (p. 209)

2. schedules (p. 215)

3. Premack (p. 208)

4. shaping (p. 213)

5. reinforcement (p. 207)

6. operant (p. 206)

7. extinction (p. 211)

8. stimulus control (p. 212)

Answers to the Short Answer Questions – Module 6.3

1. The dog would have to be shaped. First, a food reinforcement should be given whenever the dog looks toward the lever, then only when he moves toward it, and later when he touches it. Next, the dog would have to push the lever slightly to be rewarded. Finally, he would have to push it hard enough to turn on the light. (p. 213)

2. In positive reinforcement, the consequence of the behavior is that a favorable event occurs after the response. For example, money is given contingent upon some behavior. The goal is to increase the behavior that led to the positive event. In negative reinforcement, the behavior results in the removal of a disagreeable event. For example, a shock is turned off as a result of a behavior. In negative reinforcement, the goal is to increase the likelihood of the behavior that led to the removal of the disagreeable event. (p. 210, Table 6.1)

3. Skinner argued that punishment may temporarily suppress a response, but that it is of no use in the long run. However, his animals were not given a response alternative. If the punishment is immediate and consistent, punishment can be effective in the long run. (p. 210)

4. <u>Fixed ratio</u>: Reinforcement is given after a set number of responses; e.g., FR 10 means reinforcement after every 10 responses.
   <u>Variable ratio</u>: Reinforcement after some number of responses, but the number is an average; e.g., VR 10 means reinforcement is given after an average of 10 responses, but not after the 10th, 20th, etc.
   <u>Fixed interval</u>: Reinforcement is given for the first response following some time interval; e.g., FI 5 sec. means that the first response after 5 sec. has passed would be reinforced.
   <u>Variable interval</u>: Reinforcement is given after a time interval, but it is an average interval; e.g., VI 5 sec. means that the intervals would average 5 sec., but would vary. Responding will continue longer without reinforcement after one of these schedules than after reinforcement following every response (continuous). (pp. 215-216, Table 6.3)

5. This happened during the Korean War. The Chinese Communists ran essay contests, and soldiers who wrote the best essays won extra food or privileges. Soldiers who wrote negative comments about the United States were asked to elaborate on them. Many prisoners ended up denouncing the United States, making false confessions, and even revealing military secrets. Basically, a shaping process with positive reinforcements was used. (p. 217)

Answers to the Multiple Choice Questions – Module 6.3

1. a. Correct! (p. 206)
   b. Incorrect. Curves plot the course of performance, they don't cause it; errors decreased
   c. Incorrect. Visceral responses are usually automatic and classically conditioned; not relevant to cats' behavior
   d. Incorrect. Skeletal responses are usually voluntary muscle movements and operantly conditioned

2. a. Incorrect. Extinction in classical conditioning
    b. Incorrect. Could lead to spontaneous recovery in classical conditioning
    c. Correct! (p. 211)
    d. Incorrect. Chaining; can be done without extinction

3. a, b. Incorrect. Different terms for reinforcing small parts of the response
    c. Incorrect. This is how the different responses would be linked
    d. Incorrect. The whole sequence would never occur spontaneously, so reinforcement would never be given
    e. Correct! (pp. 212-213)

4. a. Incorrect. The buckling response removes an unfavorable consequence; it doesn't add a favorable one
    b. Incorrect. The buckling response does not remove a favorable consequence
    c. Incorrect. The buckling response does not add an unfavorable consequence
    d. Correct! (p. 210)

5. a. Incorrect. This was Skinner's view; however, if an alternative response is available, punishment can work
    b. Incorrect. Very severe punishment is not necessary
    c. Correct! (pp. 209-210)
    d. Incorrect. It can be effective, and may be necessary to stop dangerous behavior
    e. Incorrect. Punishment is sometimes reinforcing because it is accompanied by attention; however, this increases the behavior, not decreases it

6. a. Incorrect. Does not satisfy a basic biological need, unless you eat and digest plastic
    b. Incorrect. Shaping refers to responses, not reinforcements
    c. Correct! (p. 208)
    d. Incorrect. You are not being reinforced for a set number of responses

7. a. Incorrect. He doesn't get a bite every 10th cast; it's on the average
    b. Incorrect. Number of casts, not time, is specified
    c. Incorrect. Refers to increasing a response because an unfavorable stimulus is removed; not relevant here
    d. Correct! (p. 215)
    e. Incorrect. Continuous means reinforcement for <u>every</u> response; not true here

8. a. Correct! (pp. 214-215)
    b. Incorrect. Bud has been on continuous reinforcement and that will produce faster extinction
    c. Incorrect. Refers to addition of an unfavorable stimulus; not relevant here
    d. Incorrect. Bud has not been on any intermittent reinforcement schedule; he has been on continuous reinforcement

9. a. Incorrect. Tokens are reinforcers; she isn't being allowed to do a preferred behavior
    b. Incorrect. No favorable stimuli are being removed if she is not neat
    c. Incorrect. Tokens are secondary, not primary, reinforcers
    d. Correct! (p. 217)
    e. Incorrect. Disequilibrium refers to the fact that any behavior that has been engaged in less often than usual can be reinforcing; getting her to increase hygiene isn't doing this

Answers to the True/False Questions – Module 6.3

1. **True**: Omission training is usually known as negative punishment. (p. 210)

2. **True**: This is sometimes known as avoidance or escape learning. (p. 210)

3. **False**: This describes a variable interval schedule of reinforcement. In a variable ratio schedule reinforcement is delivered after a varying number of responses. (p. 215)

4. **False**: This describes the Premack principle. The disequilibrium principle suggests that each person has a normal, or "equilibrium" state in which we divide our time among various activities in some preferred way, and if we are removed from that state, a return to it will be reinforcing. (p. 208)

5. **False**: Primary reinforcers are reinforcing because of their own properties. (p. 208)

6. **True**: Operant conditioning principles have enjoyed widespread use in a variety of settings. (pp. 216-218)

Answers to the Fill in the Blank Questions – Module 6.4

1. Social-learning approach (p. 223)

2. self-efficacy (p. 225)

3. Vicarious (pp. 224-225)

Answers to the Short Answer Questions – Module 6.4

1. Song learning is species specific, and occurs during an early sensitive period. Classical and operant conditioning use the same CSs for many animals and both forms of learning occur in adulthood as well as in childhood. Songs are learned just by listening, but there is some form of feedback in both classical (UCS) and operant (reinforcement) learning. (pp. 222-223)

2. Much human learning occurs through imitation. The child sees his or her parents, other children, and TV personalities smoking, and they seem to be enjoying themselves. Thus, the child receives vicarious reinforcement, so he or she imitates these people and tries the behavior. (pp. 223-224)

3. Even if a person has received vicarious reinforcement for some behavior, the behavior may not be imitated unless self-efficacy is high. That is, a person must think that he or she can succeed at the behavior before trying it. When the behavior is attempted, some self-reinforcement (self-administered praise or reinforcers) will probably be necessary for the execution of the behavior to continue. (pp. 225-226)

Answers to the Multiple Choice Questions – Module 6.4

1. a. Incorrect. Visual stimuli are not easily associated with illness
    b. Incorrect. This type of long-delay learning does occur
    c. Correct! (pp. 220-222)
    d. Incorrect. Taste is the CS

2. a. Incorrect. He must have thought he was able to stop; he probably had high self-efficacy
    b. Correct! (p. 224)
    c. Incorrect. The positive benefits on his own health would be positive reinforcement, but at first he stopped because he saw his partner being reinforced
    d. Incorrect. The partner had a favorable, not an unfavorable, outcome

3. a. Incorrect. Must have high self-efficacy; think you can do it
    b. Incorrect. This is low self-efficacy; not likely to succeed
    c. Incorrect. Correct, but high self-efficacy is important too
    d. Incorrect. Correct, but probably need self-reinforcement as well
    e. Correct! (pp. 225-226)

Answers to the True/False Questions – Module 6.4

1. **True**: Conditioned taste aversion was first documented by John Garcia and his colleagues. (pp. 220-222)

2. **False**: Both can be effective tools for modifying ones behavior. (pp. 225-226)

3. **False**: Songs are learned by listening and perfected with practice. (p. 222)

Answers to Final Comprehensive Assessment

1. a (p. 193)
2. a (p. 192)
3. b (pp. 196-197)
4. d (p. 199)
5. b (p. 201)
6. d (p. 206)
7. e (pp. 212-214)
8. d (p. 210)
9. c (p. 209)
10. e (p. 208)
11. a. (p. 217)
12. b (p. 208)
13. e (pp. 215-216, Table 6.3)
14. e (p. 214)
15. a (pp. 221-222)
16. b (pp. 222-223)
17. c (p. 223)
18. c (p. 224)
19. b (pp. 217-218)
20. d (p. 225)

CHAPTER 7

MEMORY

CHAPTER OVERVIEW INFORMATION

LEARNING OBJECTIVES

By the end of Chapter 7 you should

- ✓ Be familiar with different aspects of memory
- ✓ Understand processes and techniques that improve memory storage and retention
- ✓ Be familiar with issues related to remembering, repressed memories, and false memory
- ✓ Understand processes and conditions that promote forgetting; differentiate between simple forgetting and amnesia

CHAPTER 7 OUTLINE

Chapter 7 examines the full range of memory from the different varieties of memory to long-term storage of memories to retrieval of memories to amnesia or the loss of certain memories. These aspects of memory have been discussed throughout history by philosophers and psychologists alike. The research in Chapter 7 presents contemporary views and research on these topics.

Chapter 7 is presented below in outline format to assist you in understanding the information presented in the chapter. More detailed information on any topic can be found using the page references to the right of the topic.

Module 7.1 Varieties of Memory

I. Ebbinghaus's Pioneering Studies of Memory
    A. Memory is the process of retaining information and to the information retained. (p. 231)
    B. Ebbinghaus learned nonsense syllables and forgot them quickly (pp. 233-234, Figs. 7.1 and 7.2)

II. Methods of Testing Memory
    A. How much one remembers depends upon the type of test and the amount of information provided in each test (pp. 234-236, Table 7.2)
        1. Free Recall
            a. Information must be produced from memory (p. 234, Fig. 7.3)
        2. Cued Recall
            a. Hints, or cues, are provided to help remember (pp. 234-235, Table 7.1)
        3. Recognition
            a. Several items are given and the person picks the correct one (p. 235)
        4. Savings
            a. Also known as relearning, the person relearns the material and the time is compared to the original learning time (p. 235)
        5. Implicit Memory
            a. A memory that influences behavior without conscious recognition one is using a memory (p. 235)

III. Application: Suspect Lineups as Recognition Memory
    A. Misidentification of suspects can occur in a lineup due to faulty memory (p. 236)
    B. Researchers have proposed several methods to improve accuracy of identification
        1. Avoid hinting or agreeing with a tentative choice (p. 236)

2. Record the witness's confidence immediately at the time of initial identification (p. 237)
3. Use a sequential lineup with a yes/no decision on each suspect (p. 237)

IV. The Information-Processing View of Memory
    A. Information-processing model assumes that there are three basic types of memory (p. 237, Fig. 7.4)
    B. The Sensory Store
        1. Sensory store holds a very brief image of stimuli (pp. 237-238, Fig. 7.5, Table 7.3)
    C. Short-Term and Long-Term Memory
        1. Short-term memory (p. 238, Table 7.3)
            a. A limited capacity, temporary storage of recent events that is available only a short time (p. 239)
            b. Chunking, or grouping, of information increases capacity (pp. 239-240, Fig. 7.6)
            c. Decay occurs in short-term memory if a person doesn't rehearse and seems to be caused by the brain producing a protein (p. 241, Fig. 7.9)
            d. Interference also causes forgetting from short-term memory (p. 241)
        2. Long-term memory (p. 238, Table 7.3)
            a. An unlimited capacity, permanent store of information
                i. Semantic memory is memory of general principle (p. 238)
                ii. Episodic memory is memory for specific events (p. 238)
            b. Retrieval cues help to bring out long-term memories (p. 240)

V. Working Memory
    A. Working memory temporarily stores information, but it is also a system for working with information (pp. 242-243)
        1. The phonological loop stores and rehearses speech (p. 242)
        2. The visuospatial sketchpad stores and manipulates visual and spatial information (p. 242)
        3. The central executive governs shifts of attention (p. 242)

The message: *Psychologists agree that memory consists of many processes. (p. 243)*

Module 7.2 Long-Term Memory Storage
VI. Meaningful Storage and Levels of Processing
    A. Repetition does not guarantee information will be remembered (p. 245, Fig, 7.10)
    B. According to levels of processing, the number and type of associations formed is important for later memory (pp. 245-246, Table 7.4)
        1. Superficial processing occurs with repetition of information (p. 246)
        2. Putting things into categories helps memory (p. 246)
        3. Giving meaning to material results in a deep level of processing (p. 246)

VII. Encoding Specificity
    A. The best retrieval cues are the associations formed during learning (pp. 246-247, Fig. 7.11, Table 7.5a-b)
    B. The condition of your body can be used as a retrieval cue (p. 247)

VIII. The Timing of Study Sessions
    A. Studying all at once results in an overestimation of how well the information is understood (p. 247)
    B. Studying with time between repetitions increases long-term retention (p. 248)

C. To remember for a longer time, study at various times and places with long intervals between studying thereby increasing number of retrieval cues (p. 248)

IX. The SPAR Method
   A. A systematic way to organize and study
      1. **S**-Survey to get an overview of material (p. 248)
      2. **P**-Process or read the information carefully (p. 248)
      3. **A**-Ask questions regarding the material to test understanding (p. 248)
      4. **R**-Review and test over material at later time (p. 248)

X. Emotional Arousal and Memory Storage
   A. People remember events that were emotionally arousing, although such memories may not be accurate (p. 248)
   B. Accuracy of "flashbulb memories" decreased although self-reported vividness and confidence remained high (p. 249)
   C. Results in increases in cortisol and epinephrine which increases excitation to enhance memory storage (p. 249)

XI. Mnemonic Devices
   A. Mnemonic devices allow for special encoding to help anyone to improve memory (p. 249, Fig. 7.12)
      1. Stories linking items can help (p. 250, Fig. 7,13)
      2. Method of loci involves imagining things in known places (p. 250, Fig. 7.14)

The message: *Storing information long-term is an effortful process that should occur over time.* *(p. 251)*

Module 7.3 Retrival of Memories
XII. Retrieval and Interference
   A. Ebbinghaus forgot faster than college students today because he learned so many lists (pp. 252-253, Fig. 7.15)
   B. Interference from earlier (proactive) or later (retroactive) learning can cause forgetting (p. 253, Fig. 7.16)
   C. Distinctiveness
      1. Distinctive material that stands out is remembered better than common material (p. 253)
   D. Serial Order and Retrieval
      1. The serial-order effect consists of a primacy effect and a recency effect (p. 254)
         a. The primacy effect is the tendency to remember things learned first (p. 254)
         b. The recency effect is the tendency to remember things learned last (p. 254)

XIII. Reconstructing Past Events
   A. Memory is often reconstructed from bits of memory that remain (p. 254)
   B. Reconstruction and interference in List Memory
      1. Words not present on lists of related words are inferred and "remembered" (pp. 254-255)
      2. Likelihood of including a word not presented increases with age and intermediate memory strength (p. 255)

C. Reconstructing stories
   1. Expectations are used to reconstruct stories (p. 255)
      a. Typical events are often reconstructed (p. 255)
      b. If story is retold or rehearsed it becomes more coherent and the remaining details fit the gist of the story (p. 255)
      c. Culture specific stories remember better by natives of that culture (p. 255)
D. Hindsight bias
   1. Hindsight bias refers to remembering events as consistent with the outcome (p. 256, Fig. 7.17)

XIV. The "Recovered Memory" and "False Memory" Controversy
   A. Recovered memories are reports of long-lost memories (pp. 256-257)
   B. People create false memories through the power of suggestion (pp. 258-260, Fig 7.18)
      1. People report things that were suggested and not presented (p. 259)
      2. People come to believe that events occurred when they are suggested by a relative (p. 259)
   C. Memory for Traumatic Events
      1. Some psychologists warn that repressed memories for childhood sexual abuse may actually come from therapists' suggestions (pp. 257-258)
         a. Freud defined repression as moving a memory into the unconscious, but there is not good evidence that repression occurs (p. 257)
      2. People who experienced traumatic events generally remember them (p. 258)
   D. Areas of Agreement and Disagreement
      1. Agreement on the fact that some people cannot remember abusive childhood experiences (p. 258)
      2. Disagree as to the reason being repression/disassociation or just usual forgetting of events from the past that have not been recalled (p. 258)

XV. Children as Eyewitnesses
   A. Relatively accurate under proper conditions (p. 261)
   B. Influenced by
      1. The delay between the event and questioning (p. 261)
      2. Suggestive (leading) questions (p. 261)
      3. The understandability of the questions (p. 261)
      4. Repetition of the questions (p. 261)
      5. Use of doll props (p. 261)

The message: *Everyone reconstructs memory using the essential gist and misremembering some of the details. (pp. 261-262)*

Module 7.4 Amnesia
XVI. Amnesia after Damage to the Hippocampus
   A. Amnesia is a severe loss of memory following brain damage (p. 263)
      1. Damage to the hippocampus can cause amnesia (p. 263, Fig. 7.19)
         a. Anterograde amnesia is an inability to learn new things (pp. 263-264, Fig. 7.20)
         b. Retrograde amnesia is the forgetting of events that occurred before the damage (p. 264, Fig. 7.20)
         c. Procedural memory may be spared in such amnesia (p. 264)
            i. The main problem is in memory for facts, declarative memory (p. 264)

XVII. Amnesia after Damage to the Prefrontal Cortex
   A. Damage to the prefrontal cortex produces a different type of amnesia (p. 264, Fig. 7.19)
       1. Korsakoff's syndrome occurs in chronic alcoholics who have a deficiency of vitamin B_1 (pp. 264-265)
       2. These patients have severe retrograde and anterograde amnesia (p. 264)
       3. They tend to fill in gaps in memory with confabulations (p. 265)
           a. They have trouble working with memory, or reconstructing memory (p. 265)
       4. Amnesic patients perform normally on implicit memory tasks (p. 266)
       5. Amnesia is usually selective in the type of memory being impaired (p. 266)

XVIII. Memory Impairments in Alzheimer's Disease
   A. Severe memory loss, confusion, depression and disordered thinking which generally occurs in old age caused by harmful proteins in the brain (p. 266)
       1. Although there seems to be a genetic influence, not an inevitability to have Alzheimer's (p. 266)
       2. Widespread effects on many types of memory (p. 266)

XIX. Infant Amnesia
   A. Infant amnesia refers to the fact that most adults cannot remember anything from before age 3 1/2 (p. 266)
       1. Freud argued that infantile memories are repressed (p. 266)
       2. The hippocampus may not be mature enough to store factual memories (pp. 266-267)
       3. A sense of self may be necessary before permanent memories can be formed (p. 267)
       4. Early memories may be nonverbal and we later rely on language (p. 267)
       5. Lack of retrieval cues may also contribute to lack of memories (p. 267)

The message: Severe memory loss is usually caused by brain damage although there can be an emotion problem that compounds some organic problem. (p. 267)

RELATED WEBSITES AND ACTIVITIES

Visit http://psychology.wadsworth.com/kalat_intro7e/ for online quizzing, glossary flashcards, crossword puzzles, annotated web links, and more.

LECTURE MATERIAL

Information from the text is only half of the picture. Don't forget to review your lecture material. Process each topic meaningfully. Most importantly, be sure that you understand the material in each lecture-if you don't, ask your instructor or teaching assistant.

STUDY TIP # 7: If possible, set aside time every day to study. You will need to determine what time of the day works best for you. It may be early in the morning, late at night, or sometime during the day. One recommendation is to study for 50 minutes of every hour. The other 10 minutes reward yourself with some activity you enjoy (e.g., chatting with friends, getting a cup of coffee). Even if you have only 15 minutes to study, it is still worth the effort to get out your materials and study.

TIP: Associate the lecture material with the information from the text, with things that you already know, with your personal experiences, or with real-life applications. Type or neatly re-write your notes. Make sure they are detailed and organized. Make comments on your notes. Then write questions to cover each concept.

CHAPTER MODULE ASSESSMENTS

Module 7.1 Varieties of Memory
Answer these questions soon after reading the **Module 7.1: Varieties of Memory**. There are several formats to the assessments. Answers to all questions appear on pp. 144-145.

Fill in the Blank
Provide a term(s) which best completes the statement below. Answers appear on p. 144.

1. A test of _____ memory asks you to identify the correct item from several choices.

2. The capacity of _____ memory is approximately seven items, plus or minus two.

3. The German psychologist _____ founded the experimental study of memory.

4. The memory for specific events in a person's life, generally including details of when and where they happened, is _____ memory.

5. The _____ model of memory suggests that human memory works similar to that of a computer.

6. The _____ stores and manipulates visual and spatial information in working memory.

Short Answer
The following questions require a short written answer (3-7 sentences). Answers appear on p. 144.

1. Describe the research done by Ebbinghaus, including one of his findings.

2. Describe two ways that short-term and long-term memory differ.

3. Describe working memory. How does it relate to reading comprehension?

Multiple Choice
Circle the best answer below. Check your answers on pp. 144-145. If your answer was incorrect, try to write why it was incorrect. Check your reasons on pp. 144-145.

1. The questions in this exercise are using what method to measure your memory?
   a. recognition
   b. cued recall
   c. free recall
   d. savings
   e. relearning

2. Which memory store can only store images for less than a second?
   a. short-term memory
   b. long-term memory
   c. sensory store
   d. episodic memory store

3. You've just looked up a phone number and held it in memory while you dialed it. Now, the operator comes on and asks you what number you dialed and you are unable to tell her. What has happened?
   a. the number is still in your sensory store
   b. the number has faded from short-term memory
   c. the number is now in long-term memory
   d. the number was lost because you chunked it too much

4. Practice in short-term memory tasks can:
   a. expand short-term memory capacity
   b. actually hurt long-term memory
   c. help sensory memory as well as short-term memory
   d. improve the ability to chunk

5. Working memory:
   a. is broader than short-term memory involving a system of processing as well a storage
   b. occurs after a memory has been consolidated from short-term memory to long-term memory
   c. is the same thing as the phonological loop
   d. consists of memory for specific events in a person's life

6. Almost all memory researchers agree on which of the following?
   a. long-term memory should be divided into episodic and semantic
   b. source amnesia is the main cause of forgetting from long-term memory
   c. memory that stays in short-term store long enough is consolidated into long-term memory
   d. the visuospatial sketchpad is a separate system than the phonological loop
   e. memory is not a single store that we dump things into and later take them out

True/False
Select the best answer by circling *T for True* or *F for False*. Check your answers on p. 145.

1. **T or F** Memory of general principles is episodic memory.

2. **T or F** Semantic memory is memory of general principles.

3. **T or F** Research has shown that the brain produces a protein to weaken short-term memory traces to avoid permanent storage of the information.

4. **T or F** Chunking decreases the amount of information that someone can remember.

5. **T or F** Researchers suggest that to improve accuracy of identification of suspects in a lineup that police should encourage and agree with a witness' tentative choice.

Module 7.2 Long-Term Memory Storage
Answer these questions soon after reading the **Module 7.2: Long-Term Memory Storage**.
There are several formats to the assessments. Answers to all questions appear on pp. 145-147.

Fill in the Blank
Provide a term(s) which best completes the statement below. Answers appear on p. 145.

1. The relatively permanent storage of most meaningful information occurs in _____ memory.

2. The _____ principle proposes suggests that how easily we can retrieve a memory depends on the number and type of associations we form to it.

3. A _____ device is any memory aid that is based on encoding each item in a special way.

4. The _____ principle would explain why when Amorfus learned the word orange, he thought of it as a color not as a fruit; now he can not remember it with fruit as a cue.

Short Answer
The following questions require a short written answer (3-7 sentences). Answers appear on p. 146.

1. Describe two characteristics of material that affect ease of memorizing, and give an example of each.

2. Describe the effects of emotional arousal on memory.

3. According to the levels-of-processing principle, why is it useless to simply repeat a definition over and over?

4. Describe how the timing of study affects later memory.

5. Why does forgetting occur according to the encoding specificity principle?

6. Explain how you would use the method of loci to remember a grocery list.

Multiple Choice
Circle the best answer below. Check your answers on pp. 146-147. If your answer was incorrect, try to write why it was incorrect. Check your reasons on pp. 146-147.

1. According to the levels-of-processing principle of memory, which of the following should be remembered best?
   a. a word that is repeated several times in short-term memory
   b. a word for which you produced a rhyme
   c. a word that you looked at to decide if it had an e in it
   d. a word that you related to yourself

2. If you want to remember something for a long time, what should you do?
   a. study it immediately before the test
   b. eat chocolates right before studying
   c. avoid self-monitoring of understanding
   d. study under condition that are as different as possible as the actual test conditions
   e. study several times with long intervals between studying

3. When you learned the word "spade," you thought of it as a type of card. Now you're trying to remember the word and you are given "shovel" as a cue, but it doesn't help you to remember. The best explanation is:
   a. encoding specificity principle
   b. working memory is different from reference memory
   c. depth-of-processing principle
   d. retroactive interference

4. The method of loci involves:
    a. avoiding mnemonic devices because they produce interference
    b. imagining what you want to remember in places that you already know
    c. use of the recency effect
    d. taking something that you know well, like the face of a coin, and using it to associate what you want to remember

True/False
Select the best answer by circling *T for True* or *F for False*. Check your answers on p. 147.

1. **T or F** The SPAR method recommends to **S**urvey the material to get an overview.

2. **T or F** Mnemonic devices like the method of loci can be used to improve memory.

3. **T or F** Research examining "Flashbulb" memories found that the accuracy of people's memories did not decrease over time. That is, memories were as accurate years later as they were shortly after the event.

4. **T or F** If you want to remember something in the long term you should study and review under varying conditions with substantial intervals between study sessions.

Module 7.3 Retrieval of Memories
Answer these questions soon after reading the **Module 7.3: Retrieval of Memories**. There are several formats to the assessments. Answers to all questions appear on pp. 147-149.

Fill in the Blank
Provide a term(s) which best completes the statement below. Answers appear on p. 147.

1. Mary remembers few facts about an important Civil War battle, so she just fills in the rest with what should have happened using _____.

2. A likely explanation for why John forgot the Spanish that he learned in high school because he studied French in college is _____.

3. Freud believed that memories of painful events were moved into the unconscious mind through the process of _____.

4. Pat has forgotten his new address because it is similar to his old address. _____ has caused Pat to forget his address.

5. The tendency to remember unusual items better than common items can be attributed to the _____ of the unusual items.

6. The tendency to remember well the first items on a list is known as the _____ effect.

7. Our tendency to mold our recollection of past events to fit how events turned out later is referred to as _____ bias.

Short Answer

The following questions require a short written answer (3-7 sentences). Answers appear on pp. 147-148.

1. Give one example of forgetting by retroactive interference and one example of forgetting by proactive interference.

2. Discuss three reasons for normal forgetting.

3. What is meant by reconstruction in memory? Give an example.

4. How is the suggestibility of memory related to the false memory controversy?

Multiple Choice

Circle the best answer below. Check your answers on p. 148. If your answer was incorrect, try to write why it was incorrect. Check your reasons on p. 148.

1. After Ebbinghaus had been learning and recalling lists of nonsense syllables for months, he began to study forgetting. He learned a list and then tried to recall it after 24 hours. He forgot much more of the list than an average college student would. What is the best explanation for this?
   a. his declarative memory was fine, but his semantic memory was poor
   b. Ebbinghaus was probably less intelligent than the average student
   c. retroactive interference; the earlier lists caused rapid forgetting of the later lists
   d. proactive interference; the earlier lists caused rapid forgetting of the later lists
   e. Ebbinghaus had probably developed Alzheimer's disease

2. After learning who was the murderer in a mystery novel, the reader thinks back and decides that she was pretty sure who actually did it after the very first chapter. This is an example of:
   a. savings
   b. retrograde amnesia
   c. von Restorff effect
   d. hindsight bias

3. False memories:
   a. are controversial when they are remembered in therapy after having been "repressed"
   b. can be implanted for emotional, real-life events, but not for simpler laboratory events
   c. are most controversial when the client has always known that she was abused
   d. are most easily implanted if the event is highly unusual for a person
   e. may develop because children have little memory for traumatic events

4. Which of the following has <u>not</u> been shown to influence children's eyewitness testimony?
   a. the delay between the event and questioning
   b. suggestive or leading questions
   c. the understandability of the questions
   d. use of doll props
   e. whether the person asking the questions is a man or a woman

5. Which of the following is true about ease of memorizing?
   a. people who have more practice in memorizing similar things remember better
   b. distinctive events are easier to remember than less distinctive ones
   c. words that have little meaning are easier than words that are meaningful because there is less interference
   d. words that show the von Restorff effect are not well remembered

True/False
Select the best answer by circling *T for True* or *F for False*. Check your answers on p. 149.

1. **T or F** Repression is the process of moving a memory, motivation, or emotion from the unconscious to the conscious mind.

2. **T or F** The tendency to remember unusual items better than more common items is known as free recall.

3. **T or F** Increased recall of items that occur at the beginning of a list is known as the recency effect.

4. **T or F** Children are able to provide relatively accurate recall under appropriate conditions.

5. **T or F** People retelling stories generally add details to make the story coherent.

Module 7.4 Amnesia
Answer these questions soon after reading the **Module 7.4: Amnesia**. There are several formats to the assessments. Answers to all questions appear on pp. 149-150.

Fill in the Blank
Provide a term(s) which best completes the statement below. Answers appear on p. 149.

1. A person with Korsakoff's syndrome can not remember new things and is experiencing _____ amnesia.

2. H. M. has a poor memory for things that happened within the 3 years before his operation. He is experiencing _____ amnesia.

3. One area of the brain believed to be important in the formation of new memories is the
   _____.

4. An elderly person exhibiting severe memory loss, confusion, depression and disordered thinking caused by harmful proteins in the brain is likely suffering from _____.

5. The phenomenon of most adults not remembering much from before the age 3 or 4 is known as _____.

Short Answer

The following questions require a short written answer (3-7 sentences). Answers appear on p. 149.

1. What is the difference between retrograde and anterograde amnesia? From which type of amnesia did H. M. suffer?

2. Discuss the types of memory that are spared in most types of amnesia.

Multiple Choice

Circle the best answer below. Check your answers on p. 150. If your answer was incorrect, try to write why it was incorrect. Check your reasons on p. 150.

1. Damage to the hippocampus results in:
   a. in inability to learn new facts
   b. a loss of procedural memory
   c. anterograde, but no retrograde amnesia
   d. a total loss of all long-term memories developed before the damage
   e. total amnesia

2. A list of words is presented. Which would be an implicit test of the words?
   a. present a long list of words, half new and half old; ask subjects to say whether each word is old or new
   b. ask subjects to write down all the words they remember
   c. give the first three letters of the words and ask subjects to complete the stems with any word that comes to mind
   d. ask the subjects to relearn the words after some time period

3. Which of the following is characteristic of frontal lobe amnesia such as that associated with Korsakoff's syndrome?
   a. confabulation is common
   b. people remember when and where events occurred but they can't remember the details of the events
   c. people lose their sense of self and hence they can't remember
   d. procedural learning is the first to show the effects of amnesia
   e. it is particularly evident when the details from stories are tested

4. On which task would Korsakoff's patients do the best?
   a. describing their present life's situation, i.e., children's ages, length of marriage, location of present home
   b. describing what they had for dinner the night before
   c. remembering a list of words presented in the laboratory
   d. completing word stems with words that were previously presented
   e. describing what happened to them before age 3

True/False
Select the best answer by circling *T for True* or *F for False*. Check your answers on p. 150.

1. **T or F** Most patients suffering from amnesia still possess many of their procedural memories.

2. **T or F** At the later stages Alzheimer's disease people will show widespread memory deficits.

3. **T or F** One possible explanation for infant amnesia is that the hypothalamus has not fully developed and therefore impairs the ability to form memories.

FINAL COMPREHENSIVE CHAPTER ASSESSMENT TEST

Check your answers on p. 150.

1. Susan learned German in college but she has not used it for two years. During this time, she has been studying French. Mary also learned German in college and she hasn't used it for two years either, but she has not learned any other languages in the two years. Who should remember German better and why?
   a. Mary; she will have less retroactive interference
   b. Susan; she will have less proactive interference
   c. Mary; she will have more retroactive interference
   d. Susan; she will have less retroactive interference
   e. Mary; she will have less proactive interference

2. Many students are dismayed because they feel that they have forgotten everything they learned in some courses. However, some weak memories are probably left. Which method would be most likely to show those weak memories?
   a. relearning
   b. cued recall
   c. recognition
   d. recall
   e. von Restorff effect

3. If you are given an English word and asked to give the French equivalent, your memory is being tested by:
   a. cued recall
   b. implicit test
   c. free recall
   d. recognition
   e. savings

4. If you meet someone and use her correct name immediately but cannot remember it a half-hour later, the name probably was in your:
   a. sensory store
   b. episodic memory
   c. short-term memory
   d. long-term memory
   e. semantic memory

5. If you glance at a bright scene on television and close your eyes and still see the exact image for less then a second, the image is in your:
   a. sensory store
   b. procedural memory
   c. long-term memory
   d. short-term memory
   e. episodic memory

6. Why can people hold about seven 5-letter words (35 letters) in short-term memory, but only seven unrelated letters?
   a. they use chunking so that each word is one unit
   b. words are tested by implicit memory; letters by explicit memory
   c. the seven letters are held in long-term memory, but the words are held in short-term memory
   d. the seven letters are held in short-term memory, but the words are held in long-term memory
   e. unrelated letters decay much faster than meaningful words

7. Why did Peterson and Peterson have subjects count backward during the delay interval in their experiment on short-term memory?
   a. to prevent passive decay
   b. to prevent rehearsal
   c. to prevent the use of visual imagery
   d. to interfere with the sensory store
   e. to increase the amount of proactive interference

8. The concept of working memory differs from the traditional concept of short-term memory in that working memory:
   a. does not store information, short-term memory is a storage system
   b. comes after the sensory store; short-term memory comes before it
   c. is forgotten because of interference; short-term memory forgotten because of decay
   d. has a limited capacity; short-term memory does not
   e. includes a processing system along with storage; short-term memory just stores information

9. According to levels-of-processing theory, which will lead to the best memory?
   a. repeating a word over and over for 5 sec.
   b. counting the number of vowels in a word
   c. looking to see whether a word contains an "e"
   d. producing a rhyme for a word
   e. producing a definition for a word

10. According to the encoding specificity principle, what type of cue will be best for the word *iron*, which you learned along with *sweep* and *wash*?
    a. metals
    b. i---
    c. had an "o"
    d. household chores
    e. rhymes with "my urn"

11. The Bahrick family studied foreign language vocabulary on a moderately frequent basis (every 2 weeks) or on an infrequent basis (every 8 weeks). The moderately frequent study led to:
    a. faster learning, but poorer retention
    b. slower learning, but better retention
    c. slower learning and poorer retention
    d. faster learning and better retention
    e. a total inability to learn

12. John needed to remember the last 10 presidents of the United States. He generated an image of each of the presidents located somewhere in his house. John used:
    a. the method of loci
    b. the peg method
    c. retroactive interference
    d. savings

13. The patient H. M.:
    a. has damage to the cerebral cortex
    b. could not remember any information from before his operation
    c. has no short-term memory
    d. has great difficulty learning new facts
    e. cannot learn any new skills

14. Infant amnesia occurs because:
    a. childhood memories are repressed
    b. the hippocampus is immature so long-term memories aren't stored
    c. infants and young children don't have a sense of self yet
    d. early memories are nonverbal and later memories are verbal
    e. all of the above may have been proposed, but there are problems with each explanation

15. Which of the following is likely to occur in our recall of an event?
    a. incorrect suggestions given after the event will wipe out memory for the original event
    b. details that don't fit in with the rest of the story will be omitted or distorted
    c. it is either recalled word-for-word or not recalled at all
    d. we are very accurate at dating events based on their sharpness in memory
    e. the middle part is likely to be remembered better than the beginning and the end

16. A lineup measures memory in what way?
    a. recall
    b. cued recall
    c. savings
    d. relearning
    e. recognition

17. Which of the following is true about false memories?
    a. people distort things they've seen; they don't "add" things to memory because of suggestions
    b. more than half of the people tested in "lost in the mall study" believed that personal events occurred when they were only suggested
    c. memories are more likely to be implanted if they fit with one's personal experience than if they are not related
    d. children are less likely to have memories implanted than adults

18. The serial-order effect is characterized by which of the following effect(s)?
    a. primacy Effect
    b. Secondary Effect
    c. Recency Effect
    d. a and c

19. Reports of long-lost memories, prompted by clinical techniques, are known as
    a. hindsight biases
    b. recovered memories
    c. mnemonics
    d. repressed memories

20. When you look at something briefly, then blink your eyes open and shut as quickly as possible, you cannot describe every detail of what you saw before the image fades. This very brief storage of sensory information is called the sensory store. It is also sometimes known as
    a. iconic memory
    b. plutonic memory
    c. short-term memory
    d. none of the above

ANSWERS AND EXPLANATIONS FOR CHAPTER MODULE ASSESSMENTS

Answers to the Fill in the Blank Questions – Module 7.1

1. recognition (p. 235)

2. Short-term (p. 239)

3. Ebbinghaus (p. 231)

4. episodic (p. 238)

5. Information-processing model (p. 237)

6. visuospatial sketchpad (p. 242)

Answers to the Short Answer Questions – Module 7.1

1. Ebbinghaus wanted to study how associations are formed in memory. He used nonsense syllables because they had no prior associations (as he thought; it turns out that they do). He would memorize a list and then test himself. He measured how quickly he forgot a list of syllables. He found that he forgot rapidly, forgetting about half of the syllables after an hour and still more after 24 hours. (pp. 231-234)

2. Capacity: Only about seven chunks fit in short-term memory; long-term memory capacity is vast. (pp. 234-235)
   Length of time that information is available: Information is available for only a short time in short-term memory; it becomes less available after attention has shifted; information is potentially retrievable forever in long-term memory. (pp. 238-240)

3. Working memory both stores information and works with current information. It may be thought of as one's present region of attention. The central executive governs shifts of attention. The phonological loop stores and rehearses verbal information. The visuospatial sketchpad stores and manipulates visual and spatial information. People who can't hold as much in their phonological loops have more trouble understanding complex sentences than people who have larger phonological loops. (pp. 242-243)

Answers to the Multiple Choice Questions – Module 7.1

1. a. Correct! (p. 235)
   b. Incorrect. Would give you cues but have you produce response
   c. Incorrect. Would have you produce answers in any order
   d. Incorrect. Would have you relearn material and compare with time to learn originally
   e. Incorrect. Same as d

2. a. Incorrect. Lasts for 20-30 sec. without rehearsal
    b. Incorrect. Lasts indefinitely
    c. Correct! (p. 237)
    d. Incorrect. Type of long-term memory for personal events

3. a. Incorrect. Moved out of sensory store before you could use it
    b. Correct! (pp. 239-241)
    c. Incorrect. Unlikely or you would remember it
    d. Incorrect. Chunking allows you to remember more in short-term memory, not less

4. a. Incorrect. More information can be learned, but capacity itself is not changed
    b. Incorrect. No evidence for this
    c. Incorrect. Sensory memory is not affected by practice
    d. Correct! (p. 239)

5. a. Correct! (p. 242)
    b. Incorrect. Is involved in consolidation; doesn't come after it
    c. Incorrect. The phonological loop is one part of working memory, not the whole concept
    d. this is episodic memory

6. a-d. Incorrect. Some theorists believe each of these statements, but there is wide agreement
        only on statement e
    e. Correct! (p. 243)

Answers to the True/False Questions – Module 7.1

1. **False**: Episodic memory is memory for specific events in a person's life, generally including details of when and where they happened. (p. 238)

2. **True**: Semantic memory is memory of general principles where people usually do not remember the exact source of the information. (p. 238)

3. **True**: The brain does produce a protein that weakens or destroys short-term memory traces. (p. 241)

4. **False**: A person using chunking will group items into meaningful sequences or clusters to increase the amount of information they can recall. (p. 239)

5. **False**: Researchers suggest that it would be better if police refrained from agreeing with a witness' tentative choice. (p. 236)

Answers to the Fill in the Blank Questions – Module 7.2

1. long-term (p. 245)

2. levels-of-processing (p. 245)

3. mnemonic (p. 249)

4. encoding specificity (p. 246)

Answers to the Short Answer Questions – Module 7.2

1. Things that are meaningful and have lots of associates are remembered better than things that are not. For example, you can remember material presented in your own language better than material presented in a language that you do not understand. Material that is emotionally arousing is remembered better than material that is less arousing. However, information learned during emotional arousal is not always completely accurate. (pp. 245-246, 248)

2. People often remember many details about arousing events, such as news of an assassination or some major disaster. Although the memories may be vivid and intense, they are not necessarily accurate. Exciting events may be remembered because certain norepinephrine synapses are stimulated and because the sympathetic nervous system is aroused. (pp. 248-249)

3. Rote repetition results in a very superficial level of learning. Studies have shown that simple repetition does not lead to an increase in later memory for the material. A deeper encoding in terms of meaning and understanding is necessary for later memory. Remember the SPAR system-- Process meaningfully. (p. 246)

4. Timing effects have to do with spacing study over long periods of time, or learning right before a test. Spacing learning sessions over weeks results in slower learning than learning all in one session. However, the spaced learning will be remembered longer than the massed learning. Thus, to remember a long time, learning should be spaced over several sessions. (pp. 247-248)

5. The principle of encoding specificity argues that you must use retrieval cues that are similar to the way you originally thought about the material. If you place a word in memory in one way (e.g., thinking of ball as a dance) and try to pull it out in way (e.g., thinking of ball as a round, bouncy object), you won't retrieve it. (p. 245)

6. First, I would learn a list of 20 locations in order, buildings on a walk around campus, for example. Then I would imagine each item that I want to buy in one of those locations. For example, if the administration building comes first and I want to buy tomatoes, I would imagine tomatoes smeared all over the building. Then in the store, I would take an imaginary walk and "see" each thing that I want to buy. (p. 250)

Answers to the Multiple Choice Questions – Module 7.2

1. a. Incorrect. Rote repetition does little good
   b. Incorrect. Fairly superficial level of processing
   c. Incorrect. Very superficial level of processing
   d. Correct! (p. 246)

2. a. Incorrect. This will produce good performance in the short run, but not for the long-term
   b. Incorrect. This may raise blood glucose briefly but not it won't help long-term memory
   c. Incorrect. Self-monitoring of understanding is necessary for good learning
   d. Incorrect. The encoding specificity principle states that the best memory will occur when the conditions of study and testing are as *similar* as possible
   e. Correct! (p. 248)

3. a. Correct! (p. 246)
   b. Incorrect. This is a problem with retrieval cues, not differences in memory store
   c. Incorrect. The word should have been processed semantically; you can't retrieve it now
   d. Incorrect. No new learning occurred during the interval; it's a retrieval problem

4. a. Incorrect. Method of loci is a mnemonic system
   b. Correct! (p. 250)
   c. Incorrect. Very few people can remember detailed images; anyone can use method of loci
   d. Incorrect. Might help if you knew the face of a coin better than most people do, but it is not the method of loci

Answers to the True/False Questions – Module 7.2

1. **True**: Surveying to get an overview of the material is the first step in the SPAR method. The other steps include **P**rocessing of the material, **A**sking questions, and **R**eviewing. (p. 248)

2. **True**: When practiced, any mnemonic device has the potential of improving memory. (pp. 249-250)

3. **False**: Research shows that people's accuracy decreases over time, while confidence in their memories does not. (p. 249)

4. **True**: Research has shown these to be effective in increasing memory. (p. 248)

Answers to the Fill in the Blank Questions – Module 7.3

1. reconstructive memory (p. 254)

2. retroactive interference (p. 253)

3. repression (p. 257)

4. proactive interference (p. 253)

5. distinctiveness (p. 253)

6. primacy (p. 254)

7. hindsight (p. 256)

Answers to the Short Answer Questions – Module 7.3

1. Retroactive interference: Last week you studied theories of learning and this week you are studying theories of interference. You forget the theories of learning because you learned about interference. Proactive interference: Last week you learned how to use the NIFTY-1 word processing program and this week you learned how to use the SUPER-W program. Your memory for the SUPER-W program will be impaired, because the NIFTY-1 will interfere. (p. 253)

2. Interference is one explanation for forgetting. People forget specific information because of other similar information that they learned before it (proactive interference) or because of other information learned after it (retroactive interference). A second explanation is that the information learned between the first information (primacy effect) and the last information (recency effect) is not remembered as well. A third possibility is that the information to be remembered was not very distinctive and therefore was forgotten. (pp. 252-254)

3. We tend to fill in the gaps of memories by inserting things that should be true. We omit or distort other details to fit with our expectations. For example, students remember a Native American folk tale as more consistent with their expectations than it really was. People may omit unexpected events and include events that should have happened even though they did not. (pp. 254-255)

4. Experiments show that people will incorporate false information from questions about events into their memory of the events themselves. Whether the memories actually change, or whether people have trouble identifying the source of the suggested information is not clear. The false memory controversy surrounds clients' remembering childhood sexual abuse during therapy. Some psychologists believe that certain therapeutic techniques suggest that abuse occurred when it did not and the client comes to believe this is an actual memory and not just a suggestion. (pp. 256-258)

Answers to the Multiple Choice Questions – Module 7.3

1. a. Incorrect. Ebbinghaus measured declarative memory, and it was poor
    b. Incorrect. He was very creative for his times
    c. Incorrect. This is the reason, but it's <u>proactive</u>
    d. Correct! (p. 256)
    e. Incorrect. Doubtful; his memory was generally good

2. a. Incorrect. Refers to faster relearning the second time; no relearning here
    b. Incorrect. Forgetting of earlier material; material here is reconstructed
    c. Incorrect. Memory for distinctive things; reconstruction occurred here
    d. Correct! (p. 253)

3. a. Correct! (p. 254)
    b. Incorrect. When lists of related words are presented in the laboratory, people falsely "remember" non-presented words
    c. Incorrect. These cases probably involve real, not false, memories
    d. Incorrect. It is just the opposite; events that fit in with one's normal life are more easily implanted
    e. Incorrect. Children who have experienced traumatic events remember them fairly well

4. a-d. Incorrect. All of these have been shown to influence recall.
    e. Correct! (p. 260)

5. a. Incorrect. The earlier material would cause proactive interference
    b. Correct! (p. 255)
    c. Incorrect. Meaningful words are more easily associated
    d. Incorrect. Refers to distinctive events; these are easier

Answers to the True/False Questions – Module 7.3

1. **False:** Repression is the process of moving a memory, motivation, or emotion from the conscious to the unconscious mind. (p. 257)

2. **False:** The tendency to remember unusual items better than more common items is based on distinctiveness of those uncommon items. Free recall is a method of testing memory by asking someone to produce a certain item without substantial hints, as on an essay or short-answer test. (p. 253)

3. **False:** A recency effect is observed when recall of the <u>last</u> few items is increased relative to the middle items. A primacy effect is observed when recall of the <u>first</u> few items is increased relative to the middle items. (p. 254)

4. **True:** When children are questioned under the appropriate conditions, they are able to give relatively accurate accounts of events. (p. 260)

5. **True:** People do add details to stories that will fit the gist even though those details were not part of the original event. (p. 255)

Answers to the Fill in the Blank Questions – Module 7.4

1. anterograde (p. 263)

2. retrograde (p. 264)

3. hippocampus (p. 263)

4. Alzheimer's disease (p. 266)

5. infant amnesia (p. 266)

Answers to the Short Answer Questions – Module 7.4

1. Retrograde amnesia means a loss of memory for events that occurred before the onset of the amnesia. Anterograde means an inability to learn new things, or to form new long-term memories. H. M.'s biggest problem was anterograde amnesia; he couldn't learn new facts. Although he had some trouble remembering events that happened a few years before his operation, H. M. could generally remember things that occurred before his amnesia. (p. 264, Fig. 7.20)

2. People with amnesia generally perform normally on tests that do not require explicit remembering. These implicit memory tests ask participants to simply respond to some stimuli that they have experienced before, like giving words for word fragments. Generally, the people with amnesia give as many previously seen words as normal participants do. People with amnesia are usually normal on procedural memory tasks. They remember how to do things even though they may not remember having learned to do them. (pp. 265-266)

Answers to the Multiple Choice Questions – Module 7.4

1. a. Correct! (p. 263)
    b. Incorrect. New skills can be learned
    c. Incorrect. Some retrograde amnesia for memories occurring just before the brain damage
    d. Incorrect. Some memories acquired long before the damage are normal
    e. Incorrect. No, because of b and d

2. a. Incorrect. Recognition; an explicit test
    b. Incorrect. Recall; an explicit test
    c. Correct! (p. 266)
    d. Incorrect. Relearning; an explicit test
3. a. Correct! (pp. 264-266)
    b. Incorrect. They have trouble remembering when and where events occurred
    c. Incorrect. This is one explanation for childhood amnesia, not for frontal lobe amnesia
    d. Incorrect. Procedural learning is rarely affected by amnesia
    e. Incorrect. True of the amnesia of old age; Korsakoff's have problems with important parts also

4. a., b. Incorrect. They confabulate, mixing old memories with guesses; such episodic memory is very poor
    c. Incorrect. Word lists containing more than about seven items cannot be remembered
    d. Correct! (p. 266)
    e. Incorrect. They would not be able to do this because of infantile amnesia

Answers to the True/False Questions – Module 7.4

1. **True**: Most patients suffering from amnesia have problems with declarative memory or remembering facts. (p. 264)

2. **True**: Many different types of memory are impaired at the later stages of Alzheimer's disease. (p. 266)

3. **False**: Although the hypothalamus is not yet matured, it is likely that an immature hippocampus is the brain structure primarily responsible for memory. (pp. 266-267)

Answers to Final Comprehensive Assessment

1. a (p. 253)
2. a (p. 235)
3. a (p. 234)
4. c (pp. 238-239)
5. a (p. 237)
6. a (pp. 239-240)
7. b (p. 241)
8. e (p. 242)
9. e (pp. 245-246)
10. d (p. 246)

11. a (pp. 247-248)
12. a (p. 250)
13. d (p. 263)
14. e (pp. 266-267)
15. b (p. 255)
16. e (p. 235)
17. c (pp. 258-259)
18. d (p. 254)
19. b (p. 257)
20. a (p. 257)

CHAPTER 8

COGNITION AND LANGUAGE

CHAPTER OVERVIEW INFORMATION

LEARNING OBJECTIVES

By the end of Chapter 8 you should

- ✓ Be familiar with the three fundamental processes of cognition
- ✓ Have an increased understanding of the techniques of problem solving and development of expertise; and an increased awareness of common errors of thought
- ✓ Be familiar with theories of language evolution and learning in humans; understanding the cognitive and social purposes of language

CHAPTER 8 OUTLINE

Chapters 6 and 7 explored the topics of how we **LEARN** (Chapter 6) and store information in **MEMORY** (Chapter 7). Chapter 8 completes the picture by exploring how we USE the information we retrieve from our memories. Included in Chapter 8 are the topics of attention, categorization, problem-solving, expertise, errors, and language.

Chapter 8 is presented below in outline format to assist you in understanding the information presented in the chapter. More detailed information on any topic can be found using the page references to the right of the topic.

Module 8.1 Categorization and Attention

I. Methods of Research in Cognitive Psychology
    A. Cognitive psychologists study how people think and gain knowledge (p. 273)
        1. People are unaware of their thought processes (p. 273, Fig. 8.1)

II. Categorization
    A. Categories are used to group similar things (p. 274)
    B. Ways of Describing a Category
        1. There are several different theories about the arrangement of categories (pp. 274-276)
            a. Categories are organized around prototypical members (pp. 274-275)
    C. Conceptual Networks and Priming
        1. Related concepts activate each other through a conceptual network in memory (pp. 275-276, Fig. 8.2)
        2. Spreading activation causes priming of related concepts (p. 276, Fig 8.3)

III. Cross-Cultural Studies of Concepts
    A. Different cultures may have different names for the same objects (p. 276)
    B. Different cultures create similar categories for the differently named objects (p. 277, Fig. 8.4)

IV. Attention
    A. Attention, or a tendency to respond or remember certain stimuli, can shift and causes increases in brain processing (p. 277)
    B. Preattentive and Attentive Processes
        1. Objects that differ drastically from others immediately stand out (pp. 277-278, Figs. 8.5 and 8.7)
        2. Identification of an object amongst similar objects requires attention (pp. 278-279, Figs. 8.6-8.7)
    C. The Stroop Effect
        1. The Stroop effect shows how preattentive processes in reading can interfere with performance (p. 279, Fig. 8.8)

V. Attention Limits Over Time and Space
    A. Attention is limited in the number of objects and space over which it can be distributed (p. 280, Fig. 8.9)
    B. Change Blindness
        1. People frequently fail to notice subtle changes, changes that occurred during eye blinks or eye movements (pp. 281-282, Figs. 8.10-8.11)
    C. Shifting attention
        1. Cell phone use while driving causes shifts in attention (pp. 282-283)
        2. Video game players learn to broaden attention which is both beneficial and detrimental (p. 283)
    D. The Attentional Blink
        1. People will ignore a stimulus when presented shortly after a previous stimulus (p. 283)

The message: Measuring mental events is not easy but it can be accomplished. (p. 283)

Module 8.2 Problem Solving, Expertise, and Error
VI. Expertise
    A. Practice Makes (Nearly) Perfect
        1. Experts have a lot of practice in their fields (pp. 285-287)
    B. Expert Pattern Recognition
        1. Experts recognize common patterns in their fields quickly (p. 287, Fig. 8.12)
            a. They remember organized material from their areas easily (p. 287)
        2. Experts solve problems quickly by selecting relevant information (p. 287)

VII. Problem Solving
    A. Problem solving involves four phases (p. 287, Fig. 8.13)
    B. Understanding and Simplifying a Problem
        1. Problems need to be understood and simplified (pp. 287-288)
    C. Generating Hypotheses
        1. Hypotheses should be generated (pp. 288-289)
            a. Algorithms can be used to generate all possibilities (p. 288)
            b. Heuristics generate likely possibilities (p. 288)
    D. Testing Hypotheses and Checking the Results
        1. Hypotheses should be tested and results checked (p. 289, Fig. 8.15)
    E. Generalizing Solutions to Similar Problems
        1. Solutions should be generalized to similar problems (p. 289)
            a. People often fail to generalize to similar problems (pp. 289-291, Figs. 8.16-8.17)

VIII. Special Features of Insight Problems
    A. Some problems are solved insightfully (p. 291)
    B. Sudden or Gradual Insights?
        1. People may be making progress before a solution is found (pp. 291-292)
    C. The Characteristics of Creativity
        1. Creative people are probably only creative in their own fields (pp. 292-293)

IX. Reasoning by Heuristics
    A. Using heuristics to reason will sometimes be effective as well as ineffective (p. 293)
    B. The Representativeness Heuristic and Base-Rate Information
        1. People often use representativeness and not base rate (pp. 293-294, Table 8.1)
    C. The Availability Heuristic
        1. People overuse availability in memory to judge frequency (pp. 294-295, Table 8.1)
            a. People overestimate likelihood of an event that they can easily recall (p. 294)

X. Other Common Errors in Human Cognition
    A. Intelligent people will accept erroneous information as accurate (p. 295)
    B. Overconfidence
        1. People overestimate confidence on difficult questions and underestimate confidence on easy questions (pp. 295-296)
    C. Attractiveness of Valuable but Very Unlikely Outcomes
        1. People prefer a unlikely chance at a fortune to a small sure gain (p. 296)
    D. Confirmation Bias
        1. People often do not consider alternative hypotheses but seek support for their original hypothesis (pp. 296-297, Fig. 8.19)
        2. Functional fixedness is the tendency to adopt a single approach or method (p. 297, Fig. 8.20)
    E. Framing Questions
        1. The way a question is worded affects its answer (pp. 297-298)
            a. People are more willing to take risks when dealing with a loss than with a gain (p. 298, Fig. 8.21)
    F. The Sunk Cost Effect
        1. People are willing to do things they would not otherwise do because of the prior investment in the activity (p. 299)

The message: *Learning about common cognitive errors may help us make better decisions. (p. 299)*

Module 8.3 Language
XI. Precursors to Language in Nonhumans
    A. Language and human's ability to produce and transform language makes us unique (p. 302, Figs. 8.22-8.23)
    B. Some animals have learned rudimentary human language (pp. 303-304, Fig. 8.24)
        1. Chimps use symbols but they don't show flexibility (p. 304)
        2. Pygmy chimps show more flexible use of language (p. 304, Fig. 8.25)

XII. Human Specializations for Learning Language
    A. Language and General Intelligence
        1. Humans are specialized for learning language (pp. 304-305)
        2. Language ability is not based solely on intelligence (p. 305)
    B. Language Learning as a Specialized Capacity
        1. People possess an innate ability to acquire language (p. 305)
            a. Brain activity increases in language areas for natural rules (pp. 305-306)
        2. Young infants are skilled in some language processes (p. 306)
    C. Language and the Human Brain
        1. Some areas of the brain are critical for language comprehension and production (pp. 306-307, Fig. 8.26)
    D. Stages of Language Development
        1. Children progress through different stages of language ability (pp. 307-308, Table 8.2)
            a. Most follow natural progression regardless of challenges or opportunities achieving adult competency by age 4 (p. 308, Fig. 8.27)
    E. Children Exposed to No Language or Two Languages
        1. Experience with language during child development is important (p. 308)
            a. Deaf and bilingual children show the importance of the language environment during development (p. 308)
            b. Bilingual children take longer to master two languages (p. 309)

XIII. Understanding Language
    A. Understanding a Word
        1. People hear the same sounds differently, depending upon context (pp. 309-310)
        2. Missing sounds in words are filled in by the brain (pp. 309-310)
    B. Understanding Sentences
        1. Comprehension is influenced by knowledge, context and grammar (p. 310, Fig. 8.28)
    C. Limits to Our Language Understanding
        1. Embedded sentences and those containing negatives result are difficult to understand (p. 311)
    D. Monitoring Understanding
        1. Good and poor reader vary in their ability to monitor their understanding (p. 312)

XIV. Reading
    A. Reading is complicated too, but most are experts at reading (p. 312)
    B. Word Recognition
        1. Whole words are read faster than individual letters (pp. 312-313, Figs. 8.30-8.31)
        2. The connectionist model involves interactive activation of higher-order and lower-order units (p. 313, Figs. 8.32-8.33)
    C. Reading and Eye Movements
        1. Effective readers process sound and meaning information of words (p. 313, Fig. 8.34)
        2. Eyes jump in saccades while reading (pp. 314-315)
            a. Nothing can be seen while the eye is moving (p. 314)
            b. Readers take in about 11 letters per fixation (pp. 314-315)
                i. Part of the next word is processed while each word is being read (p. 315)
                ii. Some languages have a shorter span or fixation than English (p. 315)
            c. Speed readers seem to be more efficient in their reading (p. 315)

The message: *Although nonhuman primates show some use of language, only humans are language "experts." (pp. 315-316)*

RELATED WEBSITES AND ACTIVITIES
Visit http://psychology.wadsworth.com/kalat_intro7e/ for online quizzing, glossary flashcards, crossword puzzles, annotated web links, and more.

LECTURE MATERIAL
Information from the text is only half of the picture. Don't forget to review your lecture material. Process each topic meaningfully. Most importantly, be sure that you understand the material in each lecture-if you don't, ask your instructor or teaching assistant.

STUDY TIP # 8: Set up study groups. Studying in groups of two or three can be very effective if your study group members are of like ability and everyone is prepared before the group meets.

TIP: Associate the lecture material with the information from the text, with things that you already know, with your personal experiences, or with real-life applications. Type or neatly re-write your notes. Make sure they are detailed and organized. Make comments on your notes. Then write questions to cover each concept.

CHAPTER MODULE ASSESSMENTS

Module 8.1 Categorization and Attention
Answer these questions soon after reading the **Module 8.1: Categorization and Attention**. There are several formats to the assessments. Answers to all questions appear on pp. 166-167.

Fill in the Blank
Provide a term(s) which best completes the statement below. Answers appear on p. 166.

1. Hearing or thinking about a concept primes you to think about other related concepts. Priming of the related concepts occurs as a result of _____.

2. A way of extracting information automatically and simultaneously across a large portion of the visual field results from the use of _____ processes.

3. Categories such as vehicle can be defined by _____ such as car, train, airplane, and boat.

4. Psychologists who study how people think, acquire knowledge, and solve problems are _____ psychologists.

5. A(n) _____ occurs when people ignore a stimulus when presented shortly after another stimulus.

Short Answer
The following questions require a short written answer (3-7 sentences). Answers appear on p. 166.

1. Behaviorists argue that thinking cannot be studied because there is no way to measure it. Give an example of an experiment which could be used to argue against that view.

2. Explain how a person would know that a robin is a bird according to the prototype view and according to the conceptual network approach.

3. The use of cell-phones has skyrocketed in the last few years. Concerns regarding the safety of talking on a cell-phone while driving have also increased. Discuss the research regarding the safety of using cell-phones while driving.

4. Discuss the conditions under which presenting two stimuli will result in the detection of only one of the stimuli.

Multiple Choice
Circle the best answer below. Check your answers on p. 167. If your answer was incorrect, try to write why it was incorrect. Check your reasons on p. 167.

1. The topic that would be least likely to be studied by a psychologist interested in cognition is how people:
   a. plan a vacation
   b. use their imagination to describe a scene
   c. change their behavior following reinforcement
   d. become experts on a new topic

2. Which of the following is an example of the use of conceptual networks in categorizing?
   a. a dog must have lungs because it is a mammal; mammals are animals; animals have lungs
   b. a dog is an animal because it has fur, a tail, and lungs
   c. a dog is an animal because it is similar to an average animal
   d. a dog is an animal because I memorized that fact in childhood

3. When people decide whether two objects that differ in orientation are the same or not:
   a. the difference in orientation has no effect
   b. they act as if they are watching a model rotate in their heads
   c. responses are faster if the two objects are in very different orientations than if they are in similar orientations
   d. people report that they do not use visual images

4. An attentional blink is most likely to occur when:
   a. two stimuli are separated by a fraction of a second
   b. two stimuli are separated by a few seconds
   c. two stimuli are separated by a few minutes
   d. only one stimulus is presented

5. Finding the X in this display **OOOXOOOOO** is easier (and faster) than finding the X in this display **WHVXKYMZN**. The reason is:
   a. processing circles is easier than processing angles
   b. preattentive processes (automatic and parallel search) can be used in the first display
   c. attentive processes (serial search) can be used in the first display
   d. interference from the Stroop effect

True/False
Select the best answer by circling *T for True* or *F for False*. Check your answers on p. 167.

1. **T or F** People listening to a cell-phone on one ear switch their attention to that side of their body.

2. **T or F** Change blindness refers to the phenomenon of people detecting subtle changes to scene or in their environment.

3. **T or F** Although cultures may have different names for different objects, most create similar categories for those objects.

4. **T or F** Cognitive psychologists waste time and energy by creating elaborate and precise experiments to measure cognitive ability when they could just ask people to describe their own cognitive processes.

Module 8.2 Problem Solving, Expertise, and Error
Answer these questions soon after reading the **Module 8.2: Problem Solving, Expertise, and Error**. There are several formats to the assessments. Answers to all questions appear on pp. 167-170.

Fill in the Blank
Provide a term(s) which best completes the statement below. Answers appear on p. 167.

1. The _____ heuristic is the tendency to assume that, if an item is similar to members of a particular category, it is probably a member of that category itself.

2. A _____ is a strategy for simplifying a problem or for guiding an investigation.

3. The _____ effect occurs when we do something we would not otherwise choose to do, because we have already invested money or effort into it.

4. Data about the frequency or probability of a given item occurring is known as _____ information.

5. The tendency to adhere to a single approach to a problem or a single way of using an item is known as _____.

Short Answer
The following questions require a short written answer (3-7 sentences). Answers appear on p. 168.

1. Describe one way in which experts differ from novices.

2. Describe one strategy that a problem solver can use to understand a problem.

3. Explain the difference between an algorithm and a heuristic.

4. Discuss research on generalization of problem solution to other similar problems.

5. Discuss the characteristics of creative problem solving.

6. Under what conditions are people likely to be overconfident about their predictions?

7. Many people fail to consider alternative hypotheses when trying to solve a problem. Give one example of this.

8. Give an example of how rephrasing a situation involving risks would affect people's acceptance of risk.

Multiple Choice

Circle the best answer below. Check your answers on p. 169. If your answer was incorrect, try to write why it was incorrect. Check your reasons on p. 169.

1. Experts:
   a. excel mainly because they quickly recognize familiar patterns
   b. are better at all types of memory tasks involving material from their area than novices
   c. are born with special talent
   d. solve problems better than novices almost entirely because they have more "tools" to use

2. Which of the following would be <u>least</u> useful in solving a problem that you cannot answer quickly?
   a. try to answer a related or simplified question
   b. start to generate hypotheses
   c. try to solve a simpler version
   d. start with the assumption that the problem is not solvable

3. When people are asked to solve problems that are similar to just-solved ones, they:
   a. easily apply the same principles to the new problem
   b. apply the same principles if they have seen only one example, but don't if they've seen many examples
   c. sometimes use the prior experience if they had a variety of different examples
   d. can apply materials from a specific discipline, such as physics, to a more general discipline, such as math, but not vice versa

4. Creative problem solving is:
   a. a talent; either you have it or you don't
   b. unrelated to prior knowledge; discoveries are made without reliance on accumulated data
   c. similar to insight in that it is sudden and unrelated to a gradual move toward a solution or a discovery
   d. based, in part, on the availability of prior data
   e. both b and c

5. A patient shows most of the symptoms of a very rare disease and many of the symptoms of a common one. The doctor decides that it must be the very rare disease. In her decision, she has ignored:
   a. base-rate information
   b. the similarity of the symptoms to those in each category
   c. the fact that there may be an alternative hypothesis
   d. a heuristic that would be useful in solving the problem

6. The availability heuristic would lead to which error?
   a. thinking that a test for a rare disease that is 99% accurate would call only a few well people "sick"
   b. taking a risk when a question is phrased in terms of loss but not in terms of gain
   c. deciding that a student is a math major because he wears glasses, carries a calculator in his pocket, and is sort of a nerd even though only 1% of all students are math majors
   d. thinking that you are more likely to die in a plane than in a car crash because you have read about so many plane crashes lately
   e. saying you are 99% sure you're correct when the actual likelihood is 70%

7. People generally:
   a. avoid taking risks when considering a loss
   b. avoid taking risks when considering a gain
   c. take risks when considering a gain
   d. avoid risks in all cases if lives are involved, but take them if money is involved

True/False
Select the best answer by circling *T for True* or *F for False*. Check your answers on pp. 169-170.

1. **T or F** Compared to a novice, an expert in an area is able to recognize patterns more quickly.

2. **T or F** Algorithms are used to reduce the complexity of a problem by generating a subset of likely possibilities.

3. **T or F** People readily generalize the solution of one problem to another similar problem.

4. **T or F** People often make progress on insight problems without realizing it.

Module 8.3 Language
Answer these questions soon after reading the **Module 8.3: Language**. There are several formats to the assessments. Answers to all questions appear on pp. 170-171.

Fill in the Blank
Provide a term(s) which best completes the statement below. Answers appear on p. 170.

1. A speech disorder that is caused by damage to the temporal lobe and results in impaired language comprehension describes the effects of _____ aphasia.

2. A _____ is a unit of sound that is part of a word and can be a single letter or a combination of letters.

3. A genetic form of mental retardation that does not impair language ability is _____ syndrome.

4. Quick eye movements that occur during reading and take your eyes from one fixation point to another are called _____.

Short Answer
The following questions require a short written answer (3-7 sentences). Answers appear on p. 170.

1. Early attempts to teach language to non-human primates were not very successful, but later attempts have been more successful. Explain why.

2. The linguist Noam Chomsky and his followers have suggested that people are born with a built-in mechanism for learning language -- the language acquisition device. What was their argument in its favor? What additional evidence could you use to support their idea?

3. What is known about the role of context in the understanding of words with missing phonemes?

4. Describe the word-superiority effect and explain how the connectionist model can handle it.

Multiple Choice
Circle the best answer below. Check your answers on pp. 170-171. If your answer was incorrect, try to write why it was incorrect. Check your reasons on pp. 170-171.

1. "Visiting relatives can be tiresome" can either mean that the relatives are visiting you or you are visiting the relatives. Thus, this sentence has:
   a. two deep structures and one surface structure
   b. two surface structures and one deep structure
   c. deep structures that are identical to surface structures
   d. deep structures that are unrelated to surface structures

2. The most recent attempts to teach language to animals have shown that:
   a. chimps can learn language and use it in the same way as children
   b. animals that supposedly understand and use language are really only using subtle cues
   c. young bonobos have shown evidence of actual language learning
   d. watching and imitating other animals who are being taught disrupts learning

3. Most psychologists believe that humans are specialized for language learning. Which of the following is support for that belief?
   a. the human brain contains areas specifically important for language comprehension
   b. children progress through stages of language learning
   c. deaf children deprived of language experience make up their own sign language
   d. all of the above provide support for human language specialization

4. Which of the following shows evidence that context affects our understanding of words?
   a. lecturers in scientific areas use fewer uhs and ers than lecturers in the humanities
   b. if there is a delay between a word with a missing first letter and the word that clarifies it (such as *ent and forest), people don't report the appropriate word (tent)
   c. adding a label such as "not cyanide" makes students less likely to select the container
   d. the word "rose" can refer to a flower or the past tense of rise depending on other words around it

5. During a fixation in reading, people:
   a. take in less than during a saccade
   b. can take in long sentences
   c. keep their eyes stationary for several seconds
   d. take in a window of about 11 characters

True/False
Select the best answer by circling *T for True* or *F for False*. Check your answers on p. 171.

1. **T or F** In language the basic unit of meaning is a grapheme.

2. **T or F** A person experiencing difficulty in using and understanding language especially grammatical devices is likely suffering damage to Broca's area.

3. **T or F** The ability to recognize letters faster than words is termed the word-superiority effect.

4. **T or F** Bilingual children are able to master two languages faster than children learning just one language.

FINAL COMPREHENSIVE CHAPTER ASSESSMENT TEST

Check your answers on p. 171.

1. Mental activity can best be measured by:
   a. asking people what they are thinking
   b. directly observing it
   c. having people judge how long it would take them to do a task
   d. measuring how long it takes to answer questions
   e. none of the above; it cannot be measured and cannot be studied scientifically

2. Categories are:
   a. very similar from culture to culture
   b. absolute so that an object either is or is not a clear member of a category
   c. completely organized by levels such that each feature is stored at the lowest possible level and not repeated at higher levels
   d. activated by related concepts
   e. clearly defined by critical features

3. According to the conceptual network view of categorization, which would take longer to respond "true" to: "A blackpoll warbler can fly" or "A bird can fly"?
   a. "A bird can fly," because it is more general
   b. "A blackpoll warbler can fly," because you need to infer that a blackpoll warbler is a bird
   c. "A bird can fly," because it is a more typical statement
   d. "A blackpoll warbler can fly," because it is lacking some of the features of a typical bird

4. In Shepard and Metzler's study in which students decided whether two drawings of blocks were the same or different, students:
   a. were more accurate in responding "same" than "different"
   b. took longer to say "same" when the two objects were many degrees different in orientation than when they were only a few degrees different
   c. took longer to say "same" when the two objects were only a few degrees different in orientation than when they were many degrees different
   d. made so many errors (over 97%) that reaction times were meaningless
   e. reacted as if they could not use mental images

5. A film producer decides to re-shoot a scene from a movie three weeks after it was originally shot. Unfortunately, the costume originally worn by one cast member is no longer available and cannot be exactly duplicated. However, the crew is able to get a similar costume. When viewers watch the movie they do not recognize the subtle differences in the costume. This is a result of?
   a. an attentional blink
   b. an attentional shift
   c. change blindness
   d. none of the above

6. People can do two things as fast as one thing if:
   a. they are able to perform tasks in series, rather than in parallel
   b. one task is so routine that is requires no attention
   c. the response to one task follows the other one by 200 ms
   d. they are responses to complex stimuli
   e. both tasks require cognitive effort

7. When chess experts were shown a chess board and asked to recall the pieces, they:
   a. recalled more poorly than novices; apparently their expertise got in the way
   b. remembered better than novices whether the pieces were arranged as in a game or randomly
   c. remembered more poorly than novices if the pieces were arranged as in a game, but better if they were arranged randomly
   d. remembered better than novices if the pieces were arranged as in a game, but about the same if they were arranged randomly

8. In which situation would a heuristic be most useful?
   a. you have no hypotheses about how to solve a problem
   b. you have committed yourself to one hypothesis
   c. you cannot think of a way to test a hypothesis
   d. you keep generating the same incorrect hypothesis
   e. you have too many hypotheses to test

9. Which of the following would be most useful in helping to understand a problem?
   a. try to answer a related or simplified question
   b. try to add complexity to the problem; think of many instances rather than just a few
   c. keep trying to retrieve the factual information; avoid making estimates of the answer
   d. sit back and try to use insight to solve the problem

10. Students who learned how to solve progression problems in physics were later asked to solve very similar math problems. They:
   a. solved them very quickly because they noted the similarity
   b. did not use their learning on the math problems; evidently they associated the solutions entirely with physics
   c. solved the math problems more quickly than students who learned math first and then were given physics problems
   d. gave correct solutions if the problems involved rigid things like guns and bullets, but not if water and hoses were used in the examples

11. Evidence that solutions to insight problems may involve a gradual progression toward the solution is shown by:
   a. people's inability to say whether or not they will be able to solve such problems
   b. people's ability to indicate whether or not problems have solutions, even without being able to solve them
   c. the fact that some people are never able to solve some insight problems
   d. the inability of students to calculate Kepler's results

12. Which of the following is an example of base-rate information?
   a. the population consists of 10,000 mosquitoes and 2 rare kwiny bugs
   b. the kwiny bug looks like a mosquito except it is a bit bigger
   c. the mosquito flies a bit faster than the kwiny bug
   d. a particular specimen looks exactly like a kwiny bug
   e. the bite of the kwiny bug soothes the skin rather than irritating it

13. You are quite sure that it rains every time you wash your car. In fact, this is probably not true, but it is most related to which heuristic?
   a. representativeness
   b. base-rate
   c. avoiding risk
   d. availability
   e. overconfidence

14. If you are like most people, which would you be more likely to select as your prize in a quiz show?
    a. win $5,000
    b. take a 25% chance of winning $20,000 with a 75% chance of winning nothing
    c. lose $2,000 that you've won
    d. take a 50% chance of winning $10,000 with a 50% chance of winning nothing
    e. all of the above are equally likely; people do not agree on their choices

15. "Mary chased the man" and "The man was chased by Mary" have:
    a. a unique transformational grammar
    b. two deep structures but only one surface structure
    c. totally arbitrary speech sounds
    d. two surface structures but only one deep structure

16. Chimpanzees can:
    a. learn spoken language, but teaching them is very difficult
    b. learn to use many symbols in sign language
    c. not learn anything that resembles human language because they lack intelligence
    d. not learn sign language but they can learn spoken language
    e. learn and use language in the same way as children

17. The language acquisition device
    a. is a built-in mechanism for acquiring language in humans
    b. is a computer that generates sentences and answers questions
    c. is the typewriter used by bonobos when they learn to speak
    d. is the computer terminal used by the gorilla Koko when she "spoke" on the internet

18. The Stroop effect occurs because:
    a. it is very difficult to see the colors of ink
    b. people are so used to reading words that they cannot suppress the habit
    c. people do not take the frequency of things in the population into account
    d. people's thoughts are related to their categories

19. When students hear a sentence with part of a word missing, they report:
    a. exactly what was missing
    b. hearing a word that fits the sentence no matter when the relevant context word appears
    c. hearing the whole word, even the missing letter
    d. hearing the word with those sounds that occurs most frequently in the language, independently of context

20. Which of the following is consistent with the word-superiority effect?
    a. you can find letters faster by searching for letters rather than by reading words
    b. you can recognize the difference between C and J alone faster than in COIN and JOIN
    c. you can recognize the difference between C and J faster in XQCF and XQJF than in COIN and JOIN
    d. a single letter can be identified faster when people read the whole word than when they focus attention on the critical letter
    e. all of the above are consistent

ANSWERS AND EXPLANATIONS FOR CHAPTER MODULE ASSESSMENTS

Answers to the Fill in the Blank Questions – Module 8.1

1. spreading activation (p. 276)

2. preattentive (pp. 277-278)

3. prototypes (pp. 274-275)

4. cognitive (p. 273)

5. attentional blink (pp. 281-282)

Answers to the Short Answer Questions – Module 8.1

1. The time that thought processes take can be measured. More complex processes take longer than simple ones. For example, Shepard and Metzler presented pictures of three-dimensional objects and asked subjects if they were the same or different. Each pair of objects was in the same orientation, or one was turned some amount relative to the other. The time to say "same" depended upon the difference in orientation. It appeared that subjects actually imagined one of the pictures turning in their head and then matched the image with the other picture. The farther they had to turn it, the longer it took, just as it would if they were actually moving an object. (pp. 273-274)

2. The prototype view argues that people categorize by comparing objects with typical instances of categories. For <u>bird</u>, typical birds are robins and sparrows, so a person could quickly compare an actual robin with the prototypical bird, see the similarity, and call a robin a bird. The conceptual network approach would argue that we determine that a robin is a bird by noticing that robin is subordinate to (beneath) bird in the hierarchy in memory. (pp. 274-276)

3. Attention research examining the effects of talking on a cell-phone while driving indicate that person tends to shift their attention toward the side of the body where they have the phone instead of straight ahead. Research also shows that a conversation on a cell phone requires more attention than a conversation with another person in the car and that cell-phone conversations decrease a driver's attention to signs and increases the risk of accidents. (pp 282-283)

4. If a second stimulus is presented within 100 – 700 msec of the previous stimulus, many participants fail to detect the second stimulus. This effect is known as the attentional blink. There are several possible explanations. One explanation is that the second stimulus is not detected due to the brain being engaged in the "binding" process for the first stimulus. (p. 283)

Answers to the Multiple Choice Questions – Module 8.1

1. a. Incorrect. Planning is part of cognition
    b. Incorrect. Imaging is part of cognition
    c. Correct! (p. 273)
    d. Incorrect. Acquiring knowledge is part of cognition

2. a. Correct! (pp. 275-276)
    b. Incorrect. Using features to categorize
    c. Incorrect. Prototype view of categorization
    d. Incorrect. True, but how is that fact represented in memory?

3. a. Incorrect. The larger the difference in orientation, the longer the time
    b. Correct! (pp. 273-274)
    c. Incorrect. The closer together the orientations, the shorter the time
    d. Incorrect. People say that they do compare images in this task

4. a. Correct! (p. 283)
    b. Incorrect. An attention blink will occur only after a brief delay (less than 100 msec)
    c. Incorrect. An attention blink will occur only after a brief delay (less than 100 msec)
    d. Incorrect. Two stimuli must be presented.

5. a. Incorrect. Preattentive processes operate equally well on all kinds of features (find O in
       XXXOXXXX vs. QCPODBSG)
    b. Correct! (p. 277)
    c. Incorrect. Attentive processes are used in the second display
    d. Incorrect. The response to the target stimulus X is the same in both displays

Answers to the True/False Questions – Module 8.1

1. **True**: Research has shown that people do in fact switch their attention. (p. 282)

2. **False**: Change blindness occurs when people <u>do not</u> detect changes. (p. 281)

3. **True**: Cultures may have many different names for objects but people tend to categorize
    them similarly. (pp. 276-277)

4. **False**: People generally cannot accurately describe their own cognitive processes so creating
    experiments to evaluate those processes are essential. (p. 273)

Answers to the Fill in the Blank Questions – Module 8.2

1. representativeness (p. 293)

2. heuristic (p. 288)

3. sunk cost (p. 299)

4. base-rate (p. 294)

5. functional fixedness (p. 297)

Answers to the Short Answer Questions – Module 8.2

1. Experts recognize and remember organized patterns relevant to their expertise more quickly and accurately than novices. (pp. 285-287)

2. Try to solve a simpler version of the problem. If there are many objects involved, try to solve it with only one or two. (pp. 287-288)

3. An algorithm is a mechanical, repetitive procedure that will eventually lead to a correct answer. It tests all possible hypotheses. Heuristics are strategies for simplifying a problem. They are "rules of thumb" for solving various problems that often lead to correct answers. (p. 288)

4. People are often very poor at generalizing. They may be able to use probability to solve simple problems, such as those involving coin tosses, but they are poor at applying the same principles to real-world problems. People are better at generalizing if they have seen several different types of examples of problems than if they have only seen one type of example. Mathematics transfers to physics, but physics doesn't transfer to mathematics. We know that mathematics is applicable to many different areas, but we don't assume that this is true for physics. (pp. 289-291)

5. Creative contributions involve both good solutions to problems and the selection of appropriate problems. Guessing that problems are important and solvable is part of creative problem solving. The formation of great theories may depend on having the appropriate data and persistence to keep trying to solve the problem, and not on some special talent. Creative individuals often sense that the old ways are not quite right, and they throw themselves into the work. (pp. 292-293)

6. People tend to be overconfident when they predict events that are quite uncertain. This is particularly true about predictions of one's own performance. Students are overconfident about their performance in courses and athletes predict they'll have better seasons than they have. Government officials express great confidence in their predictions of future events, but they are actually no more accurate than people outside of the government. (pp. 295-296)

7. If subjects are told to find the rule for generating number sequences and are given 2,4,6 as an example, they immediately decide that the rule is "add 2" and ask if 6, 8, 10 or 190, 192, 194 fit the rule. They may not consider the alternative that any increasing sequence might be correct. (pp. 296-297)

8. People are more likely to accept a plan in which 200 out of 600 will live than a plan in which there is a one-third chance that all will live and a two-thirds chance you will save no one. However, if it is phrased as 400 out of 600 will die vs. a one-third chance that no one will die and a two-thirds chance that all will die, people prefer the second version. Phrasing in terms of gain (living) or loss (dying) changes people's willingness to accept risk. (pp. 297-298)

Answers to the Multiple Choice Questions – Module 8.2

1. a. Correct! (p. 287)
    b. Incorrect. Not all memory tasks; they don't remember random arrangements better, just organized ones
    c. Incorrect. Experts need to put in about 10 years of practice
    d. Incorrect. Also know which "tools" to use and when to use them

2. a-c. Incorrect. These should help problem solution
    d. Correct! (p. 287)

3. a. Incorrect. Often the very same principles would work, but they are not used
    b. Incorrect. Seeing several examples makes generalization <u>more</u> likely
    c. Correct! (pp. 289-290)
    d. Incorrect. Research shows just the opposite

4. a. Incorrect. Scientific discoveries may be based more on having available data than on talent
    b. Incorrect. Access to prior data is important
    c. Incorrect. Solutions to insight problems may first involve "getting warm"; creative discoveries may also be based on study of data and be gradual
    d. Correct! (p. 292)
    e. Incorrect. Both b and c are incorrect

5. a. Correct! (p. 293)
    b. Incorrect. The similarity of the symptoms and the diseases was considered
    c. Incorrect. She did consider an alternative, the more common disease
    d. Incorrect. She doesn't need to simplify; the number of hypotheses is small

6. a. Incorrect. Base-rate fallacy; ignoring how many people 1% of a large number actually is
    b. Incorrect. Letting framing of questions affect decisions
    c. Incorrect. Use of representativeness; ignoring base rate
    d. Correct! (p. 294)
    e. Incorrect. This is overconfidence

7. a. Incorrect. They are willing to take risks when a loss is involved
    b. Correct! (p. 298)
    c. Incorrect. They tend to avoid risks if a gain is involved
    d. Incorrect. Situations involving lives and money show similar effects

Answers to the True/False Questions – Module 8.2

1. **True**: One distinguishing characteristic of an expert is that they do recognize patterns within their expertise faster than novices. (p. 287)

2. **False**: An algorithm generates all possibilities. A heuristic generates a subset of likely possibilities. (p. 288)

3. **False**: Very infrequently do people transfer the solution of one problem to another similar problem without explicit instructions to do so. (pp. 289-290)

4. **True**: Research suggests that people will make progress even though they feel they do not know the solution. (pp. 291-292)

Answers to the Fill in the Blank Questions – Module 8.3

1. Wernicke's (p. 306, Fig. 8.26)

2. phoneme (p. 313)

3. Williams (p. 305)

4. saccades (pp. 314-315)

Answers to the Short Answer Questions – Module 8.3

1. Very early attempts to teach spoken language to chimpanzees failed because chimpanzees do not have the appropriate vocal apparatus to speak. Later attempts to teach sign language or other symbols were more successful, although some scientists argued that the chimps simply imitated symbols used by their trainers. The chimps created nothing like a sentence. More recent attempts have used pygmy chimpanzees known as bonobos. These animals use symbols to describe objects and to relate past events. They make creative requests, but still they don't form full sentences. Bonobos may have greater language ability than other chimps, or learning by observation and imitation may be more effective than more formal training. (pp. 303-304)

2. The original observation was that the language that children hear does not provide enough information for them to learn the rules of grammar; therefore, children must be born with such rules. However, that argument does not explain how children learn different grammars associated with different languages in different cultures. Additional evidence for something like an innate language acquisition device could include the existence of specialized areas of the brain, developmental stages of language development, and effects of early experience (effects of deafness and bilingualism). (pp. 305-308)

3. Context can help to identify words with missing phonemes, but the appropriate context word must come soon after the word with missing sounds. Delayed context, however, can change your interpretation of a sentence, even if you have misinterpreted a word. (pp. 309-310)

4. Letters can be identified in words faster than alone. According to the connectionist model, incoming letters activate units corresponding to the letters, which in turn activate higher-level word units. Letter units aren't activated enough to identify the letters. However, the word units increase the activation of the lower-level letter units, allowing identification of the letters. (pp. 312-313)

Answers to the Multiple Choice Questions – Module 8.3

1. a. Correct! (p. 302)
    b. Incorrect. The sentence itself is the surface structure; there's only one
    c. Incorrect. Deep structure is the meaning; different from surface structure
    d. Incorrect. They are not the same, but they are related

2. a. Incorrect. Chimps' language wasn't as flexible as human children's language
    b. Incorrect. Not true with the bonobos; they followed instructions given over headphones
    c. Correct! (p. 304)
    d. Incorrect. It probably helped young bonobos to learn

3. a-c. Incorrect. Each of these provides support for the idea that humans are specialized for language learning
    d. Correct! (pp. 304-308)

4. a. Incorrect. Not because of context but because there are fewer ways to say things in scientific areas than in the humanities
    b. Incorrect. This is an example where context does not affect understanding; context must come soon after an ambiguous word to clarify it
    c. Incorrect. Evidence for the difficulty of understanding negatives; not necessarily evidence for context
    d. Correct! (pp. 309-310)

5. a. Incorrect. Saccades are eye movements; nothing is taken in during them
    b. Incorrect. Only about 11 characters
    c. Incorrect. Fixations last from about 100 ms. to about 1 sec.
    d. Correct! (pp. 314-315)

Answers to the True/False Questions – Module 8.3

1. **False**: The basic unit of meaning in language is termed a morpheme. (p. 313)

2. **True**: Patients suffering from damage to Broca's area exhibit a difficulty in using and understanding language although they do not completely lose the ability. (p. 306)

3. **False**: The word-superiority effect refers to the ability of people to recognize words faster than individual letters. (pp. 312-313)

4. **False**: Since the child is mastering two languages it actually takes longer than mastering a single language. (p. 309)

Answers to Final Comprehensive Assessment

1. d (p. 273)
2. d (p. 274)
3. b (p. 275)
4. b (pp. 273-274)
5. c (p. 281)
6. b (p. 282)
7. d (p. 287)
8. e (p. 288)
9. a (p. 288)
10. b (p. 289)

11. b (p. 290)
12. a (p. 293)
13. d (p. 294)
14. a (p. 298)
15. d (p. 302)
16. b (p. 304)
17. a (p. 305)
18. b (p. 279)
19. c (p. 309)
20. d (p. 312)

CHAPTER 9

INTELLIGENCE AND ITS MEASUREMENT

CHAPTER OVERVIEW INFORMATION

LEARNING OBJECTIVES

By the end of Chapter 9 you should

- ✓ Be familiar with definitions of intelligence and problems of defining what intelligence actually is
- ✓ Be knowledgeable about the different types of IQ tests and their attributes
- ✓ Understand the process of developing IQ tests and the areas of debate related to these tests

CHAPTER 9 OUTLINE

Chapter 9 examines the topic of intelligence and how psychologists test it. The interesting thing is that psychologists are not really sure what these tests measure even though there are several tests designed to measure intelligence. Some researchers suggest that we have a single intelligence with component parts. Another suggests that we have both crystallized and fluid intelligence. Still others propose multiple intelligences that are at least partially independent from each other. Thus, there is no real agreement on what intelligence is or is not! There is however good agreement on how to evaluate tests. These evaluations examine reliability, validity, and utility. Also explored in Chapter 9 is the role of nature and nurture on intelligence.

Chapter 9 is presented below in outline format to assist you in understanding the information presented in the chapter. More detailed information on any topic can be found using the page references to the right of the topic.

Module 9.1 Intelligence and Intelligence Tests
I. What is Intelligence?
    A. Original tests were developed to measure the ability to do well in school (p. 323)

II. IQ Tests
    A. Intelligence tests attempt to measure probable performance in school (p. 324)
        1. The intelligence quotient (IQ) involves dividing mental age by chronological age (p. 324)
    B. The Stanford-Binet Test
        1. Stanford-Binet asks questions that can be answered at different ages (p. 324, Table 9.1)
    C. The Wechsler Tests
        1. Wechsler tests give scores on verbal and performance (p. 325, Fig. 9.1)
    D. Culture-Reduced Testing
        1. Raven's Progressive Matrices makes minimal use of language and facts (pp. 325-326, Fig. 9.2)

III. The Relationship Between IQ Tests and Intelligence
    A. Defining intelligence is difficult, so we can not tell if the tests measure it (p. 326)
        1. This definition is too narrow (p. 326)

B. Spearman's Psychometric Approach and the g Factor
  1. Spearman suggested that there is a general factor (g) in mental ability (pp. 326-327, Fig. 9.3, Table 9.2)
  2. Spearman allowed that each task also requires specific abilities (pp. 326-327)
C. Possible Explanations for g
  1. The g Factor could be related to mental speed, ability of neurons to change, attention and visual processing, or working memory (pp. 327-328)
D. Fluid Intelligence and Crystallized Intelligence
  1. Cattell distinguished between fluid and crystallized intelligence (p. 328, Table 9.2)
E. Gardner's Theory of Multiple Intelligences
  1. Gardner argued that people have multiple intelligences (p. 329, Table 9.2)
F. Sternberg's Triarchic Theory of Intelligence
  1. Sternberg's triarchic theory has three components of intelligence (pp. 329-330, Table 9.2)
     a. Cognitive processes within an individual (Analytical) (p. 330)
     b. Identification of situations that require intelligence (Creative) (p. 330)
     c. Relationship between intelligence and the outside world (Practical) (p. 330)
  2. Critics have suggested the components of the triarchic theory are correlated thereby measuring some of the same ability (p. 330)

The message: Test scores give overall summaries of abilities which can be useful but must be interpreted cautiously. (p. 331)

Module 9.2 Evaluation of Intelligence Tests
IV. The Standardization of IQ Tests
  A. Tests are standardized so that a process is established for administration and interpretation (p. 332)
  B. Norms are established so that scores corresponding to percentiles can be determined (p. 332)
     1. Mean and standard deviation are established (pp. 332-333, Fig. 9.5)
  C. The Distribution of IQ Scores
  D. Restandardizations and the Flynn Effect
     1. Tests are restandardized as society changes (pp. 333-334)
        a. Tests are harder today than they used to be (pp. 333-334)

V. Evaluation of Tests
  A. Reliability
     1. Reliability refers to the repeatability of the test (pp. 334-335, Figure 9.6, Table 9.3)
        a. A correlation coefficient is used to measure reliability (pp. 334-335)
  B. Validity
     1. Validity refers to whether a test measures what it claims to measure (p. 329, Table 9.3)
        a. Content validity refers to whether questions accurately represent the information (p. 335)
        b. Construct validity refers to whether the test results correspond to theoretical expectations (p. 336)
        c. Predictive validity refers to whether test scores predict behavior (p. 329)
           i. Correlated IQ with school performance (p. 336)
           ii. Scores must vary over a substantial range for high predictive validity (p. 336)
  C. Utility
     1. Utility refers the practical usefulness of a test (p. 337, Table 9.3)

D. Interpreting Fluctuations in Scores
  1. Test scores can fluctuate, especially if reliability is low (p. 337)

VI. Heredity, Environment, and IQ Scores
  A. Intelligence is influenced both by heredity and environment (p. 337)
  B. Family Resemblances
    1. People who are closely related have more similar IQ scores than more distant relatives (pp. 337-338, Fig. 9.7)
  C. Identical Twins Reared Apart
    1. Identical twins adopted into different families have similar IQs, but the environments are usually similar and may magnify the genetic effect (p. 338)
  D. Twins and Single Births
    1. IQs of identical twins are more similar than fraternal twins which are more than single birth siblings (p. 338)
  E. Adopted Children
    1. Adopted children's IQs correlate with their biological parents' IQs although there is a small effect of the environment (pp. 338-339, Fig. 9.8)
  F. Gene Identification
    1. Numerous genes have small effects on IQ, but so does environment (p. 339)

VII. Gender and Ethnic Differences in IQ scores
  A. Groups differ in mean performance on IQ tests (pp. 339-340)
    1. Males and females have similar means, but males show more variability (p. 340)
    2. There are some differences among ethnic groups on tests (p. 340)
      a. First generation immigrants do not perform as well as their children and grandchildren (p. 340)
        i. Likely due to language barriers (p. 340)
      b. Differences among ethnic groups may not have a genetic basis (p. 340)
  B. Are IQ Tests Biased?
    1. Tests are biased against a group if they systematically underestimate abilities (p. 340)
      a. Single items may be biased if they do not correlate with the whole test for a group of people (p. 341, Fig. 9.9)
      b. Tests may be biased if they underestimate the performance of a group of people (pp. 341-342)
      c. IQ tests predict performance in school equally well for minority groups and European Americans with the same test score (p. 342)
        i. This does not mean there are differences in innate ability (p. 342)
  C. Test Anxiety and Stereotype Threat
    1. Ethnic minorities may worry more about the effects of performing badly which may cause test anxiety and poor performance (p. 342)
  D. Genetics?
    1. Not clear whether ethnic differences in IQ are influenced by genetics (pp. 342-343)
      a. African-American children raised in European-American homes score only slightly higher than the average for African-American children (pp. 343-344, Fig. 9.10)
      b. The degree of European ancestry in African Americans does not predict IQ scores (p. 345)

The message: Researchers continue to make progress in measuring and understanding IQ is influenced by both genes and environment. (pp. 345-346)

RELATED WEBSITES AND ACTIVITIES

Visit http://psychology.wadsworth.com/kalat_intro7e/ for online quizzing, glossary flashcards, crossword puzzles, annotated web links, and more.

LECTURE MATERIAL

Information from the text is only half of the picture. Don't forget to review your lecture material. Process each topic meaningfully. Most importantly, be sure that you understand the material in each lecture-if you don't, ask your instructor or teaching assistant.

STUDY TIP #9: Become an active learner in class. Prepare for class by reading the relevant chapters in the text, completeing the relevant chapters in the study guide, and reviewing your notes from the last lecture. Sit in the front of the classroom to avoid distractions, hear what the instructor is saying, and see what the instructor is writing.

TIP: Associate the lecture material with the information from the text, with things that you already know, with your personal experiences, or with real-life applications. Type or neatly re-write your notes. Make sure they are detailed and organized. Make comments on your notes. Then write questions to cover each concept.

CHAPTER MODULE ASSESSMENTS

Module 9.1 Intelligence and Intelligence Tests
Answer these questions soon after reading the **Module 9.1: Intelligence and Intelligence Tests**. There are several formats to the assessments. Answers to all questions appear on pp. 184-185.

Fill in the Blank
Provide a term(s) which best completes the statement below. Answers appear on p. 184.

1. The general term for a measure of a person's probable performance in school is called
    _____.

2. The _____ is used for children and gives scores on subabilities.

3. Intelligence consisting of acquired skills and knowledge and the application of that knowledge to the specific content of a person's experience is termed _____?

4. An IQ test for <u>adults</u> that was originally developed by David Wechsler is the _____ .

5. The psychometric approach to intelligence testing, which features the measurement of individual differences, was pioneered by _____.

6. One example of a culture reduced intelligence test that does not rely on being able to speak English is Raven's _____.

7. According to Sternberg's _____ theory of intelligence, intelligence consists of three different aspects of ability.

8. The _____ IQ test was first modified for use with English speaking persons by Terman and other psychologists.

9. According to Spearman, all intelligent abilities have an area of overlap or general ability that he labeled the _____ .

Short Answer
The following questions require a short written answer (3-7 sentences). Answers appear on p. 185.

1. Explain how the theories of intelligence of Spearman and Cattell are similar and how these two theories differ from Gardner's theory.

2. How does Sternberg's theory differ from those of Cattell and Spearman?

3. Describe the WISC-IV and the WAIS-III and explain how they differ from the Stanford-Binet.

4. Explain why Raven's Progressive Matrices should be more "culture-fair" than the Stanford-Binet and the Wechsler tests.

Multiple Choice
Circle the best answer below. Check your answers on p. 185. If your answer was incorrect, try to write why it was incorrect. Check your reasons on p. 185.

1. The *g* factor identified by Spearman:
    a. consists of tasks that girls excel in
    b. involves crystallized intelligence
    c. involves dealing with abstract concepts and perceiving relationships
    d. is all the knowledge that a person has acquired
    e. is evidence for defining intelligence as independent abilities

2. Which of the following is <u>not</u> part of Sternberg's triarchic theory?
   a. crystallized and fluid intelligence must be distinguished
   b. identification of situations that require intelligence
   c. relationship between intelligence and the outside world
   d. cognitive processes within an individual

3. A person who is an outstanding singer, but cannot remember a short grocery list, can best be explained by which theory of intelligence?
   a. Spearman's *g*
   b. the Flynn effect
   c. Gardner's theory of multiple intelligences
   d. Stanford-Binet's IQ theory

4. IQ tests are:
   a. measures of innate potential
   b. explanations for why people do well or poorly in school
   c. useless for predicting school success
   d. not very reliable
   e. measurements of current performance

5. How do the Wechsler tests differ from the Stanford-Binet?
   a. the WISC-IV has an average of 200; Stanford-Binet is 100
   b. WISC-IV can be used with adults; Stanford-Binet cannot
   c. Wechsler tests give scores on more component abilities than the Stanford-Binet
   d. Wechsler tests don't involve factual information; Stanford-Binet test does
   e. Wechsler tests give only a single score; Stanford-Binet gives multiple scores

6. How are the Progressive Matrices different from the Wechsler tests?
   a. they require knowledge of more specific facts
   b. they can be used with blind people
   c. they make minimal use of language
   d. they provide scores on several distinct abilities
   e. they are not as "culture-fair"

True/False
Select the best answer by circling *T for True* or *F for False*. Check your answers on p. 185.

1. **T or F** Fluid intelligence is characterized by the ability to perceive relationships, solve unfamiliar problems, and gain new knowledge.

2. **T or F** The WAIS-III intelligence test for adults contains both verbal and performance items.

3. **T or F** Spearman suggested that there is a general factor (*g*) in mental ability.

4. **T or F** IQ tests were originally developed to predict job performance.

5. **T or F** Critics of Sternberg's Triarchic theory have suggested the components of the theory are correlated and measure some of the same ability.

Module 9.2 Evaluation of Intelligence Tests
Answer these questions soon after reading the **Module 9.2: Evaluation of Intelligence Tests**.
There are several formats to the assessments. Answers to all questions appear on pp. 186-188.

Fill in the Blank
Provide a term(s) which best completes the statement below. Answers appear on p. 186.

1. A test is said to have construct _____ if what it measures corresponds to a theoretical construct (e.g., intelligence).

2. Someone with an IQ score of 130 would be described as _____ .

3. The tendency for IQ scores to increase each decade is known as the _____ effect.

4. The _____ of a test is defined as the repeatability of its scores.

5. The process of establishing rules for administering a test and interpreting its scores is called _____ .

6. A person's perceived fear that they may do something that supports an unfavorable belief about a group they belong to describes _____.

Short Answer
The following questions require a short written answer (3-7 sentences). Answers appear on pp. 186-187.

1. What does it mean to standardize a test? Why must tests be restandardized periodically?

2. Discuss the relationship between reliability and validity.

3. Discuss the differences between content, construct, and predictive validity. How do these concepts differ from utility?

4. What type of evidence would be necessary to decide that a specific test item is biased against a group of individuals?

5. Discuss whether IQ tests are biased against groups of people.

6. Describe how the role of genetics in a characteristic, such as IQ, can be studied.

7. Discuss evidence related to the role of environment in the differences in IQ between African Americans and European Americans.

Multiple Choice
Circle the best answer below. Check your answers on pp. 187-188. If your answer was incorrect, try to write why it was incorrect. Check your reasons on pp. 187-188.

1. Susan, who is 10, performs better than 84% of the other 10-year-olds who took the Stanford-Binet. Her IQ would be:
   a. 84
   b. 16
   c. 100
   d. 116

2. To standardize a test means to:
   a. check to see if people get the same score twice
   b. establish the rules for administering the test and for interpreting its scores
   c. see if the test predicts what it is supposed to predict
   d. make sure that all items are very similar, so that if people get one correct, they will get all correct

3. I have designed a new test for admission to law school. I measure the size of a person's wrist, and if it is larger than 85% of the people's, the student is admitted. My test has:
   a. reliability but not validity
   b. validity but not reliability
   c. content validity but not reliability
   d. neither reliability nor validity
   e. both reliability and validity

4. If a test has construct validity, it means that the test:
   a. predicts a certain behavior in a setting outside of the test
   b. has utility
   c. contains questions that accurately represent the information that the test is supposed to measure
   d. measures a concept that corresponds to a theoretical expectation

5. Research has shown that IQ tests are biased against:
   a. females as compared to males
   b. twins who were reared apart and unrelated people
   c. African Americans and East Asians
   d. non-English-speaking immigrants to the U.S.

6. Identical twins are more similar in IQ scores than fraternal twins whether they were raised together or apart. Which of the following is consistent with the conclusion that IQ is determined by heredity?
   a. twins whose parents thought they were fraternal but who really are identical are only as similar as other identical twins
   b. parents treat identical twins more similarly than they treat fraternal twins
   c. environments of twins reared apart are actually very similar
   d. twins are exactly the same age; random pairs of children are not

7. Which of the following provides evidence against genetics in the IQ difference between European and African Americans?
   a. there is no correlation between IQ scores and amount of European ancestry in African Americans
   b. African Americans consistently score lower than whites
   c. African-American children adopted into upper-middle class homes score only slightly higher on IQ tests than other African-American children
   d. African-American children's test scores do not improve when they are tested by an African-American tester using appropriate dialect

True/False
Select the best answer by circling *T for True* or *F for False*. Check your answers on p. 188.

1. **T or F** A good test is described as having utility if it has been demonstrated to be useful for a practical purpose such as selecting better job candidates.

2. **T or F** Identical twins adopted into different families have similar IQs.

3. **T or F** IQ scores for African-American adolescent children raised in European-American homes are only slightly higher than the average for European-American children.

4. **T or F** A test is said to be biased against a group if it underestimates the group's performance.

5. **T or F** IQs of adopted children in adolescence are more like their adopted parents than their biological parents.

Check your answers on p. 188.

1. Which of the following is most consistent with Spearman's theory of intelligence?
   a. intelligence consists of a general ability to perceive and manipulate relationships, plus some specific abilities
   b. intelligence consists entirely of factual information
   c. intelligence consists of cognitive processes, identification of situations requiring intelligence, appropriate use of intelligence in the world
   d. intelligence consists of unrelated specific abilities
   e. intelligence consists of the ability to plan approaches to problems

2. Jimmy remembers things well and has learned skills taught in the first grade. However, he does not have much potential to go far beyond these very basic skills. Jimmy has:
   a. high fluid intelligence but low crystallized intelligence
   b. a high *g* factor but low crystallized intelligence
   c. a low *g* factor and high fluid intelligence
   d. high fluid intelligence and high crystallized intelligence
   e. low fluid intelligence

3. A 30-year-old adult who has an IQ of 130 did what on the Stanford-Binet?
   a. performed as well as the average 39-year-old
   b. performed better than half of the other adults
   c. performed toward the left end of the normal distribution
   d. performed better than most other adults
   e. performed as well as the average 23-year-old

4. If a child has separate scores on Verbal Comprehension, Perceptual Reasoning, Working Memory, and Processing Speed, she must have taken which test?
   a. WAIS-III
   b. WISC-IV
   c. Raven's Progressive Matrices
   d. Stanford-Binet
   e. TAT

5. Theoretically, why should the Progressive Matrices test be more culture-fair than the Wechsler tests?
   a. the matrices have more subtests
   b. the matrices are balanced so that males and females score about the same
   c. the matrices call for no verbal responses and no specific information
   d. the matrices are more interesting than the Wechsler tests
   e. the matrices have much higher reliability than the Wechsler tests

6. IQ tests:
   a. measure differences among people; they do not explain them
   b. probably measure a single quantity
   c. measure inborn limits and capacities
   d. are based on precise meanings of "intelligence"
   e. explain why some people do better in school than others

7. To say that someone is in the 70th percentile on a test means that she:
   a. scored higher than 70% of the norm group
   b. is 2 standard deviations above the mean
   c. got 70% of the questions correct on the test
   d. falls within the "gifted" range of intelligence
   e. falls within the "retarded" range of intelligence

8. I have a test that accurately predicts who will learn statistics quickly. My test has:
   a. predictive validity but not reliability
   b. content validity but not predictive validity
   c. predictive validity and reliability
   d. neither validity nor reliability
   e. reliability but not predictive validity

9. Which of the following is evidence for a biased test item?
   a. a judge suggests that African-American children may respond differently than European-American children because of differences in their cultures
   b. the item is missed by most test-takers
   c. the item correlates well with the entire test
   d. the item correlates with the entire test better for one group than for another group

10. The Stanford-Binet and the Wechsler tests are biased against people who do not speak English well because:
   a. such people do better in school and on the job than their scores predict
   b. such people score lower than the average population
   c. such people do about the same in school as other people with the same score
   d. the tests do not have high content validity for them
   e. the tests are too reliable for them

11. The difference between the IQs of African- and European Americans:
   a. has been increasing in the last few years
   b. is about 25 points on the Wechsler tests
   c. predicts differences in their school grades
   d. is not caused by environmental differences
   e. is greater when African Americans who have more European ancestry are compared European Americans

12. If genetics plays no role in a trait, then:
   a. identical twins reared in very different environments should be more similar than unrelated people
   b. fraternal twins reared together should be much more similar than identical twins reared together
   c. adopted children should look more like their biological parents than their adoptive parents
   d. identical twins reared apart should be less similar than fraternal twins reared together
   e. disadvantaged children adopted in higher-income homes should perform the same as other disadvantaged children

13. Identical twins reared apart are more similar in IQ than fraternal twins reared apart. A researcher who believes in the influence of environment more than heredity might explain this in what way?
    a. identical twins are more similar genetically
    b. the environments of the identical twin pairs were more similar
    c. the identical twins were raised in genuinely different environments
    d. the adoptive parents of the fraternal twin pairs were more similar than the adoptive parents of the identical twin pairs
    e. both c and d

14. African-American children reared in upper middle-class European-American homes scored:
    a. higher than the average of European-American children on IQ tests
    b. about 15 points lower on IQ tests than the average of African-American children
    c. about the same as other African-American children in Minnesota
    d. much higher than the average African-American child in the United States
    e. much higher than European-American children adopted into the same homes

15. Performance on Raven's Progressive Matrices and amount of European ancestry in African-American children are:
    a. highly correlated, giving good evidence for the importance of environment in race differences in IQ
    b. highly correlated, giving good evidence for the importance of genetics in race differences in IQ
    c. uncorrelated, giving evidence that genetics may not be important in ethnic differences in IQ
    d. negatively correlated, giving good evidence for the importance of genetics in ethnic differences in IQ
    e. uncorrelated, giving good evidence for the importance genetics in ethnic differences in IQ

ANSWERS AND EXPLANATIONS FOR CHAPTER MODULE ASSESSMENTS

Answers to the Fill in the Blank Questions – Module 9.1

1. IQ or Intelligence Quotient (p. 324)

2. WISC-IV (p. 325)

3. crystallized (p. 328)

4. WAIS-III (p. 325)

5. Spearman (pp. 326-327)

6. Progressive Matrices (pp. 325-326)

7. Triarchic (pp. 329-330)

8. Stanford-Binet (p. 324)

9. *g* factor (pp. 327-328)

Answers to the Short Answer Questions – Module 9.1

1. Spearman's and Cattell's theories assume that people use the same components of intelligence in tasks in different areas. Although they disagree on what or how many components of intelligence there are, they assume that the same components are used in different tasks. Gardner, on the other hand, assumes that there are different types of intelligence that are used for different tasks. (pp. 326-328, Table 9.3)

2. Sternberg focuses less on the structure of intelligence and more on its function. He asks how people process information and engage in intelligent behavior. Sternberg's theory has three components: the cognitive processes that occur within an individual, the ability to identify repeated and novel situations and to make correct responses to them, and the ability to adapt to or change the environment. (pp. 326-330, Table 9.2)

3. The WISC-IV is the children's version and the WAIS-III is the adult's version. They include a number of different parts to assess different types of knowledge and abilities. The Stanford-Binet yields an overall IQ score, along with three subscores. However, it doesn't report as many subcomponents as the Wechsler tests. (pp. 324-325)

4. The matrices involve very little language, so a person who does not understand English or who has poor verbal skills can still complete the tests (assuming they can understand the instructions). They also do not test specific knowledge, but rather ask people to look for relationships among nonverbal items, so they should be less dependent upon what a person has been taught than the other tests. (pp. 325-326)

Answers to the Multiple Choice Questions – Module 9.1

1. a. Incorrect. General intelligence, not gender-specific
    b. Incorrect. Part of intelligence--skills and knowledge one a already has; *g* argues for general factor
    c. Correct! (p. 325)
    d. Incorrect. Includes ability to acquire new knowledge also
    e. Incorrect. Spearman argued that there is a general factor

2. a. Correct! (pp. 329-330)
    b-d. Incorrect. General abilities included in triarchic theory

3. a. Incorrect. General ability; implies similar strengths on all tasks
    b. Incorrect. Flynn effect refers to changes from one generation to another; see next module
    c. Correct! (p. 329)
    d. Incorrect. The IQ is a measure of intelligence; not a theory

4. a. Incorrect. No reason to assume this
    b. Incorrect. They don't explain performance, although they are reasonable predictors
    c. Incorrect. Predict school success fairly well
    d. Incorrect. Have high reliability
    e. Correct! (p. 323)

5. a. Incorrect. Both have means of 100
    b. Incorrect. WISC-IV is the children's test
    c. Correct! (pp. 324-325)
    d. Incorrect. Both test some factual knowledge
    e. Incorrect. Wechsler tests give scores on several component abilities

6. a. Incorrect. No specific facts are tested
    b. Incorrect. Neither test can be used with blind individuals
    c. Correct! (pp. 324-326)
    d. Incorrect. Matrices provide only one score
    e. Incorrect. Presumably they are more fair because they do not require many language skills and they do not test facts

Answers to the True/False Questions – Module 9.1

1. **True**: Fluid intelligence is the power to reason and use information. (p. 328)

2. **True**: The WAIS-III intelligence test has an average score of 100. It provides subscores on various abilities. (pp. 324-325)

3. **True**: Spearman suggested that people have a general ability that can be observed in many different areas and abilities. (pp. 326-327)

4. **False**: IQ tests were originally developed to predict performance in school. (p. 323)

5. **True**: Critics have suggested that since components are correlated they may be measuring some general ability. (p. 330)

Answers to the Fill in the Blank Questions – Module 9.2

1. validity (p. 336)

2. gifted (p. 332)

3. Flynn (pp. 333-334)

4. reliability (pp. 334-335)

5. standardization (p. 332)

6. stereotype threat (p. 342)

Answers to the Short Answer Questions – Module 9.2

1. Standardization sets norms, or determines the mean performance and sets up the standard deviation. It also involves the selection of test items that test a variety of information but that all correlate to the total score. Over the years, some items become too easy, so they must be changed so that not everyone gets them correct. (pp. 332-333)

2. Reliability refers to the consistency of a test or how likely it is that a person will get the same score twice. A test can be very reliable (showing high consistency) but still not be useful or valid. A test that is not reliable, however, cannot be valid, because if the scores vary too much, they cannot predict performance. (pp. 334-335)

3. Generally, validity refers to whether a test measures what it is supposed to measure. A test has content validity if its questions represent the information that the test is supposed to measure. Construct validity refers to whether the test results are consistent with what would be expected from a theoretical construct. Predictive validity indicates that the test predicts behavior in a setting outside of the test. Utility refers to whether a test is useful, that is, whether its results can aid in improving selection or education. (pp. 335-336)

4. An item is biased if it systematically underestimates the abilities of one group relative to another, that is, if it is easy for individuals from one group but difficult for another group. An item may also be biased if it correlates with the whole test score better for one group than for another. For example, if an item using a football field is answered correctly more often by men than by women and if the item correlates with the entire test better for men than for women, then the item is probably biased against women and it should be replaced by another item. (p. 341)

5. A biased test systematically underestimates the performance of a group, so a person should perform better than the test score would predict. This is true for immigrants who do not speak English as their first language. It is also true of older women who take college entrance tests. They do better in college than the tests predict. Some ethnic groups score higher on standardized tests than other ethnic groups. This does not necessarily mean the tests are biased, however, because they do tend to predict school performance for the ethnic groups. School grades, however, may be biased and unfair for someone from a culture other than the majority culture. (pp. 341-342)

6. The role of genetics can be estimated by comparing differences in IQ for people who are either very similar or different in genetics and environment. If the role of genetics is high, people who are very similar genetically (such as identical twins) should be very similar in IQ no matter how different their environments are. If the role of genetics is low, similarity in environment should predict similarity in IQ. (pp. 342-345)

7. African-American children adopted into upper middle-class European-American families have IQs that are slightly above the averages for non-adopted African-American children. However, the size of the environmental effect here is disappointing. The amount of European ancestry in African-American children does not predict their IQs; it should if genes associated with European Americans produce higher IQs. (pp. 343-345)

Answers to the Multiple Choice Questions – Module 9.2

1.   a. Incorrect. Performs better than 84%; this is not her score
     b. Incorrect. Performed worse than 16%; this is not her score
     c. Incorrect. This is average; she performed better than 50%
     d. Correct! (pp. 332-333)

2.   a. Incorrect. Test-retest reliability; not part of standardization
     b. Correct! (p. 332)
     c. Incorrect. Validity; not part of standardization
     d. Incorrect. Tests need a variety of items; items should be correlated with each other, but not all the same

3.   a. Correct! (pp. 334-336)
     b. Incorrect. Will not predict performance, but is reliable because the same value would obtain every time
     c. Incorrect. Questions don't represent information a law student knows; is reliable, see b
     d. Incorrect. It is reliable; see b
     e. Incorrect. Not valid-see b and c above

4.   a. Incorrect. This is predictive validity
     b. Incorrect. Means that test is useful for practical purposes
     c. Incorrect. This is content validity
     d. Correct! (p. 336)

5.   a. Incorrect. Females score about the same as males on IQ tests although males scores are more variable
     b. Incorrect. Genetics is irrelevant in bias
     c. Incorrect. East Asians have higher than average scores and African Americans have lower than average scores but an intelligence test is only biased if it under predicts school performance
     d. Correct! (p. 340)

6.   a. Correct! (p. 338)
     b, c. Incorrect. Environmental explanations for identical-twin similarities
     d. Incorrect. Explains why twins' IQs are more similar than random pairs, but not why identical twins are more similar than fraternal twins

7. a. Correct! (p. 345)
    b. Incorrect. Does not say anything about genetics or environment
    c. Incorrect. These results show a disappointingly small environmental influence; they do not argue against genetics
    d. Incorrect. Does not argue against genetics

Answers to the True/False Questions – Module 9.2

1. **True**: A test with utility provides scores that are helpful to be worth using. (p. 337)

2. **True:** Adopted identical twins do have similar IQ, but the environments are usually similar and may magnify the genetic effect. (p. 338)

3. **False:** Their IQs are slightly higher than other African-American children but not as high as European-American children. (pp. 343-344)

4. **True:** Tests are biased when they systematically underestimate a group's performance. (p. 340)

5. **True:** As young children they their IQs correlate with the adopted parents but as they mature their IQs correlate more with their biological parents. (pp. 338-339)

Answers to Final Comprehensive Assessment

1. a (pp. 326-327)
2. e (p. 328)
3. d (p. 324)
4. b (pp. 324-325)
5. c (pp. 325-326)
6. a (p. 324)
7. a (p. 332)
8. c (pp. 334-336)
9. d (p. 341)
10. a (p. 340)
11. c (p. 340)
12. d (p. 338)
13. b (p. 337)
14. c (pp. 343-344)
15. c (p. 345)

CHAPTER 10

HUMAN DEVELOPMENT

CHAPTER OVERVIEW INFORMATION

LEARNING OBJECTIVES

By the end of Chapter 10 you should

- ✓ Be familiar with the process and importance of early development including the prenatal environment
- ✓ Be familiar with the major theories of human cognitive and moral development
- ✓ Understand theories and principles of psychosocial development
- ✓ Have an increased awareness of the many influences on human development

CHAPTER 10 OUTLINE

Chapter 10 includes topics students find exciting and interesting (that is not to say that students do not find the other chapters exciting and interesting). Developmental psychologists are interested in exploring changes in behavior and experience across the life span. That is, from birth (and earlier) until death or from cradle to grave, how does our behavior and experience change? Topics explored in Chapter 10 include the role of prenatal development; thinking and reasoning development; social and emotional development; and the influences of many other conditions (e.g., birth order, cultural influences) on development.

Chapter 10 is presented below in outline format to assist you in understanding the information presented in the chapter. More detailed information on any topic can be found using the page references to the right of the topic.

Module 10.1 Getting Started: From Genetics Through Infancy

I. Research has shown that identical twins reared separately are more similar than fraternal twins (p. 33, Figs. 10.1-10.2)

II. Genetic Principles
   A. Chromosomes are transmitted from one generation to the next (p. 354, Figs. 10.3-10.4)
      1. Genes are sections of chromosomes which direct development (p. 354, Fig. 10.3)
      2. Single genes can determine some behaviors (p. 355, Fig. 10.5)
      3. Genes are dominant or recessive (p. 355, Fig. 10.5)
   B. Sex-linked and Sex-Limited Genes
      1. Some genes are different from males and females (p. 355)
         a. Sex chromosomes determine sex (p. 355, Fig. 10.6)
         b. Sex-linked genes are found on the X chromosome (p. 355, Fig. 10.7)
         c. Sex-limited genes affect one sex more than the other (p. 356)
   C. Identifying and Localizing Genes
      1. Technology exists to identify genes that increase likelihood of developing a condition (e.g., Alzheimer's) (p. 356)
   D. Estimating Heritability in Humans
      1. Differences among individuals due to genetics are measured by heritability (p. 356)
         a. Identical and fraternal twins can be compared (pp. 356-357, Fig. 10.8)
         b. Adopted children can be compared with their biological and adoptive parents (p. 357)

III. How Genes Influence Behavior
  A. Genetics can influence many types of behavior (p. 357)
  B. Direct and Indirect Influences
     1. Just because something is under genetic control does not mean that the environment cannot alter it (p. 357-358)
     2. Heredity and the environment interact (p. 358, Fig. 10.9)
  C. Phenylketonuria: Modifying Genetic Effect Through Diet
     1. PKU is a genetic disorder that can be altered by the environment (p. 358)

IV. The Fetus and the Newborn
  A. Prenatal development depends upon the health of the mother (p. 358)
     1. Low birth weight babies may do poorly because they have other disadvantages (p. 358, Fig. 10.10)
     2. Fetal alcohol syndrome is marked by stunted growth and other abnormalities (p. 359; Fig. 10.11)

V. Behavior Capacities of the Newborn
  A. Newborn's capacities are limited, but they do have some sensory and learning abilities (p. 360)
  B. Newborns' Vision
     1. They spend more time looking human faces than at other objects (p. 360, Fig. 10.12)
     2. Infants show a fear of heights soon after they begin to crawl (p. 361)
  C. Newborns' Hearing
     1. Young infants can discriminate one sound from another (p. 361, Fig. 10.13)
  D. Infants' Learning and Memory
     1. Very young infants show learning and memory (p. 361)
        a. They respond more to their mother's than to an unfamiliar voice (p. 361)
        b. They can learn a response and remember it for days (p. 362, Fig. 10.14)

The message: Researchers have discovered that genes can influence development and that infants have many capacities even though their motor control is poor. (p. 362).

Module 10.2 Childhood Thinking and Reasoning
VI. Research Designs for Studying Development
  A. There are two main types of research designs for studying development (p. 364, Table 10.1)
     1. Cross-sectional designs compare groups of different ages at one time (p. 364, Table 10.1)
     2. Longitudinal designs compare the same individuals when they are at different ages (p. 364, Table 10.1)
        a. This allows the researcher to know who has left the study (pp. 364-365)
  B. Sequential Designs
     1. Combines the advantages of the cross-sectional and longitudinal designs (pp. 365-366)
  C. Cohort Effects
     1. Cohort effects refer to differences due to the time of growing up rather than age (p. 366, Fig. 10.16)

VII. Jean Piaget's View of Development
  A. Piaget studied how children's thought processes differ from those of adults (p. 366)
     1. Behavior is based on schemata that change with development (p. 367)
     2. Development occurs through assimilation and accommodation (p. 367)
  B. Piaget proposed four stages of development (p. 367, Table 10.3)

VIII. Piaget's Sensorimotor Stage
  A. Sensorimotor stage lasts from birth to 1 1/2 years (p. 368, Table 10.2)
     1. Children begin to develop a concept of self (p. 368, Fig. 10.17)
     2. Children lack object permanence (pp. 368-370, Fig. 10.18-10.19)

IX. Piaget's Preoperational Stage
  A. Preoperational stage lasts from 1 1/2 to 7 years (p. 370, Table 10.2)
  B. Egocentrism: Understanding Other People's Thoughts
     1. Preoperational children tend to have egocentric thought (p. 370)
     2. Preoperational children develop an understanding of other people's knowledge (pp. 370-372, Figs. 10.20-10.21)
  C. Distinguishing Appearance from Reality
     1. Early preoperational stage children accept that appearances are reality (p. 372)
     2. Early preoperational stage children unable to map environments under most conditions (pp. 373-374, Fig. 10.22)
  D. Developing the Concept of Conservation
     1. Concept of conservation is not understood (pp. 374-375, Table 10.2, Fig. 10.23)

X. Piaget's Concrete Operations Stage and Formal Operations Stage
  A. Concrete operations stage lasts from 7 to 11 years (p. 374, Table 10.2, p. 376)
     1. Children can perform mental operations on concrete objects (p. 375)
  B. Formal operations stage begins at age 11 (p. 374, Table 10.2)
     1. Now children use logical and systematic planning for abstract problems (p. 375)
  C. Are Piaget's Stages Distinct?
     1. Children may have abilities related to later stages, but they may only be able to use them on simpler tasks (p. 376, Fig. 10.24)
  D. Differing Views: Piaget and Vygotsky
     1. Vygotsky argued the children have a zone of proximal development that is important in education (p. 377)

XI. The Development of Moral Reasoning
  A. Kohlberg's Measurements of Moral Reasoning
     1. Kohlberg suggested that moral reasoning develops in stages (p. 377, Table 10.4, Figs. 10.24-10.25)
  B. Limitations of Kohlberg's Views
     1. Kohlberg has been criticized (p. 380)
        a. Kohlberg's studies looked at moral reasoning from a "justice" orientation, not a "caring" orientation (p. 380, Table 10.5)
        b. Reasoning is just the beginning; does it lead to moral behavior? (pp. 380-381)

The message: *The universe is complicated and children construct hypotheses to understand it. (p. 381).*

Module 10.3 Social and Emotional Development

XII. Erikson's Description of Human Development (Table 10.6)
   A. Erikson proposed eight stages of social and personality development (pp. 383-384, Table 10.6)
      1. Basic trust vs. mistrust occurs first (p. 383)
      2. Autonomy vs. shame and doubt occurs from about ages 1 to 3 (p. 383, Table 10.6)
      3. Initiative vs. guilt occurs from about ages 3 to 6 (p. 383, Table 10.6)
      4. Industry vs. inferiority is the conflict from ages 6 to 12 (p. 383, Table 10.6)
      5. Adolescents face a conflict between identity vs. role confusion (p. 383, Table 10.6)
      6. Intimacy vs. isolation is the conflict of young adults (p. 383, Table 10.6)
      7. Generativity vs. stagnation occurs in middle adulthood (p. 383, Table 10.6)
      8. The conflict in old age is between ego integrity vs. despair (p. 383, Table 10.6)

XIII. Infancy and Childhood
   A. Infants develop attachments to their mothers (pp. 384-385)
      1. Infants differ in their styles of attachments to parents and care-givers (p. 384)
      2. Research suggest that genetics and parent responsiveness affect style (p. 385)
         a. The effects on children may differ in different ethnic groups (p. 385)

XIV. Social Development in Childhood and Adolescence
   A. Forming friendships is important for social and emotional development (p. 385, Fig. 10.28)
      1. Children tend to be popular, rejected, or controversial (p. 385)
   B. Adolescence begins when the body shows signs of sexual maturation (p. 385)
      1. Western culture promotes prolonging of adolescence compared to other societies (p. 386)
   C. Identity Development
      1. An identity crisis occurs as adolescents decide who they are and what kind of lives they will lead (p. 386)
         a. Resolution of crisis occurs via several possible processes (p. 387)
   D. The "Personal Fable" of Teenagers
      1. Adolescents believe they are "special"; bad things will not happen to them (p. 387)
         a. Teens often do not use contraceptives, thinking the will not become pregnant (p. 387)

XV. Adulthood and the Midlife Transition
   A. Adults wonder what they will achieve and contribute to society and their families (p. 388)
      1. Most adults are satisfied current state, but reassess whether situations and personal goals (p. 388)
      2. People become aware that they will not accomplish their goals and have a midlife transition (p. 388)

XVI. Old Age
   A. A problem in old age is maintaining dignity and self esteem (pp. 388-389)
      1. Adjustment to retirement can be a problem (p. 389)
      2. Older people desire to maintain control over their lives (p. 389)

XVII. The Psychology of Facing Death
    A. Death is a principal source of anxiety (p. 389)
    B. People try to avoid thinking about death through a variety of ways (pp. 389-390)

The message: People confront different crises at different ages, but decisions made at one age affect later life. (p. 390)

Module 10.4: Temperament, Family, Gender, and Cultural Influences on Development

XVIII. Temperament and Lifelong Development
    A. Temperaments differ at birth and remain fairly consistent across lifespan (p. 391, Fig. 10.26)
        1. Genetics and environment play a role because monozygotic twins raised together are more similar in temperament than dizygotic twins and monozygotic twins raised apart from each other (p. 392)

XIX. The Family
    A. Birth Order and Family Size
        1. Birth order may have some small effects on development (p. 392)
        2. Family size inversely correlated with IQ (pp. 392-393, Fig. 10.27)
    B. Effects of Parenting Styles
        1. Parents may be authoritative, authoritarian, permissive, or uninvolved (p. 393)
        2. Parenting style has a small effect on child's behavior (pp. 393-394)
    C. Parental Employment and Child Care
        1. The quality of daycare and quality of home life affect development (pp. 394-384)
        2. One of these must be of high quality for satisfactory development (pp. 395-395)
    D. Nontraditional Families
        1. Although the evidence is not conclusive, nontraditional families do not produce children different from traditional families (p. 395)
    E. Parental Conflict and Divorce
        1. Children have difficulty following divorce, especially in the beginning (p. 396)
            a. Boys tend to become more aggressive and girls react negatively to a stepfather, if mother remarries (p. 396)

XX. Gender Influences
    A. On average, men and women are different from each other cognitively, socially and emotionally (pp. 396-397)
    B. Cognitive Differences
        1. Females tend to be better at language and men are better on spatial tasks (p. 397)
    C. Differences in Social Situations
        1. Most sex differences emerge in social situations (pp. 397-398)
        2. Boys' play is more competitive than girls' (pp. 397-398)
    D. Reasons Behind Gender Differences
        1. Adults treat boys differently than girls, but differences could also be due to biological differences (p. 398)

XXI. Ethnic and Cultural Influences
    A. Minority children face different pressures than others (p. 398)
        1. Immigrants undergo acculturation (p. 398)
        2. Minority groups may show full assimilation to American culture or they may develop biculturalism (pp. 398-399)

The message: *Temperament, family influences, gender, and ethnic and cultural diversity lead to a diversity of behavior. (p. 399).*

RELATED WEBSITES AND ACTIVITIES
Visit http://psychology.wadsworth.com/kalat_intro7e/ for online quizzing, glossary flashcards, crossword puzzles, annotated web links, and more.

LECTURE MATERIAL
Information from the text is only half of the picture. Do not forget to review your lecture material. Process each topic meaningfully. Most importantly, be sure that you understand the material in each lecture-if you don't, ask your instructor or teaching assistant.

**STUDY TIP # 10: To study for an exam set up a schedule of activities that need to be completed. Instead of your schedule ending on the day of the exam, have your schedule end a day or two before the exam day. Your anxiety will be reduced because you will have finished your studying early and if you need to do some additional studying it can be done in the one or two days prior to the exam.

**TIP: Associate the lecture material with the information from the text, with things that you already know, with your personal experiences, or with real-life applications. Type or neatly re-write your notes. Make sure they are detailed and organized. Make comments on your notes. Then write questions to cover each concept.

CHAPTER MODULE ASSESSMENTS

Module 10.1 Getting Started: From Genetics Through Infancy
Answer these questions soon after reading the **Module 10.1: Getting Started: From Genetics Through Infancy**. There are several formats to the assessments. Answers to all questions appear on pp. 207-208.

Fill in the Blank
Provide a term(s) which best completes the statement below. Answers appear on p. 207.

1. The hereditary material of animals is contained in _____ of the cell nucleus.

2. A gene located on the X chromosome is known as an X-linked or _____ gene.

3. An estimate of the variance within a population that is due to heredity is known as _____.

4. Identical twins have identical genetic material, while _____ develop from separate zygotes.

5. A person showing a decreased response to a repeated stimulus is showing _____.

6. Babies who have stunted growth accompanied by other physical deformities and cognitive deficits likely suffer from _____.

Short Answer
The following questions require a short written answer (3-7 sentences). Answers appear on p. 207.

1. What are the advantages of locating specific genes that are related to specific characteristics?

2. What have studies involving identical and fraternal twins shown about the role of genetics in behavior?

3. Describe the relationship between low birth weight and later development.

4. For many years, it was thought that newborn infants could not learn. Describe some evidence that shows that infants can learn.

Multiple Choice
Circle the best answer below. Check your answers on p. 208. If your answer was incorrect, try to write why it was incorrect. Check your reasons on p. 208.

1. If neither F. Lat nor his wife can curl their tongue, which of the following would be evidence for high heritability of tongue-curling?
   a. none of their children will be able to curl their tongue
   b. half of their children will probably be able to curl their tongue
   c. all of their children should be able to curl their tongue
   d. either b or c, depending on whether F. Lat and his wife are heterozygous or homozygous

2. Men are much more likely to be color-blind than women because this is a sex-linked trait. This means that:
   a. the gene is sex limited; although both sexes carry it, it is more likely to show up in men
   b. it is not carried on a chromosome
   c. it is carried on the Y chromosome
   d. it is carried on the X chromosome

3. How could genetics affect people's preferences for dairy products?
   a. a single gene is directly responsible for the food preference
   b. genes control the ability to digest lactose
   c. genes produce differences in taste buds, which produce differences in food preferences
   d. genetics does not control this taste preference; it depends purely upon culture

4. Low-birth-weight babies typically show low achievement and often have behavior problems. The best reason for this is:
   a. impaired brain development
   b. that the mother is usually malnourished during pregnancy
   c. that the mother is usually unmarried
   d. that they have a number of disadvantages

5. Which of the following is true of infants vision?
   a. infants are immediately capable of depth perception
   b. infants look at light and dark patterns more than human faces
   c. infants are unable to control their eye movements
   d. infants look at human faces more than at other patterns

6. When an infant sucks, the sound "ba" is produced. He increases his sucking rate and then decreases it as the sound is repeated. The experimenter then changes the sound to "pa." What is the infant likely to do?
   a. continue sucking at the same rate because he ca not discriminate any speech sounds
   b. decrease his sucking rate because the new sound catches his attention
   c. continue sucking at the same rate because he ca not discriminate "pa" and "ba"
   d. increase his sucking rate because he hears a new sound

True/False
Select the best answer by circling *T for True* or *F for False*. Check your answers on p. 208.

1. **T or F** Identical twins reared separately show only as many similarities as fraternal twins reared separately.

2. **T or F** Development of the fetus can be significantly affected by the health of the mother.

3. **T or F** Babies as young as two months are able to demonstrate a level of learning and memory.

Module 10.2 Childhood Thinking and Reasoning
Answer these questions soon after reading the **Module 10.2: Childhood Thinking and Reasoning**. There are several formats to the assessments. Answers to all questions appear on pp. 209-210.

Fill in the Blank
Provide a term(s) which best completes the statement below. Answers appear on p. 209.

1. According to Vygotsky, every child has a zone of _____, which is the distance between what the child can do alone and what they can do with the help of others.

2. Specific stages in the development of moral reasoning with the highest stage being a universal ethical principle orientation has been proposed by _____.

3. A _____ is an organized way of interacting with objects in the world.

4. Children under the age of four often display _____ thinking, or the inability to understand someone else's point of view.

5. Groups of individuals of different ages all are compared simultaneously in a _____ study.

6. The idea that objects continue to exist even when we do not see or hear them is known as _____.

Short Answer
The following questions require a short written answer (3-7 sentences). Answers appear on p. 210.

1. Explain what Piaget meant by the terms "assimilation" and "accommodation."

2. Describe how a child in the concrete operations and a child in the formal operations stage would decide which two colors of paint would make a certain shade of brown.

3. Briefly describe Kohlberg's theory of moral development.

Multiple Choice
Circle the best answer below. Check your answers on pp. 210-211. If your answer was incorrect, try to write why it was incorrect. Check your reasons on pp. 210-211.

1. Piaget interpreted infants' not reaching for a hidden object as a failure in object permanence. The correct explanation for this is that infants:
   a. do not know that objects continue to exist even when we ca not see them
   b. may concentrate so much on seen objects than they ignore unseen ones
   c. quickly forget where things are hidden
   d. may show object permanence under some test conditions but not others

2. An infant takes a new rubber ducky and immediately puts it in her mouth in exactly the same way as she sucks her rattle. Piaget would say that:
   a. accommodation of the ducky to the sucking schema has occurred
   b. assimilation of the ducky to the sucking schema has occurred
   c. the infant is in the preoperational stage
   d. the infant has added a new schema to handle the ducky
   e. the infant is in the zone of proximal development

3. Children gain some concept of self during the first stage of development. What is the evidence for this?
   a. infants over 1 1/2 years touch a spot of rouge on their face when they see themselves in the mirror
   b. infants over 1 1/2 years touch the red spot on the mirror when they see themselves with rouge on their face
   c. 4-year-olds select the same cup as an informed adult rather than an uninformed adult
   d. children tend to draw a pile of blocks as they see them even when you ask them to draw the blocks as you see them from the other side

4. I take two equal-sized cans of Coke and pour one into a tall, thin glass and another into a shorter, fatter glass. Janie then tells me that there is more coke in the tall, thin glass. Janie is:
   a. in the concrete operations stage
   b. in the sensorimotor stage
   c. in the formal operations stage
   d. in the preoperational stage
   e. showing conservation

5. Several studies have been done to determine whether children who fail Piaget's tasks can pass the same tasks when they are set up more simply. After such practice, children can often pass the more difficult versions of the tasks. This shows that:
   a. the stages are distinct; children are either in one or the other
   b. the shift between the stages is sudden
   c. transitions from one stage to the next require a major reorganization of the child's way of thinking
   d. each stage seems to merge gradually into the next stage
   e. both a and b

6. John feels that he should be helpful to a new employee because one day that employee may become his boss and he would want his boss to owe him. John's moral reasoning is in which of Kohlberg's stages?
   a. social-contract legalistic
   b. universal ethical principle
   c. law and order
   d. instrumental relativist
   e. punishment and obedience

7. A weakness of Kohlberg's theory is:
   a. people often go back to earlier stages
   b. high-level moral reasoning does not necessarily go with moral behavior
   c. people progress through the stages in very different orders
   d. the differences between men's and women's moral reasoning are very great
   e. it emphasizes a "caring" approach to moral reasoning too heavily

8. An investigator wished to study the relationship between intelligence and age in adults. She started with a group of 40 20-year-olds and tested their intelligence. She (and later her students) continued to test this group every 5 years for the next 60 years. What type of study is this?
   a. longitudinal
   b. cohort
   c. cross-sectional
   d. a combination of longitudinal and cross-sectional

True/False
Select the best answer by circling *T for True* or *F for False*. Check your answers on p. 210.

1. **T or F** A child in the formal operations stage uses logic and systematic planning to solve problems.

2. **T or F** Assimilation is the process by which a child changes her schema to fit new information.

3. **T or F** A longitudinal design is best for a study that can be accomplished in one session.

Module 10.3 Social and Emotional Development
Answer these questions soon after reading the **Module 10.3: Social and Emotional Development**. There are several formats to the assessments. Answers to all questions appear on pp. 211-212.

Fill in the Blank
Provide a term(s) which best completes the statement below. Answers appear on p. 211.

1. Psychologists who examine the early relationship between infants and their mothers are studying the concept of _____.

2. The belief that one is special and that bad things only happen to other people is called the

   _____.

3. The reassessment of personal goals that occurs for many people in the middle of their life is called a _____.

4. When one has explored the outcome of having various possible identities and then makes their own decisions about their life choices they have achieved _____.

5. We may cope with death by avoiding thinking about it and by affirming a worldview that provides self-esteem, hope and value in life which is consistent with _____ theory.

Short Answer
The following questions require a short written answer (3-7 sentences). Answers appear on p. 211.

1. Describe how a securely attached infant reacts in the Strange Situation test and also in other real-world situations.

2. Discuss the "personal fable" of teenagers.

3. Describe the midlife transition.

4. Discuss how people adjust to retirement.

Multiple Choice
Circle the best answer below. Check your answers on pp. 211-212. If your answer was incorrect, try to write why it was incorrect. Check your reasons on pp. 211-212.

1. Perplexity is 16 years old. She is trying to decide whether she wishes to apply herself in school so that she can enter medical school or whether she wants to have fun in school and not bother about a career. Perplexity is in which of Erikson's stages?
   a. ego integrity vs. despair
   b. generativity vs. stagnation
   c. intimacy vs. isolation
   d. industry vs. inferiority
   e. identity vs. role confusion

2. Controversial children are those who are:
   a. popular with other children, but not with parents
   b. avoided by other children
   c. popular when young, but become rejected when they get older
   d. liked by some children, but rejected by others

3. Chris has been told by her parents that she must become a plumber in the family plumbing business. Which of the following best describes Chris' process in development of her identity?
   a. identity moratorium
   b. identity foreclosure
   c. identity diffusion
   d. identity achievement

4. Compared to other societies Western society encourages adolescents to:
   a. stay in school longer
   b. postpone marriage and family
   c. postpone career
   d. all of the above

True/False
Select the best answer by circling *T for True* or *F for False*. Check your answers on p. 212.

1. **T or F** Most people try to avoid thinking about death and instead affirm a view which provides hope.

2. **T or F** Kohlberg divided the human life into eight stages of social and emotional development.

3. **T or F** An adolescent who has reached firm decisions about his identity without much thought or input could be described as reaching identity foreclosure.

Module 10.4 Temperament, Family, Gender, and Cultural Influences on Development
Answer these questions soon after reading the **Module 10.4: Temperament, Family, Gender, and Cultural Influences on Development**. There are several formats to the assessments. Answers to all questions appear on pp. 212-213.

Fill in the Blank
Provide a term(s) which best completes the statement below. Answers appear on p. 212.

1. The ability to alternate between membership in one culture and membership in another is

   _____.

2. The transition to feeling a part of the culture of one's new country is_____.

3. People differ markedly in their _____ or tendency to be active or inactive, outgoing or reserved.

4. The fact that women do better on some tasks than men and men do better than women on other tasks is evidence for _____.

Short Answer

The following questions require a short written answer (3-7 sentences). Answers appear on p. 212.

1. Briefly, describe the effects of day care on the development of children.

2. Describe the situations in which sex differences are most likely to occur.

3. Describe the effects of birth order and family size on development.

Multiple Choice

Circle the best answer below. Check your answers on p. 213. If your answer was incorrect, try to write why it was incorrect. Check your reasons on p. 213.

1. Differences in temperament that exist in infancy are:
   a. largely gone by the time a child is 7
   b. due to the environment; genetics plays no role
   c. unrelated to measures of fear tested a few months later
   d. fairly consistent through childhood

2. Following divorce:
   a. almost all children act depressed for more than 5 years
   b. girls have more adjustment problems than boys, particularly if they live with their mother
   c. adjustment is best if children live with the opposite-sex parent
   d. African-American children have more adjustment problems than European-American children
   e. boys become aggressive toward other children

3. Gender roles are:
   a. gradually disappearing in today's society
   b. mostly defined by biology
   c. likely influenced both by biological and cultural aspects
   d. almost entirely learned from parents

4. An authoritarian parenting style is associated with:
   a. withdrawn children
   b. children who have a lack of self-control
   c. children who are socially cooperative
   d. withdrawn or assertive children depending upon the ethnic group
   e. African-American children doing well in school; European-American children doing poorly.

True/False
Select the best answer by circling *T for True* or *F for False*. Check your answers on p. 213.

1. **T or F** Boys' play is usually more competitive than girls' play.

2. **T or F** Parenting style has huge effects on children's behavior.

3. **T or F** The effects of birth order are significant within a family and influence things such as IQ.

4. **T or F** Results of studies examining the effects of nontraditional families on development are inconclusive regarding whether children in these families are different than children from traditional families.

FINAL COMPREHESIVE CHAPTER ASSESSEMENT TEST

Check your answers on p. 213.

1. If a gene shows its effects more in one sex than the other because certain hormones activate it, the gene is said to be:
   a. sex limited
   b. recessive
   c. dominant
   d. sex linked
   e. chromosomal

2. Which of the following statements would be most conclusive?
   a. similarities in monozygotic twins raised apart must be genetic
   b. lack of resemblance in some trait for monozygotic twins indicates a non-genetic influence
   c. similarities between adopted children and their adoptive parents indicates a genetic influence
   d. preferences and attitudes cannot be genetic because they are psychological
   e. if something is under genetic control, it cannot be modified by the environment

3. Infants with low birth weight:
   a. may catch up in development to infants with higher birth weights if they experience similar environments
   b. have irreversible brain damage
   c. tend to be overachievers; have higher academic achievement than higher-birth-weight counterparts
   d. usually have environments that are similar to infants with higher birth weights
   e. have a lower risk of dying than heavier infants

4. An infant's response to a sound ("ba") decreases every time she hears it. She is showing evidence of
   a. habituation
   b. disinhibition
   c. blocking
   d. none of the above

5. An infant sees a toy car go down a slope and emerge from behind a screen in either a possible (a hidden box is above the slope) or impossible (a hidden box blocks the slope) situation. What happened?
   a. infants stared longer at the possible than at the impossible event
   b. infants stated equally long at both events
   c. infants over 6 months stated longer at the impossible event; infants under 6 months stared longer at the possible event
   d. because infants do not have object permanence, they did not stare at either event; they assumed that the car was gone when it went behind the screen
   e. infants stared longer at the impossible than at the possible event

6. Which of the following is an example of egocentric thought, as Piaget described it?
   a. Johnny argues that his sister should not touch his toys
   b. Michael draws a pile of blocks as he sees them, even when ask to draw how they would look from your side
   c. Diane looks for the candy under the cup indicated by an "informed" adult
   d. Susie grasps at the new puppy and tries to shake him like a rattle
   e. Jamie does not hunt for Easter eggs because he assumes that hidden objects are gone

7. Susie in answer d in the above question is showing:
   a. a lack of conservation
   b. assimilation
   c. concrete operational thought
   d. object permanence
   e. an inability to accommodate

8. A child in the formal operations stage can do which of the following that cannot be done by a child in the concrete operations stage?
   a. show conservation
   b. have the concept of object permanence
   c. be able to assimilate
   d. solve problems systematically
   e. distinguish between "pa" and "ba"

9. Piaget argued that children in the preoperational stage fail conservation tasks because they lack the necessary mental processes. More recent research has shown that:
   a. the relevant mental processes emerge suddenly at a particular age
   b. children who can show conservation of number with a few items fail when the number is increased
   c. giving children water to pour and balls of clay to squash speeds up their understanding of conservation
   d. Piaget overestimated the abilities of young children
   e. children fail the tasks only because they do not understand the questions

10. The military overthrows a dictator because he gives rights to a minority and the law states that they have no rights. The military's moral reasoning is probably at what level?
    a. law and order
    b. punishment and obedience
    c. social contract
    d. interpersonal concordance
    e. universal principles

11. A weakness of Kohlberg's theory is that:
    a. people seem to progress through the stages in the same order
    b. people usually do not go back to earlier stages
    c. in societies throughout the world, people begin at Kohlberg's first stage
    d. differences between males and females are not great
    e. criminals often show high-level moral reasoning, but their behavior is not moral

12. Today's 20-year olds score higher on an IQ test than today's 60-year olds. To say that this is due to a cohort effect means that:
    a. IQ declines with age
    b. the groups of 60-year olds is a dull group and the 20-year olds are a bright group
    c. the effects are due to the longitudinal design
    d. there is a correlation, but cause cannot be determined
    e. the effects may be due to health and education differences while the groups were growing up

13. Michael is 21 and he is trying to decide whether to marry now or wait until he has finished graduate school. He is in which of Erikson's stages?
    a. intimacy vs. isolation
    b. identity vs. role diffusion
    c. ego integrity vs. despair
    d. generativity vs. stagnation
    e. identity foreclosure vs. identity achievement

14. Authoritarian parents tend to have children who:
    a. lack a sense of social responsibility
    b. get mixed reactions from their peers, liked by some but rejected by others
    c. show self-reliance and self-control
    d. are withdrawn
    e. have serious identity crises

15. Adolescence is sometimes characterized as a period of "storm and stress". Which of the following is most true about the "storm and stress" of this period?
    a. varies substantially across cultures
    b. are most common in teens who are particularly obedient to their parents
    c. occur during the midlife transition
    d. occur only for teenagers who believe strongly in the personal fable

16. Dr. Frodul has just turned 41. He decides that his life is not going anywhere. He has always wanted to backpack through Europe so he quits his job, buys a backpack and takes off to Europe. Dr. Frodul has experienced:
    a. a "honeymoon period"
    b. a failure in gender role identity
    c. an autonomy vs. shame and doubt crisis
    d. midlife transition
    e. an ego integrity vs. despair crisis

17. John has worked the same job for the last 45 years. John has centered his entire life around his job. When John retires which of the following will he likely experience?
    a. a sense of loss
    b. increased stress
    c. a personal fable
    d. identity foreclosure

18. In which situation will a child probably develop most normally?
    a. the child comes from a disadvantaged home and day care is poor
    b. the child comes from a disadvantaged home and stays at home with mother
    c. the parents have just been divorced and the mother goes to work for the first time
    d. the child comes from a disadvantaged home and goes to a good day care

19. Research examining the differences in boys and girls show that in social situations:
    a. boys play more competitively than girls
    b. girls play more competitively than boys
    c. boys and girls are about equal in their competitive play
    d. boys play more cooperatively if only boys are playing

20. If an immigrant to the United States is able to alternate between his native culture and that of the United States, he is showing:
    a. biculturalism
    b. total assimilation
    c. bilingualism
    d. difficulty with acculturation
    e. gender identity

ANSWERS AND EXPLANATIONS FOR CHAPTER MODULE ASSESSMENTS

Answers to the Fill in the Blank Questions – Module 10.1

1. chromosomes (p. 354)

2. sex-linked (p. 355)

3. Heritability (p. 356)

4. fraternal (p. 356)

5. habituation (p. 361)

6. fetal alcohol syndrome (p. 359)

Answers to the Short Answer Questions – Module 10.1

1. Finding a specific gene for a genetic disorder would allow a person to know that they will develop the disease and to plan accordingly. If genes can be identified, researchers may be able to develop a treatment to undo the damage. Problems may be preventable before they begin. (p. 356)

2. Identical twins, who share the same genetics, are more similar in characteristics such as having a predisposition toward certain conditions than fraternal twins, who are less similar genetically. Even identical twins separated at birth and reared apart are very similar. They often share interests and hobbies. These similarities are not conclusive evidence for genetics because the twins shared the prenatal environment. (pp. 353-354)

3. Children who are born with low birth weight tend to have lower academic achievement and behavior problems later in life. This does not mean the low birth weight causes these problems, however. The postnatal environments of low birth weight children are often not very good. When twins who vary in birth weight are compared, the twin with low birth weight tends to catch up to the heavier twin, suggesting that low birth weight per se may not be the cause of later problems. (pp. 358-359)

4. Infants less than 3 days old could turn on a tape recording of their mother's voice by sucking on a nipple at certain times and certain rates. By sucking at different times and rates, they could turn on a recording of another woman's voice. The infants increased their sucking in order to turn on their mother's voice, but they decreased it when it resulted in turning on the other woman's voice. This shows that the infants recognized their mother's voice and they learned what to do to turn it on. The fact that the recognized their mother's voice so early suggests that the infants had learned their mother's voice even before birth. (p. 361)

Answers to the Multiple Choice Questions – Module 10.1

1. a. Correct! (p. 355)
    b. Incorrect. Would occur if one was heterozygous and the other homozygous for not curling; one ca not be heterozygous because curling is dominant
    c. Incorrect. Would occur if both carried two genes (homozygous) for tongue curling; ca not be because neither can do it
    d. Incorrect. Because tongue curling is dominant, it would show up with one gene; they must both have two recessive genes for an inability to curl

2. a. Incorrect. Located on the X chromosome; capable of altering either sex
    b. Incorrect. All genes are carried on chromosomes
    c. Incorrect. The Y chromosome is smaller and does not carry this gene at all; that is why a male is color-blind if he gets the gene from his mother
    d. Correct! (p. 355)

3. a. Incorrect. Genes control the taste preference indirectly, not directly
    b. Correct! (p. 358)
    c. Incorrect. Differences in taste buds do not explain this
    d. Incorrect. Cultures do differ in their preference for milk products, but this is genetically controlled

4. a. Incorrect. Probably not, because when twins are compared in the same environment the low-birth-weight twin usually catches up to the higher-birth-weight one
    b. Incorrect. True, but this is not necessarily the cause of the poor development later
    c. Incorrect. True, but mother's marital status per se does not cause the later problems
    d. Correct! (p. 358)

5. a. Incorrect. Depth perception develops later as a result of experience
    b. Incorrect. They spend time looking at both but have a preference for faces
    c. Incorrect. They are capable of controlling their eye movements
    d. Correct! (p. 360)

6. a. Incorrect. Infants can discriminate speech sounds
    b. Incorrect. New sounds are novel and infants increase their sucking rate
    c. Incorrect. Infants do discriminate between "pa" and "ba"
    d. Correct! (p. 361)

Answers to the True/False Questions – Module 10.1

1. **False**: Research suggests that identical twins reared separately are <u>more</u> similar than fraternal twins reared separately. (p. 353)

2. **True**: Since the fetus is dependent on the mother, any unhealthy aspects of the mother can affect the prenatal environment. (p. 358)

3. **True**: Babies of this age have learned to kick to activate a mobile and remember how to activate it days later. (p. 362)

Answers to the Fill in the Blank Questions – Module 10.2

1. proximal development (p. 377)

2. Kohlberg (p. 377)

3. schema (p. 367)

4. egocentric (p. 370)

5. cross-sectional (p. 364)

6. object permanence (pp. 368-370)

Answers to the Short Answer Questions – Module 10.2

1. Children try to use old ways of behaving in new situations. In Piaget's terms, they assimilate objects to a specific schema (an organized way of interacting with the world). Sometimes these old ways do not quite work, so they need to modify their behavior in order to interact with a new object. This modification of a schema is called accommodation. (p. 367)

2. The concrete operations child would haphazardly select two colors and mix them. This child might try some combinations twice and never try other combinations. The formal operations child would test pairs of colors systematically--mix #1 with #2, #3, #4, #5, #6, #7, and #8.Then she would mix #2 with #3, #4, #5, #6, #7, and #8. This systematic process would be continued until the correct combination was found. (p. 375)

3. As children grow older, their moral reasoning becomes less related to immediate rewards and punishments and more related to abstract principles. There are six stages, with the highest level of morality based on ethical principles such as a respect for human life and justice. Kohlberg argues that these changes occur because the child becomes more and more able to reason abstractly. (p. 377)

Answers to the Multiple Choice Questions – Module 10.2

1. a. Incorrect. Piaget's explanation; could be correct, but so could b or c
    b. Incorrect. Possibly correct, but so are a and c
    c. Incorrect. Possibly correct, but so are a and b
    d. Correct! (pp. 369-370)

2. a. Incorrect. An old schema was applied here because she sucked in exactly the same way; accommodation involves modifying an old schema
    b. Correct! (p. 367)
    c. Incorrect. An infant is in the sensorimotor stage
    d. Incorrect. An old schema, sucking, was used
    e. Incorrect. This is Vygotsky's term for the distance between what children can do themselves and what they can do with help

3. a. Correct! (p. 368)
   b. Incorrect. This shows that they do not understand that it is themselves in the mirror; no concept of self
   c. Incorrect. Shows they understand other people's knowledge; not evidence for concept of self; 4-year old not in first stage of development
   d. Incorrect. An example of egocentric thought

4. a. Incorrect. If so, she should know they are the same
   b. b. Incorrect. If so, she should not be able to talk
   c. Incorrect. She would show conservation at this age
   d. Correct! (p. 371, Fig. 10.20)
   e. Incorrect. She is not showing conservation (notice the term is not conversation)

5. a. Incorrect. Shows that the distinction is less certain; children appear to be in one stage on one task, but in the next stage on another task
   b. Incorrect. The shift appears to be more gradual
   c. Incorrect. Piaget's belief; this contradicts it; child shows thought patterns from both stages at same time
   d. Correct! (p. 372)
   e. Incorrect. Both a and b are wrong; they are Piaget's beliefs, which these results contradict

6. a. Incorrect. He is not arguing that it's best for society
   b. Incorrect. He is not thinking about highest ethical principles
   c. Incorrect. He is not doing it because it is the law
   d. Correct! (p. 377, Table 10.4)
   e. Incorrect. There are no immediate consequences

7. a. Incorrect. People usually do not go back
   b. Correct! (pp. 380-381)
   c. Incorrect. People progress in the same order
   d. Incorrect. There are some sex differences, but they are not great
   e. Incorrect. Kohlberg's levels are based on a "justice" orientation

8. a. Correct! (p. 364)
   b. Incorrect. Cohort effects refer to similarities in environment while growing up; occur with cross-sectional studies
   c. Incorrect. A cross-sectional design would have tested different-age people all at once
   d. Incorrect. It is purely longitudinal; same people tested many times

Answers to the True/False Questions – Module 10.2

1. **True**: Using logic and systematic planning to solve problems are characteristics of a child in Piaget's formal operations stage. (p. 375)

2. **False**: Accommodation is the process of changing a schema to fit new information. (p. 367)

3. **False**: Since participants are only available for one session, a cross-sectional design is better. (p. 364)

Answers to the Fill in the Blank Questions – Module 10.3

1. attachment (pp. 384-385)

2. personal fable (p. 387)

3. midlife transition (p. 388)

4. identity achievement (p. 387)

5. terror management (pp. 389-390)

Answers to the Short Answer Questions – Module 10.3

1. In the Strange Situation, a mother and an infant come into a room with many toys. Then a stranger enters and the mother leaves the room. Later the mother returns. A securely attached infant uses the mother as a base for exploration, showing her toys and making eye contact with her. When the mother leaves, the infant may cry, but only a little. When the mother returns, the infant goes to her with apparent delight, cuddles with her, and then returns to the toys. Such infants also show secure attachment patterns to fathers, grandparents, and other care-givers. They relate well to playmates. (p. 384)

2. Teenagers are likely to believe that they are special and that bad things only happen to other people, not to them. This has been called the "personal fable"; it may lead to risky behaviors such as having sex without contraceptives. (p. 387)

3. People realize that they may never be able to meet some of the goals that they have not yet met. Illusions are discarded and people may become discontented. They may accept this and channel their energies into things they can accomplish or they may change their routine and modify their lives. Others may become depressed and turn to alcohol as a means of escape. (p. 388)

4. People who had activities and interests outside of work adjust better than people without such outside interests. There is often a period immediately after retirement when people enjoy doing things they never had time for before. They may soon realize that they cannot achieve all of their goals, and may set more realistic goals. Older people need to feel that they have control of their lives, even if their health begins to deteriorate. (p. 389)

Answers to the Multiple Choice Questions – Module 10.3

1. a. Incorrect. This conflict occurs during old age
   b. Incorrect. This conflict occurs during middle age
   c. Incorrect. This conflict occurs during young adulthood; she's only 14
   d. Incorrect. This conflict occurs during preadolescent years
   e. Correct! (p. 386, Table 10.6, p. 384)

2. a. Incorrect. Definitions refer to children's liking, not parents'
   b. Incorrect. These are called "rejected" children
   c. Incorrect. Status tends to be fairly consistent from year to year
   d. Correct! (p. 385)

3. a. Incorrect. An identity is not selected
   b. Correct! (p. 398)
   c. Incorrect. Identity has not been given real consideration and thus person has no sense of identity
   d. Incorrect. After exploring possible identities one is selected by the person

4. a. Incorrect. Since b and c are also correct, D is the best answer
   b. Incorrect. Since a and c are also correct, D is the best answer
   c. Incorrect. Since a and b are also correct, D is the best answer
   d. Correct! (p. 386)

Answers to the True/False Questions – Module 10.3

1. **True**: As a way to cope with the inevitability of death people often try to ignore thinking about it. (pp. 388-390)

2. **False**: Erikson proposed we go through these eight stages of social and emotional development. (pp. 383-384, Table 10.6)

3. **True**: In identify foreclosure is a state of reaching firm decisions about one's identity without much thought or consideration. (p. 387)

Answers to the Fill in the Blank Questions – Module 10.4

1. biculturalism (pp. 398-399)

2. acculturation (p. 398)

3. temperament (p. 391)

4. gender influences (pp. 396-397)

Answers to the Short Answer Questions – Module 10.4

1. In many cultures, it is not expected that mothers will stay home with their young infants; however, in North America and Europe, this was the prevalent custom. Children who come from good homes develop adequately either at home or in a good day care center. Children from disadvantaged homes who have good day care actually develop better than the same children who stay at home with their mothers. Very early day care is not harmful if it is of good quality. (pp. 394-395)

2. Important differences between males and females emerge in social situations. Boys compete with each other, whereas girls tend to cooperate. Boys exchange insults and make threats and boasts. Girls exchange compliments and make suggestions rather than demands. (pp. 397-398)

3. Research has shown that birth order effects within a family are not significant. That is, on average the oldest child does not have a higher IQ than other children. However, research has also shown that IQ and family size are inversely correlated. As family size increases, IQ decreases. (pp. 392-393)

Answers to the Multiple Choice Questions – Module 10.4

1. a. Incorrect. Differences are still there at 7 1/2
    b. Incorrect. Monozygotic twins are more similar than dizygotic, so genetics plays a role
    c. Incorrect. More difficult infants were more afraid later
    d. Correct! (p. 391)

2. a. Incorrect. Some did, but many felt better after a year or two
    b. Incorrect. Boys had more problems
    c. Incorrect. Generally better with same-sex parent
    d. Incorrect. It is the opposite; European-American children seem to have more problems
    e. Correct! (p. 396)

3. a. Incorrect. May be changing, but differences are still there
    b. Incorrect. A few aspects are, but most are not biological
    c. Correct! (p. 398)
    d. Incorrect. Also role models, television, other children

4. a. Incorrect. Related to authoritarian European-American parents, but not African-American parents; d is a better answer
    b. Incorrect. Related to a permissive parenting style
    c. Incorrect. Related to an authoritative parenting style
    d. Correct! (p. 398)
    e. Incorrect. Related to an authoritative parenting style; it's European-American children who are likely to do well in school

Answers to the True/False Questions – Module 10.4

1. **True**: Boys' play on average is more competitive than girls play. This may be due to both genetics and the way parents differentially treat boys and girls. (p. 398).

2. **False**: Results of studies examining the relationship between adopted children and their parents show that the effects of parenting are not as large as once thought. (p. 393)

3. **False**: Birth order effects on IQ are not significant within a family. (p. 392)

4. **True**: No conclusive results have been obtained to determine whether a difference exists, although the results so for suggest no strong influence (p. 395)

Answers to Final Comprehensive Assessment

1. a (p. 356)
2. b (pp. 353, 357)
3. a (p. 358)
4. a (p. 361)
5. e (p. 369)
6. b (p. 370)
7. b (p. 367)
8. d (p. 375)
9. b (p. 376)
10. a (p. 377)

11. e (p. 380)
12. e (p. 366)
13. a (p. 384, Table 10.6)
14. c (p. 393)
15. a (p. 386)
16. d (p. 388)
17. a (p. 389)
18. d (pp. 394-395)
19. a (pp. 397-398)
20. a (pp. 398-399)

CHAPTER 11

MOTIVATION

CHAPTER OVERVIEW INFORMATION

LEARNING OBJECTIVES

By the end of Chapter 11 you should

- ✓ Understand the fundamental principles of motivation
- ✓ Increase your knowledge of the complex influences on hunger motivation
- ✓ Increase your knowledge of the complex influences on human sexual behavior
- ✓ Be familiar with theories of motivation and their application to work environments

CHAPTER 11 OUTLINE

Chapter 11 explores why we do what we do or, put another way, what motivates us daily and as throughout our lives. General theories of motivation are discussed. Hunger, sexual, and work motivation are also explored in detail.

Chapter 11 is presented below in outline format to assist you in understanding the information presented in the chapter. More detailed information on any topic can be found using the page references to the right of the topic.

Module 11.1 General Principles of Motivation

I. Properties of Motivated Behaviors
  A. Motivated behaviors are goal-directed (p. 407)

II. Views of Motivation (Table 11.1)
  A. Motivation as an Energy
    1. Lorenz believed that instinctive energy compels behavior (p. 408, Fig 11.1)
  B. Drive theories
    1. Drive-reduction theories propose that motivation is an internal state or irritation that energizes behavior (p. 408)
      a. Flaws of theories include role of seeking new experiences and external stimulation (p. 408)
  C. Homeostasis
    1. Homeostasis is the maintenance of biological conditions at an optimum level (p. 408)
  D. Incentive Theories
    1. Incentive theories propose that incentives "pull" organisms (p. 409)
  E. Intrinsic and Extrinsic Motivations
    1. Intrinsic motivation involves engaging in a behavior for its own sake; extrinsic motivation includes rewards and punishments (pp. 409-410, Fig. 11.2)
      a. An Overjustification Effect occurs when intrinsic motivation to perform some task declines as a result of giving more extrinsic motivation than necessary (pp. 409-410)

III. Delay of Gratification
    A. Sometime people are motivated to defer a smaller immediate event for a larger later event (p. 410)
        1. Children usually select immediate reward, older people select the later reward (p. 410)
        2. Selection of immediate or later event depends on the type of event being considered (pp. 410-411)

The message: *There are many types of motivation. (p. 411)*

Module 11.2 Hunger Motivation

IV. The Physiological Mechanisms of Hunger
    A. Hunger is partly controlled by physiological mechanisms (p. 412)
    B. Short-Term Regulation of Hunger
        1. Hunger is controlled by glucose in blood stream (p. 413, Fig. 11.3)
            a. Insulin promotes movement of nutrients out of the bloodstream into cells (p. 413)
                i. If insulin is low, as in diabetes, nutrients enter cells very slowly (pp. 413-414, Figs. 11.4-11.5)
                ii. If insulin is consistently high, glucagon can not move glucose back into the bloodstream (p. 414)
            b. Glucagon converts stored energy back into blood glucose (p. 413)
    C. Long-Term Regulation of Hunger
        1. Variation in daily weight occurs, but is stable over time due to set point (pp. 414-415)
        2. The amount of leptin controls the brain to keep weight near set point (p. 415, Fig. 11.6)
    D. Brain Mechanisms of Hunger and Satiety
        1. Hypothalamus is important in regulating weight (pp. 415-416, Fig. 11.7)
            a. Lateral hypothalamus is critical for starting meals (p. 415)
            b. Ventromedial hypothalamus controls the speed of digestion and insulin secretion (p. 415)
                i. Damage results in rapid digestion and weight gain (p. 415, Fig.11.8)
            c. Paraventricular hypothalamus is important for sensing a sense of fullness (pp. 415-416)
                i. Damage results in person regularly eating enormous meals (p. 416)

V. Social and Cultural Influences on Eating
    A. Cultural
        1. U.S. society more obese today than previously due to a variety of factors (p. 416)
        2. Other populations influenced by the U.S. culture also showing signs of obesity (p. 416, Fig. 11.9)
    B. Social
        1. People eating as part of group will eat longer and consume twice as much food compared to dining alone (p. 416)

VI. Easting Too Much or Too Little
    A. Eating disorders occur through a combination of social and physiological influences (pp. 416-417)
    B. Obesity
        1. Obesity is an excessive accumulation of body fat (p. 417)
        2. Approximately 65% of U.S. population is obese (30%) or overweight (35%) (p. 417)
        3. People sometimes overeat in response to emotional problems (p. 417)
            a. This probably is not a cause of obesity (p. 417)
        4. Genetics are involved in obesity (p. 417)
        5. Overweight people may expend less energy (p. 417)
    C. Losing Weight
        1. The best way to lose weight is to eat less and exercise more (p. 418)
        2. External assistance can benefit some in their effort to lose weight (p. 418)
    D. The Effect of Intentional Weight Loss on Appetite
        1. Women are more likely to be dissatisfied with their appearance (pp. 418-419)
        2. People in U.S. concerned more about eating healthy, but report eating unhealthy (p. 419)
        3. Women and men have different perspectives of attractive figures of the opposite sex (p. 419, Fig. 11.10)
        4. Dieting requires a great deal of self-regulation and perseverance (pp. 419-420)
    E. Anorexia Nervosa
        1. Anorexia nervosa involves steady weight loss (p. 420)
            a. Occurs in .3% of young women and much lower in other groups (p. 420)
            b. Social pressure to be thin, biochemical abnormalities, genetics, and parent's psychiatric history contribute to anorexia (pp. 420-421)
            c. An evolutionary mechanism may contribute to onset (p. 421)
    F. Bulimia Nervosa
        1. Bulimia involves eating binges (p. 421)
        2. Occurs in 1% of young women and .1% of adult men and is increasing (p. 422)
        3. Binge eating includes many sweets and fats with little protein (p. 422)
        4. Culture, self-starvation, and eating sweets following food deprivation may contribute to developing bulimia. Similar to drug addiction (p. 422)
        5. Emotional influences not consistently linked to causing bulimia (p. 422)

VII. Motives for Food Selection
    A. Food selection depends upon physiological, social, and cognitive factors (pp. 422-423)
    B. Food Selection Based on Taste
        1. Some taste preferences are biologically based (p. 423)
    C. Preference for Familiar Foods
        1. People prefer familiar foods with familiar tastes (pp. 423-424)
    D. Learned Associations with Food
        1. Taste aversions develop to foods that preceded illness and to foods that evoke repulsive associations (p. 425, Fig. 11.11)

The message: *Our motivation to eat and what to eat are influenced by a complex mixture of physiological, social, and cognitive forces. (p. 425)*

Module 11.3 Sexual Motivation

VIII. What Do People Do, and How Often?
    A. Sexual motivation depends upon physiological drive and incentives (p. 426)
    B. The Kinsey Survey
        1. Human sexual behavior shows great variability (p. 427)
            a. People think that excessive means "more than they do" (p. 427)
    C. Contemporary Surveys
        1. Frequency of different sexual activities as "very appealing" varies (p. 427, Fig. 11.12)
        2. Men more likely to masturbate frequently and look for casual sex opportunities (p. 427)
        3. Women more likely than men to adopt new partner's pattern and switch between homosexuality and heterosexuality (p. 427)
        4. Some similarities in sexual behaviors are present across cultures (p. 427, Fig. 11.13)
        5. Cohorts differ in the reported number of sex partners (pp. 427-428, Fig 11.14)
    D. Sexual Behavior in the Era of AIDS
        1. AIDS has made people more cautious in their sexual behavior (pp. 428-429)
    E. Sexual Arousal
        1. Sexual arousal involves four physiological stages (excitement, plateau, climax, resolution) (p. 430, Fig. 11.15)
    F. Sexual Dysfunction
        1. Some people, more likely women than men, experience sexual difficulties (p. 430)
        2. Viagra allows muscles controlling blood flow in the penis to relax to achieve erection (p. 430)

IX. Sexual Anatomy and Identity
    A. Gender identity is the sex a person regards him or herself (p. 430)
    B. Sexual anatomy starts out similar but the final outcome is determined by testosterone (male hormone) during early development (p. 431, Fig. 11.16)
        1. Intersexes have anatomies that appear intermediate between male and female (pp. 431-432, Fig 11.17)

X. Sexual Orientation
    A. Sexual orientation is a preference for male or female partners (p. 432, Fig. 11.18)
        1. The number of homosexuals is difficult to determine but may be around 2.8% for men and 1.4% for women and is similar across some cultures (p. 433, Fig. 11.19)
        2. Many homosexuals are well adjusted and content (p. 434)
        3. Genetics my play a role in a homosexual orientation (p. 434, Fig. 11.20)
        4. A section of the anterior hypothalamus is smaller in homosexual men (pp. 435-436, Fig. 11.21)

The message: *Sexual motivation results from a combination of biological factors and experiences. (p. 436)*

Module 11.4: Work Motivation

XI. Goals and Deadlines
   A. Setting deadlines and goals affect performance (pp. 438-439)
   B. High and Low Goals
     1. The most effective goal is one that is high and reasonable (p. 439)
     2. Goals are most effective when committed to publicly, when feedback is received regarding progress, and when the reward is perceived to be worth the effort (p. 439, Fig. 11.22)

XII. Job Design and Job Satisfaction
   A. Two Approaches to Job Design
     1. Theory X suggests that jobs should be simple and foolproof leaving little, if anything, up to the employee (p. 440, Fig. 11.23)
     2. Theory Y suggests that jobs should be enriching and meaningful with responsibility given to the employee (p. 440)
   B. Job Satisfaction
     1. Job satisfaction is related to how well one performs their job (p. 441)
     2. Genetics may play a role in satisfaction in general (p. 441)
     3. Older workers express more satisfaction than younger workers (p. 441, Fig. 11.24)
   C. Pay and Job Satisfaction
     1. Amount a person is paid for performing some job is important but people also work for more intrinsic reasons (p. 441)
     2. Employees seek to receive fair salary and exhibit less desirable behaviors if they perceive they are not being paid fairly (p. 441)

XIII. Leadership
   A. Usually one of two types
     1. Transformational leader articulates vision and motivates subordinates to move organization ahead (p. 442)
     2. Transaction leader focuses on the organization becoming more efficient at what they are doing (p. 442)

The message: *Striving for excellence, being competitive, and achieving goals are the motivators of work. (p. 442)*

RELATED WEBSITES AND ACTIVITIES

Visit http://psychology.wadsworth.com/kalat_intro7e/ for online quizzing, glossary flashcards, crossword puzzles, annotated web links, and more.

LECTURE MATERIAL

Information from the text is only half of the picture. Don't forget to review your lecture material. Process each topic meaningfully. Most importantly, be sure that you understand the material in each lecture-if you don't, ask your instructor or teaching assistant.

**STUDY TIP # 11: Use the comprehensive chapter assessment test as practice for an upcoming exam. Use only half of the questions from each chapter. That way you will get two opportunities to check your performance. Use the day or two you have set aside before the exam (see Chaper 10 Tip) to take the practice test. Complete the practice test under similar conditions to the real one (e.g., no notes or books). Check your performance. If you do not do well, review the topics you did not do well on and when sufficiently prepared take the second practice test.

TIP: Associate the lecture material with the information from the text, with things that you already know, with your personal experiences, or with real-life applications. Type or neatly re-write your notes. Make sure they are detailed and organized. Make comments on your notes. Then write questions to cover each concept.

CHAPTER MODULE ASSESSMENTS

> **Module 11.1 General Principles of Motivation**
> Answer these questions soon after reading the **Module 11.1: General Principles of Motivation**. There are several formats to the assessments. Answers to all questions appear on pp. 230-231.

Fill in the Blank
Provide a term(s) which best completes the statement below. Answers appear on p. 230.

1. The maintenance of an optimum level of biological conditions within an organism is called _____.

2. External stimuli that pull us towards certain actions are _____.

3. Both animals and humans strive to reduce their needs and drives, such as hunger, as much as possible is proposed by _____ theories.

4. A motivation to do an act for its own sake is a(n) _____ motivation.

Short Answer
The following questions require a short written answer (3-7 sentences). Answers appear on p. 230.

1. What do motivated behaviors have in common?

2. Explain how motivation involves both physiological drives and incentives.

Multiple Choice
Circle the best answer below. Check your answers on p. 230. If your answer was incorrect, try to write why it was incorrect. Check your reasons on p. 230.

1. Which of the following is <u>not</u> consistent with a drive theory of motivation?
   a. a very hungry animal will work harder than a less hungry animal
   b. a hungry animal will seek food to achieve need reduction
   c. a rat will run faster to get tasty food than to get less-tasty food
   d. a thirsty child will produce many behaviors

2. Which of the following is an example of an extrinsically motivated behavior?
   a. you eat something quickly because it tastes so good
   b. a college student spends hours on a paper because the topic is so interesting
   c. a worker works extra hard because a bonus is expected soon
   d. a monkey figures out how to open a device "just for the fun of it"

3. Chris has won the lottery and has the option of receiving $1,000,000 immediately or $15 million dollars over 20 years. Chris opts for the $15 million dollar option. Which of the following is Chris demonstrating?
   a. intrinsic motivation
   b. drive-reduction
   c. delayed gratification
   d. homeostasis

True/False
Select the best answer by circling *T for True* or *F for False*. Check your answers on pp. 230-231.

1. **T or F** An incentive is an external stimulus that "pulls" an animal.

2. **T or F** Extrinsic motivation is based on rewards and punishments separate from the act itself.

3. **T or F** Homeostasis is the effort to reduce some drive.

4. **T or F** Intrinsic motivation is engaging in an act for its own sake.

5. **T or F** An overjustification effect results in an increase in inherent interest in doing an act after rewards are withdrawn.

Module 11.2 Hunger Motivation
Answer these questions soon after reading the **Module 11.2: Hunger Motivation**. There are several formats to the assessments. Answers to all questions appear on pp. 231-233.

Fill in the Blank
Provide a term(s) which best completes the statement below. Answers appear on p. 231.

1. The excessive accumulation of body fat is known as _____.

2. The hormone _____ increases the flow of glucose and other nutrients into body cells.

3. The most abundant sugar in the blood, and an important source of energy for all parts of the body, including the brain is _____ .

4. A condition in which a person refuses to eat adequate food and steadily loses weight is

   _____ _____.

5. New research examining bulimia nervosa suggests that some of the behaviors are similar to those experiencing _____ _____.

6. The hormone responsible for maintaining long-term body weight is _____.

Short Answer

The following questions require a short written answer (3-7 sentences). Answers appear on p. 231.

1. Discuss factors involved in people's food preferences.

2. Explain how insulin levels are related to hunger.

3. Discuss two reasons for obesity.

4. Explain how anorexia nervosa and bulimia are similar and how they differ.

Multiple Choice

Circle the best answer below. Check your answers on p. 232. If your answer was incorrect, try to write why it was incorrect. Check your reasons on p. 232.

1. Taste preferences in humans:
    a. develop during the 2nd year of life
    b. can be related to abnormal biological functioning
    c. are purely psychological; they are not related to biology
    d. are almost always related to the amount of nutrition in food
    e. are very similar across ethnic groups

2. A person with uncontrolled diabetes has low insulin levels. Which is most likely?
    a. a high percentage of what the person eats will be stored as fats
    b. the person probably has low glucagon levels
    c. the person has damage to the ventromedial hypothalamus
    d. a low percentage of each meal is converted to fats

3. A physician argues that overweight people have high set points and, therefore, cannot lose weight. By this he means that:
    a. their brain mechanisms are maintaining a constant, high weight
    b. they are set in their ways and unlikely to change through diets
    c. they have damage to the lateral hypothalamus
    d. satiety occurs too quickly in overweight people

4. Damage to which structure will result in a rat that loses a lot of weight and then maintains a very low body weight?
    a. ventromedial hypothalamus
    b. lateral hippocampus
    c. lateral hypothalamus
    d. ventromedial hippocampus

5. It has been argued that people become overweight because they eat to overcome emotional problems. Which of the following is true about this argument?
    a. it is true, because people "binge" when they are anxious
    b. it is probably not the reason for their being overweight, because overweight people do not have more emotional problems than normal-weight people
    c. it is probably true, because most overweight people have low self-esteem
    d. it is true, genetics has been linked to the increased anxiety and consequently to obesity

6. In a study, one group of dieters were seated near snacks and told to help themselves while watching a video. Snacks for a second group were placed 10 feet away. The dieters from the first group did not eat any snacks during the video but reported being tempted by the snacks. All of the dieters then rated the taste of ice cream. They were told they could eat as much as they wanted. Results showed that the first group of dieters:
    a. ate the minimum amount of ice cream to perform the taste test
    b. ate <u>more</u> ice cream than the second group of dieters
    c. ate <u>less</u> ice cream than the second group of dieters
    d. ate <u>the same</u> amount of ice cream than the second group of dieters

7. Anorexia nervosa:
    a. results in very low energy levels
    b. is most common in women over 25
    c. is usually accompanied by a pathological fear of fatness
    d. occurs in women with poor self-control
    e. involves frequent episodes of binge eating

True/False
Select the best answer by circling *T for True* or *F for False*. Check your answers on pp. 232-233.

1. **T or F** One estimate suggests that approximately 35% of Americans are obese or overweight.

2. **T or F** The best way to lose weight is to eat less and exercise more.

3. **T or F** One hypothesis regarding what triggers anorexia suggests that normal dieting can trigger a mechanism causing hyperactivity and decreases in eating.

4. **T or F** Bulimics finishing a fasting period are less likely to begin the next meal with desserts or snack foods.

Module 11.3 Sexual Motivation
Answer these questions soon after reading the **Module 11.3: Sexual Motivation**. There are
several formats to the assessments. Answers to all questions appear on pp. 233-234.

Fill in the Blank
Provide a term(s) which best completes the statement below. Answers appear on p. 233.

1. The sex that a person regards him or herself as being regardless of their biological physical
   sex characteristics is their _____ .

2. People with a sexual anatomy that appears intermediate between male and female are known
   as _____.

3. The final physiological stage of sexual arousal is known as _____.

Short Answer
The following questions require a short written answer (3-7 sentences). Answers appear on p.
233.

1. Name and describe Masters and Johnson's four stages of sexual arousal.

2. Discuss evidence that suggests a role for genetics in homosexuality.

3. Discuss the genitalia development of a fetus and the hormones that influence development.

Multiple Choice
Circle the best answer below. Check your answers on pp. 233-234. If your answer was incorrect,
try to write why it was incorrect. Check your reasons on pp. 233-234.

1. How is the sex drive similar to hunger?
   a. both depend on physiological drives and incentives
   b. both drives are easily aroused in the absence of incentives
   c. incentives for both vary greatly, and people understand other people's preferences
   d. Masters and Johnson described four similar stages of arousal for both drives

2. In his pioneering research on sexuality, Kinsey found that:
   a. people agreed pretty much on what was excessive masturbation
   b. number of orgasms for an individual person declines with age
   c. the range of variation in male sexual activity was great; the range of variation in female sexual activity was very limited
   d. most people consider their behavior normal and anything above that to be excessive
   e. about 2.8% of the men reported themselves as being homosexual

3. Vaginal intercourse:
   a. is less likely to result in the transmission of the AIDS virus than anal intercourse
   b. will not lead to transmission of the AIDS virus, even if one partner is infected, so heterosexuals have nothing to fear
   c. has been less affected by the threat of AIDS than by the threat of other venereal diseases
   d. is safe between homosexual males if a condom is worn

4. Homosexuality in men:
   a. may occur because the mother secretes estrogen during pregnancy
   b. means that a man would prefer to be a woman
   c. was taboo in ancient Greek and Roman society
   d. appears to be related to genetics
   e. is caused by a part of the anterior hypothalamus being small

5. Viagra was introduced to help men achieve an erection. Viagra works by
   a. inhibiting the excitement phase
   b. relaxing muscles in penis that allow for blood flow to achieve an erection
   c. causing men to have prolonged resolution phases
   d. none of the above

True/False
Select the best answer by circling *T for True* or *F for False*. Check your answers on p. 234.

1. **T or F** One estimate suggests that approximately 50% of people find having sex with a stranger "very appealing".

2. **T or F** After finding a new sexual partner, women are more likely to maintain their old partner's patterns instead of adopting their new partner's patterns.

3. **T or F** Most people will stay sexually active into their 70s.

Module 11.4 Work Motivation
Answer these questions soon after reading the **Module 11.4: Work Motivation**. There are several formats to the assessments. Answers to all questions appear on pp. 234-235.

Fill in the Blank
Provide a term(s) which best completes the statement below. Answers appear on p. 234.

1. The most effective goals are both _____ and _____.

2. A _____ leader is someone who articulates a vision, is intellectually stimulating, and motivates others.

3. The _____ approach to job design, or Theory Y, proposes that people like to take responsibility for their work, enjoy variety in their job, and feel a sense of accomplishment.

4. Most employees seek a salary that they perceive to be _____ given the type and amount of work they are performing.

Short Answer
The following questions require a short written answer (3-7 sentences). Answers appear on pp. 234-235.

1. Contrast a transformational and transactional leadership styles.

2. Compare and contrast the two approaches to job design and the different assumptions about employees that each approach makes.

3. Identify and describe variables influencing job satisfaction.

Multiple Choice
Circle the best answer below. Check your answers on p. 235. If your answer was incorrect, try to write why it was incorrect. Check your reasons on p. 235.

1. Nicholas has just been hired as the new manager of a five star restaurant. He has found an organization that lacks a plan and operates very inefficiently. Nicholas is well versed in making restaurants more efficient and implements an incentive plan to help workers achieve maximum efficiency. Nicholas' leadership style is likely?
   a. transactional
   b. transformational
   c. transcendental
   d. transmittal

2. Kate has been in her current job for five years and feels that for the work she does that she is significantly underpaid. Based on the research, which of the following behaviors is Kate likely to exhibit?
   a. she will start looking for a new job
   b. she is likely to stop being a "good citizen" on the job
   c. she is less likely to help other workers
   d. all of the above

3. Austin has made a goal to perform better in school during the upcoming semester. Which of the following are likely to help Austin in achieving his goal?
   a. he commits to it in front of his family and friends
   b. he works with his professors to get timely feedback on his progress
   c. he perceives that the reward of doing well (e.g., graduating and getting a good paying position) is worth the effort
   d. all of the above

True/False
Select the best answer by circling *T for True* or *F for False*. Check your answers on p. 235.

1. **T or F** Research examining the effectiveness of deadlines/got found that students who set deadlines/goals had enhanced performance.

2. **T or F** Joe has a GPA of 2.0 over his first 4 semesters. He is setting his goal on earning a 4.0 this semester. Thus, he is likely to achieve his goal.

3. **T or F** Job satisfaction is determined by the amount a person is paid.

4. **T or F** A job that includes a simple task that does not require much responsibility on the part of the employee is likely to have been designed using Theory X of job design.

FINAL COMPREHENSIVE CHAPTER ASSESSMENT TEST

Check your answers on p. 236.

1. Drive reduction theory argues that people and animals act:
   a. in order to find an outlet for excessive libido
   b. because they are pulled by incentives
   c. because they develop specific hungers for particular behaviors
   d. because they have a kind of irritation that energizes behaviors
   e. differently depending upon their level in the hierarchy of needs

2. Ravin is having stomach contractions, there is little food in his intestines, and the amount of glucose and fats in his bloodstream is low. He immediately takes off for the nearest fast-food restaurant and orders two jumbo bacon-cheese burgers. He eats until he can eat no more. At this point, his stomach feels full and some food has reached his intestines. This process of bringing the body into equilibrium is:
   a. an overjustification effect
   b. homeostasis
   c. an incentive system
   d. a breakdown in libido
   e. instinctive energy

3. Which of the following best supports an incentive view of motivation?
   a. a hungry rat runs to the end of a maze to get food
   b. a thirsty child turns on the garden hose to get water
   c. a woman eats a piece of birthday cake although she is not hungry
   d. a bear licks its paw to remove a thorn
   e. a diver surfaces as quickly as is safe when he runs out of air

4. A fifth-grader has just learned how to do some simple programming on his dad's computer. Now, his class at school is learning programming and he gets gold stars for doing well. If the overjustification effect occurs, what is likely to happen this summer when he no longer gets stars for programming?
   a. he will work less hard than before the reward
   b. he will continue at about the same rate as before he was rewarded
   c. he will work harder than before the reward

5. Research on delay of gratification suggests
   a. children are usually successful in delaying gratification
   b. children usually select the immediate reward
   c. adults always select the delayed gradification
   d. none of the above

6. A rat has a much higher than average weight, it seems to be hungry all the time, and most of what it eats is stored as fat. This rat probably has damage to the:
   a. set point
   b. lateral hypothalamus
   c. libido
   d. ventromedial hypothalamus
   e. insulin-producing center

7. Which of the following is least likely to cause a person to be overweight?
   a. high levels of insulin
   b. expending less energy than normal-weight people
   c. damage to the ventromedial hypothalamus
   d. depression

8. Injecting insulin in a person whose levels are normal will result in:
   a. a decrease in appetite
   b. a high percentage of each meal being stored as fat
   c. the body's fat supplies being converted to glucose
   d. a low percentage of each meal being stored as fat
   e. both c and d

9. Fallon and Rozin conducted a study in which men and women indicated the body figure they thought the opposite sex would prefer. They found
   a. women accurately selected the female body figure men preferred
   b. men accurately selected the male body figure women preferred
   c. both a and b
   d. neither a nor b

10. Which of the following is true of anorexia nervosa?
    a. it is more common among Asian cultures than among Western cultures
    b. it is related to sexuality in women, but not in men
    c. there is almost always damage to the lateral hypothalamus
    d. it reflects a pathological fear of fatness
    e. it involves frequent binge eating

11. Which of the following is true about sexual behavior?
    a. Kinsey found that most people had similar sexual behaviors
    b. Kinsey found that homosexual experiences were very rare, particularly in men
    c. a higher percentage of women than men report an interest in various sexual activities
    d. the percentage of people having multiple sex partners increases with age
    e. most people think their sexual behavior is normal; anything in excess of it is excessive

12. In today's society in the United States:
    a. about 15% of the people report a predominantly homosexual orientation
    b. about 80% of the heterosexuals having multiple sexual partners use condoms consistently
    c. people in their 50s and 60s report having sex less often than younger people
    d. the threat of AIDS has not really changed sexual behavior
    e. there are more homosexual women than men

13. What is the order of Masters and Johnson's four stages of sexual arousal?
    a. plateau, excitement, climax, resolution
    b. excitement, plateau, orgasm, resolution
    c. plateau, climax, resolution, excitement
    d. resolution, excitement, orgasm, plateau
    e. excitement, orgasm, plateau, resolution

14. Homosexual men:
    a. developed their homosexuality because they were exposed to estrogen as fetuses
    b. have a mistaken sexual identity
    c. are less common than homosexual women
    d. are more likely to have a homosexual brother if they are identical twins instead of fraternal twins

15. People considered intersexes have
    a. more siblings that are males than females
    b. a sexual anatomy that appear intermediate between male and female
    c. parents that are likely to have been intersexes
    d. none of the above

16. Which person is most likely to have the highest level of job satisfaction?
    a. Al, who is paid well, but is not very good at his job
    b. Alan, who is paid what he considers a fair salary and finds intrinsic value in performing his job
    c. Alice, who, in general, is not very satisfied with anything
    d. Albert, who has only been in his job for three years

17. Joan has been selected as the next president of Pennyfield College. The board selected her because she best fit their desire to have a transformational leader. Which of the following characteristics would Joan least likely have?
    a. a focus on details
    b. an ability to inspire and motivate faculty and staff
    c. a focus on making Penneyfield College more efficient
    d. a plan for improving the fairness of salaries

18. Which person will probably be most successful in getting high grades?
    a. Jane, who has an IQ of 90, but who says she will get all A's
    b. Greta, who will do her best
    c. Maria, who says she will try to pass all her courses
    d. Helen, who had mostly As last semester and who publicly says she will get all A's
    e. Sally, who says she will get all A's, but who never is in class to find out how she is doing

19. The new widget factory is opening soon in your hometown. Making widgets is a very boring since the manufacturing process is simple and straightforward. Potential employees have been screened by the widget factory and most are bright, imaginative and responsible workers. According to Theory X, what will be the likely outcome of hiring mostly bright, imaginative and responsible workers?
    a. the factory will be very successful
    b. the workers are likely to produce new and improved widgets
    c. the workers will likely become bored and unproductive
    d. none of the above

20. Why are older workers more likely to be satisfied with their jobs than younger workers?
    a. older workers have better and higher-paying jobs
    b. younger workers are from a cohort that are harder to please
    c. younger workers start in the wrong job and find a more suitable one later
    d. all of the above

ANSWERS AND EXPLANATIONS FOR CHAPTER MODULE ASSESSMENTS

Answers to the Fill in the Blank Questions – Module 11.1

1. homeostasis (p. 408)

2. incentives (p. 409)

3. drive-reduction (p. 408)

4. intrinsic (pp. 409-410)

Answers to the Short Answer Questions – Module 11.1

1. Motivated behaviors are directed at reaching a goal. However, they vary from time to time, from situation, and from person to person. Most behavior is motivated by more than one thing. (p. 407)

2. Motivation depends upon a drive to reduce needs; e.g., when a person is hungry she seeks food. Homeostasis is the idea that we are motivated to maintain a state of equilibrium, keeping states fairly constant. But motivation also depends on incentives, or external stimuli; e.g., a person may eat snacks because they are there and look good, not because she is hungry. The overjustification effect occurs because people do some things because of intrinsic motivation and adding an external incentive might actually reduce their tendency to do them. (pp. 408-409)

Answers to the Multiple Choice Questions – Module 11.1

1. a, b, d. Incorrect. All consistent with drive theory
   c. Correct! (p. 408)

2. a, b, d. Incorrect. All intrinsically motivated; there is no external reward
   c. Correct! (pp. 409-410)

3. a. Incorrect. There is not anything intrinsically motivating about selecting one option over the other
   b. Incorrect. Chris does not have some internal state that selecting one option over the other would reduce
   c. Correct! (p. 410)
   d. Incorrect. Selecting the second option will not maintain some biological condition at optimal levels

Answers to the True/False Questions – Module 11.1

1. **True**: Incentives prompt the animal to engage in some behavior. (p. 409)

2. **True**: This is the definition of extrinsic motivation. (pp. 409-410)

3. **False**: Homeostasis is the maintenance of equilibrium. (p. 408)

4. **True**: This is the definition of intrinsic motivations. (pp. 409-410)

5. **False**: An overjustification effect results in a decrease in inherent interest not an increase. (pp. 409-410)

Answers to the Fill in the Blank Questions – Module 11.2

1. obesity (p. 417)

2. insulin (p. 413)

3. glucose (p. 413)

4. anorexia nervosa (p. 420)

5. drug addiction (p. 422)

6. leptin (p. 415)

Answers to the Short Answer Questions – Module 11.2

1. Bodily needs can affect taste preferences; e.g., if a person has a salt deficiency, salty foods may be preferred. People generally prefer familiar tastes; they tend to like foods that are flavored in ways that they are used to. Associations can affect food preferences; people will avoid foods that are associated with repulsive things, even though the foods are perfectly nutritious. (pp. 422-425)

2. When insulin levels in the bloodstream are low, glucose does not enter the body's cells and people feel hungry. When insulin levels are moderate, glucose enters the body's cells and people are not very hungry. When insulin levels are high, glucose enters the body's cells but a high percentage of it is converted into fat; people feel hungry. (pp. 413-414, Figs. 11.4-11.5)

3. First, there is some evidence for a genetic component to obesity. One study found that overweight families bought more food overall and more high-fat foods at the supermarket than families with average sized people. A second study found that babies born to overweight mothers were more inactive during their first 3 months and became overweight when compared to infants of normal weight mothers. Similar to the babies mentioned above, overweight people may expend less energy than normal-weight people. People with the lowest energy expenditure were the most likely to gain weight. (p. 417)

4. Anorexics and bulimics both starve themselves, but bulimics also have periods of eating binges after which they may force themselves to vomit. Thus, bulimics alternate between starving and eating binges, but anorexics just starve themselves. Both groups have an exaggerated fear of becoming fat, and both are preoccupied with food. Both disorders are more common in women than in men. (pp. 420-422)

Answers to the Multiple Choice Questions – Module 11.2

1. a. Incorrect. Some preferences are present at birth
    b. Correct! (p. 423)
    c. Incorrect. Abnormal biological conditions can influence preferences, such as a need for salt if the boy excretes salt too quickly
    d. Incorrect. We often reject unfamiliar, nutritious foods
    e. Incorrect. Ethnic groups may differ in their food preferences

2. a. Incorrect. Fats are stored when insulin is high
    b. Incorrect. Has the opposite effect as insulin; not low in both
    c. Incorrect. This would produce high insulin levels
    d. Correct! (p. 413)

3. a. Correct! (pp. 414-415)
    b. Incorrect. May be true, but it isn't what is meant by "set point"
    c. Incorrect. This would result in low body weight, not high
    d. Incorrect. Satiety means feeling full, so this would result in low weight

4. a. Incorrect. Damage to this structure increases insulin, which converts glucose to fat and makes an animal hungry; causes weight gain
    c. Correct! (p. 415)
    b, d. Incorrect. Hippocampus is involved in memory

5. a. Incorrect. People do binge, but this is not the cause of obesity; it usually happens in people who are dieting
    b. Correct! (p. 417)
    c. Incorrect. This is true for a minority of overweight people, but not the majority
    d. Incorrect. Genetics plays a factor in obesity but it results in increased secretion of a protein and not in anxiety

6. a. Incorrect. They ate more than the minimum
    b. Correct! (pp. 419-420)
    c, d. Incorrect. They actually ate more ice cream than the second group "what-the-heck" effect led them to eat more; they had already gone off their diets

7. a. Incorrect. Energy levels tend to be very high
    b. Incorrect. Most common in teenage years and early 20s
    c. Correct! (p. 420)
    d. Incorrect. Anorexic women usually have high self-control
    e. Incorrect. Bulimia; anorexics usually eat little food

Answers to the True/False Questions – Module 11.2

1. **False**: Research suggests that nearly **65%** of Americans are obese or overweight. (p. 417)

2. **True**: Controlling weight is best accomplished by decreasing caloric intake and expending more energy through exercise. (p. 418)

3. **True**: This hypothesis draws parallels between the eating and exercise behavior of elk migrating and anorexics. (p. 421)

4. **False**: Bulimics are <u>more</u> likely to start the next meal with desserts or snacks. (p. 422)

Answers to the Fill in the Blank Questions – Module 11.3

1. gender identity (p. 431)

2. intersexes (pp. 431-432)

3. resolution (p. 430)

Answers to the Short Answer Questions – Module 11.3

1. <u>Excitement</u>: Penis becomes erect, vagina is lubricated, breathing becomes rapid and deep, heart rate, blood pressure increase.
   <u>Plateau</u>: Excitement remains fairly constant.
   <u>Climax or orgasm</u>: Excitement becomes intense followed by relief in the form of orgasm.
   <u>Resolution</u>: Body returns to unaroused state. (p. 430, Fig. 11.15)

2. If one twin is homosexual, then the other twin is more likely to be homosexual if the pair is identical than if the pair is fraternal. Homosexuality has greater concordance among fraternal twins than among adopted brothers. (p. 434, Fig. 11.20)

3. Genitalia development is unisex very early on in the development of the fetus. Around eight weeks of gestation the genitalia start to develop into male or female structures depending on the levels of testosterone. Male fetuses will secrete higher levels of testosterone than females. In the presence of higher testosterone levels the unisex structure will develop into a penis and scrotum. In the presences of lower levels of testosterone the unisex structure will develop into a cliotis and labia. Female fetuses will secrete more estrogen during this time which influences the development of internal female components. (pp. 431-432)

Answers to the Multiple Choice Questions – Module 11.3

1. a. Correct! (p. 426)
   b. Incorrect. For many people, the sex drive is only aroused in the presence of incentives; people get hungry whether or not they see food
   c. Incorrect. Incentives probably vary more for the sex drive; people don't understand others' preferences
   d. Incorrect. They described the stages of sexual arousal

2. a. Incorrect. People varied greatly in what they thought was excessive
   b. Incorrect. Cannot tell; Kinsey's sample was cross-sectional so he interviewed different people at different ages
   c. Incorrect. Females also showed a great deal of variability
   d. Correct! (p. 427)
   e. Incorrect. Kinsey actually reported that 13% were homosexual; a more recent survey found 2.8%

3. a. Correct! (pp. 428-429)
   b. Incorrect. Transmission can occur, although it is less likely than with anal intercourse
   c. Incorrect. AIDS has had more effect on sexual practices because it is life threatening
   d. Incorrect. Only women have vaginas; two males cannot have vaginal intercourse

4. a. Incorrect. Estrogen is secreted, but testosterone is important for male development
    b. Incorrect. This is sexual identity; usually not related to sexual orientation
    c. Incorrect. They considered it typical for men to engage in occasional sexual activities with other men
    d. Correct! (p. 434, Fig. 11.20)
    e. Incorrect. This was smaller in homosexual men, but it may not be the cause; homosexual life-style may cause brain difference

5. a. Incorrect. Viagra does not inhibit the excitement phase
    b. Correct! (p. 430)
    c. Incorrect. Prolonged resolution is not a result of taking Viagra
    d. Incorrect. Facilitates penile blood flow necessary for erection as described in answer b

Answers to the True/False Questions – Module 11.3

1. **False**: Research suggests that significantly less than 10% of people find having sex with a stranger to be "very appealing". (p. 427, Fig. 11.12)

2. **False**: Women are actually more likely than men to adopt her new partner's patterns. (p. 427)

3. **True**: Most people will remain sexually active into their 70s if they are healthy and have a healthy and willing partner. (p. 427)

Answers to the Fill in the Blank Questions – Module 11.4

1. high, attainable (p. 439)

2. transformational (p. 442)

3. human relations (p. 440)

4. fair (p. 441)

Answers to the Short Answer Questions – Module 11.4

1. A leader with a transformational style articulates a vision, is intellectually stimulating and is able to motivate subordinates to move the organization towards that vision. On the other hand, a leader with a transactional style focuses on the organization becoming more efficient at what they are already doing, by paying subordinates to work more effectively. Although there are two different styles, a leader may exhibit both or neither of these styles and still provide effective leadership. (p. 442)

2. In designing jobs one must consider many variables but the most important is recognition of the type of employees. Two theories have been proposed that make different recommendations based on assumptions regarding the type of employee. The scientific-management approach (Theory X) assumes that most employees are lazy, indifferent and uncreative. Thus, jobs should be simple and foolproof leaving little, if anything, up to the employee. Conversely, the human-relations approach (Theory Y) assumes that employees like variety, a sense of accomplishment and a sense of responsibility. Thus, jobs should be enriching and meaningful with responsibility given to the employee. (p. 440)

3. Several variables influence job satisfaction. One such variable is how well a person performs their job. A person that performs their job well usually has higher levels of job satisfaction than someone who does not perform their job well. Genetics may also play a role in that a person with a positive disposition in general will have greater job satisfaction. Age also seems to play a role in that, on average, older workers are more satisfied than younger workers. Finally, being paid a fair wage also contributes to job satisfaction. (p. 441)

Answers to the Multiple Choice Questions – Module 11.4

1. a. Correct! (p. 442)
   b. Incorrect. A transformational leader focuses on a vision and motivating employees to achieve that vision
   c. Incorrect. Not discussed in this chapter
   d. Incorrect. Not discussed in this chapter

2. a. True, she will likely start looking for a new job, but b and c are also true
   b. True, she will likely not do those little extra things for which she is not compensated, but a and c are also true
   c. True, she will likely not be as collegial as she once was, but a and b are also true
   d. Correct! (p. 441)

3. a. True, public commitment does increase the likelihood of achieving a goal, but b and c are also true
   b. True, receiving timely feedback also increases the likelihood of achieving a goal, but a and c are also correct
   c. True, having a perception that the goal is worth the work increases the likelihood of achieving the goal, but a and b are also correct
   d. Correct! (pp. 438-439)

Answers to the True/False Questions – Module 11.4

1. **True**: Students who set deadlines performed better than those who did not set deadlines. (pp. 438-439)

2. **False**: Joe is unlikely to earn a 4.0 since this goal is not reasonable attainable given his past performance. (p. 439)

3. **False**: Pay is one of the variables that influence job satisfaction, but other more intrinsic reasons also influence job satisfaction. (p. 441)

4. **True**: Theory X, or the scientific-management approach, suggests designing jobs that are simple and does not place much responsibility in the employee. (p. 440)

Answers to Final Comprehensive Assessment

1. d (p. 408)
2. b (p. 408)
3. c (p. 409)
4. a (pp. 409-410)
5. b (p. 410)
6. d (p. 415)
7. d (p. 417)
8. b (p. 414)
9. d (p. 419, Fig. 11.10)
10. d (p. 420)
11. e (p. 427)
12. c (pp. 427-428)
13. b (p. 430)
14. d (p. 434)
15. b (pp. 431-432)
16. b (p. 441)
17. b (p. 442)
18. d (p. 439)
19. c (p. 440)
20. d (p. 441)

CHAPTER 12

EMOTIONS, STRESS, AND HEALTH

CHAPTER OVERVIEW INFORMATION

LEARNING OBJECTIVES

By the end of Chapter 12 you should

- ✓ Increase your understanding of the influence and theories of emotions
- ✓ Understand the origin and nature of sadness, anger, violence, happiness, fear and anxiety
- ✓ Understand cognitive, experiential and behavioral influences on health and illness
- ✓ Further understand cognitive and behavioral strategies for coping with stress

CHAPTER 12 OUTLINE

STRESS!!! How many times during a semester do you feel "stressed out"? How do you cope with the stress you experience? Stress, and strategies to cope with it, are discussed in Chapter 12. Chapter 12 also explores other types of emotions including happiness, joy, sadness, fear, anxiety, anger and aggressiveness. You have probably experienced all of these. Chapter 12 presents interesting research on each of these emotions.

Chapter 12 is presented below in outline format to assist you in understanding the information presented in the chapter. More detailed information on any topic can be found using the page references to the right of the topic.

Module 12.1 The Nature of Emotions
I.   Emotions are difficult to define or distinguish from motivations (p. 449)
   A. Most definitions include the dimensions of physiology, cognition, phenomenology, and actions (p. 449)

II. Measuring Emotion
   A. Self Reports
      1. Self reported emotions are quick and easy, but not necessarily reliable (p. 449)
   B. Behavioral Observations
      1. Infer emotion from behavior(s) especially involuntary expressions of emotions called micro expressions (p. 449)
   C. Physiological Measures
      1. Emotion is related to physiological arousal (p. 449)
         a. Autonomic nervous system is involved in emotion (pp. 449-450, Fig. 12.1)
            i.   Sympathetic nervous system increases arousal (p. 450, Figs. 12.1, 12.4)
            ii. Parasympathetic nervous system decreases arousal (pp. 450-451, Fig. 12.1)
         b. Several parts of the brain are active during different emotions (p. 451, Fig. 12.2)

III. Emotion, Arousal, and Actions
   A. The postulated relationship between physiological arousal and experiencing the emotion differs for different theories (p. 452)

B. The James-Lange Theory of Emotions
   1. James-Lange theory proposes that sympathetic arousal is necessary to feel an emotion (p. 452)
      a. People with decreased arousal levels report less intense emotions (p. 452)
      b. People made to experience the physical effects (e.g., postural and facial) of an emotion showed signs of experiencing that emotion (pp. 452-453, Fig. 12.3)
C. Schachter and Singer's Theory of Emotions
   1. We probably cannot determine our emotional state by differences in physiological states (pp. 453-454)
   2. Schachter and Singer proposed that emotion is the label given to arousal and that people will report strong emotions appropriate for the situation (p. 454, Figs. 12.4-12.5)
      a. A problem with their experiment is that people given placebo injections also felt emotion (p. 454, Fig. 12.5)

IV. The Range of Emotions
A. Many basic emotions have been proposed and vary across cultures (p. 455)
   1. Basic emotions should emerge early in life, be similar across cultures, and have its own biological basis and facial expression (pp. 455-456)
B. Producing Facial Expressions
   1. Facial expressions can communicate emotional states (p. 456, Fig. 12.6)
   2. Different facial patterns occur for involuntary and voluntary smiles (p. 456, Fig. 12.7a-b)
C. Understanding Facial Expressions
   1. Some facial expressions are innate and almost universal (pp. 457-458, Figs. 12.8-12.11)
   2. Some problems with methodology and photo stimuli (p. 458, Fig 12.12)
D. Do Facial Expressions Indicate Basic Emotions?
   1. Facial expressions do not always indicate a basic emotion (pp. 459-460, Figs. 12.12-12.15)

V. Emotions and Moral Decisions
A. Making a decision following emotions will usually lead to moral decision (pp. 460-461, Fig. 12.16)

VI. Decisions by People with Impaired Emotions
A. Physical damage to the brain can impair emotions which leads to poor decisions (p. 461, Fig. 12.17)

VII. Emotional Intelligence
A. We use our knowledge about emotions in making decisions (p. 462)
B. Difficult and challenging to independently measure like academic intelligence (pp. 462-463)

The message: *Measuring all four components of emotions requires multiple research efforts. (p. 463)*

Module 12.2 A Survey of Emotions

VIII. Happiness, Joy, and Positive Psychology
- A. The relatively new field of Positive psychology explores ways of enriching life (p. 465)
    1. People perform a self-evaluation regarding their life as pleasant, interesting and satisfying (p. 465)
- B. Influence of Wealth
    1. Wealth plays some role in a person's perceived happiness but it is not clear how much of a role and it varies across cultures (p. 465, Fig. 12.18)
    2. Measuring some index of both wealth and happiness may not produce reliable data (pp. 465-466)
    3. People receiving a windfall of money report higher levels of happiness initially but over time their happiness rating becomes "normal" (p. 465)
- C. Other Influences
    1. Happiness is influenced by temperament or personality, marital status, goals in life, health, religion, how trustworthy one perceives others, emotion stability, and control (p. 467)

IX. Sadness
- A. Usually results from a sense of loss (p. 467)
- B. Crying
    1. Acceptability varies across cultures; women cry more than men; increases sympathetic nervous system arousal, and seems to serve no purpose (p. 467)
- C. "Depressive Realism"
    1. Sadness can facilitate viewing circumstances more realistically and making better decisions resulting from lower self-confidence (p. 468)

X. Fear and Anxiety
- A. Similar to each other, but fear is in response to immediate danger and anxiety results from long lasting sense of something bad will happen (p. 468)
- B. Measuring Anxiety
    1. Measured by measuring any changes in the startle reflex (p. 468)
    2. Changes can be a result of learning and are controlled by the amygdala (p. 468, Fig. 12.19)
    3. People with damage to amygdala still feel fear but exhibit less startle to stimuli (p. 468)
- C. Anxiety, Arousal, and Lie Detection
    1. Not very accurate in detecting lies without polygraph (p. 469)
        a. Polygraph measures sympathetic arousal (p. 469, Fig 12.20)
            i. Polygraph administrators can identify lying more accurately than most people, but they also identify innocent people as lying. (pp. 469-470, Fig. 12.21)
            ii. Not perfect so results are not admissible in court, not used for national security clearance, nor used by private employers in the hiring process (p. 470)
- D. Alternative Methods of Detecting Lies
    1. Measure blood flow to the face which increases when lying (p. 470, Fig 12.22)
    2. Guilty-knowledge test reduces number of innocent people identified as lying (pp. 470-471)
    3. Observing behaviors of people lying one sees a calm and happy expression but also some micro expressions of fear (p. 471)

XI. Anger and Aggressive Behavior
   A. Understanding anger and violence is important for humanity (p. 471)
   B. Relationship of Anger to Aggression
      1. Anger usually does not lead to physical aggression (pp. 471-472)
   C. Causes of Anger
      1. The frustration-aggression hypothesis proposes that anger is displayed when an individual is frustrated (p. 472)
      2. All unpleasant events may lead to the impulse to fight or flee (p. 472)
   D. Individual Differences in Anger and Aggression
      1. Violence not related to low self-esteem, but rather a result of threatening of a person's high self-esteem (p. 472)
      2. Genetics, physical abuse as a child, witnessing physical abuse, neighborhood violence, lack of guilty feeling, smaller pre-frontal cortex, weaker response to arousal, cigarette smoking of mother during pregnancy, and previous violent behaviors all are correlated with the tendency toward violence (p. 472, Fig. 12.23)
   E. Sexual Aggression and Violence in Relationships
      1. Both men and women can be violent in relationship. Women more violent (but less severe violence) than men (p. 473)
      2. Rape is sexual contact without consent. It may be obtained through violence, threat, intimidation, or as a result of the influence of drugs/alcohol (p. 473)
         a. Generally unreported especially by women raped by a person she knew (p. 474)
         b. Rapists are self-centered and have a history of hostility and violence against both men and women (p. 474)
   F. Controlling Anger and Violence
      1. Methods available to help people control displays of anger (p. 475)

XII. Other Emotions
   A. Include surprise, anger, disgust, contempt, (reactions to different offenses); embarrassment, shame, guilt, and pride ("self-conscious" emotions) (p. 475)

The message: *We experience many types of emotions both positive and negative which add to the richness of our lives. (p. 476)*

Module 12.3 Stress, Coping, and Health
XIII. Stress
   A. Health psychology is concerned with how behaviors influence health and wellness (p. 476)
   B. Stress results from a variety of experiences (p. 476)
   C. Selye's Concept of Stress
      1. Selye's concept of stress is that it is the response of the body to demands. (p. 476)
         a. Responses to stress are alarm, resistance, and exhaustion. (p. 477)
            i. Persistent stress can lead to weakness, fatigue, loss of appetite and generalized lack of interest (p. 477)
   D. Post-Traumatic Stress Disorder
      1. Posttraumatic stress disorder results from extreme stress (p. 477)
         a. Talking about event immediately does not affect development of PTSD (p. 477)
   E. Measuring Stress
      1. We must be able to measure stress to look at its effects on health (p. 478)
         a. Social Readjustment Rating Scale is one measure of stressful events (p. 478)
            i. This scale is subject to many criticisms (p. 478)
      2. Stress depends upon how events are interpreted (p. 478, Fig. 12.24 and Table 12.1)

XIV. Coping with Stress
    A. Monitoring strategies involve attending to a stressful event and trying to take effective action whereas blunting strategies help manage our reaction to stress (p. 479)
    B. Problem-based (Monitoring) Strategies
        1. Predictability and control reduce stress (p. 480)
            a. We assume that things will not get worse (p. 480)
            b. We can prepare for predictable events (p. 480)
        2. Inoculation involves practice coping with a small-scale or simulated stressful experience (pp. 480-481)
    C. Emotion-based (Blunting) Strategies
        1. Reinterpretation of a situation to view it more positively can reduce stress (p. 481)
        2. Relaxation can reduce stress (p. 481)
        3. Exercise can reduce stress (pp. 481-482)
        4. Distraction can help to reduce pain (p. 482)

XV. Stress and Illness
    A. Psychosomatic illnesses are related to stress (p. 482)
    B. Heart Disease
        1. Heart disease is related to a Type A personality type (pp. 482-483, Fig. 12.25)
    C. Cancer
        1. Stress may influence the immune system and be weakly related to cancer (p. 484)
        2. Social support strengthens immune system and improves survival time (p. 484)

The message: *Although we experience stressors throughout our life we usually find some way to cope with the stress we experience. (p. 484)*

RELATED WEBSITES AND ACTIVITIES

Visit http://psychology.wadsworth.com/kalat_intro7e/ for online quizzing, glossary flashcards, crossword puzzles, annotated web links, and more.

LECTURE MATERIAL

Information from the text is only half of the picture. Don't forget to review your lecture material. Process each topic meaningfully. Most importantly, be sure that you understand the material in each lecture-if you don't, ask your instructor or teaching assistant.

STUDY TIP # 12: Determine if your exam will mainly consist of objective questions (e.g., True/False, Matching, Multiple Choice, Fill in the Blank, etc.) or conceptual questions (e.g., short answer or essay). For objective questions you will want to focus on details instead in the information. For conceptual questions you will want a more general focus on topics and issues.

TIP: Associate the lecture material with the information from the text, with things that you already know, with your personal experiences, or with real-life applications. Type or neatly re-write your notes. Make sure they are detailed and organized. Make comments on your notes. Then write questions to cover each concept.

CHAPTER MODULE ASSESSMENTS

Module 12.1 The Nature of Emotions
Answer these questions soon after reading the **Module 12.1: The Nature of Emotions**. There are several formats to the assessments. Answers to all questions appear on pp. 253-254.

Fill in the Blank
Provide a term(s) which best completes the statement below. Answers appear on p. 253.

1. _____ is the ability to perceive, imagine, and understand emotions and to use that information effectively in decision making.

2. According to the _____ theory, emotion is the perception of a change in the body's physiological state.

3. The _____ nervous system consists of the sympathetic and parasympathetic nervous systems.

4. _____ are very brief and involuntary facial expressions of different emotions.

Short Answer
The following questions require a short written answer (3-7 sentences). Answers appear on p. 253.

1. Describe the research that suggests how emotions might be related to decision making.

2. Schachter and Singer's experiment on cognitive factors in emotion is frequently cited, but what problem is there in the interpretation of that experiment?

3. Describe what happened in the study in which subjects were made to frown smile by holding pens in their lips.

4. What has been found when facial expressions are studied in different cultures?

5. Describe the methods used to measure emotions.

Multiple Choice
Circle the best answer below. Check your answers on pp. 253-254. If your answer was incorrect, try to write why it was incorrect. Check your reasons on pp. 253-254.

1. In a study in which young heterosexual men rated the attractiveness of Sports Illustrated swimsuit models, researchers found that the highest ratings were given
   a. for only the first two models, after which their ratings were lower
   b. when they thought their heartbeat was accelerating
   c. if men rated them in the morning as compared to rating them in the afternoon
   d. if the men were placed undo stress

2. When hiking, you suddenly notice a rattlesnake preparing to embed his fangs into you. You promptly beat all known records for the 40-yard dash to get away. According to the James-Lange theory, you:
   a. are afraid because you perceive your heart pounding and you are running away
   b. run away because you are afraid
   c. decide that you are afraid at the same time as your body reacts to the fear
   d. have probably been classically conditioned to fear rattlesnakes

3. Research examining the role of the brain in emotions found
   a. a different and distinct part of the brain becomes active for each emotion
   b. any given emotion will elicit brain activity in several brain areas which may also be active for other emotions
   c. the prefrontal cortex is inactive for all emotions
   d. left hemispheric activity is greater for "happy" emotions and right hemisphere is more active for "sad" emotions

4. How does Schachter and Singer's theory of emotions differ from the James-Lange view?
   a. body states are not relevant in the Schachter-Singer theory
   b. body states and the perception of emotion are independent in the Schachter-Singer view
   c. a given body state always leads to the same emotion in the Schachter Singer theory
   d. a given body state may lead to different emotions depending upon interpretation in the Schachter-Singer theory
   e. Schachter and Singer argue that facial expressions can induce emotions; James-Lange theory says they cannot

5. In different cultures, gestures and facial expressions:
   a. are similar enough that many can be identified cross-culturally
   b. are used in exactly the same situations
   c. are very different; most of the expressions in some cultures are unknown in other cultures
   d. are the same but their interpretation is very different

True/False
Select the best answer by circling *T for True* or *F for False*. Check your answers on p. 254.

1. **T or F** Primates, including humans, use facial expressions to communicate emotional states.

2. **T or F** It is very difficult to distinguish between an involuntary and a voluntary smile because both use all of the same muscles around the mouth and eyes.

3. **T or F** Facial expressions are used by almost everyone even those people who have never directly seen or heard them because the people are deaf and blind.

4. **T or F** Using emotional reactions is usually reliable to guide in making moral decisions.

Module 12.2 A Survey of Emotions
Answer these questions soon after reading the **Module 12.2: A Survey of Emotions**. There are several formats to the assessments. Answers to all questions appear on pp. 254-256.

Fill in the Blank
Provide a term(s) which best completes the statement below. Answers appear on pp. 254-255.

1. The part of the brain that is believed to control emotions such as fear and anxiety is the
   _____.

2. The _____ is a modified version of the polygraph test that produces more accurate results.

3. _____ is the study of the features that enrich life, such as hope, creativity, courage, spirituality, and responsibility.

4. _____ is sexual contact obtained through violence and threats.

5. The _____ hypothesis suggests that frustration - a failure to obtain something that one expected - leads to aggressive behavior.

Short Answer
The following questions require a short written answer (3-7 sentences). Answers appear on p. 255.

1. Why is happiness difficult to measure in a behavioral way? What problems does this cause for the study of happiness?

2. Describe the original frustration-aggression hypothesis and Berkowitz's modification of it.

3. Describe factors that are related to the accuracy of prediction of violent behavior.

4. Describe what the role of wealth is in happiness.

5. Explain how a lie-detector test is supposed to work and describe a better way to arrange the test.

Multiple Choice

Circle the best answer below. Check your answers on pp. 255-256. If your answer was incorrect, try to write why it was incorrect. Check your reasons on pp. 255-256.

1. The polygraph test:
   a. measures only the electrical conduction of the skin
   b. is close to 90% accurate in detecting lies
   c. is most accurate when the guilty-knowledge test is used
   d. is no more accurate than a person trying to detect lying
   e. is a measure of parasympathetic nervous system activity

2. Which of the following is most consistent with the frustration-aggression hypothesis?
   a. a person who is insulted sometimes attacks the person who insulted him; but at other times, he leaves the room
   b. a foul odor makes someone run from a room
   c. a man who is locked out of his house kicks a passing dog
   d. a rat that can avoid shocks does not attack another rat even though it is frequently shocked

3. Violent behavior:
   a. can be accurately predicted with interviews
   b. can be prevented by severe punishment during childhood
   c. is likely to occur in people who have stronger than normal physiological responses to arousal
   d. is unrelated to the amount of violence watched on television
   e. is associated with not feeling guilty after hurting someone

4. Which of the following is true regarding violence in a relationship?
   a. men commit more violent acts than women do
   b. women commit more violent acts than men do
   c. men and women commit an equal number of violent acts in a relationship

5. A rapist is likely to use which of the following in order to rape a woman
    a. violence
    b. threat
    c. intimidation
    d. any or all of the above

True/False
Select the best answer by circling *T for True* or *F for False*. Check your answers on p. 256.

1. **T or F** Rape is almost always reported to the authorities.

2. **T or F** Violent people are more likely to also have low self-esteem.

3. **T or F** For most people, becoming angry does not lead to physical aggression.

4. **T or F** A seemingly reliable alternative to a polygraph to determine if someone is lying, is to examine blood flow to the person's face.

5. **T or F** A person with damage to their amygdala is likely to experience an increase in the startle reflex.

Module 12.3 Stress, Coping, and Health
Answer these questions soon after reading the **Module 12.3: Stress, Coping, and Health**.
There are several formats to the assessments. Answers to all questions appear on pp. 256-258.

Fill in the Blank
Provide a term(s) which best completes the statement below. Answers appear on p. 256.

1. _____ is the nonspecific response of the body to any demand made upon it.

2. The _____ personality includes behavior such as hostility and impatience and has been linked to an increased risk of heart disease.

3. Monitoring and blunting are two major categories of _____ , which are people's strategies for dealing with stress.

4. People who have endured extreme stress and feel prolonged anxiety and depression may be diagnosed with _____ .

5. According to _____ the body goes through three specific stages in its response to stress.

6. _____ is concerned with how an individual's behavior can enhance health and prevent illness and how behavior contributes to recovery from illness.

Short Answer

The following questions require a short written answer (3-7 sentences). Answers appear on p. 257.

1. Describe the effects of prolonged stress on the body.

2. Explain some of the problems that are associated with the conclusion that the Social Readjustment Rating Scale predicts illness.

3. Explain how cancer might be considered a psychosomatic illness.

4. Describe how predictability and control can help in coping with stress.

5. How can exercise help to reduce stress?

Multiple Choice

Circle the best answer below. Check your answers on pp. 257-258. If your answer was incorrect, try to write why it was incorrect. Check your reasons on pp. 257-258.

1. According to Selye, what are the stages that the body goes through in response to stress?
   a. resistance, alarm, general adaptation syndrome
   b. exhaustion, alarm, resistance
   c. general adaptation syndrome, resistance, alarm
   d. alarm, resistance, exhaustion

2. PTSD:
   a. is a fairly new disorder seen only since the Vietnam War
   b. occurs only in cases involving tough combat
   c. develops anytime someone experiences severe stress
   d. may involve nightmares, constant unhappiness, anger, and guilt

3. The Social Readjustment Rating Scale:
   a. measures the number of unpleasant events in a person's life
   b. measures the stressful events that cause illness
   c. is related to the likelihood of illness
   d. is a very accurate way to measure stress

4. Psychosomatic illnesses:
   a. are imagined illnesses
   b. are illnesses such as heart disease that are related to stress
   c. occur because emotions lead directly to illness
   d. are not caused by genes and toxic substances

5. What does the most recent evidence say about people with Type A personalities?
   a. they are more likely to get cancer than Type B people
   b. when they are also hostile there is a link with heart disease
   c. they usually live in cultures where time is not very important
   d. they usually experience less stress

6. Which of the following would be effective in dealing with a stressful situation, such as a loss of a job?
   a. keep the person distracted by constantly thinking about working
   b. convince the person that others were really at fault
   c. have the person join a support group whose members have all lost jobs
   d. make the person understand that he really had no control over the situation
   e. have the person think about other people who are better off

7. Which of the following is not true about predictability? It:
   a. can make it easier to cope because we can prepare for it at the right time
   b. may not be helpful if you cannot do anything about the event
   c. may make an event less stressful if we also perceive that we have control
   d. helps coping only if people actually exert control over the event

True/False
Select the best answer by circling *T for True* or *F for False*. Check your answers on p. 258.

1. **T or F** The field of Health Psychology is concerned with how people's behavior is related to physical well-being.

2. **T or F** The coping method of exposing oneself to a small amount of stress before a greater stress situation is known inoculation.

3. **T or F** A person who is always on the go, doing many things at once, trying to win at everything is likely to have a Type B personality.

4. **T or F** People perceive events as less stressful if they think they have no control over them.

5. **T or F** Distraction can be an effective method to reduce stress.

Check your answers on p. 258.

1. Your sympathetic nervous system has just been activated. What are you most likely to do?
   a. fall asleep
   b. breathe harder and perspire
   c. slow your breathing and heart rate
   d. increase your salivation and digestion rate
   e. feel sorry for something in your environment

2. Researchers examine John's brain while he has a happy experience and a sad experience. Which of the following patterns of brain activity would be observed?
   a. separate and independent patterns of activity would be observed for the two emotions
   b. the patterns of activity would be exactly the same
   c. there would be separate, but somewhat overlapping patterns of activity
   d. no activity would be observed

3. Which question is a polygraph examiner likely to ask in a guilty-knowledge test?
   a. Have you ever stolen anything?
   b. Did you steal the money from the grocery store on March 21?
   c. Did you rob the gas station as well as the grocery store?
   d. How much money was taken from the store? $50? $100? $200? $1,000?
   e. Are you lying?

4. Godzilla, Frankenstein, a werewolf, King Kong, the creature from the black lagoon, and Dracula all enter your room. How does the James-Lange theory relate your emotions to your behavior?
   a. you perceive the stimuli, are afraid, run away, and then respond physiologically
   b. you feel afraid, and this causes increased sympathetic arousal, which will produce a running response
   c. the stimuli provoke a specific sympathetic nervous system response that you label as "fear"
   d. you aren't really afraid, because epinephrine would be secreted and it produces "cold" emotions
   e. your thalamus simultaneously activates your sympathetic nervous system and sends a message to your cortex that indicates fear

5. Which of the following results from Schachter and Singer's experiment are inconsistent with their theory about cognitive interpretation of emotion?
   a. the groups that were informed about the drug's effects showed little emotion
   b. participants who were not informed about the drug's effects showed euphoria in that condition and anger in the "angry" condition
   c. the same physiological state was interpreted differently by different participants
   d. participants who got a placebo showed almost as much emotion as participants who got epinephrine

6. Forcing people to make facial expressions by having them move specific facial muscles or holding pencils in their mouths:
   a. does not result in any change in emotions, because there is no sympathetic nervous system arousal
   b. tends to make people feel happier or sadder
   c. makes people sadder, but has no effect on behavior, such as the ratings of cartoons
   d. has some behavioral results, but they are almost entirely due to demand characteristics

7. Across cultures, facial expressions and gestures:
   a. are similar, but people from one culture cannot interpret expressions from another culture
   b. are the same, because they are entirely controlled by genetics
   c. are similar in westernized cultures, but totally different in non-Western cultures, such as Japan
   d. can be identified with perfect accuracy
   e. are similar, but the frequencies with which they are used differ

8. Happiness differs from anger in that:
   a. people who say they are happy all mean about the same thing; people who say they are angry may mean different things
   b. happiness involves sympathetic nervous system arousal; anger does not
   c. anger has more observable behaviors associated with it than happiness
   d. when people become happy, it does not always lead to observable behavior; when people become angry it usually leads to observable physical attacks

9. How are anger and aggression related?
   a. people become aggressive far more often than they become angry
   b. when people became angry at family and friends, they usually also display aggression toward them
   c. aggression is more context specific, in that the same level of anger will not always trigger aggression
   d. anger is related to how much violence one watches on television, but actual aggression is not

10. Berkowitz proposed a theory of aggression that is more comprehensive than frustration-aggression theory. Which of the following best describes his theory?
    a. all aggression is caused by frustration, which occurs when a motivated behavior is disrupted
    b. unpleasant stimuli that lead to aggression do so automatically
    c. both frustration and biological factors are important in aggression
    d. all unpleasant events give rise to the impulse to fight or flee; circumstances determine which will happen
    e. aggression will only occur when something goes wrong and there is no one to blame

11. According to Selye's theory of stress, a person who has had many long-lasting stressful events during the past few months is likely to:
    a. be in the resistance stage
    b. develop weakness, fatigue, and a general lack of interest
    c. be in the alarm stage
    d. be less susceptible to disease than someone not so stressed

12. Who is likely to have the highest score on the Social Readjustment Rating Scale?
    a. Oblivia, who just took out a mortgage of $50,000
    b. Dr. Quaalude, who just got married
    c. Erasmus, who just got married and who changed his job
    d. Perplexity, who just graduated from college

13. Which of the following conclusions from the Social Readjustment Rating Scale is most appropriate?
    a. high stress scores cause illness
    b. day-to-day problems are more related to illness than major crises are
    c. there is a relationship between high stress scores and illness
    d. people of different ages and circumstances respond in a similar manner to the stressful events on the scale
    e. events that people worry about but that do not happen produce the highest scores on the scale

14. People with Type A personality:
    a. are more likely to live in countries in which time is not important and the pace is relaxed than in more time-conscious countries such as the United States
    b. show less increase in heart rate and blood pressure in competitive situations than people with Type B personality
    c. vary in how they handle work assignments, but not in how they behave in leisure activities, such as fishing
    d. develop heart disease because they avoid competitive tasks
    e. often are driven and impatient and have too many things going on simultaneously

15. Which is true about the relationship between emotional states and cancer?
    a. emotional factors are more important in cancer than genes and exposure to toxic substances
    b. severe depression may play a role in cancer by suppressing the immune system
    c. studies consistently show that stress in humans increases the spread of cancer
    d. cancer is most related to anger, rather than to impatience and competitiveness as originally thought
    e. stress influences the onset of cancer more than the course of the cancer following the onset

16. Which is the least likely explanation for why prediction and control can help in coping with stress?
    a. prediction allows an animal or human to prepare for the event
    b. control helps people, but only if they actually exert control, such as turning off an annoying noise
    c. a predictable and controllable event probably will not get any worse; an unpredictable event might
    d. if an event is predictable or controllable, a human or animal does not need to be in a constant state of preparation
    e. if an event is controllable, a human or animal can work harder to control it if it does get worse

17. A person who fears dental work is given a series of mild shocks to the teeth before going to the dentist to help her in coping with the stress associated with dental work. The technique being used here is:
    a. social support
    b. distraction
    c. inoculation
    d. control
    e. exercise

18. A man who has a stroke partially as a result of living a stressful life begins to take time "to smell the roses". He is coping by:
    a. monitoring
    b. distraction
    c. inoculation
    d. relaxation
    e. social support

19. Which of the following is not true about crying?
    a. the acceptability varies across cultures
    b. women tend to cry more than men
    c. it increases sympathetic nervous system activity
    d. it makes a person feel better

20. Alex is sad and experiencing a "depressive realism". Which of the following is she most likely to experience?
    a. her decisions will be more realistic
    b. her decisions will be less realistic
    c. she will be unable to make any decisions
    d. she will likely defer making a decision until she is no longer sad

Answers to the Fill in the Blank Questions – Module 12.1

1. Emotional intelligence (p. 462)

2. James-Lange (p. 452)

3. autonomic (pp. 450-451)

4. Micro expressions (p. 449)

Answers to the Short Answer Questions – Module 12.1

1. Damage to the prefrontal cortex seems to result in a loss of emotion. In addition, people who have such damage have trouble making decisions and following plans. One hypothesis is that problems with decision-making occur because of the inability to experience emotions. The patients can not follow through and imagine how they would feel if they made one decision or another, or how they would feel after carrying out a plan. (p. 461)

2. Participants who were given placebo injections showed about as much emotion as subjects who were given epinephrine. Therefore, an appropriate conclusion may be that people in a euphoria situation act happy and people in an anger situation act angry. (p. 454)

3. Participants who were made to smile by holding a pen between their teeth rated cartoons as funnier than subjects who were make to frown by holding a pencil in their lips. (pp. 452-453)

4. Facial expressions are pretty much the same, although their frequency and the situations in which they are used differ somewhat. People from one culture are fairly accurate in their interpretations of other cultures' expressions. (pp. 457-458)

5. Emotions are difficult to measure because they cannot be directly observed rather they must be inferred from other observable behaviors. For example, self-report of what people are thinking and feeling, observations of behavior, and most notably measurement of physiological responses are all used to infer emotions. (pp. 449-451)

Answers to the Multiple Choice Questions – Module 12.1

1.
   a. Incorrect. Order of the models was not unimportant
   b. Correct! (pp. 454-455)
   c. Incorrect. Time of day was not tested
   d. Incorrect. Stress was not tested

2. a. Correct! (p. 452)
   b. Incorrect. Commonsense view; James-Lange is opposite
   c. Incorrect. This would be consistent with another theory of emotion
   d. Incorrect. May be true, but irrelevant to James-Lange

3. a. Incorrect. There is not just one area of the brain exclusively responsible for an emotion
   b. Correct! (p. 451, Fig. 12.2)
   c. Incorrect. It is likely active for most emotions
   d. Incorrect. No research looking at hemispheric specialization was cited in the text

4. a. Incorrect. Body states are necessary for an emotion
   b. Incorrect. Perception does depend upon body state
   c. Incorrect. Different emotions can come from same body state, depending upon interpretation
   d. Correct! (pp. 453-454)
   e. Incorrect. Both theories would agree that expressions might be related to body states, but these theories are aimed at physiological arousal

5. a. Correct! (pp. 457-458)
   b. Incorrect. Similar expressions are used, but they may be used in somewhat different circumstances
   c. Incorrect. Many of the expressions are very similar
   d. Incorrect. People of different cultures can interpret each other's expressions fairly accurately

Answers to the True/False Questions – Module 12.1

1. **True**: Primates rely on using facial expressions to communicate emotions with each other. (p. 456)

2. **False**: An involuntary smile includes muscles activity around the mouth and eyes. Most voluntary smiles only use the mouth muscles. (p. 456)

3. **True**: Experience does play a role in the facial expression we use to express emotion. However, people never having experienced those expressions still use appropriate facial expressions to express certain emotions. (p. 457)

4. **True**: Emotions seem to be relatively reliable in deciding whether some decision is right or wrong. (pp. 460-461)

Answers to the Fill in the Blank Questions – Module 12.2

1. amygdala (p. 468)

2. guilty knowledge (pp. 470-471)

3. Positive psychology (p. 465)

4. Rape (p. 473)

5. frustration-aggression (p. 472)

Answers to the Short Answer Questions – Module 12.2

1. Although anger is often linked to specific behaviors, happiness is not linked to specific behaviors. This means that the only way to measure happiness is to ask people if they are happy. People have different criteria for happiness, and so one person's low rating may actually mean the same level of happiness as another person's higher rating. (pp. 465-466)

2. Whenever individuals experience frustration (because something prevents them from reaching some goal), they respond with aggression. Berkowitz modified this by saying that all unpleasant events lead to the impulse to fight or flee. Whether one fights or flees depends upon the circumstances. (p. 472)

3. Predictions based on specific biographical information, such as physical abuse during childhood, history of committing violent acts, genetics, witnessing physical abuse, neighborhood violence, lack of a feeling of guilt after doing something bad, smaller pre-frontal cortex, weaker response to arousal, cigarette smoking of mother during pregnancy seem to play a role in predicting violent behavior. (p. 472)

4. Many people suggest being wealthy would make them happier however the amount depends on current income. Obviously having enough money plays a role in a person's perceived happiness but it is not clear how much of a role. Moreover, the degree to which it plays a role varies across cultures. Measuring some index of both wealth and happiness is not easy to do and results in unreliable data to interpret. One interesting finding is that people winning the lottery initially report higher levels of happiness but over time their happiness rating becomes average (p. 465, Fig. 12.18)

5. When a person is nervous, the sympathetic nervous system increases breathing rate, heart rate, and sweating. The polygraph measures these variables, which should be higher when a person is lying than when telling the truth. However, polygraph tests result in a number of errors in which innocent people are called guilty. (37% in one study). The "guilty-knowledge" test helps to eliminate these. It asks about specific facts that only the guilty party would know, so an innocent person would not be judged guilty. (pp. 469-470)

Answers to the Multiple Choice Questions – Module 12.2

1.
   a. Incorrect. Measures heart rate and breathing rate also
   b. Incorrect. Will accurately detect lying about 75% of the time, but will also "detect" innocent people
   c. Correct! (pp. 470-471)
   d. Incorrect. It is more accurate than people
   e. Incorrect. It measures sympathetic activity

2.
   a. Incorrect. Consistent with Berkowitz' theory that unpleasant events lead to either fighting or fleeing
   b. Incorrect. An unpleasant event but no evidence of frustration
   c. Correct! (p. 472)
   d. Incorrect. Even unpleasant stimuli do not always lead to aggression

3. a. Incorrect. Interviews are only a little better than chance
   b. Incorrect. Severe punishment may increase future violent behavior
   c. Incorrect. Likely to occur in people with <u>weaker</u> than normal responses
   d. Incorrect. Watching violence is associated with violent behavior
   e. Correct! (p. 472)

4. a. Incorrect. Men commit fewer, but more severe acts of violence
   b. Correct! (p. 473)
   c. Incorrect. Women actually commit more than men.
   d. Incorrect. Since answer b is correct

5. a. Incorrect. Although some do use violence, b and c are also correct
   b. Incorrect. Although some do use threat, a and c are also correct
   c. Incorrect. Although some do use intimidation, a and b are also correct
   d. Correct! (p. 473)

Answers to the True/False Questions – Module 12.2

1. **False**: Rape is generally unreported especially if the perpetrator is someone the victim knows. (p. 474)

2. **False**: Research has shown that low self-esteem is not the cause of violence in people. (p. 472)

3. **True**: Most people are able to control their anger and restrain themselves from engaging in physical aggression towards someone. (pp. 471-472)

4. **True**: Recent research has shown that when a person lies, there is an increase in blood flow to the face. (p. 470, Fig 12.22)

5. **False**: The person will actually have a decrease in the startle reflex but will still experience fear. (p. 468)

Answers to the Fill in the Blank Questions – Module 12.3

1. Stress (p. 476)

2. Type A (pp. 482-483)

3. coping styles (p. 479)

4. PTSD (p. 477)

5. Seyle (p. 476)

6. Health psychology (p. 476)

Answers to the Short Answer Questions – Module 12.3

1. According to Selye, reactions to stress go through an alarm, a resistance, and an exhaustion phase. This final phase leads to general adaptation syndrome, which results in weakness, fatigue, loss of appetite, and loss of interest. Continuing stress results in an increase in epinephrine in the body. Posttraumatic stress disorder may result from prolonged exposure to traumatic experiences. (p. 477)

2. People who score higher on this scale are more likely to become ill; but the scale asks about symptoms of illness, so, of course, people with higher scores are more likely to be ill. The scale does not ask about stress from unchanging problems, such as poverty. It also ignores stress from things you worry about, but that do not happen. It may be inappropriate to add together the scores from various events. Having three mildly stressful events is probably not the same as having one very stressful event. In addition, the same event may be stressful for some people but not for others. (p. 478)

3. People's behavior influences the onset and spread of cancer. Lung cancer is related to smoking. Women who examine their breasts can detect breast cancer early to prevent spreading. Severe depression affects the immune system, making depressed people more vulnerable to the spread of tumors. After the onset of cancer, stress weakens the ability of the immune system to attack cancer cells. However, social support does strengthen the immune system and improves survival time and quality of life (p. 484)

4. We assume that a predictable event will not get any worse or, if we have control, that we can control it if it does. We are able to prepare ourselves for predictable events. We need not be constantly aroused if an event is predictable; we can relax during "safe" periods. However, if we cannot do anything about a predictable negative event, we may prefer not to know about it. (p. 480)

5. Exercise can help relaxation. It is particularly helpful to deal with nervousness about an upcoming stressful event. Exercise also helps because people who are in good physical condition react less strongly to stressful events than people who are not in such good condition. (pp. 481-482)

Answers to the Multiple Choice Questions – Module 12.3

1. a, c. Incorrect. Alarm is first; general adaptation syndrome is the result of last phase
   b. Incorrect. Alarm is first; exhaustion is last
   d. Correct! (p. 477)

2. a. Incorrect. It has been recognized following wars throughout history
   b. Incorrect. Can occur following extreme stress due to any cause
   c. Incorrect. Does not develop in everyone having the same stressful experience
   d. Correct! (p. 477)

3. a. Incorrect. Pleasant events can be stressful, too
   b. Incorrect. Events may not cause illness; this is a correlation
   c. Correct! (p. 478)
   d. Incorrect. It is probably not very accurate

4. a. Incorrect. Not imagined; they are physiologically very real
    b. Correct! (p. 482)
    c. Incorrect. Emotions don't lead directly to illness; they lead to other behaviors that may increase illness
    d. Incorrect. Cancer can be considered a psychosomatic illness, but its primary causes are genetic and toxic substances

5. a. Incorrect. More likely to get heart disease than Type B
    b. Correct! (pp. 482-483)
    c. Incorrect. Probably more likely in cultures where time is important because they are always in a hurry
    d. Incorrect. On average they usually have more stress in their lives

6. a. Incorrect. Distraction is usually used for pain; the person should think about something other than the problem
    b. Incorrect. This would make it worse; it would increase perceived loss of control
    c. Correct! (pp. 480-482)
    d. Incorrect. Lack of control usually increases, not decreases stress
    e. Incorrect. Needs to think of people who are worse off

7. a-c. Incorrect. All are true
    d. Correct! They do not actually have to exert control; they just need to perceive that they can exert control (p. 480)

Answers to the True/False Questions – Module 12.3

1. **True**: Health Psychology is interested in the link between behavior and enhancing health and preventing or recovery from illness. (p. 476)

2. **True**: Using inoculation can reduce the perception of stress. (pp. 480-481)

3. **False**: These are all characteristics associated with a Type A personality. (pp. 482-483)

4. **False**: Actually, if people perceive they have control over the event, it will be perceived as less stressful. (p. 480)

5. **True**: Having someone direct their attention away from the stress can result in a reduction. (p. 482)

Answers to Final Comprehensive Assessment

1. b (p. 450)
2. c (p. 451, Fig. 12.2)
3. d (pp. 470-471)
4. c (p. 452)
5. d (p. 454)
6. b (pp. 452-453)
7. e (pp. 457-458)
8. c (p. 465)
9. c (pp. 471-472)
10. d (p. 472)

11. b (p. 477)
12. c (p. 478)
13. c (p. 478)
14. e (pp. 482-483)
15. b (p. 484)
16. b (p. 480)
17. c (pp. 480-481)
18. d (p. 481)
19. d (p. 467)
20. a (p. 468)

CHAPTER 13

PERSONALITY

CHAPTER OVERVIEW INFORMATION

LEARNING OBJECTIVES

By the end of Chapter 13 you should

- ✓ Be familiar with the major personality theories
- ✓ Increase your understanding of personality traits versus states
- ✓ Have a basic understanding of the process and problems in personality assessment

CHAPTER 13 OUTLINE

A person may be extraverted or introverted. They may seek out new ideas and experiences or they may feel comfortable with ideas and experiences they already know. They may show self-discipline or they may let themselves "go". Who we are and how we behave is brought out through our personality. Chapter 13 examines personality theories, personality traits, and methods used to assess personality. Some thought provoking ideas and research are presented.

Chapter 13 is presented below in outline format to assist you in understanding the information presented in the chapter. More detailed information on any topic can be found using the page references to the right of the topic.

Module 13.1 Personality Theories

I. Debate has raged throughout recent history as to whether people are inherently good or bad (p. 491, Fig. 13.1)

II. Personality consists of consistent ways in which people's social behaviors differ (p. 491)

III. Sigmund Freud and the Psychoanalytic Approach
  A. Personality is the interplay of conflicting forces, some of which are unconscious (p. 491)
  B. Freud's Search for the Unconscious
    1. Freud developed psychoanalysis which explains and deals with the interplay of conscious and unconscious forces (p. 492, Fig. 13.2)
      a. Unconscious holds memories, emotions, and thought which we may be unaware although they affect behavior (pp. 492-493)
      b. Freud's evidence was based on his inferences (p. 493)
        i. His interpretation with respect to the role of sex and sexual abuse and fantasies changed (p. 493)
          (i) Oedipus complex occurs when little boys develop sexual interest in mother and aggression towards father (p. 493)
        ii. Freud did not seek parsimonious explanations (p. 493)
  C. Stages of Psychosexual Development in Freud's Theory of Personality
    1. Strong, pleasant excitement resulting from body stimulation was psychosexual pleasure (p. 494)
    2. Libido was psychosexual energy which could be fixated at some level of psychosexual development if normal development was blocked (p. 494)

3. Freud proposed five stages of psychosexual development (pp. 494-495, Table 13.1)
   a. Oral stage-- libido focused on stimulation of mouth (pp. 494-495)
   b. Anal stage-- libido focused on bowel movements (p. 495)
   c. Phallic stage-- libido focused on genitals (p. 495)
   d. Latent period-- libido is suppressed (p. 495)
   e. Genital stage-- libido focused on sexual intercourse (p. 495)
4. Evaluation of the theory has not generally been supportive (p. 495)

D. Freud's Description of the Structure of Personality
1. Personality consists of conflicting parts-- id, ego, superego (p. 495)

E. Defense Mechanisms Against Anxiety / Freud's Legacy
1. Defense mechanisms keep some thoughts from consciousness (pp. 495-496, Fig. 13.3)
   a. Repression-- motivated forgetting (p. 496)
   b. Denial-- refusal to believe facts (p. 496)
   c. Rationalization-- try to prove that actions are rational (p. 496)
   d. Displacement-- diverting behavior to less threatening target (p. 496)
   e. Regression-- a return to more juvenile means of escaping (p. 496)
   f. Projection-- attributing one's own undesirable characteristics to others (p. 497)
   g. Reaction formation-- presenting the self as opposite (p. 497)
   h. Sublimation-- transformation of unacceptable urges into acceptable, even admirable, ones (p. 497)

F. Freud's Legacy
1. Freud's contribution was seemingly significant at the time, but over the years many have re-examined his contributions and discount many of them (pp. 497-498)

G. Neo-Freudians
1. Neo-Freudians have remained faithful to some aspect of Freud's theory and changed others (p. 498)

IV. Carl Jung and the Collective Unconscious
A. Jung's psychodynamic theory argues for an unconscious that reflects the experiences of human ancestors with more emphasis on people's search for meaning in life (pp. 498-499, Fig. 13.4)
1. He added the concept of the collective unconscious and archetypes (p. 498)

V. Alfred Adler and Individual Psychology
A. Adler emphasized the whole person not the parts and suggested that people are guided by a natural striving for superiority (p. 500)
B. Adler's Description of Personality
1. Adler's individual psychology proposed that people try to overcome weaknesses (p. 500)
   a. Striving for superiority is a main motivation in life via a style of life (p. 500)
C. Adler's View of Psychological Disorders
1. Mental illnesses come from faulty, selfish life styles (pp. 500-501)
   a. People need to develop a social interest (pp. 500-501)
D. Adler's Legacy
1. The ideas of inferiority complex and mental health as a positive state have become part of the common culture (p. 501)

VI. The Learning Approach
A. Most of personality is learned in a situation-by-situation basis (p. 501)
1. Gender roles are learned because of society's expectations (pp. 501-502, Fig. 13.5)

VII. Humanistic Psychology
   A. Humanistic psychology emphasizes consciousness, values and abstract beliefs (p. 502)
      1. Humanists do not use determinism and reductionism to explain behavior (p. 503)
   B. Carl Rogers and the Goal of Self-Actualization
      1. Rogers believed that people naturally try to achieve self-actualization, the achievement of full potential (p. 503)
         a. Children develop a self-concept (actual self), but they also have an ideal self (p. 503)
         b. People should relate to others with unconditional positive regard (p. 503)
   C. Abraham Maslow and the Self-Actualized Personality
      1. Maslow described the self-actualized personality (p. 504)
      2. Possess accurate perception of reality; independence, creativity, and spontaneity; acceptance of themselves and others; problem-centered outlook; enjoyment of life; good sense of humor (p. 504)

The message: *Personality theory has a rich history which has led to new and interesting attempts to understand and measure personality. (p. 504)*

Module 13.2 Personality Traits
VIII. Psychologists investigate how people differ (p. 506)
   A. Nomothetic approach seeks general laws about behavior (p. 506)
   B. Idiographic approach concentrates on intensive studies of individuals (p. 506)

IX. Personality Traits and States
   A. Psychologists distinguish between traits and states (p. 506)
      1. A trait is a consistent, long-lasting tendency in behavior (p. 506)
      2. A state is a temporary activation of behavior (p. 506)

X. The Search for Broad Personality Traits
   A. Psychologists try to identify broad personality traits (p. 507)
      1. Internal v. external locus of control is one of those broad traits (p. 507, Table 13.2)
         a. Internal locus people believe they are in control of life (p. 507)
         b. External locus people believe external forces control life (p. 507)
   B. Issues in Personality Measurement
      1. Difficult to get accurate and reliable measures of ever changing personality (p. 507)
      2. Most studies relate actual behavior to responses on questionnaire (pp. 507-508)
   C. An Example of Measurement Problems: Self-esteem
      1. Measuring self-esteem difficult because of the varying definitions of it (p. 508)
      2. Research suggests
         a. People whose self-esteem has been raised are less likely to feel depressed (p. 508)
         b. Raising self-esteem has little effect on aggressive behavior (p. 508)
         c. Raising self-esteem decreases performance in school or work (p. 508)

XI. The Big Five Model of Personality
   A. Derivation of The Big Five Personality Traits
      1. Many researchers agree on the "big five" personality traits (p. 509)
         a. Neuroticism is the tendency to experience unpleasant emotions easily (p. 509)
         b. Extraversion is the tendency to seek new experiences and enjoy company (p. 509)
            i. Introverts and extraverts instructed to act extraverted felt happier (p. 509)
            ii. Introverts and extraverts instructed to act introverted felt less happy (p. 509)
         c. Agreeableness is a tendency to be compassionate (p. 509)

       d. Conscientiousness is a tendency to show self-discipline (pp. 509-510)

       e. Openness is the tendency to enjoy being exposed to new ideas (p. 510)

  B. Criticisms and Problems

    1. There are also problems with the concept of "big five" (pp. 510-511)

       a. Most data depend on written responses to questionnaires (p. 510)

       b. The selection of five, rather than 3 or 14, traits is arbitrary (p. 510)

       c. Some traits do not exist or vary much in some cultures (p. 510)

       d. The five-factor structure is not theoretically satisfying (p. 511)

XII. The Origins of Personality

  A. Heredity and Environment

    1. Heredity has a moderate influence on personality (pp. 511-512)

       a. Monozygotic twins are more similar than dizygotic twins on some traits (p. 511, Fig. 13.6)

       b. Biological parents are more similar to their children than adoptive parents (p. 511, Fig. 13.7)

       c. Personality variation may come from the unshared environment, the part the differs among family members (pp. 511-512)

  B. Age and Historical Era

    1. Personality fairly consistent over time and becomes more fixed as we age (p. 512)

    2. Older people more conscientious, less extraverted, less neurotic, more agreeable (pp. 512-513)

    3. Inter-generational differences also exist in group personality and anxiety data (p. 513)

The message: *Individual personalities are all different and individuals may show different personalities in different situations. (p. 513)*

Module 13.3 Personality Assessment

XIII. People accept general and vague personality descriptions of themselves (pp. 515-516)

XIV. Standardized Personality Tests Objective Personality Tests

  A. Standardized personality tests are administered according to specified rules and they are scored in prescribed ways (p. 515)

    1. Objective personality tests are based on simple pencil and paper responses (p. 515)

  B. The Minnesota Multiphasic Personality Inventory

    1. The MMPI measures tendencies toward psychological disorders (p. 516, Table 13.3)

       a. Constructed by comparing people with mental illness and people who did not have mental illnesses (p. 516)

  C. Revisions of the Test

    1. The MMPI-2 is a recent revision of the MMPI (p. 517, Fig. 13.8)

    2. The MMPI-A is used for adolescents (p. 517)

  D. Generalizability of the MMPI

    1. The same norms are used for different ethnic groups, although this may not be appropriate (p. 517)

  E. Detection of Deception

    1. MMPI includes a lie scale and measures other types of deception (p. 518)

  F. Uses of the MMPI

    1. Test results classify people, but do not tell anything about degree of disorder (p. 518)

XV. Projective Techniques
   A. Projective tests ask people to respond to ambiguous stimuli (pp. 518-519)
   B. The Rorschach Inkblots
      1. Rorschach invented the inkblot test (p. 519, Fig. 13.9)
         a. Its interpretation may depend on the psychologist's expectations (p. 519)
         b. An objective scoring method has improved reliability (pp. 519-520)
         c. Problems with standardization, administration, ethnic differences, interrater reliability, and scale validity still exist (p. 520)
   C. The Thematic Apperception Test
      1. Thematic Apperception Test (TAT) involves telling stories about pictures (pp. 520-521, Fig. 13.10)
         a. It has low reliability perhaps because it measures present concerns (p. 521)
   D. Less Common Projective Techniques
      1. Handwriting analysis tells us little about personality (p. 521)

XVI. Research on Possible Implicit Personality Tests
   A. The Emotional Stroop Test
      1. The Emotional Stroop Test may allow objective measurement of anxieties (pp. 521-522)
   B. The Implicit Association Test
      1. Measures whether people respond faster to a category that combines some topic with pleasant or unpleasant words (pp. 522-523)

XVII. Uses and Misuses of Personality Tests In Closing: Trying to Measure Personality
   A. Use of test scores in isolation could result in making faulty decisions (p. 523, Fig 13.11)
   B. Test scores should be used appropriately and in concert with other information (p. 523)

XVIII. Personality Tests in Action: Criminal Profiling
   A. Criminal profiling, at best, has limited success (p. 524)
      1. Studies have not found consistent pattern between crime and criminal (p. 524)
      2. Professional profilers not much more accurate than others in profiling a criminal (pp. 524-525)
      3. Profiles are usually so general that people misinterpret their accuracy (p. 525)

The message: Personality tests can only measure a few aspects of personality. (pp. 525-526)

RELATED WEBSITES AND ACTIVITIES

Visit http://psychology.wadsworth.com/kalat_intro7e/ for online quizzing, glossary flashcards, crossword puzzles, annotated web links, and more.

LECTURE MATERIAL

Information from the text is only half of the picture. Don't forget to review your lecture material. Process each topic meaningfully. Most importantly, be sure that you understand the material in each lecture-if you don't, ask your instructor or teaching assistant.

STUDY TIP # 13: Access any websites associated with your textbook. There are many excellent study tools available for free at these sites. See the URL above for the text site.

TIP: Associate the lecture material with the information from the text, with things that you already know, with your personal experiences, or with real-life applications. Type or neatly re-write your notes. Make sure they are detailed and organized. Make comments on your notes. Then write questions to cover each concept.

CHAPTER MODULE ASSESSMENTS

Module 13.1 Personality Theories
Answer these questions soon after reading the **Module 13.1: Personality Theories**. There are several formats to the assessments. Answers to all questions appear on pp. 275-277.

Fill in the Blank
Provide a term(s) which best completes the statement below. Answers appear on p. 275.

1. The term _____, which describes someone with exaggerated feelings of weakness and inadequacy, was first used by Alfred Adler.

2. _____ psychologists believe that people are motivated by a natural desire for self-actualization.

3. _____ disagreed with Freud's emphasis on sexuality and believed that an important source of conflict in personality was found in the relationship between parent and child.

4. The ego uses _____ that push threatening feelings into the unconscious.

5. According to Freud, the _____ is the repository of thoughts, feelings, and memories that even though we are unaware of them, affect our behavior.

6. Jung believed that we had a _____ unconscious, which contained memories of the experiences of our ancestors.

7. Freud believed that all male children went through a stage called the _____ when they develop sexual feelings towards their mother and aggressive impulses towards their father.

8. According to Freud, _____ is a form of psychosexual energy that flows through various body parts as a person develops.

Short Answer
The following questions require a short written answer (3-7 sentences). Answers appear on pp. 275-276.

1. Discuss the basic difference between the psychodynamic and humanistic approaches to personality.

2. Describe Freud's five stages of sexual development.

3. Explain why people use defense mechanisms.

4. How did Jung and Freud disagree?

5. Describe Adler's individual psychology.

6. Describe Freud's ideas regarding libido, how it could become fixated, and the effects on behavior if it became partially fixated.

Multiple Choice

Circle the best answer below. Check your answers on pp. 276-277. If your answer was incorrect, try to write why it was incorrect. Check your reasons on pp. 276-277.

1. Which personality theorist has a view most similar to that of Hobbes, who argued that humans are selfish and must be restrained by government?
    a. Maslow
    b. Rogers
    c. Adler
    d. Freud

2. According to learning approach, gender roles
    a. are at least partially learned by observation
    b. result from being raised in a single parent home
    c. are genetically determined
    d. are taught formally by society

3. Which of the following is <u>not</u> characteristic of the self-actualized personality?
    a. treat people with unconditional positive regard
    b. a good sense of humor
    c. a self-centered outlook
    d. an accurate perception of reality
    e. follow own impulses

4. According to Freud's psychodynamic theory:
    a. all neurotic behavior can be traced to sexual abuse
    b. libido focuses on different parts of the body
    c. catharsis is what happens if the libido becomes fixated
    d. the unconscious has no thoughts, memories or emotions
    e. the unconscious never manifests itself in everyday life

5. According to Freud, the Oedipus complex occurs during which stage?
    a. phallic stage
    b. oral stage
    c. anal stage
    d. genital stage
    e. latent stage

6. Dan is angry with his boss, but he goes home and yells at his wife, who becomes crabby with her daughter, who starts tormenting the dog. What defense mechanism is being used?
    a. repression
    b. regression
    c. reaction formation
    d. projection
    e. displacement

7. John sees an attractive young woman. His _____ wants to have sex with her immediately; his _____ says absolutely not, he shouldn't even think such thoughts; his _____ tries to mediate between the other two.
    a. id, superego, ego
    b. superego, ego, id
    c. id, libido, superego
    d. id, ego, superego
    e. ego, id, libido

8. Karen Horney, an influential neo-Freudian, differed with Freud's views on:
    a. the existence of an ego
    b. the importance of peak experiences
    c. the importance of unconditional positive regard
    d. the importance of sexual motivation
    e. the role of self-actualization

9. Which of the following is <u>not</u> a correct pairing?
    a. Adler--collective unconscious
    b. Jung--universal symbols in art, religions, and dreams
    c. Adler--individual psychology
    d. Adler--inferiority complex
    e. Horney--importance of cultural influences

10. Adler believed that:
    a. we inherit archetypes as part of our collective unconscious
    b. each person is aware of his or her own style of life
    c. people with a strong social interest are very outgoing and friendly
    d. everyone has a natural striving for superiority
    e. personality theorists should study the parts of personality

True/False
Select the best answer by circling *T for True* or *F for False*. Check your answers on p. 277.

1. **T or F** According to Maslow, a self-actualized person should have an accurate perception of reality.

2. **T or F** There is significant evidence that the defense mechanism repression is widely employed to forget threatening memories or events.

3. **T or F** Neo-Freudians accepted Freud's ideas in their entirety and added to it.

Module 13.2 Personality Traits
Answer these questions soon after reading the **Module 13.2: Personality Traits**. There are several formats to the assessments. Answers to all questions appear on pp. 277-279.

Fill in the Blank
Provide a term(s) which best completes the statement below. Answers appear on p. 277.

1. One of the "big five" personality traits which describes individuals who tend to seek out new experiences and enjoy the company of others is _____.

2. The _____ approach to personality seeks to discover general laws about how an aspect of personality affects behavior.

Short Answer
The following questions require a short written answer (3-7 sentences). Answers appear on p. 278.

1. Discuss the topic of self-esteem including the difficulties in measuring and some of the research results.

2. Discuss the difference between the nomothetic and idiographic approaches to personality.

3. What type of support has been obtained for the "big five" personality traits?

4. Discuss the role of family environment in personality.

Multiple Choice
Circle the best answer below. Check your answers on pp. 278-279. If your answer was incorrect, try to write why it was incorrect. Check your reasons on pp. 278-279.

1. John always seems to be fidgety and anxious. John's anxiety is probably:
   a. state anxiety
   b. trait anxiety
   c. the result of extraversion
   d. the result of too much openness to experience

2. Which of the following is <u>not</u> one of the "big five" personality dimensions?
   a. androgyny
   b. extraversion
   c. agreeableness
   d. openness to experience
   e. neuroticism

3. A valid criticism of the "big five" personality traits is that:
   a. the traits change a great deal with age
   b. the traits do not correlate with each other very well
   c. the trait structure works well for women but not for men
   d. choosing only 5 traits is arbitrary

4. What is the role of imitating parents in personality development?
   a. it is strong because adopted children's personalities are much like their adopted parents'
   b. it is strong because adopted children's personalities correlate with their biological parents more than with their adoptive parents
   c. it is strong because unrelated children growing up in the same family are very similar
   d. it is weak because dizygotic twin pairs are more similar than monozygotic pairs
   e. it is weak because parents and their adopted children's personalities do not correlate

5. Introverts that are instructed to act extraverted
   a. were unable to act as extroverts
   b. felt greater levels of sadness
   c. felt uncomfortable and were even more introverted
   d. felt happier

True/False
Select the best answer by circling *T for True* or *F for False*. Check your answers on p. 279.

1. **T or F** Personality states are personality characteristics that are persistent over time.

2. **T or F** Over the decades the anxiety level of children has increased beyond the level once observed in mental hospital patients.

3. **T or F** Openness to new experience decreases with age in all countries.

4. **T or F** Kerry believes that she controls what happens in her life. Kerry would be classified as having an internal locus of control.

Module 13.3 Personality Assessment
Answer these questions soon after reading the **Module 13.3: Personality Assessment**. There are several formats to the assessments. Answers to all questions appear on pp. 279-280.

Fill in the Blank
Provide a term(s) which best completes the statement below. Answers appear on p. 279.

1. The _____ is a type of projective test that asks a person to make up stories about a series of pictures.

2. The Emotional Stroop Test is one example of an _____ personality test.

3. The _____ is the most widely used tests of personality.

4. A _____ personality test is administered according to specific rules and the results are interpreted in a prescribed fashion.

5. Projective psychological tests, like the _____ test, examine an individual's responses to ambiguous stimuli such as inkblots.

Short Answer
The following questions require a short written answer (3-7 sentences). Answers appear on p. 279.

1. Describe how the developers of the MMPI guarded against lying. How do employers do a similar thing on job applications?

2. What is the problem with using tests, such as the MMPI-2, that have fairly good reliability and validity as the only means of diagnosing individuals?

3. What is criminal profiling and what does the research say about its effectiveness?

Multiple Choice
Circle the best answer below. Check your answers on p. 280. If your answer was incorrect, try to write why it was incorrect. Check your reasons on p. 280.

1. Experiments have been done in which students took tests and were given personality feedback. Generally, what was their opinion of the feedback?
   a. they believed it only if it had direct relevance to their answers on the test
   b. they rarely believed the feedback from so-called experts
   c. less than 20% rated a vague and general description as "good to excellent"
   d. about 90% rated a vague and general description as "good to excellent"
   e. about 90% rated a strange, unflattering description as "good to excellent"

2. The original MMPI:
   a. was developed by asking questions that fit with the developers' theory of personality
   b. has high validity, so that a clinician can use it alone to evaluate psychological problems
   c. asks questions that are answered differently by people with various psychological disorders and other people
   d. asks a series of open-ended questions
   e. is not valid because most people lie

3. In the Thematic Apperception Test, you would be asked to:
   a. describe what you see in inkblots
   b. tell stories about people in pictures
   c. free-associate in Freud's sense
   d. describe what people of the opposite sex are doing in pictures

4. A psychologist administering a Rorschach will:
   a. begin with very clear instructions about what the client should say
   b. only record what you say and not things you do with the cards
   c. almost always administer it using double-blind methodology
   d. show more reliability using objective scoring than using subjective interpretations
   e. be able to identify your specific disorder with about 95% accuracy

5. Which of the following best describes the results of criminal profiling?
   a. professional profilers are about 90% accurate in their profiling
   b. professional profilers are about 70% accurate in their profiling
   c. professional profilers are about 50% accurate in their profiling
   d. professional profilers are less than 50% accurate in their profiling

True/False
Select the best answer by circling *T for True* or *F for False*. Check your answers on p. 280.

1. **T or F** Results on the MMPI are used to classify people.

2. **T or F** The Thematic Apperception Test (TAT) involves people looking at ink blots and telling the test administrator what they perceive.

3. **T or F** Psychological profilers are very accurate (over 90%) in creating criminal profiles.

4. **T or F** Handwriting analyses provide accurate and detailed personality descriptions.

FINAL COMPREHENSIVE CHAPTER ASSESSMENT TEST

Check your answers on p. 281.

1. Which approach to personality would agree with Rousseau that humans are good by nature?
    a. Freud's approach
    b. psychodynamic
    c. the ancient Greeks' approach
    d. humanistic
    e. neo-Freudian

2. Behaviorism and psychoanalysis share which assumptions that differ from humanistic psychology?
    a. parsimony and reductionism
    b. determinism and parsimony
    c. "all behavior is learned" and parsimony
    d. determinism and "all behavior is learned"
    e. reductionism and determinism

3. Which one of the following is **not** a structure in Freud's description of personality:
    a. ego
    b. meta ego
    c. id
    d. super ego

4. Unconditional positive regard means:
    a. encouraging a person to act on every impulse
    b. leading a person toward self-actualization
    c. trying to change behavior rather than thoughts
    d. complete, unqualified acceptance of a person
    e. a natural drive to achieve one's own potential

5. Maslow thought that people with self-actualized personalities showed all <u>except</u>:
    a. openness to all kinds of experiences
    b. avoidance of ambiguous perceptions
    c. independence and creativity
    d. good sense of humor
    e. treating people with unconditional positive regard

6. Carl has recently worked with a group to increase his low self-esteem. Which of the following is likely to happen?
   a. he will do better in school
   b. he will experience a decrease in his normally aggressive behaviors
   c. both a and b
   d. neither a nor b

7. Johnny, who is 8, has absolutely no interest in girls or anything related to sex. According to Freud, Johnny would be in what stage?
   a. latent
   b. anal
   c. oral
   d. genital
   e. phallic

8. Mr. Ku absolutely hates people of other races, yet he sets up free food programs and medical clinics in areas where they live. Which defense mechanism is he using?
   a. denial
   b. reaction formation
   c. displacement
   d. projection
   e. repression

9. John, an introvert, is told that he must go out and introduce himself and carry on a brief conversation with at least 5 new people a day for a week. At the end of the week, how will John most likely feel?
   a. upset because he found it very anxiety provoking
   b. tired from talking to so many people
   c. happier than he would usually feel
   d. all of the above are equally likely

10. In the revision of his theory, what did Freud believe about sexual abuse?
   a. it was responsible for all neurotic behavior
   b. sexual abuse rarely occurs, because patients almost never report it
   c. sexual abuse is the cause of sublimation
   d. sexual abuse is part of the collective unconscious
   e. his patients misled him into believing they had been sexually abused

11. Adler argued that:
   a. people create a master plan for reaching peak experiences
   b. universal symbols occur in art, dreams, and hallucinations
   c. penis envy occurs because of the collective unconscious
   d. everyone has a natural striving for superiority
   e. people become maladjusted if they do not have a peak experience

12. Which of the following is mispaired?
   a. style of life-Adler
   b. inferiority complex-Jung
   c. collective unconscious-Jung
   d. Oedipus complex-Freud
   e. social interest-Adler

13. Which two traits do most personality theorists agree are the most powerful?
    a. assertiveness and self-discipline
    b. neuroticism and extraversion
    c. conscientiousness and agreeableness
    d. openness to experience and extraversion
    e. conscientiousness and warmth

14. Evidence for a role of genetics in personality includes the finding that:
    a. dizygotic twins are more similar than monozygotic twins
    b. parents' level of extraversion is more similar to their biological children than to their adopted children
    c. unrelated children adopted into the same families develop similar personalities
    d. there is little relationship between arousal levels and personality
    e. unshared environments differ from one sibling to another

15. Which of the following is not necessary for a standardized test?
    a. it was developed from a specific theoretical viewpoint
    b. items are clear and unambiguous
    c. the mean and range of scores is determined for a large number of people
    d. it is administered according to specific rules
    e. the normal range of scores can be determined

16. The MMPI was devised empirically, which means that:
    a. it was based on a theory about personality disorders
    b. it was revised recently to improve its validity today
    c. items were simply given to groups having different disorders and similar answers given by similar groups were identified
    d. it was normed on many different ethnic groups
    e. it was designed to detect deception

17. Why would a psychologist use a projective test rather than just asking a person to talk about himself or herself?
    a. the projective test will be much higher in validity
    b. the projective test will make it much easier to decide if a person has a severe mental disorder
    c. the projective test should be more effective in getting a person to start talking
    d. different psychologists will come to different conclusions from an interview but not from a projective test

18. Which of the following is the psychologist least likely to do when giving a Rorschach?
    a. notice whether you rotate each card
    b. record how long you study each card
    c. suggest that you should try to see the inkblot as one object
    d. notice whether you say anything about color or movement
    e. count how many responses you give

19. The world famous Dr. Igot U. Now has been hired to develop a profile of the local serial killer. Dr. Now carefully studies all of the information available on the case and develops a profile of the killer. Given the research, which of the following is most likely to happen based on Dr. Now's profile?
    a. the profile will be very accurate and therefore the killer will be captured quickly
    b. the profile will be very accurate and therefore it will take longer to capture the killer
    c. the profile is likely to contain many inaccuracies
    d. the profile will be very inaccurate and the killer will be captured quickly

20. Which of the following is least likely a personality characteristic of an older person?
    a. will be more conscientious
    b. less extraverted
    c. more neurotic
    d. more agreeable

ANSWERS AND EXPLANATIONS FOR CHAPTER MODULE ASSESSMENTS

Answers to the Fill in the Blank Questions – Module 13.1

1. inferiority complex (p. 500)

2. Humanistic (p. 502)

3. Karen Horney (p. 498)

4. defense mechanism (pp. 495-496)

5. unconscious (pp. 492-493)

6. collective (p. 498)

7. Oedipus complex (p. 493)

8. libido (p. 494)

Answers to the Short Answer Questions – Module 13.1

1. Psychodynamic theorists agree with Hobbes that basic human instincts are selfish; these instincts are part of the id. Other parts of personality are necessary to keep these instincts from showing up fully. Humanist theorists side with Rousseau and argue that humans are good by nature; a person's full potential emerges in self-actualization. People strive for perfection, and when their true selves emerge, they are basically good, caring people. (pp. 491-503)

2. <u>Oral stage</u>: Libido attaches itself to mouth area and infant derives pleasure from sucking.
   <u>Anal stage</u>: Libido attaches itself to anal area and infant derives pleasure from bowel movements.
   <u>Phallic stage</u>: Libido is in genital area and child shows interest in genitals. Oedipus complex occurs because male child wishes to have mother's affection and get rid of father.
   <u>Latent stage</u>: Child is so traumatized by Oedipus complex that libido becomes latent or hidden. Child suppresses sexual interest.
   <u>Genital stage</u>: Libido is in genital area and child takes interest in own and others' genitals.
   (pp. 494-495, Table 13.1)

3. Personality is made up of the id, which is motivated by biological instincts; the superego, which is highly moral and punishing; and the ego, which mediates between id, superego, and reality. Ego can exclude some of id's impulses from consciousness, and thus avoid some of the guilt caused by superego. Defense mechanisms reduce anxiety by dealing with the conflict between id and superego. (p. 495)

Personality   275

4. Jung put greater emphasis on people's search for meaning in life than Freud did. Jung argued that there was a deeper level of unconscious called the collective unconscious; Freud disagreed. (pp. 498-499)

5. It is the psychology of a person as a whole. Adler argued that people strive for superiority, and if they don't succeed in overcoming helplessness in childhood they may develop an inferiority complex. The plan for achieving superiority determines a person's style of life. If a person contributes to the welfare of the human race, he or she has developed social interest. (p. 500)

6. Freud believed that people possessed libido (sexual energy) which flowed to different parts of the body at specific times during development. If normal sexual development was blocked or frustrated at any stage, part of the libido became fixated. That is, a person would continue to be preoccupied with the pleasure area associated with that stage. Freud believed that as adults, people fixated at any given level would exhibit behaviors consistent with that level. For example, someone exhibiting pleasure from eating, drinking and other oral activities (e.g., talking or smoking) might have part of their libido fixated at the oral stage. (pp. 494-495, Table 13.1)

Answers to the Multiple Choice Questions – Module 13.1

1. a. Incorrect. Believed in self-actualization, an innate goodness
    b. Incorrect. Argues that people have good, noble goals
    c. Incorrect. Many people have strong social interest
    d. Correct! (p. 491)

2. a. Correct! (p. 501)
    b. Incorrect. Although children do imitate behavior of adults of the same gender
    c. Incorrect. Although genes may play a role, learning through observation is stronger
    d. Incorrect. Society does not formally teach gender roles

3. a, b, d, e. Incorrect. All are characteristics
    c. Correct! (p. 504) They are problem centered

4. a. Incorrect. Freud once thought this, but decided it was sexual fantasies, not actual abuse
    b. Correct! (p. 494)
    c. Incorrect. Catharsis is release of tension related to unpleasant experiences; fixation means that people continue to be preoccupied with pleasure related to the stage
    d. Incorrect. Unconscious does have these, but it's less logical
    e. Incorrect. It does in slips of the tongue; unconscious motivations can influence such errors

5. a. Correct! (p. 493)
    b. Incorrect. Sensual pleasure from mouth area
    c. Incorrect. Pleasure from bowel movements
    d. Incorrect. Interest in others' and own genitals
    e. Incorrect. Sexual interest is suppressed

6. a. Incorrect. Dan would place anger with boss into unconscious
    b. Incorrect. Dan would behave in a more juvenile way
    c. Incorrect. Dan would be very friendly toward his boss to hide the anger
    d. Incorrect. Dan would argue that everyone hates his or her boss
    e. Correct! (p. 496)

7. a. Correct! (p. 495)
    b. Incorrect. Id contains sexual urge; superego is like a conscience; ego deals with reality
    c. Incorrect. Libido is general sexual energy; superego doesn't mediate, it is restrictive
    d. Incorrect. Ego is the mediator; superego is the restrictive part
    e. Incorrect. Id contains sexual urges; ego mediates and deals with reality; libido is sexual energy

8. a. Incorrect. She agreed that ego existed
    b. Incorrect. In humanistic psychology--moments when people feel truly fulfilled
    c. Incorrect. In humanistic psychology--unqualified acceptance of others
    d. Correct! (p. 498)
    e. Incorrect. Fulfillment of potential in humanistic theories

9. a. Correct! (p. 500)
    b-e. Incorrect. All are correct

10. a. Incorrect. This is Jung's idea
    b. Incorrect. People may not be aware of their style of life
    c. Incorrect. Refers to striving to benefit the human race
    d. Correct! (p. 500)
    e. Incorrect. People should be viewed as wholes

Answers to the True/False Questions – Module 13.1

1. **True**: This is one of the characteristics of Maslow's self-actualization theory. (p. 504)

2. **False**: Research by Holmes (1990) suggests that repression, if it occurs at all, occurs very infrequently. (p. 496)

3. **False**: Neo-Freudians accepted some of Freud's ideas, but changed other parts as they developed their own theories and ideas. (p. 498)

Answers to the Fill in the Blank Questions – Module 13.2

1. extraversion (p. 509)

2. nomothetic (p. 506)

Answers to the Short Answer Questions – Module 13.2

1. Over the last several years researchers have been trying to measure self-esteem with varying levels of success. Since these researchers have varying definitions of self-esteem, the tests purporting to measure self-esteem do not seem very similar. Regardless, research suggests that people whose self-esteem has been raised are less likely to feel depressed and that raising self-esteem has little effect on aggressive behavior and decreases performance in school or work (p. 508)

2. The nomothetic approach seeks general laws about how personality influences behavior. Groups of people are compared and statistical analysis is used. The results are meant to be generalized to the population. The idiographic approach focuses on intensive studies of individuals. The results are not meant to be generalized to the population. (p. 506)

3. The five-factor description characterizes personality in both men and women. It works in many languages and cultures, although some cultures may not show enough variation in some of the traits for the description to be meaningful. The "big five" traits seem to be fairly stable across age. (pp. 508-509)

4. Adopted children's personalities generally do not correlate with the personalities of their adoptive parents. Unrelated children growing up in the same home do not develop similar personalities. These findings suggest that personality development is not dependent upon family environment. However, many researchers believe that much of the variation in personality may be due to unshared environment which is the environment that differs from family member to family member. This is difficult to test. Overall, the research suggests a limited role for family environment in personality development. (pp. 511-512, Figs. 13.6, 13.7)

Answers to the Multiple Choice Questions – Module 13.2

1. a. Incorrect. Seems to be more temporary; a transient condition
    b. Correct! (p. 506)
    c. Incorrect. Directing interest in others; unrelated to anxiety
    d. Incorrect. Enjoyment of new experiences; wouldn't cause anxiety

2. a. Correct! (pp. 509-510)
    b-e. Incorrect. All are "big five" personality dimensions

3. a. Incorrect. They change very little with age
    b. Incorrect. They aren't supposed to correlate with each other; they should be nearly independent
    c. Incorrect. The traits work well for both men and women
    d. Correct! (p. 510)

4. a. Incorrect. Adopted children and their adoptive parents are not similar
    b. Incorrect. This is evidence for no family environment effect
    c. Incorrect. They are not very similar, arguing against family environment as an important influence
    d. Incorrect. Monozygotic twins are more similar, showing a genetic influence
    e. Correct! (p. 511, Fig. 13.7)

5. a. Incorrect. Introverts in the study were able to act like extroverts
   b. Incorrect. They felt happier
   c. Incorrect. They successfully acted as introverts
   d. Correct! (p. 509)

Answers to the True/False Questions – Module 13.2

1. **False**: Personality states are actually temporary in response to a specific situation. (p. 506)

2. **True**: From the 1950s to the 1980s anxiety level in children increased from 15.1 to 23.3. In the 1950s the mean anxiety level of children in a mental hospital was 20.1. (p. 513)

3. **False**: In the United States it does decrease, but in several countries it does not decrease. (p. 510)

4. **True**: People with believe they are in control of their own lives. (p. 507)

Answers to the Fill in the Blank Questions – Module 13.3

1. TAT (pp. 520-521)

2. implicit (pp. 521-522)

3. MMPI (p. 516)

4. standardized (p. 515)

5. Rorschach (pp. 519-520)

Answers to the Short Answer Questions – Module 13.3

1. Some questions should be answered the same by everyone; if you answer differently, you must be lying. The number of such answers are added up to give a score on the lie scale. Employers sometimes do a similar thing on job applications by asking applicants about experience in doing nonexistent tasks. (p. 518)

2. Tests should be used as aids and not the sole method of diagnosis. Even if a test correctly identifies 95% of the people with a disorder and incorrectly diagnoses 5% of the normal population, it is misdiagnosing more people than it is correctly diagnosing. This is because the total population of normal people is much greater than the population of people with fairly rare disorders. (p. 523)

3. Criminal profiling occurs when a trained person (e.g., psychologist or police officer) reviews the facts of a crime and generates a profile of the criminal including assumptions about the criminals personality, emotions, and motivations. Research in the area suggests that profiles are generally not very accurate. One of the reasons that the profiles are not very accurate is because of a faulty assumption that there are consistent patterns between the crimes committed and the type of criminals committing them. (pp. 524-525)

Answers to the Multiple Choice Questions – Module 13.3

1. a. Incorrect. Test questions do not have to be related to feedback
    b. c. Incorrect. 90% rated it "good to excellent"
    d. Correct! (pp. 515-516)
    e. Incorrect. Only about 20% rated this description "good to excellent"

2. a. Incorrect. Questions were chosen by trial and error; they just found questions that were answered differently by different groups
    b. Incorrect. Validity not that high; should be used with other measures
    c. Correct! (p. 516)
    d. Incorrect. Projective tests do this; MMPI is objective
    e. Incorrect. A lie scale is included, and if the score is too high, test results will not be used

3. a. Incorrect. Rorschach
    b. Correct! (pp. 520-521)
    c. Incorrect. People are given pictures because they often don't talk spontaneously
    d. Incorrect. People in pictures are mostly of one's own sex

4. a. Incorrect. The instructions are intentionally vague
    b. Incorrect. Some psychologists will record all behaviors
    c. Incorrect. They should, but most psychologists already know what disorder the person shows
    d. Correct! (pp. 519-520)
    e. Incorrect. Can tell whether people have some sort of problem but not specifically which one

5. a-c. Incorrect. Research suggests that profilers were correct less than 50% of the time
    d. Correct! (pp. 524-525)

Answers to the True/False Questions – Module 13.3

1. **True**: The MMPI can provide a classification of the person especially if they are experiencing some personality disorder. (p. 518)

2. **False**: The TAT involves telling a story about some picture stimulus. The Rorschach involves perceptions of inkblots. (pp. 520-521)

3. **False**: Research suggests that criminal profilers are usually not much more accurate in their profiles than non-professionals. (pp. 524-525)

4. **False**: Handwriting analyses are usually so general and vague such that they tell us little about personality. (p. 521)

Answers to Final Comprehensive Assessment

1. d (pp. 501-503, Fig. 13.1)
2. e (p. 503)
3. b (p. 495)
4. d (p. 503)
5. b (p. 504)
6. d (p. 508)
7. a (p. 495)
8. b (p. 497)
9. c (p. 509)
10. e (p. 493)
11. d (p. 500)
12. b (pp. 498-500)
13. b (p. 509)
14. b (p. 511)
15. a (p. 515)
16. c (pp. 515-516)
17. c (pp. 518-519)
18. c (p. 519)
19. c (pp. 524-525)
20. c (pp. 512-513)

CHAPTER 14

SOCIAL PSYCHOLOGY

CHAPTER OVERVIEW INFORMATION

LEARNING OBJECTIVES

By the end of Chapter 14 you should

- ✓ Increase your awareness of the influence of cognition on social behavior and interaction
- ✓ Understand the social processes of persuasion and attitude change
- ✓ Understand the factors that influence interpersonal attraction
- ✓ Increase your understanding of the factors that increase or decrease the influence people have upon each other
- ✓ Increase your awareness of the influence of the situation upon human behavior

CHAPTER 14 OUTLINE

Did you wash your hands the last time you used a public restroom? If you did, was it because someone else was there? If you didn't, was it because no one else was there? Social psychology examines how many of our behaviors and experiences, like hand washing in public restrooms, are influenced by the presence or implied presence of others. Social psychologists study many fascinating topics including first impressions, stereotypes, affiliation, attitudes, physical attractiveness, marriage, group processes, and obedience to name a few.

Chapter 14 is presented below in outline format to assist you in understanding the information presented in the chapter. More detailed information on any topic can be found using the page references to the right of the topic.

Module 14.1 Social Perception and Cognition

I.   Social psychologists study how people influence each other (p. 532)

II. Social perception and cognition are the processes used to gather and remember information about others and to make inferences from that information (p. 533)

III. First Impressions
   A. First impressions influence perceptions of individuals (p. 533)
   B. Can result in a change in behavior leading to the fulfillment of self-fulfilling prophesy (p. 533)

IV. Stereotypes and Prejudices
   A. Stereotypes are generalizations about groups of people (p. 534)
      1. People's judgments of others are often unreliable and inaccurate (p. 534)
   B. Aversive Racism
      1. Prejudice is a negative stereotype about a group which is usually associated with discrimination (p. 534)
      2. Aversive racism occurs when people consciously express equality of races, but still have negative feelings or unintentionally discriminate (p. 535)
      3. Ambivalent sexism when focus is on sex and not race (p. 535)

C. Implicit Measures of Stereotypes and Prejudice
   1. Several methods used to implicitly measure prejudices (pp. 535-536, Figs. 14.1-14.2)
   2. Results suggest both black and white people have an attitude favoring whites (p. 536)
   3. Other methods show implicit prejudice if participants focus on race (p. 537)
D. Overcoming Prejudice
   1. Prejudice may be overcome by having people work toward common goals since cooperation leads to friendship (p. 537)

V. Attribution
   A. Attribution is the process of assigning causes to behavior (p. 537)
   B. Internal Versus External Causes
      1. Behavior is attributed to internal (dispositional) or external (situational) causes (p. 538)
         a. Consensus information involves comparing behavior to that of others (p. 538)
         b. Consistency information involves comparing behavior across time (p. 538)
         c. Distinctiveness involves comparing behavior toward different objects or people (p. 538)
   C. The Fundamental Attribution Error
      1. We often assume that behavior results from internal causes (p. 539)
         a. The fundamental attribution error is an overemphasis on internal causes for other people (p. 539)
   D. Cultural Differences in Attribution and Related Matters
      1. Western culture relies on internal attributions, Asian cultures rely on external (p. 539)
      2. Some non-western cultures can accommodate multiple viewpoints, contradictions, change, and hindsight bias (pp. 539-540)
   E. The Actor-Observer Effect
      1. The actor-observer effect makes people more likely to attribute internal causes to other's behavior than to their own (p. 540, Fig. 14.3)
   F. Using Attributions to Manage Perceptions of Ourselves
      1. Attributions for our own behavior may produce a self-serving bias (p. 541)
         a. We may adopt self-handicapping strategies as excuses for failures (p. 541)

The message: *We make guesses about reasons for people's behaviors and those (sometimes wrong) guesses influence how we interact with others. (p. 541)*

Module 14.2 Attitudes and Persuasion
VI. Attitudes and Their Influence
   A. An attitude is a learned like or dislike of something or somebody (p. 543)
      1. Attitudes are usually measured with rating scales (p. 543, Fig. 14.4)
      2. Often attitudes are only weakly related to behavior due to impulsivity of answering, fluctuations in attitude or holding contradictory attitudes (pp. 543-544)

VII. Central and Peripheral Routes of Attitude Change and Persuasion
   A. Attitudes can be changed by central (logical) and peripheral (superficial) routes (p. 544)
   B. Delayed Influence
      1. Messages sometimes have a delayed effect on attitudes (p. 544)
         a. The sleeper effect is a delayed attitude change after an initial rejection (p. 544)
         b. Minorities can change attitudes in the long run if they are outvoted at first (p. 544, Table 14.1)

C. Ways of Presenting Persuasive Messages
    1. The way a message is presented can affect its effectiveness. Messages of doing something good or avoiding something bad are effective (p. 545, Fig. 14.5)
    2. If person listener identifies with the speaker, message is more effective (p. 546)
    3. If a group you respect endorses idea then more likely to adopt it (p. 546)
D. Audience Variables
    1. Some people are more easily persuaded than others (pp. 546-547)
        a. Intelligent people are persuaded by complex messages, but less intelligent people are more easily persuaded by poorly supported ideas (pp. 546-547)
        b. The forewarning and inoculation effects reduce persuasion (p. 547)

VIII. Strategies of Persuasion
    A. Several techniques are used to persuade us to do what other people would like us to do (pp. 547-548)
        1. The foot-in-the-door technique involves increasing a modest request to a large one (p. 547)
        2. The bait-and-switch technique begins with a large request and then scales it down to a smaller, more reasonable one (pp. 547-548)
        3. The low-ball technique begins by making a favorable deal and then making more demands (p. 548)
        4. The that's-not-all technique begins with an offer that is quickly improved (p. 548)

IX. Cognitive Dissonance
    A. Cognitive dissonance theory says that changes in behavior precede changes in attitude when the two are in conflict (p. 548, Fig. 14.6)
        1. People who lie for little money are more likely to change their attitudes than people who lie for more money (pp. 549-550, Fig 14.7)

The message*: Our attitude about something is based on its importance and the type of information we have; our behavior can be affected by persuasion strategies used by other people. (p. 550)*

Module 14.3 Interpersonal Attraction
X. Establishing Lasting Relationships
    A. Proximity and Familiarity
        1. People choose friends who live close to them; this is called proximity (p. 552)
        2. The more exposure to something, the more it is liked; this is familiarity (p. 552)
    B. Similarity
        1. People choose friends who are similar to themselves; this is similarity (p. 552)
    C. Confirmation of Self-Concept
        1. We tend to be attracted to people who confirm our self-evaluation (p. 552)
    D. The Equity Principle
        1. Exchange or equity theory says that each party should get the best deal possible in the relationship (p. 553)

XI. Special Concerns in Selecting a Mate
    A. Selection of a marriage partner is different because it may include raising children (p. 553)

B. Physical Attractiveness
    1. Physical attractiveness is important in dating, especially at first (pp. 553-554)
       a. Attractive people are judged more favorably and treated better (p. 554)
       b. In some animals attractiveness indicates good health (p. 554, Fig. 14.8)
       c. In humans no strong link between attractiveness and good health, genes and fertility (pp. 554-556, Fig 14.9-14.10)
C. Men's and Women's Preferences
    1. The sociobiological approach provides a speculative explanation for the preferences and sexual jealousies of men and women (pp. 556-557, Fig. 14.11)
       a. Men prefer younger, fertile mates for many years of producing children (p. 557)
       b. Women need mates who are fertile, healthy, and who have substantial resources (p. 557)

XII. Marriage
A. Although many marry, many end in divorce due to lack of discussing important issues (p. 558)
    1. Marriages ending in first 7 years started with unresolved problems (p. 558)
    2. Marriages ending after 7 years started strong and then people became disillusioned (p. 558)
B. Marriages That Last
    1. Characteristics of successful marriages include similar attitudes and personalities; frequent sexual relations; infrequent arguments; adequate income; wife not pregnant before marriage; couple's parents had successful marriages (p. 558)
C. Trying to Save a Marriage
    1. Marriage counseling has dubious results in saving marriage (p. 559)
    2. Recommended "open communication" may increase exchange of hostilities (p. 559)
    3. Couples that limit the expression and perception of negative emotions are more successful (p. 559)

The message: *Learning about what influences interpersonal attraction may help us make better choices of friends and spouses. (p. 559)*

Module 14.4 Interpersonal Influence
XIII. Conformity
A. Conformity is the tendency to change our behavior based on what others are doing, information we have read, or tasks we have just completed (p. 561)
B. Conformity to an Obviously Wrong Majority
    1. Many participants in Asch's research changed their answers at least once to conform with the group's wrong answer (p. 562, Figs. 14.12-14.13)
       a. Conformity occurred in groups of 3-4 as much as to a larger group (p. 562, Fig. 14.14)
       b. Having an ally reduces conformity (p. 563, Fig 14.15)
C. Cultural Differences in Conformity
    1. No reliable difference in conformity and attitudes between U.S. and Japanese participants (p. 563, Table 14.2)
       a. Must be careful of generalizations about whole culture (p. 563)

XIV. Accepting or Denying Responsibility Toward Others
    A. People sometimes accept responsibility toward others and sometimes not (p. 564)
    B. Bystander Helpfulness and Apathy
        1. Bystanders often will not help if others are present because of diffusion of responsibility or they may believe the inaction of others means they should not act as well (p. 564)
    C. Social Loafing
        1. Social loafing means working less hard when sharing work with others (p. 565)
        2. Less likely in team sports or when people perceive large benefit to the group (p. 565)

XV. Group Decision Making
    A. Decisions of groups may differ from decisions of individuals (p. 565)
    B. Group Polarization
        1. Homogenous groups usually come to more extreme decisions than individuals; this is called the group polarization effect (p. 565)
    C. Groupthink
        1. Groupthink occurs when group members do not question others' ideas and do not ask probing questions (p. 565)

The message: *Conformity can be helpful, but we need to be alert to situations when conformity can be harmful to ourselves or others. (p. 565)*

Module 14.5 The Power of the Social Situation
XVI. Much behavior is controlled by social or technological situations (p. 568)
    A. Behavior traps force people into self-defeating behaviors (p. 568)

XVII. Escalation of Conflict
    A. Escalation of conflict occurs when people continue a behavior to avoid defeat (p. 569)

XVIII. The Prisoner's Dilemma
    A. Situations like the prisoner's dilemma result in uncooperative behavior (pp. 569-570, Fig. 14.16)
        1. However the tendency to cooperate with someone who may repay the favor later is known as reciprocal altruism (p. 570)

XIX. The Commons Dilemma
    A. The commons dilemma involves overuse of limited resources (pp. 570-571)

XX. Obedience to Authority
    A. People playing the roles of "guards" in one study became abusive towards "prisoners" since they could get away with it (p. 571)
    B. Milgram found that many people showed obedience to authority and would "punish" another person (pp. 571-572, Figs. 14.17-14.18)
        1. Obedience varied based on several manipulations (pp. 572-573, Figs. 14.19-14.20)
        2. The ethical issues raised by his study resulted in clearer rules for treating research subjects (pp. 572-573)

The message: *Knowing about behavior traps can help us make better choices about social situations and environments. (p. 574)*

RELATED WEBSITES AND ACTIVITIES

Visit http://psychology.wadsworth.com/kalat_intro7e/ for online quizzing, glossary flashcards, crossword puzzles, annotated web links, and more.

LECTURE MATERIAL

Information from the text is only half of the picture. Don't forget to review your lecture material. Process each topic meaningfully. Most importantly, be sure that you understand the material in each lecture-if you don't, ask your instructor or teaching assistant.

STUDY TIP # 14: Review the Key Terms at the end of each chapter. Consider making flashcards for those key terms you do not feel you have a firm understanding of. Fold the card in half. Put the term on the front. On the inside put the definition and page number. On the back put any additional information you might want to associate with the Key Term.

TIP: Associate the lecture material with the information from the text, with things that you already know, with your personal experiences, or with real-life applications. Type or neatly re-write your notes. Make sure they are detailed and organized. Make comments on your notes. Then write questions to cover each concept.

CHAPTER MODULE ASSESSMENTS

Module 14.1 Social Perception and Cognition
Answer these questions soon after reading the **Module 14.1: Social Perception and Cognition**. There are several formats to the assessments. Answers to all questions appear on pp. 300-301.

Fill in the Blank
Provide a term(s) which best completes the statement below. Answers appear on p. 300.

1. The tendency for the first information we learn about someone to influence us more than later information is known as the _____ effect.

2. The tendency to make internal attributions for people's behavior even when we see evidence for an external influence on behavior is known as the _____ attribution error.

3. A _____ is a generalized belief or expectation about groups of people.

4. A _____ occurs when we protect our self-esteem by attributing our successes to skill and our failures to outside influences.

5. An unfavorable stereotype toward a group of people is known as _____.

Short Answer

The following questions require a short written answer (3-7 sentences). Answers appear on p. 300.

1. Discuss the factors that are important in first impressions.

2. What is an attribution, and what types of information are important in making internal and external attributions?

3. Give some reasons for why people tend to make external attributions for their own behavior and internal attributions for the behavior of others.

Multiple Choice

Circle the best answer below. Check your answers on pp. 300-301. If your answer was incorrect, try to write why it was incorrect. Check your reasons on pp. 300-301.

1. Which of the following is <u>not</u> true about forming impressions of new acquaintances?
   a. physically attractive people are likely to be judged more favorably
   b. facial expressions and body movements are more likely to be used than conflicting verbal information
   c. information that is learned first is more influential than information that is learned later
   d. information that is learned last is more influential than information that is learned earlier

2. Stereotypes probably get started because people:
   a. discount internal causes if there is an external cause as stated in the discounting principle
   b. do not remember the behavior of minority groups
   c. rely on consistency information more than distinctiveness information
   d. remember unusual behaviors of minority groups

3. The fundamental attribution error involves overemphasizing:
   a. external as opposed to internal causes of behavior
   b. distinctiveness rather than consensus information
   c. internal as opposed to external causes of behavior
   d. consensus rather than distinctiveness information

4. Self-handicapping refers to:
    a. creating external causes for our failures
    b. a tendency to attribute internal causes to others people's behavior but external causes to one's own behavior
    c. attributing emotional arousal to external stimuli
    d. creating internal causes for our successes

True/False
Select the best answer by circling *T for True* or *F for False*. Check your answers on p. 301.

1. **T or F** When making attributions Western cultures generally rely on internal attributions whereas Asian cultures generally rely on external attributions.

2. **T or F** Aversive racism occurs when people consciously express inequality of races and intentionally discriminate against that race.

Module 14.2 Attitudes and Persuasion
Answer these questions soon after reading the **Module 14.2: Attitudes and Persuasion**.
There are several formats to the assessments. Answers to all questions appear on pp. 301-302.

Fill in the Blank
Provide a term(s) which best completes the statement below. Answers appear on p. 301.

1. A state of unpleasant tension that people experience when they hold contradictory attitudes or when their behavior is inconsistent with their attitudes is _____.

2. The _____ effect occurs when simply informing participants a few minutes ahead of time that they are about to hear a persuasive speech weakens its ability to persuade them to change their attitude

3. The _____ persuasive technique involves first offering an extremely favorable deal and then making additional demands after the person has already committed to the deal.

4. The _____ route to persuasion involves careful deliberation of information before making an important decision.

Short Answer
The following questions require a short written answer (3-7 sentences). Answers appear on p. 301.

1. Describe the two routes to persuasion and discuss the conditions under which each might be used.

2. Contrast the foot-in-the-door, door-in-the-face, and that's-not-all techniques for persuasion.

3. Describe cognitive dissonance theory.

Multiple Choice
Circle the best answer below. Check your answers on p. 302. If your answer was incorrect, try to write why it was incorrect. Check your reasons on p. 302.

1. Measurement of attitudes is:
   a. often done on a Likert scale
   b. very accurate because people are aware of their attitudes
   c. similar across cultures in that people tend to use rating scales in the same way
   d. more accurate for implicit attitudes than for explicit ones
   e. useful because they accurately predict behavior

2. The central route to persuasion:
   a. is more likely to be followed for decisions that are unimportant
   b. involves paying attention to a speaker's appearance and reputation
   c. involves paying attention to the evidence and logic behind a message
   d. involves paying attention to the sheer number of arguments and not to their quality

3. How can a minority group best influence public opinion?
   a. by making themselves seem as different as possible from the public
   b. by presenting very frightening messages telling people that disaster is imminent and there is nothing they can do about it
   c. by forewarning people that they will hear a persuasive message
   d. by beginning with a weak message and then strengthening it
   e. by repeating a single, simple message over and over

4. An example of the foot-in-the-door technique is:
   a. a volunteer worker first asked me to give $100, and when I said no, she asked for $10
   b. a salesman places his briefcase in the door so that I can't close it until I have heard his spiel
   c. a beggar follows a pedestrian up the street constantly asking him for money
   d. a survey worker asks if I will answer a simple question, and after I do that, she asks if I will fill out a long questionnaire
   e. a salesman tells me the price of an item, and then immediately adds that another item will also be included in the price

5. According to cognitive dissonance theory, what is the relationship between attitude change and behavior change?
    a. attitudes must be changed before behavior can be
    b. attitude change and behavior change are unrelated
    c. behavior only changes if people are forewarned about attempts to change attitudes
    d. if behavior is changed, then attitude change will follow

True/False
Select the best answer by circling *T for True* or *F for False*. Check your answers on p. 302.

1. **T or F** The sleeper effect occurs when a person initially rejects a message but ultimately changes their attitude.

2. **T or F** Research suggests that intelligent people are persuaded by simple messages, but less intelligent people are more easily persuaded complex messages.

Module 14.3 Interpersonal Attraction
Answer these questions soon after reading the **Module 14.3: Interpersonal Attraction**. There are several formats to the assessments. Answers to all questions appear on pp. 302-303.

Fill in the Blank
Provide a term(s) which best completes the statement below. Answers appear on p. 302.

1. According to _____ theory, social relationships are transactions in which partners exchange goods and services.

2. According to one theory, _____ prefer younger, fertile mates so that they can enjoy many years of reproduction.

Short Answer
The following questions require a short written answer (3-7 sentences). Answers appear on pp. 302-303.

1. Describe three things that are important in who dates whom.

2. Describe how equity theory applies to romantic relationships and friendships.

Multiple Choice
Circle the best answer below. Check your answers on p. 303. If your answer was incorrect, try to write why it was incorrect. Check your reasons on p. 303.

1. People tend to have friends that are
    a. similar in age
    b. similar in physical attractiveness
    c. similar in political and religious beliefs
    d. similar in intelligence
    e. all of the above

2. The likelihood of developing a friendship is increased by:
    a. proximity; people who live close together are more likely to become friends
    b. familiarity; people who are very familiar as children are likely to develop romantic relationships
    c. dissimilarity because opposites attract
    d. having a dominant person who gets a better deal from the relationship than the other person

3. What is the relationship between physical attractiveness and attraction in the early stages of a dating relationship?
    a. opposites attract; generally people who are very different in attractiveness have the strongest relationships
    b. attitudes and personality are much more important than attractiveness in determining how much people like dating partners
    c. while personality and attitudes may draw two people together initially, physical attractiveness is what determines whether they stay together
    d. people like physically attractive dating partners better than unattractive ones

4. With respect to romantic partners, women are more likely than men to prefer:
    a. someone younger than themselves
    b. casual sex partners
    c. multiple partners
    d. partners who have wealth

True/False
Select the best answer by circling *T for True* or *F for False*. Check your answers on p. 303.

1. **T or F** People are more likely to be attracted to others who confirm our self-evaluation than those who hold a contrary view.

2. **T or F** Attractiveness in humans is strongly linked to good health, better genes and greater fertility.

3. **T or F** Research suggests that marriage counseling is a highly effective method to save a marriage.

Module 14.4 Interpersonal Influence
Answer these questions soon after reading the **Module 14.4: Interpersonal Influence**.
There are several formats to the assessments. Answers to all questions appear on pp. 303-304.

Fill in the Blank
Provide a term(s) which best completes the statement below. Answers appear on p. 303.

1. When we tend to feel less responsibility for doing something helpful when other people are around because we assume that others are equally able to act we are experiencing

    _____.

2. An extreme form of group polarization is also known as _____ .

Short Answer
The following questions require a short written answer (3-7 sentences). Answers appear on pp. 303-304.

1. How social loafing is related to bystander apathy?

2. Explain why the group polarization effect occurs.

Multiple Choice
Circle the best answer below. Check your answers on p. 304. If your answer was incorrect, try to write why it was incorrect. Check your reasons on p. 304.

1. In which situation would you expect a true subject to conform the most?
    a. two people give a wrong answer
    b. seven people give a wrong answer
    c. five people give a wrong answer, and one person gives the correct one
    d. four people give a wrong answer
    e. b and d would be about equal

2. Would you expect to get help faster if your car broke down on a highway that has relatively few travelers or on a busy highway?
    a. on the busy one, because of bystander intervention
    b. on the lightly traveled highway, because of the ambiguity on the busy one
    c. on the busy one, because of diffusion of responsibility
    d. on the busy one, because of social loafing
    e. on the lightly traveled one, because of diffusion of responsibility

3. A group of professors is trying to decide what to do about academically deficient students. Each writes down what he or she thinks is appropriate, but in the end the group decides on more severe action than the average recommendation of the individuals. What has happened?
   a. the group polarization effect
   b. social loafing
   c. bystander intervention
   d. a peremptory challenge
   e. volunteerism

4. Which of the following is an example of groupthink?
   a. cooperating with a group to help in a major disaster
   b. competing with a group that has different goals from yours
   c. failing to challenge the assumptions of group members
   d. gathering information before making a group decision

True/False
Select the best answer by circling *T for True* or *F for False*. Check your answers on p. 304.

1. **T or F** Asch found that participants will change their answers to the obvious wrong answer if group members have selected it as the correct answer.

2. **T or F** Groupthink occurs when groups get together to think.

Module 14.5 The Power of the Social Situation
Answer these questions soon after reading the **Module 14.5: The Power of the Social Situation**. There are several formats to the assessments. Answers to all questions appear on pp. 304-305.

Fill in the Blank
Provide a term(s) which best completes the statement below. Answers appear on p. 304.

1. A situation where people must choose between a cooperative act and an act that could benefit only themselves while hurting others is known as the _____.

2. A _____ is a situation that coerces us into self-defeating behaviors.

Short Answer
The following questions require a short written answer (3-7 sentences). Answers appear on p. 305.

1. What is the "commons dilemma?"

2. Describe Milgram's experiment on obedience and discuss what we can learn from such an experiment.

Multiple Choice
Circle the best answer below. Check your answers on p. 305. If your answer was incorrect, try to write why it was incorrect. Check your reasons on p. 305.

1. If nations act as people do in the prisoner's dilemma, what would happen in a nuclear arms race?
   a. each nation will build more weapons, because that is the best for the individual nation
   b. all nations will stop building such weapons, because this is best for each individual nation
   c. all nations will continue to build weapons, because that is best for the nations as a group
   d. communication among nations will probably increase the nuclear buildup

2. What happened in the experiment in which students could take nuts out of a bowl in which the nuts would double every 10 sec.?
   a. they competed and grabbed nuts for themselves immediately
   b. they cooperated and waited until there were many nuts and then divided them
   c. they took more nuts sooner when working as individuals than when working in a group
   d. they cooperated, just as they do in the prisoner's dilemma
   e. both b and d

3. In Milgram's experiment in which "teachers" shocked "learners":
   a. paricipants did not obey unless they were sadists
   b. many normal people continued to give shocks, although they had misgivings about it
   c. whether or not the experimenter was in the room was irrelevant for obedience
   d. more people quit the experiment when a confederate followed orders than when they worked alone

True/False
Select the best answer by circling *T for True* or *F for False*. Check your answers on p. 305.

1. **T or F** A person who is willing to help his neighbor this weekend because he will need his neighbor's help next weekend is exhibiting reciprocal altruism.

2. **T or F** Zimbardo found that "guards" in one of his studies unexpectedly behaved politely towards "prisoners" since the "guards" were generally nice people.

Check your answers on p. 305.

1. According to the primacy effect in impression formation, you will be more influenced by:
    a. physical characteristics than by nonverbal behaviors
    b. ordinary information than by unusual information
    c. information received first, rather than that received later
    d. peripheral rather than central traits
    e. nonverbal behaviors than by physical characteristics

2. 75% of the people you meet belong to group X and 25% belong to group Y. Members of both groups perform an equal number of unusual acts. When asked to decide which group does more unusual things, you will say:
    a. Group Y, because unusual acts committed by a minority group stand out
    b. Group X, because unusual acts committed by a majority group stand out
    c. Group Y, because unusual acts committed by a majority group stand out
    d. they are equivalent, because they actually are
    e. Group X, because unusual acts committed by a minority group stand out

3. Which of the following is an internal attribution?
    a. John failed the test because he had to work last night
    b. Mary forgot the party because she was so busy at work
    c. Sally invited me over for dinner because she owed me a favor
    d. Fred hung up on me because he has a short temper
    e. both a and b

4. The actor-observer effect is shown in which of the following?
    a. Jane left the party because she is not very friendly; I left it because people were using drugs
    b. Mike failed the test because it was too difficult; I failed it because I am basically stupid
    c. John dropped the tray because he is a klutz; I dropped the tray because I am clumsy
    d. Sally fell because it was slippery; I fell because my boots don't have good tread
    e. all of the above

5. People sometimes intentionally put themselves at a disadvantage on tasks so they can attribute their:
    a. successes to external factors
    b. failures to internal factors
    c. failures to external factors
    d. successes to internal factors
    e. outcomes to the fundamental attribution error

6. The measurement of attitudes:
    a. is very accurate and reliable
    b. is rarely done with subjective rating scales
    c. results in good prediction of behavior for high self-monitors
    d. may be inaccurate because people may not be aware of their attitudes
    e. is fairly constant across cultures so that a rating scale in one culture is interpreted similarly in other cultures

7. The sleeper effect refers to:
   a. persuasion via a superficial approach
   b. persuasion via careful evaluation of evidence
   c. a change in attitude by a high self-monitor
   d. changing attitudes after noticing that behaviors and attitudes don't match
   e. changing attitudes after initial rejection of a message

8. The foot-in-the-door technique is one trick to facilitate persuasion. What is another way that involves doing just the opposite?
   a. have an expert give the message
   b. start with a small request and then make a large one
   c. begin by arguing the opposite and gradually make arguments that support the desired view
   d. begin with a very large request and then scale it back
   e. make the arguments in a way that people don't know that they are being persuaded

9. According to the cognitive dissonance theory, people:
   a. will change their behavior only after their attitudes have changed
   b. try to understand and explain their behavior
   c. change their attitudes to reduce the tension that results from inconsistent attitudes and behaviors
   d. will like an activity if they receive a large payoff for doing it
   e. will dislike an activity if they avoid it because of a severe threat

10. Which of the following are people least likely to use in selecting friends
    a. similarity of the potential friend to oneself
    b. familiarity of the potential friend
    c. proximity of the potential friend
    d. anxiety of the potential friend
    e. both b and d

11. Mary and Mark just divorced after 4 years of marriage. According to the research examining divorce, the likely issue was
    a. they got married even though they had unresolved problems
    b. they started strong and then became disillusioned
    c. they waited until they were in their 30s to get married
    d. they were too similar to each other

12. In Asch's experiment, subjects were to judge the length of bars after hearing other people give a wrong answer. What happened?
    a. people rarely conformed, because the situation was not ambiguous
    b. people conformed much more if there were seven other people than if there were only three
    c. people conformed even if there was only one other person
    d. everyone conformed if there were seven other people
    e. most people did not conform if they had an "ally" who gave the correct answer

13. Under which situation would you most expect social loafing to occur?
    a. an individual shooting while playing on a basketball team
    b. a person who has a unique specialty doing something in a group
    c. people thinking up unusual uses for a brick when they know that others will know how many uses they gave
    d. people clapping as part of a group

14. The city council is discussing whether a license to operate a new bar should be approved. Each member is slightly against approval. What is the group decision likely to be and why?
    a. in favor of the license because of groupthink
    b. a split vote because of social loafing
    c. against the license because of the group polarization effect
    d. a split vote because of the group polarization effect
    e. in favor of the license because of social loafing

15. Military strategists all agreed on a plan to attack an island. No one questioned whether it was reasonable and whether they would succeed. What happened during that meeting?
    a. peremptory challenges
    b. diffusion of responsibility
    c. social loafing
    d. groupthink
    e. fundamental attribution error

16. Situations like gas wars in which one gas station lowers prices and then other nearby stations must do the same or lose customers are similar to the:
    a. dollar auction
    b. prisoner's dilemma
    c. commons dilemma
    d. door-in-the-face technique
    e. that's-not-all technique

17. If today's rules had been in effect at the time of Milgram's studies, a Human Subjects Committee might have approved his procedures. Why?
    a. few psychologists and psychiatrists predicted that subjects would actually "shock" others
    b. there was no possibility of physical harm to any participants, and that is all that concerns Human Subjects Committees
    c. researchers abide by less-strict human subjects regulations than when Milgram did his study
    d. none of Milgram's subjects were upset by the procedures, so there is no reason for concern

18. In one study examining cross cultural difference in attribution participants were shown a picture of one fish that was perceived as either leading or being chased by a school of fish. What results were observed?
    a. most Chinese thought the one fish was being chased by the school of fish
    b. most Americans thought the one fish was leading by the school of fish
    c. neither a nor b
    d. both a and b

19. Sam and Kerry are trying to save their marriage. Which of the following is correct?
    a. they should go see a marriage counselor because of the high success rate (greater than 90%) of counseling
    b. they should limit the expression and perception of negative emotions
    c. they should have "open communication" to increase exchange of hostilities
    d. see an attorney and end the marriage as soon as possible

20. Research examining cross cultural differences in conformity
    a. found no reliable differences between U.S. and Japanese participants
    b. found Japanese participants conformed more than U.S. participants
    c. found U.S. participants conformed more than Japanese participants

Answers to the Fill in the Blank Questions – Module 14.1

1. primacy (p. 533)

2. fundamental (p. 539)

3. stereotype (p. 534)

4. self-serving bias (p. 541)

5. prejudice (p. 534)

Answers to the Short Answer Questions – Module 14.1

1. First impressions are based on physical attractiveness, people's nonverbal behaviors, and information that is learned first. In addition, expectations that are derived from stereotypes about groups of people influence first impressions. (p. 533)

2. Attribution is the process of assigning causes to someone's behavior. *Consistency information* (how much a person's behavior varies), *consensus information* (how similar a person's behavior is to that of other people), and *distinctiveness information* (how much a person's behavior depends upon the situation) are important. Behaviors that are high in consistency, dissimilar to those of other people, and not distinctive to a situation are attributed to internal causes. (p. 538)

3. This actor-observer effect may occur because people who are watching someone assume that behavior results from characteristics within that person. It might occur because we know that our own behavior is not consistent across situations, but we know less about others' behavior. Another possibility is that we attribute unexpected behaviors to external events and our own behavior is not unexpected. A third explanation is that we do not see ourselves as objects, so we tend to focus on the environment, or external stimuli. (p. 540)

Answers to the Multiple Choice Questions – Module 14.1

1. a-c. Incorrect. Since these do influence impressions
   d. Correct! (p. 533)

2. a. Incorrect. Although true, such external attributions should not lead to stereotypes
   b. Incorrect. They remember unusual behaviors
   c. Incorrect. Information used to decide about internal and external attributions; not necessarily relevant to stereotypes
   d. Correct! (p. 533)

3. a. Incorrect. Since it really overemphasizes internal causes
    b, d. Incorrect. Information used in making attributions; neither distinctiveness nor
        consensus necessarily overemphasized
    c. Correct! (p. 539)

4. a. Correct! (p. 541)
    b. Incorrect. This is the actor-observer effect
    c. Incorrect. May be an example of misattribution if cause is wrong
    d. Incorrect. Refers to explanations for failure, not success

Answers to the True/False Questions – Module 14.1

1. **True**: In general, Western cultures focus more on the individual and Asian cultures focus
    more on the situation. (p. 539)

2. **False**: Aversive racism occurs when people consciously express **equality** of races, but still
    have negative feelings or **un**intentionally discriminate against that race. (p. 535)

Answers to the Fill in the Blank Questions – Module 14.2

1. cognitive dissonance (p. 548)

2. forewarning (p. 547)

3. bait-and-switch (p. 548)

4. central (p. 544)

Answers to the Short Answer Questions – Module 14.2

1. When people hear persuasive arguments, they sometimes evaluate the evidence and logic
    behind the message. This is called the central route to persuasion, and it occurs for serious
    decisions. An alternative route that is used for less serious decisions is the peripheral route to
    persuasion. People pay more attention to the speaker's appearance and reputation, and to the
    sheer number of arguments regardless of their quality. (p. 544)

2. The foot-in-the-door technique involves getting agreement for a small request first and then
    making a much larger request. The door-in-the-face technique is the opposite; begin with the
    large request and then scale down to the smaller one. The that's-not-all technique makes a
    better offer before the person has responded to the first one. With each technique, the second
    request is more likely to be agreed to than if the first was not made. (pp. 547-548)

3. The idea is that if people behave in ways that are inconsistent with their attitudes, they will
    change their attitudes. The original theory argued that tension builds up if people's behavior
    and attitudes do not match. They reduce this tension by adopting a new attitude that justifies
    their behavior. (p. 548)

Answers to the Multiple Choice Questions – Module 14.2

1. a. Correct! (p. 543)
    b. people are often unaware of attitudes
    c. Incorrect. Cultures differ in how they use rating scales
    d. Incorrect. People are unaware of implicit attitudes, so they are difficult to measure
    e. Incorrect. Attitudes often do not predict behavior

2. a. Incorrect. Peripheral is followed for unimportant decisions
    b. Incorrect. This is the peripheral route
    c. Correct! (p. 544)
    d. Incorrect. This is the peripheral route

3. a. Incorrect. Attitudes are changed more by people who are similar
    b. Incorrect. Frightening messages are usually effective only if people can do something about the disaster
    c. Incorrect. Forewarning effect reduces persuasion
    d. Incorrect. Inoculation effect reduces persuasion
    e. Correct! (p. 544)

4. a. Incorrect. This also works, but is opposite of foot-in-door
    b. Incorrect. Foot-in-door doesn't refer to forceful entry
    c. Incorrect. Foot-in-door doesn't refer to persistent asking
    d. Correct! (p. 547)
    e. Incorrect. This is the that's-not-all technique

5. a. Incorrect. Theory says the opposite
    b. Incorrect. Attitudes do change if behavior does
    c. Incorrect. Forewarning effect; decreases attitude change
    d. Correct! (p. 548)

Answers to the True/False Questions – Module 14.2

1. **True**: A sleeper effect may occur after a considerable delay following initial rejection. (p. 544)

2. **False**: Intelligent people are persuaded by complex messages, but less intelligent people are more easily persuaded by poorly supported ideas. (pp. 546-547)

Answers to the Fill in the Blank Questions – Module 14.3

1. exchange or equity (p. 553)

2. men (p. 557)

Answers to the Short Answer Questions – Module 14.3

1. Similarity is important. Couples tend to resemble each other in age, social class, religion, intelligence, etc. Proximity is important. People tend to date people who live close to them. For first dates, physical attractiveness is important; people like physically attractive dates better than less attractive dates. (pp. 552-553)

2. Equity theory assumes that social relationships are transactions in which partners exchange "goods." Each partner wants to get the best deal possible. Partners look at the pluses and minuses of relationships and decide whether the exchange seems fair. (p. 553)

Answers to the Multiple Choice Questions – Module 14.3

1. a-d. Incorrect. Since all of them are correct.
   e. Correct! (p. 552)

2. a. Correct! (p. 552)
   b. Incorrect. This is an exception to the familiarity rule; people are very familiar as children don't develop romantic relationships
   c. Incorrect. Similar people are usually attracted to each other
   d. Incorrect. Equity theory argues that both people should get a fair deal

3. a. Incorrect. Similarity is the rule; according to the equity principle, both parties should be about equally attractive
   b. Incorrect. Physical attractiveness is most important at first
   c. Incorrect. It is just the opposite; attractiveness is more important initially
   d. Correct! (pp. 553-554)

4. a. Incorrect. Men prefer younger partners who will be fertile for more years
   b. Incorrect. Men are more likely to have casual sex partners
   c. Incorrect. Men spread their genes more with multiple partners
   d. Correct! (p. 557)

Answers to the True/False Questions – Module 14.3

1. **True**: We tend to be attracted to people who confirm our self-evaluations. (p. 553)

2. **False**: Research suggests, at best, there is a weak link between attractiveness and these other variables. (pp. 554-556, Fig 14.9-14.10)

3. **False**: Marriage counseling has dubious results in saving marriage. (p. 559)

Answers to the Fill in the Blank Questions – Module 14.4

1. diffusion of responsibility (p. 564)

2. groupthink (p. 565)

Answers to the Short Answer Questions – Module 14.4

1. Both may occur because of diffusion of responsibility because people in groups do less than individuals. Bystanders are less likely to help strangers in trouble when there are more, rather than fewer, people around. They assume either that others will help or that it may not really be an emergency situation. In social loafing, people do less work in a group than alone, perhaps because their own efforts won't be evaluated. (p. 565)

2. If the members of a group generally agree on a position at the beginning, they often move toward the extreme because of diffusion of responsibility (the group is responsible, not me), because individuals hear many reasons for their position, and because they receive reinforcement from the group for agreeing. (p. 565)

Answers to the Multiple Choice Questions – Module 14.4

1.   a. Incorrect. It least three are needed for maximum conformity effect
     b. Incorrect. Conformity will occur but no more than with four people
     c. Incorrect. Having an "ally" reduces conformity
     d. Incorrect. About the same amount of conformity occurs with four and seven people
     e. Correct! (p. 562)

2.   a. Incorrect. Refers to whether people will help; not an explanation of why they help
     b. Incorrect. A car breakdown should be equally ambiguous on both types of highway
     c. Incorrect. Diffusion should lead to less help; people assume others will help
     d. Incorrect. Refers to tendency to work less hard in a group, not to whether bystanders will help
     e. Correct! (p. 564)

3.   a. Correct! (p. 565)
     b. Incorrect. Not a matter of how much effort an individual puts forth, but of a group's influence on decisions
     c. Incorrect. Refers to whether people will help; both may be due to diffusion of responsibility
     d. Incorrect. Refers to lawyers' rights to reject potential jurors; not relevant to group decision making
     e. people's tendency to help others; not relevant to group decision making

4.   a., b. Incorrect. Groupthink involves decision making
     c. Correct! (p. 565)
     d. Incorrect. Information, especially dissenting opinions, is not gathered when groupthink occurs

Answers to the True/False Questions – Module 14.4

1. **True**: Many participants in Asch's research changed their answers at least once to conform with the group's wrong answer. (p. 562, Figs. 14.12-14.13).

2. **False**: Groupthink occurs when group members do not question others' ideas and do not ask probing potentially important and difficult questions. (p. 565)

Answers to the Fill in the Blank Questions – Module 14.5

1. prisoner's dilemma (pp. 569-570)

2. behavior trap (p. 568)

Answers to the Short Answer Questions – Module 14.5

1. The commons dilemma involves overuse of limited resources due to participants taking more than their allocated share. Even in studies in which participants knew that the limited resource would increase if they waited to take their allocated share, participants did not wait and immediately exhausted the limited resource. (pp. 570-571)

2. Students served as teachers in what they thought was an experiment on obedience. They presented word pairs to a "learner" who made many mistakes in his recall of the pairs. Students were to administer a higher shock level following each mistake. Over half of the students continued and administered the highest shock level. This shows that people have such great respect for authority that they may carry out unreasonable and dangerous instructions. (pp. 571-572)

Answers to the Multiple Choice Questions – Module 14.5

1. a. Correct! (pp. 569-570)
    b. Incorrect. Best for group, not individuals; if one country has weapons and others don't, that country can dominate
    c. Incorrect. Not best for group; possibility of nuclear war
    d. Incorrect. Communication should foster cooperation

2. a. Correct! (pp. 570-571)
    b. Incorrect. Cooperative response, but not what people do
    c. Incorrect. Groups are usually more greedy than individuals
    d. Incorrect. In this commons dilemma and the prisoners dilemma, people behave competitively
    e. Incorrect. b and d are wrong

3. a. Incorrect. Over half obeyed; they were "normal"
    b. Correct! (pp. 571-572)
    c. Incorrect. Obedience increased when the experimenter was in the room
    d. Incorrect. Obedience increased when a confederate obeyed

Answers to the True/False Questions – Module 14.5

1. **True**: Reciprocal altruism is the tendency to cooperate with someone who may repay the favor later. (p. 570)

2. **False**: Zimbardo actually found that the "guards" became abusive towards the "prisoners" since they could get away with it. (p. 571)

Answers to Final Comprehensive Assessment

1. c (p. 533)	8. d (p. 547)	15. d (p. 565)
2. a (p. 534)	9. c (p. 548)	16. a (p. 568)
3. d (p. 538)	10. d (pp. 552-553)	17. a (pp. 572-573)
4. a (p. 540)	11. a (p. 558)	18. d (p. 539)
5. c (p. 541)	12. e (p. 563)	19. b (p. 559)
6. d (p. 543)	13. d (p. 565)	20. a (p. 563)
7. e (p. 544)	14. c (p. 565)	

CHAPTER 15
ABNORMALITY, THERAPY, AND SOCIAL ISSUES

CHAPTER OVERVIEW INFORMATION

LEARNING OBJECTIVES
By the end of Chapter 15 you should

- ✓ Understand the nature of abnormal behavior and the problems of defining and classifying it
- ✓ Be familiar with the major schools and methods of psychotherapy
- ✓ Have an awareness of the legal issues that affect the living conditions and treatment of the mentally ill

CHAPTER 15 OUTLINE
Chapter 15 reviews some of the topics related to abnormal behavior. Included in the chapter are overviews on abnormal behavior and psychotherapies used to address abnormal behavior. Also presented is a discussion of the social and legal aspects of treating abnormal behavior.

Chapter 15 is presented below in outline format to assist you in understanding the information presented in the chapter. More detailed information on any topic can be found using the page references to the right of the topic.

Module 15.1 Abnormal Behavior: An Overview
I. Defining Abnormal Behavior
    A. Defining abnormal behavior can be difficult (pp. 581-582)
    B. Cultural Influences on Abnormality
        1. Different disorders occur in different cultures (pp. 582-583)
        2. Suggestion/imitation may play a role in some disorders including dissociative identity disorder (DID) (p. 583)
    C. The Biopsychosocial Model
        1. Abnormal behavior has biological, psychological and sociological aspects (p. 583)
            a. Biological influences and disorders may contribute to abnormal behavior (p. 583)
            b. Psychological influences and experiences may contribute to abnormal behavior (p. 584)
            c. Sociological influences and interactions may contribute to abnormal behavior (p. 584)

II. Classifying Psychological Disorders
    A. DSM-IV classifies disorders and provides acceptable labels (p. 584)
    B. DSM-IV Classifications
        1. DSM-IV has five axes of classification (p. 584)
    C. Axis I Disorders
        1. Axis I lists disorders that have an onset after infancy and have some likelihood of recovery (p. 584, Table 15.1)
            a. Attention deficit disorder (ADD) is an example of an Axis I disorder (p. 584)
                i. Characterized by distraction, impulsiveness, and moodiness (p. 584)
            b. Attention-deficit hyperactivity disorder (ADHD) similar to ADD but also characterized by fidgetiness (p. 584)
            c. Approximately 3-10% of children, mostly boys, usually outgrow (p. 585)
            d. May have some biological cause (p. 585)

  e. Treatment includes stimulant drugs and behavioral interventions (p. 585)

  f. Performance on impulsivity tasks is also affected (pp. 585-586)

 D. Axis II Disorders

  1. Axis II lists disorders that persist throughout life (p. 586, Table 15.2)

   a. Personality disorders are inflexible ways of interacting (p. 586)

 E. Axis III lists physical disorders (p. 584)

 F. Axis IV indicates how much stress the person has had to endure (p. 584)

 G. Axis V evaluates level of functioning (p. 584)

 H. The Importance of Differential Diagnosis

  1. DSM-IV allows clinicians to make differential diagnoses (p. 586)

 I. Criticisms of DSM-IV

  1. People often have symptoms that do not fit in a disorder classification (p. 586)

   a. Many people endure some diagnosable disorder at some point in their lives (p. 587, Fig. 15.1)

    i. Percent of people who "have a problem" depends upon classification of borderline cases (p. 587)

  2. Symptoms may be related to specific situation and not indicative of disorder (p. 588)

The message: *People who qualify for psychological diagnoses are not very different from normal (p. 588)*

Module 15.2 Psychotherapy: An Overview

III. Historical Trends in Psychotherapy

 A. Psychotherapy is a treatment to address psychological issues and includes a personal relationship between a therapist and client (p. 590)

 B. Has changed since mid-1900's due to advances in treatment, costs, and insurance (p. 590)

IV. Psychoanalysis

 A. Freud developed psychoanalysis to bring out unconscious material to conscious levels and to produce a catharsis (p. 591, Fig. 15.2)

 B. Free Association

  1. Free association--patient says whatever comes to mind (p. 591)

 C. Transference

  1. Transference--patient reacts to therapist as someone else (p. 592)

V. Behavior Therapy

 A. Behavior therapists assume that behavior is learned and can be unlearned (p. 592)

 B. Therapy starts with goals and attempts to achieve those through learning (p. 592)

  1. Bed-wetting can be helped through classical conditioning (p. 592, Fig. 15.3-15.4)

VI. Therapies That Focus on Thoughts and Beliefs

 A. Some therapies focus on thoughts and beliefs (p. 593)

 B. Cognitive Therapies

  1. Cognitive therapy strives to have people discover their inappropriate beliefs and change them (p. 593, Table 15.3)

  2. Rational-emotive therapy assumes that abnormal behavior is due to irrational thoughts (p. 593, Table 15.3)

 C. Cognitive-Behavior Therapy

  1. Cognitive-behavior therapy attempts to change behavior but puts emphasis on people's interpretations of situations (p. 594, Table 15.3)

VII. Humanistic Therapy
   A. Person-centered therapy is the best-known humanistic therapy (p. 594, Table 15.3)
      1. The therapist provides an atmosphere in which the client can freely explore feelings (p. 595)

VIII. Family Systems Therapy
   A. Family systems therapy involves working with the entire family (p. 595, Table 15.3)

IX. Other Trends in Psychotherapy
   A. New methods make therapy less costly and less time-consuming (p. 596)
      1. Many therapists combine approaches and use eclectic therapy (p. 596)
   B. Brief Therapy
      1. Brief therapies usually have time limits (p. 596)
      2. Expectations on progress are set (pp. 596-597)
      3. HMOs sometimes force therapy to be too brief (p. 597)
   C. Group Therapy
      1. Group therapy sessions are less expensive and they allow individuals to relate to others with similar problems (p. 597)
   D. Self-Help Groups
      1. Self-help groups do not include a therapist (p. 597)
      2. Some self-therapies effective when dealing with mild problems (p. 598)

X. Comparing Therapies and Therapists
   A. The effectiveness of therapy can be determined by comparing treated and non-treated people (pp. 598-599)
      1. Psychotherapy patients improve more than nontreated people (pp. 598-599, Fig. 15.5)
      2. All kinds of therapies are helpful (p. 599)
         a. The type of therapist is not critical in US and Germany (p. 600, Fig. 15.6)
         b. Experienced therapists are not necessarily better than non-professionals (p. 600)
            i. However, professional therapists are always willing to listen and they keep conversations confidential (p. 600)
            ii. Trained therapists can diagnose biological problems (p. 600)
   B. Is More Treatment Better?
      1. More therapy sessions do not necessarily mean more improvement, but can be somewhat more beneficial (p. 601, Fig. 15.7)
   C. Similarities Among Psychotherapeutic Methods
      1. Effectiveness of psychotherapy primarily depends on the client (p. 601)
      2. Therapies help because they rely on a therapeutic alliance between therapist and client (p. 601)
         a. Commitment to change by the client is necessary (p. 602)
   D. Advice for Potential Clients (p. 602)
      1. Seeking out help is not shameful and therapists can be found in phone book (p. 602)
      2. Seek out therapist with similar cultural and religious background (p. 602)
      3. Expect some improvement in 6-8 weeks (p. 602)
      4. Be wary of unscrupulous therapists (p. 602)

The message: Various types of therapy are about equally effective but some therapists differ in effectiveness and therapy is more education based than medicine based. (p. 602)

Module 15.3 Social and Legal Aspects of Treatment

XI. Deinstitutionalization
    A. Older mental hospitals were bleak and provided to satisfy patients' basic needs (p. 604)
        1. Drugs and advances in psychotherapy allow hospitals to offer short-term care (p. 604)
        2. Deinstitutionalization refers to moving people from hospitals to community-based treatment centers (p. 604)
            a. Mixed results of moving to deinstitutionalization (p. 604)

XII. Involuntary Commitment and Treatment
    A. A person who is dangerous to society can be involuntarily committed to a mental institution (p. 605)
        1. Once committed, patients can still refuse treatment (p. 605, Fig 15.8)

XIII. The Duty to Protect
    A. Therapist must notify authorities if client is a danger to a specific individual (p. 606)

XIV. The Insanity Defense
    A. People are not responsible for their behavior if they are "insane" (p. 606)
        1. Under the M'Naghten rule, people must not realize that they are committing a crime (p. 607)
        2. Patients found not guilty by reason of insanity usually stay in mental hospital as long as they would have went to prison (p. 607)
        3. Some states experimenting with alternatives to insanity plea (p. 607)

XV. Preventing Mental Illness
    A. Community psychologists attempt to prevent disorders from occurring or from becoming worse (p. 608)
        1. Prevention is preferred to intervention and maintenance (p. 608)
            a. Several actions possible to increase prevention. Some feasible others not (p. 608)

The message: *The insanity defense and other legal issues are complicated, difficult topics that require political decisions by society as a whole. (p. 609)*

RELATED WEBSITES AND ACTIVITIES

Visit http://psychology.wadsworth.com/kalat_intro7e/ for online quizzing, glossary flashcards, crossword puzzles, annotated web links, and more.

LECTURE MATERIAL

Information from the text is only half of the picture. Don't forget to review your lecture material. Process each topic meaningfully. Most importantly, be sure that you understand the material in each lecture-if you don't, ask your instructor or teaching assistant.

**STUDY TIP # 15: While reading the textbook you should consider underlining (with a pencil) and annotating in the margins. This will let you review the material more easily later. You can also incorporate your annotations in your notes. Underline only the details that you find important. DO NOT overdo underlining otherwise there will be more information underlined than not underlined.

TIP: Associate the lecture material with the information from the text, with things that you already know, with your personal experiences, or with real-life applications. Type or neatly re-write your notes. Make sure they are detailed and organized. Make comments on your notes. Then write questions to cover each concept.

CHAPTER MODULE ASSESSMENTS

Module 15.1 Abnormal Behavior: An Overview
Answer these questions soon after reading the **Module 15.1: Abnormal Behavior: An Overview**. There are several formats to the assessments. Answers to all questions appear on pp. 319-320.

Fill in the Blank
Provide a term(s) which best completes the statement below. Answers appear on p. 319.

1. Uniform definitions and standards for making diagnoses of psychological disorders can be found in the _____.

2. The _____ model emphasizes that abnormal behavior has three major aspects - biological, psychological, and sociological.

3. _____ of the DSM-IV is used to classify personality disorders and mental retardation.

4. A _____ is a maladaptive, inflexible way of dealing with the environment and other people.

Short Answer
The following questions require a short written answer (3-7 sentences). Answers appear on p. 319.

1. Discuss the three components of the biopsychosocial model of abnormal behavior.

2. Describe how DSM-IV categorizes psychological disorders.

3. Discuss the Axis I disorders of ADD and ADHD including treatment.

Multiple Choice

Circle the best answer below. Check your answers on pp. 319-320. If your answer was incorrect, try to write why it was incorrect. Check your reasons on pp. 319-320.

1. The American Psychiatric Association's definition of psychological disorder is:
   a. anything that is different from average
   b. behavior associated with distress, disability, or with increased risk of death, pain, or loss of freedom
   c. patterns of behavior that a particular culture regards as troublesome or unacceptable
   d. any unusual behavior that is caused by a biological disorder

2. According to DSM-IV, if someone has an Axis I disorder:
   a. the disorder is a part of the person himself or herself and therapy is unlikely to help
   b. the person is doing worse now than at some point in the past
   c. there is a physical problem, such as diabetes
   d. he or she would also score high on the Axis V scale of level of functioning

3. Which of the following is considered in the Biopsychosocial model of abnormal behavior?
   a. biological influences and disorders
   b. psychological influences and experiences
   c. sociological influences and interactions
   d. all of the above

True/False

Select the best answer by circling *T for True* or *F for False*. Check your answers on p. 320.

1. **T or F** Cultural influences may play a role in abnormal behavior since some different cultures sometimes have different disorders.

2. **T or F** Axis I disorders usually last throughout a lifetime whereas Axis II disorders are shorter lived.

3. **T or F** Psychologists using the DSM-IV can easily distinguish between disorders.

Module 15.2 Psychotherapy: An Overview
Answer these questions soon after reading the **Module 15.2: Psychotherapy: An Overview**. There are several formats to the assessments. Answers to all questions appear on pp. 320-322.

Fill in the Blank

Provide a term(s) which best completes the statement below. Answers appear on p. 320.

1. A treatment for psychological disorders that involves a personal relationship between a trained therapist and a client is _____.

2. Freud's style of therapy was known as _____ and is considered to be the first type of "talking" therapy.

3. Therapists who focus on communication patterns within families and work with the entire family are _____ therapists.

4. Therapists who assume that human behavior is learned and can be unlearned are _____ therapists.

5. About half of all therapists today describe themselves as _____ which means that they use a combination of treatment methods depending on the client's problem and circumstances.

6. The therapy that focuses on changing an individual's thoughts and beliefs is _____ therapy.

7. Groups such as Alcoholics Anonymous which provide support for people with similar problems without using a trained therapist are _____ groups.

Short Answer
The following questions require a short written answer (3-7 sentences). Answers appear on pp. 320-321.

1. If you go to a therapist who uses psychoanalysis, what would you expect?

2. How does humanistic or person-centered therapy differ from the psychoanalytic therapy that you described above?

3. Treating people in groups has become increasingly common. Describe three types of such treatment.

4. Evaluate the effectiveness of psychotherapy.

5. Discuss the things that all forms of psychotherapy have in common.

Multiple Choice
Circle the best answer below. Check your answers on pp. 321-322. If your answer was incorrect, try to write why it was incorrect. Check your reasons on pp. 321-322.

1. In psychoanalysis:
    a. the therapist uses hypnosis to gain access to the patient's unconscious
    b. the therapist explains the universal meaning of symbols in a dream
    c. the therapist uses free association to censor embarrassing thoughts
    d. the patient may begin to treat the therapist as someone else when transference occurs

2. How do behavior therapies differ from psychoanalysis and humanistic therapies?
    a. behavior therapists attack the behavior, not the thoughts
    b. behavior therapies dwell more on the discovering hidden meanings than the other two
    c. behavior therapists tend to stick with the same procedure longer (even its not working) than the other two
    d. the goals of behavior therapy are broader and more vague than the goals of the other two

3. Bed-wetting has been treated most effectively with:
    a. classical conditioning
    b. psychoanalysis
    c. aversion therapy
    d. rationale-emotive therapy

4. How does rational-emotive therapy differ from cognitive therapy?
    a. cognitive therapy deals with changing cognitions; rational-emotive therapy deals mainly with changing emotions, with the idea that changes in thoughts will follow
    b. cognitive therapists usually use Freud's methods; rational-emotive therapies don't
    c. rational-emotive believes emotions lead to thoughts; cognitive believes thoughts lead to emotions
    d. rational-emotive therapists often contradict their patients' irrational beliefs; cognitive therapists have patients explore evidence behind their thoughts

5. Person-centered therapy:
    a. tries to increase the incongruence between a person's self-concept and his or her ideal self
    b. tries to direct a person toward worthy goals
    c. directs the client away from inappropriate thoughts toward more appropriate ones
    d. includes unconditional positive regard
    e. was pioneered by Ellis

6. A therapist helps his clients to set specific goals for changing behavior, and then he works with them to change their interpretation of problems. What type of therapy is this?
    a. rational-emotive therapy
    b. family systems therapy
    c. cognitive-behavior therapy
    d. person-centered therapy
    e. aversion therapy

7. Dr. Ron Jr. often has his client free associate; sometimes tries to get them to understand whether they are playing the role of child, adult, or parent; uses reinforcement for appropriate behavior; and tries to get them to change their irrational thoughts. Dr. Ron Jr. is a(n):
   a. psychoanalyst
   b. eclectic therapist
   c. multiple personality
   d. family therapist
   e. brief therapist

8. What is the advantage of family systems therapy?
   a. it is cheaper because the whole family shares the expense
   b. a deadline is used so both therapist and the family are motivated to bring therapy to a successful conclusion
   c. communication and unreasonable demands within a family can be dealt with
   d. a therapist is not needed; people "treat" each other

9. Which of the following is true about the effectiveness of psychotherapy?
   a. people who receive no therapy improve at about the same rate as people who are treated
   b. people who receive psychotherapy show greater improvement than about 80% of untreated people
   c. therapy works best with patients who have vague, general complaints
   d. success depends a lot on the therapy; some are much better than others
   e. experienced therapists produce much more improvement than less experienced ones

10. In all psychotherapies:
   a. the therapist does most of the talking
   b. clients must make some commitment to change
   c. the more coordinated the treatment, the more improvement
   d. the therapist and client concentrate on the reasons behind behaviors

True/False
Select the best answer by circling *T for True* or *F for False*. Check your answers on p. 322.

1. **T or F** The type of therapist one sees is critical to the success of psychotherapy.

2. **T or F** Behavior therapy is based on the idea that abnormal behavior is learned and therapy is the process by which that learning is undone or replaced.

3. **T or F** Psychotherapy has changed significantly since the mid 1900s due to advances in treatments and changes in insurance.

4. **T or F** It is always the case that receiving more therapy will be more effective than receiving less therapy.

Fill in the Blank
Provide a term(s) which best completes the statement below. Answers appear on p. 323.

1. The process by which a person can be hospitalized against their will if they are found to be a danger to themselves or others is known as _____.

2. _____, such as educating pregnant mothers against using alcohol, is used by community psychologists in an attempt to stop disorders from starting.

3. Psychologists who focus on the needs of groups rather than individuals and use a variety of prevention strategies are _____ psychologists.

Short Answer
The following questions require a short written answer (3-7 sentences). Answers appear on p. 323.

1. How have mental hospitals changed since the 1950s?

2. Discuss the issues related to whether a psychologically disturbed person can refuse treatment.

Multiple Choice
Circle the best answer below. Check your answers on p. 323. If your answer was incorrect, try to write why it was incorrect. Check your reasons on p. 323.

1. State mental hospitals:
   a. were originally designed for people needing short-term care
   b. have had a steady increase in patients since 1950
   c. are more costly than alternative care
   d. promote psychological adjustment better than alternative care

2. Patients with mental disorders:
   a. must be confined to mental institutions if they are seriously disordered
   b. cannot be convicted of a crime
   c. can refuse the right to treatment even if they have been involuntarily committed to a hospital
   d. were not discharged from hospitals during deinstitutionalization

3. In which case should a person be called insane according to the original M'Naghten rule?
   a. Fred understood that he was committing a crime, but he couldn't stop himself
   b. John, who has brain damage, did not know that what he was doing was wrong
   c. Michael, who is schizophrenic, says that he knew what he was doing was wrong, but he could not control his impulses
   d. Brian committed a bizarre crime that he agreed was wrong, but that is the only evidence for insanity

4. Which of the following is true regarding the "duty to protect"?
   a. a therapist must protect the client against family influences
   b. clients must protect themselves from unscrupulous therapists
   c. a therapist must contact the authorities if a client makes a threat against a specific person
   d. a therapist must contact the authorities if a client makes a general threat

True/False
Select the best answer by circling *T for True* or *F for False*. Check your answers on p. 324.

1. **T or F** Criminals found not guilty by reason of insanity usually stay in mental hospital as long as they would have went to prison.

2. **T or F** Deinstitutionalization refers to moving people from community-based treatment centers to hospitals.

3. **T or F** Community psychologists attempt to prevent disorders from occurring or from becoming worse through various procedures.

FINAL COMPREHENSIVE CHAPTER ASSESSMENT TEST

Check your answers on p. 324.

1. Dissociative identity disorder (DID):
   a. is another term for schizophrenia
   b. means that the person has a single, seriously disordered personality
   c. is one of the most common mental disorders
   d. is diagnosed less often now than in the past
   e. means that one has several distinct personalities

2. What is the problem with statistics about the frequencies of mental disorders?
   a. they may be misleading because psychological disorders are a matter of degree
   b. it is impossible to give differential diagnoses to psychological disorders
   c. too many people show no symptoms at all
   d. there are no accepted guidelines for diagnosis
   e. both b and d

3. Which of the following is not an axis of DSM-IV?
   a. list of disorders that involve use of addictive substances
   b. list of disorders that last throughout life
   c. list of physical disorders
   d. evaluation of how much stress a person must endure
   e. evaluation of person's overall level of functioning

4. A therapist asks you to free associate to some different stimuli. The therapist is probably using which therapy?
   a. humanistic
   b. person-centered
   c. psychoanalysis
   d. nondirective
   e. behavioral

5. A client is angry that the therapy does not seem to be helping and he tells the therapist, "I'm going to stop coming if things don't get better soon". A therapist using person-centered therapy is likely to respond:
   a. you are angry with me because you are treating me like your father
   b. thinking that everything must work quickly is irrational
   c. you must not let such thoughts enter your mind or the therapy will never work
   d. think about what you can do to make me happy
   e. so you don't think this is helping; tell me more

6. Which type of therapy focuses more on changing what people do than what they think?
   a. behavior therapy
   b. rational-emotive therapy
   c. cognitive therapy
   d. psychoanalysis
   e. person-centered therapy

7. Cognitive therapists differ from rational-emotive therapists in that they:
   a. try to help people substitute more favorable beliefs; rational emotive therapists don't
   b. focus more on past experiences than rational-emotive therapists
   c. focus on behavior much more than rational-emotive therapists
   d. try to get clients to examine the evidence underlying their beliefs; rational emotive therapists often tell clients their thoughts are irrational
   e. cognitive therapists treat the family as a unit; rational emotive therapists treat individuals

8. Why might self-help groups be preferred over other types of group therapy?
   a. the treatment takes place over a strictly limited period of time
   b. people can work on how they relate to others
   c. all members are available to one another at any time, without charge
   d. self-help group leaders have greater education and experience
   e. self-help groups treat the entire family and not an individual alone

9. Brief therapy:
   a. is used with psychoanalysis more than with other methods
   b. is suitable for clients with vague problems
   c. can be conducted by psychiatrists but not psychologists
   d. usually makes a client begin dealing with main problems promptly
   e. involves a time limit set by the therapist, but that is unknown to the client

10. All psychotherapists:
    a. only treat people with identifiable psychological disorders
    b. try to get clients to commit to making changes
    c. concentrate on getting clients to understand the reasons behind their behaviors
    d. try to change clients' irrational thoughts
    e. allow therapy to go on as long as is necessary

11. State mental hospitals:
    a. have shifted from having a goal of short-term care to long-term custody
    b. usually provide therapy by psychologists and psychiatrists
    c. provide much better care than community health centers
    d. are often bleak places and have decreased in number
    e. have received large increases in funding as their goals have changed

12. Deinstitutionalization has:
    a. successfully moved most patients from mental institutions to community-based care
    b. may have helped to increase the number of homeless people
    c. forced states to plan adequate alternatives for care and housing
    d. resulted in more cost to states because alternative care is more expensive than hospitals
    e. has been unsuccessful because populations in mental institutions have actually increased rather than decreased

13. Which of the following is true?
    a. people who are involuntarily committed can still refuse treatment
    b. fewer people would be judged insane by the M'Naghten Rule if the burden was relaxed
    c. the laws concerning involuntary commitment are the same from state to state
    d. psychiatrists consider most psychologically disturbed people to be legally insane

14. A community psychologist practicing prevention would **not** do which of the following?
    a. outlaw smoking in public places and educate people about the risks of smoking
    b. educate women about the importance of prenatal care
    c. decrease education opportunities for those who do not deserve them
    d. work to ban toxins that can cause brain damage
    e. open high quality day care centers

ANSWERS AND EXPLANATIONS FOR CHAPTER MODULE ASSESSMENTS

Answers to the Fill in the Blank Questions – Module 15.1

1. DSM-IV (p. 584)

2. biopsychosocial (p. 583)

3. Axis II (p. 586)

4. personality disorder (p. 586)

Answers to the Short Answer Questions – Module 15.1

1. One component is that psychological disorders result from biological disorders, including things like genetics, brain damage, hormonal abnormalities, disease, and the effects of drugs. The psychological component is that people react unfavorably to events. The disorder then is in the way they act or feel. The third component involves how other people act toward or expect of a mentally ill person. (pp. 583-584)

2. Clients are classified along five axes. Axis 1 lists disorders that have a particular time of onset and a realistic probability of recovery. Axis 2 lists disorders that persist throughout life, such as personality disorders and mental retardation. Axis 3 lists physical disorders, such as diabetes or cirrhosis of the liver. Axis 4 involves an evaluation of stress. Axis 5 is an overall evaluation of the person's level of functioning. (p. 584)

3. Attention deficit disorder (ADD) is characterized by distraction, impulsiveness, moodiness, and an inability to follow through on plans. Attention-deficit hyperactivity disorder (ADHD) similar to ADD but also has another characteristic of fidgetiness. Approximately 3-10% of children in the US are diagnosed as ADD/ADHD and nearly 70% of them are boys. Although treatment includes the use of stimulant drugs and behavioral interventions, many children outgrow this condition. (pp. 584-585)

Answers to the Multiple Choice Questions – Module 15.1

1.   a. Incorrect. This would include unusually happy or successful people too
     b. Correct! (p. 582)
     c. Incorrect. Some societies may be intolerant of behaviors that are quite normal in other societies
     d. Incorrect. Biological causes are only one point of view

2. a. Incorrect. This describes Axis II, things like mental retardation and personality disorders
   b. Correct! (p. 584)
   c. Incorrect. Physical problems are on Axis III
   d. Incorrect. A person with an Axis I disorder would be unlikely to score highly on the level of functioning scale
3. a-c. Incorrect. Since all three are considered
   d. Correct! (p. 583)

Answers to the True/False Questions – Module 15.1

1. **True**: Different disorders unique to specific cultures or areas can be found throughout the world. (pp. 582-583)

2. **False**: Axis II disorders usually persist throughout a lifetime whereas Axis I disorders will likely respond to treatment. (p. 586)

3. **False**: Although the DSM-IV allows for differential diagnoses, many disorders have overlapping symptoms and therefore are not unambiguously identified. (p. 587)

Answers to the Fill in the Blank Questions – Module 15.2

1. psychotherapy (p. 590)

2. psychoanalysis (p. 591)

3. family (p. 595)

4. behavior (p. 592)

5. eclectic (p. 596)

6. cognitive (p. 593)

7. self-help (p. 597)

Answers to the Short Answer Questions – Module 15.2

1. The therapist would ask me to lie down on a couch and say anything that comes to mind. I would be asked to free associate and not censor or omit anything. The therapist would interpret what I say. He would also expect me to show transference. (pp. 591-592)

2. The humanistic therapist would not try to interpret or direct the therapy as the psychoanalytic therapist would. The humanistic therapist would not look for unconscious motives, but rather she would allow the client to explore his own feelings. The humanistic therapist would show unconditional positive regard and be totally accepting of everything the client says. In person-centered therapy, the "cure" comes from the client himself; in psychoanalytic therapy, the "cure" comes from the interpretation and direction of the therapist. (pp. 594-595, Table 15.3)

3. In group therapy, a small group of people with similar problems are treated at once. They can spread the cost of the therapy among group members and they also can work on interpersonal relationships. Self-help groups are similar to group therapy, except there is no therapist. People talk with each other and try to help each other. Family systems therapy is a special type of group therapy in which entire families are treated to improve communication and interaction among family members. Each family member often has problems, and all must be resolved for an individual to be helped. (p. 595, 597)

4. An early assessment of therapy suggested that treated people were no better off than people who were not treated. However, more recent studies have shown that the average psychotherapy patient improves more than 80% of all untreated people. All the common, mainstream therapies are about equal in effectiveness. (pp. 598-599)

5. Psychotherapy requires a commitment to change one's life. A therapeutic alliance is formed between the therapist and the client that is characterized by acceptance, caring, respect, and attention. Clients talk about beliefs, emotions, and actions and gain self-understanding. The therapist conveys an expectation that the client will improve. Actual improvement, however, may depend largely on the client's commitment to work on problems outside the therapy sessions. (pp. 601-602)

Answers to the Multiple Choice Questions – Module 15.2

1.   a. Incorrect. Freud used hypnosis at first, but then he decided it didn't work
     b. Incorrect. What each symbol means to the individual is important
     c. Incorrect. Thoughts are totally uncensored; person says whatever comes to mind
     d. Correct! (p. 592)

2.   a. Correct! (p. 592)
     b. Incorrect. Psychoanalysis searches for hidden meanings, and behavior therapy does not
     c. Incorrect. Behavior therapists often change after a few sessions if something isn't working; psychoanalysts and humanists change much less
     d. Incorrect. Goals are more specific

3.   a. Correct! (p. 592)
     b. Incorrect. Psychoanalysis is ineffective for bed-wetters
     c. Incorrect. Punishments for bedwetting aren't very effective
     d. Incorrect. A "talk" therapy; usually used with adults

4.   a. Incorrect. Both deal with changing thoughts or beliefs
     b. Incorrect. Neither use Freud's methods
     c. Incorrect. Both believe that cognitions must be changed
     d. Correct! (p. 593)

5.   a. Incorrect. Tries to increase <u>congruence</u>--a match between self-concept and ideal self
     b. Incorrect. It is nondirective--therapist encourages client to seek own goals
     c. Incorrect. Nondirective; all the person's thoughts are appropriate in the therapy setting
     d. Correct! (p. 594)
     e. Incorrect. Carl Rogers; Ellis pioneered rational-emotive therapy

6. a. Incorrect. Would try to change irrational beliefs, but not necessarily set goals for changing behavior
    b. Incorrect. Would work with several family members
    c. Correct! (p. 594)
    d. Incorrect. Wouldn't set behavioral goals; wouldn't try to change interpretations
    e. Incorrect. Emphasis here is on changing interpretations, not punishing inappropriate behavior

7. a. Incorrect. He may be, but he uses more types of therapy
    b. Correct! (p. 596)
    c. Incorrect. Unlikely, unless a distinct personality goes with each of his therapies
    d. Incorrect. Not necessarily; unless he treats families rather than individuals
    e. Incorrect. Not necessarily; his therapy may go on for a long period with no deadline

8. a. Incorrect. Reason why group therapy developed; family would probably pay costs for individual therapy anyway
    b. Incorrect. Maybe, but only if brief therapy is used
    c. Correct! (p. 595)
    d. Incorrect. True with a self-help group; therapist involved in family therapy

9. a. Incorrect. Recent studies show that treated people do better
    b. Correct! (pp. 598-599)
    c. Incorrect. Works best with specific, clear-cut problems
    d. Incorrect. Studies show that various forms of therapy produce similar results
    e. Incorrect. They produced about equal benefits

10. a. Incorrect. True for some therapies, not for others
    b. Correct! (p. 602)
    c. Incorrect. This wasn't true in the Fort Bragg study; the well-coordinated program was just more expensive
    d. Incorrect. Not true for all therapies, especially not behavior therapy

Answers to the True/False Questions – Module 15.2

1. **False**: Research suggests that the type of therapist is not critical to the success of psychotherapy both in the US and in Germany. (p. 600, Fig. 15.6)

2. **True**: Behavior therapists focus on the behavior and how it was learned. They then use therapeutic techniques to change the behavior. (p. 592)

3. **True**: Early on only people who could afford psychotherapy were likely to seek it out. With advances in treatment including drugs and changes in insurance including HMOs, who seeks therapy and for how long has been affected. (p. 590)

4. **False**: More therapy sessions do not necessarily mean more improvement, but more therapy can sometimes be more beneficial. (p. 601)

Answers to the Fill in the Blank Questions – Module 15.3

1. involuntary commitment (p. 605)

2. Prevention (p. 608)

3. community (p. 608)

Answers to the Short Answer Questions – Module 15.3

1. Older mental hospitals were large hospitals built by states to house severely disturbed people who would probably never return to society. These hospitals often resembled prisons. The advent of antidepressant and anti-schizophrenic drugs has reduced the number of long-term residents so that the mental hospital population declined. The goal now is to supply short-term care until the patient can return home. Community mental health centers and halfway houses have become alternatives to large state hospitals. These types of care are effective, but many people who would have been in large hospitals are now in nursing homes, prisons, or they are homeless. (p. 604)

2. Some people with psychological disturbances fail to recognize that there is anything wrong with them. One argument is that such people should be treated. The arguments against such treatment are that families often put unwanted relatives in institutions. With "involuntary commitment" psychologically disturbed people who are considered dangerous to society can be put in mental hospitals against their will, but they can still refuse treatment once committed. (pp. 604-605)

Answers to the Multiple Choice Questions – Module 15.3

1. a. Incorrect. Were originally intended for long-term, even lifelong care
   b. Incorrect. The number has dropped because of drugs
   c. Correct! (p. 604)
   d. Incorrect. Other forms of care are often more effective

2. a. Incorrect. Not true in many states; in some states they must be dangerous to themselves or others
   b. Incorrect. Many people have mental disorders; very few are legally insane
   c. Correct! (p. 605)
   d. Incorrect. Many mentally ill people were discharged and they now live in nursing homes, prisons, are homeless, or are struggling

3. a. Incorrect. Not according to original rule; he had to be unaware that what he had done was wrong
   b. Correct! (p. 607)
   c. Incorrect. He knew he had done wrong
   d. Incorrect. He knew he was wrong and committing a bizarre crime does not necessarily mean he was insane

4. a. Incorrect. The therapist/client relationship may also include family
   b. Incorrect. Although clients should be cautious of unscrupulous therapists
   c. Correct! (p. 606).
   d. Incorrect. The client would needs to make a threat against a specific person

Answers to the True/False Questions – Module 15.3

1. **True**: Convicted criminals usually do spend as much time in the hospital as they would in prison. (p. 607)

2. **False**: Deinstitutionalization is actually the process of moving people from hospitals to community-based treatment centers. (p. 604)

3. **True**: Community psychologists examine how they can help a larger group. (p. 608)

Answers to Final Comprehensive Assessment

1. e (p. 583)
2. a (p. 587)
3. a (p. 584)
4. c (p. 591)
5. d (p. 595)
6. a (p. 592)
7. d (p. 593)
8. c (p. 597)
9. d (p. 596)
10. b (p. 602)
11. d (p. 604)
12. b (p. 604)
13. a (p. 605)
14. c (p. 608)

CHAPTER 16

SPECIFIC DISORDERS AND TREATMENTS

CHAPTER OVERVIEW INFORMATION

LEARNING OBJECTIVES

By the end of Chapter 16 you should

- ✓ Understand the nature and treatment of anxiety and avoidance disorders
- ✓ Increase your understanding of the nature and treatment of substance-related disorders
- ✓ Increase your understanding of the nature and treatment of affective disorders
- ✓ Increase your understanding of the nature and treatment of schizophrenia

CHAPTER 16 OUTLINE

The topics examined in Chapter 16 are some of the most fascinating and provocative. Many students cannot wait until this chapter is presented in the course. Topics range from phobias to schizophrenia to alcohol and drug addiction to depression. As you have read, a sizeable percentage of the population will experience one (or more) of these conditions sometime during their lifetime.

Chapter 16 is presented below in outline format to assist you in understanding the information presented in the chapter. More detailed information on any topic can be found using the page references to the right of the topic.

Module 16.1 Anxiety and Avoidance Disorders
I. Disorders Characterized by Excessive Anxiety
    A. Many psychological disorders are marked by fear, anxiety and attempts to avoid anxiety (p. 615)
    B. Generalized Anxiety Disorder (GAD)
        1. Generalized anxiety disorder involves exaggerated worries (p. 615)
        2. Affects about 5% of population, but responds to antidepressants & relaxation (p. 615)
    C. Panic Disorder (PD)
        1. Panic disorders involve a fairly constant state of anxiety plus occasional panic attacks and over response to mild stressors (pp. 615-616)
        2. 1-3% of adults have it; common in your adults; may have genetic component (p. 616)
        3. Hyperventilation is a key symptom, it may trigger other symptoms (p. 616, Fig. 16.1)
        4. Treatment includes psychotherapy and antidepressant drugs (p. 616)
            a. Social phobia involves an avoidance of other people (p. 616)
            b. Agoraphobia is an excessive fear of open places (p. 616)

II. Disorders Characterized by Exaggerated Avoidance
    A. Avoidance behaviors are resistant to extinction (p. 617)
        1. Avoidance behaviors persist long after the response is unnecessary (p. 617)
    B. Phobias
        1. Phobias are strong fears that interfere with everyday living (p. 617)
            a. 11% of the population suffers from a phobia at some time (p. 618)
            b. Mostly young adults suffer and to relatively common things (p. 618, Fig. 16.2)
            c. May be learned via classical conditioning (e.g., Albert B.) (pp. 618-620, Fig. 16.3)

            d. Phobias may also develop by observing fearful others (pp. 619-620)

     i. Observers need to know what the fearful other is frightened of to develop a fear (pp. 619-620, Fig. 16.4)

   e. People may be prepared to develop some phobias (p. 620)

   f. Phobias may develop due to lack of experience with object (p. 620)

     i. People develop phobias most easily to unpredictable and uncontrollable objects (p. 620)

   g. Systematic desensitization using virtual reality and flooding are effective therapies for phobias (p. 621, Fig. 16.5-16.6)

   h. Phobias and other anxieties may be treated with drugs (p. 622)

     i. Benzodiazepines relieve anxiety, relax muscles, and induce sleep (p. 622)

      (i) They facilitate transmission at synapses using GABA (p. 622)

 C. Obsessive-Compulsive Disorder

  1. Obsessive-compulsive disorder involves unwelcome thoughts and repetitive behaviors (p. 622)

   a. Estimated 2-3% of people have it usually in mild form, usually young intelligent people who are hardworking and perfectionistic (p. 622)

   b. There is some evidence for a biological basis (p. 622)

   c. Obsessions may stem from trying not to think of something (p. 622)

   d. Common compulsions include cleaning and checking excessively (pp. 622-623, Table 16.1)

     i. May result from inability to remember previous check (p. 623)

   e. Psychotherapy and drugs may help (p. 624)

     i. Exposure therapy exposures people to the situation and prevents the rituals from being performed (p. 624)

     ii. Clomipramine which prolongs the neurotransmitter serotonin seems to help some people (p. 624)

The message: *Emotions, cognitions, and the link between them are important in excessive anxieties. (pp. 624-625)*

Module 16.2 Substance-Related Disorders

III. Substance Dependence (Addiction)

 A. Substance dependence (addiction) occurs when a person cannot quit a self-destructive habit (p. 626)

  1. Most addictive drugs stimulates dopamine receptors in the brain area called nucleus accumbens (pleasure receptors) (p. 626)

  2. Addiction may cause brain activity, or brain may be active due to addiction (pp. 626-627)

 B. What Motivates Addictive Behavior?

  1. Pleasure seeking initially; escape from unpleasant feelings; provides relief from internal stress, may explain motivation to continue using (p. 627)

  2. Addicts continuing "wanting", even though there is little pleasure (liking) (p. 627)

   a. Likely due to changes in brain areas, tolerance and sensitization (p. 627)

 C. Is Substance Dependence a Disease?

  1. Not sure due to a lack of a definition of what constitutes disease (p. 628)

  2. Does not follow other diseases in that it varies along a continuum, the "disease" does not get progressively worse, and may respond better to non-medical therapy (p. 628)

 D. Nicotine Dependence

  1. Nicotine stimulates same brain areas as other addictive drugs (p. 628)

  2. Low-nicotine cigarettes do not deliver lower nicotine levels (p. 628, Fig 16.7)

IV. Alcoholism
    A. Some people may be predisposed for alcoholism (pp. 628-629)
    B. Genetics and Family Background
        1. Genetics plays some role in alcoholism (p. 629)
            a. Type I alcoholism develops over years; equally affects men and women; usually in response to life experiences not genetics (p. 629, Table 16.3)
            b. Type II alcoholism develops by age 25, affects men more than women, more severe, and shows a strong genetic influence (p. 629, Table 16.3)
        2. Poor family conditions and culture increase risk of alcoholism (p. 629)
            a. Sons of alcoholics respond differently to alcohol than others (p. 629)
                i. Alcohol provides more stress reduction for sons of alcoholics than for others (pp. 629-630, Fig. 16.8)
                ii. Sons of alcoholics underestimate how much they have drunk (p. 630)
                iii. Young men who underestimate intoxication level are more likely to become alcoholics later than those who report more intoxication (p. 630)
    C. Treatments
        1. Treatments for addictions are only moderately successful (pp. 630-631)
            a. Alcoholics Anonymous uses self-help groups (p. 631)
            b. Antabuse makes people ill if they drink (p. 631)
            c. Whether alcoholics can learn to drink in moderation is controversial (pp. 631-632)
            d. Contingency management uses a behavioral approach and is effective (p. 632)

V. Opiate Dependence
    A. Onset is rapid and seems to be influenced by genetics (p. 632)
    B. Treatments
        1. Methadone is the most common treatment for opiate addiction (pp. 632-633), Table 16.4)
        2. Buprenorphine, an alternative to methadone, provides longer stimulation (p. 633)

The Message: Drug and alcohol use and abuse occurs in society. It is not clear what the effects of changing laws would be. (p. 633)

Module 16.3 Mood Disorders
VI. Depression
    A. Major depression is experienced most of each day for months and involves little interest, little pleasure, and little reason for productive activity (p. 634)
        1. Affects sleeping pattern which in turn increases depression (p. 634, Fig. 16.9)
        2. Cry less, affects 5% of adults within any year; 10-20% over lifetime (p. 634)
        3. SAD-depressed repeatedly during a season of the year (p. 634, Fig. 16.10)
            a. Light therapy seems to be effective for SAD (p. 635)
    B. Genetic Influences
        1. Some people may be genetically predisposed to depression (p. 635)
        2. Likely to have relative with psychological abnormality (p. 635, Fig 16.11)
    C. Gender Differences
        1. Depression is more common in women than in men (pp. 635-636)
            a. May result from more negative events in women's lives (p. 636)
            b. Women may ruminate more about depression more than men (p. 636)
    D. Events That Precipitate Depression
        1. Unpleasant events often cause depression especially those that cause humiliation and guilt (p. 636)
            a. Some people are more vulnerable than others (p. 636)

E. Cognitive Aspects of Depression
  1. Depressed people may focus on the unpleasant side of life (p. 636)
     a. People may become depressed because of their attributions for failure (p. 637)
        i. People who make internal attributions for failure have a pessimistic explanatory style (p. 637)
F. Treatments
  1. Mild depression effectively treated with exercise, activity and regular sleep schedule (p. 637)
  2. Most people will get better spontaneously or through treatment (p. 637, Fig 16.12)
  3. Psychotherapy
     a. Interpersonal therapy focuses on coping with current or recent difficulties (p. 638)
     b. Aaron Beck pioneered cognitive therapy for depression (p. 638)
        i. Clients are invited to examine evidence for their beliefs (p. 638)
        ii. Clients encouraged to become more active and do things (p. 638)
  4. Medications
     a. There are three main classes of drugs (p. 638, Fig. 16.13)
        i. Tricyclics block reabsorption of neurotransmitters (p. 638)
        ii. SSRIs block the reuptake of serotonin (p. 638)
        iii. Monoamine oxidase inhibitors (MAOIs) block metabolic breakdown of released neurotransmitters (p. 638)
        iv. Atypical antidepressants include St. John's wort (p. 638)
     b. Take 2-3 weeks to have an effect possibly by affecting neuronal growth (p. 638)
  5. Cognitive therapy is slightly more effective than drugs, but drugs are faster and cheaper than therapy (p. 639)
  6. Electroconvulsive therapy (ECT) produces a convulsion, which quickly alleviates depression (p. 640, Fig. 16.14)
     a. Why it works is unclear but focused ECT is as effective as whole-brain ECT (p. 640)
     b. It is controversial because its effects may only be temporary and it has a history of being misused (p. 640)

VII. Bipolar Disorder
  A. People with bipolar disorder alternate between mania and depression (p. 640)
     1. In the manic phase, people follow impulses and are very active (p. 640)
     2. Bipolar I disorder people have at least an episode of mania (p. 640)
     3. Bipolar II disorder people have major depression and hypomania (p. 640)
     4. About 1% of population will experience it, with a strong genetic component (p. 640)
  B. Self-Report
     1. People describe their internal feelings during both stages of bipolar disorder (p. 641)
  C. Drug Therapies
     1. Lithium and anticonvulsant drugs are effective by blocking brain chemical (pp. 641-642)

VIII. Mood Disorders and Suicide
  A. Depression can lead to suicide but it varies along demographics (p. 642, Fig. 16.15)
     1. Risk factors are present to identify people at risk for suicide (p. 643, Table 16.5)

The message: Psychological disorders have much overlap. Depression is more than sadness; it is an inability to feel happy. Today psychologists successfully fight depression with drugs and psychotherapy. (p. 643)

Module 16.4 Schizophrenia

IX. Symptoms

    A. In schizophrenia, the emotions and the intellect seem to be separated (p. 645, Fig. 16.16)

    B. A person with schizophrenia exhibits deterioration of daily activities and must have two of five significant symptoms (e.g., hallucinations, delusions, etc.) and must not suffer from other conditions (p. 645)

    C. Positive and Negative Symptoms

        1. Symptoms of schizophrenia are positive and negative (p. 645)

            a. Positive symptoms are symptoms that are present and include hallucinations, delusions, and thought disorders (p. 645)

            b. Negative symptoms are symptoms that are not present such as lack of emotional expression and lack of social interaction (p. 645)

                i. People with mostly negative symptoms tend to have more consistent symptoms, an earlier onset, and worse job performance (p. 646)

    D. Hallucinations

        1. Hallucinations occur when sensory experiences do not correspond to the outside world (p. 646)

    E. Delusions

        1. Delusions are unfounded beliefs about persecution, grandeur or reference (p. 646)

        2. Psychologists should be cautious about diagnosing schizophrenia based primarily on occasional delusions or hallucinations since they occur in "normal" people as well (p. 646)

    F. Disordered Thinking

        1. People with schizophrenia show loose and idiosyncratic associations (p. 646)

        2. Have problems with abstract concepts and process information at literal level (pp. 646-647)

X. Types and Prevalence

    A. Types of Schizophrenia

        1. Catatonic includes movement disorders (p. 647, Fig. 16.18)

        2. Disorganized is characterized by incoherent speech, lack of social relationships, and odd behavior (p. 647)

        3. Paranoid includes elaborate hallucinations and delusions of persecution and grandeur (p. 647)

        4. Undifferentiated has basic symptoms without any special features (p. 647)

        5. Residual is for people who are partly, but not fully recovered from schizophrenia (p. 647)

    B. Prevalence

        1. Schizophrenia afflicts about 1% of people at some point in their lives (p. 648)

        2. Rate increased from 1700s until 1950 when it stopped increasing (p. 648)

        3. Varies across cultures but is more common in cities than small towns (p. 648)

        4. Gradual onset usually in teens and 20s; men outnumber women 7:5 (p. 648)

XI. Causes

    A. Schizophrenia has multiple causes (p. 648)

    B. Genetics

        1. Genetics and prenatal environment may predispose people to schizophrenia (p. 648, Fig. 16.19)

            a. No study has definitively identified gene that may cause schizophrenia (pp. 648-649)

            b. Could result from mutated genes, hence incidence rate stays at about 1% (p. 649)

C. Brain Damage
   1. Differences in some brain structures are seen in schizophrenics (pp. 649-650, Fig. 16.20)
      a. These differences may be a result of alcohol abuse or other conditions (p. 650)
D. The Neurodevelopmental Hypothesis
   1. Schizophrenia may originate with impairments developed before or at time of birth (p. 650)
      a. Impairments may result from difficult labor/delivery; poor nourishment during pregnancy; mother had infection/virus/fever during pregnancy; an Rh incompatibility between mother and child; unusually small baby; or serious head injury (p. 650)
      b. People born in winter or early spring more likely to develop schizophrenia (p. 650)

XII. Therapies
   A. Psychotherapy provides some relief by controlling stress (p. 651)
   B. Medications
      1. Antipsychotic drugs are effective in treating schizophrenia (p. 651, Fig. 16.21)
         a. They work by blocking dopamine receptors (p. 651)
            i. Excessive dopamine may be the underlying cause of schizophrenia (p. 651)
            ii. The underlying cause may be deficient stimulation of glutamate synapses (pp. 651-652)
         b. Tardive dyskinesia (a movement disorder) is a side effect (p. 652)
            i. Atypical antipsychotic drugs do not produce tardive dykinesia (p. 652)
   C. Family
      1. Expressed emotion by family can sometimes influence relapses (p. 652)
         a. Recent research suggests expressed emotion is a reaction to patients past behavior not the cause of it (p. 652)

The message: *People who are diagnosed with schizophrenia may be very different so researchers wonder whether schizophrenia may be several disorders. (p. 652)*

RELATED WEBSITES AND ACTIVITIES

Visit http://psychology.wadsworth.com/kalat_intro7e/ for online quizzing, glossary flashcards, crossword puzzles, annotated web links, and more.

LECTURE MATERIAL

Information from the text is only half of the picture. Don't forget to review your lecture material. Process each topic meaningfully. Most importantly, be sure that you understand the material in each lecture-if you don't, ask your instructor or teaching assistant.

STUDY TIP # 16: Studying for a final exam can be stressful. Find out whether the final is comprehensive. If it is, review for the exam by reviewing each of the Comprehensive tests at the end of each chapter.

TIP: Associate the lecture material with the information from the text, with things that you already know, with your personal experiences, or with real-life applications. Type or neatly re-write your notes. Make sure they are detailed and organized. Make comments on your notes. Then write questions to cover each concept.

CHAPTER MODULE ASSESSMENTS

Module 16.1 Anxiety and Avoidance Disorders
Answer these questions soon after reading the **Module 16.1: Anxiety and Avoidance Disorders**. There are several formats to the assessments. Answers to all questions appear on pp. 343-344.

Fill in the Blank
Provide a term(s) which best completes the statement below. Answers appear on p. 343.

1. A _____ is a strong, persistent fear of a specific object that is extreme enough to interfere with normal living.

2. A therapy used for treating phobias that involves gradually exposing someone to the object they fear is _____.

3. About 5% of all people experience _____ disorder, a state of almost constant exaggerated worry, at some time in their lives.

4. An excessive fear of open or public places characterizes _____.

5. _____ such as Valium and Xanax are used to treat a variety of anxiety disorders and work by increasing the action of GABA, an inhibitory neurotransmitter, in the brain.

Short Answer
The following questions require a short written answer (3-7 sentences). Answers appear on p. 343.

1. Explain how superstitions are related to phobias.

2. Describe the experiment with monkeys in which they learned fear by watching other monkeys who were afraid.

3. Describe how systematic desensitization might be used to treat someone who fears elevators. How might this be modified to use virtual reality technology?

4. Describe an experiment that shows how memory in obsessive-compulsive "checkers" may differ from that of normal people.

Multiple Choice
Circle the best answer below. Check your answers on p. 344. If your answer was incorrect, try to write why it was incorrect. Check your reasons on p. 344.

1. Mary occasionally experiences severe chest pains, sweating, faintness and shaking. At first she thought she was having heart attacks but her doctor says she is fine. Mary likely suffers from:
   a. phobia
   b. obsessive-compulsive disorder
   c. panic disorder
   d. dissociative disorder
   e. a lack of generalized anxiety

2. Which of the following is a phobia?
   a. Jean looks the other way when the cobra bites the hero in the movie
   b. Mary tries to squash the spiders in her hotel room in a slum area so they don't bite her
   c. Gladys looks around fearfully as she goes to the bank in a "bad" area with a large sum of money
   d. Susan has stopped gardening because there might be a snake outside
   e. all of the above are phobias

3. Watson and Rayner made a loud sound at the same time that Little Albert saw a white rat. Albert came to fear white rats. Which of the following is true?
   a. the sound is the CS; the rat is the UCS
   b. fear to the sound is the CR; fear to the rat is the UCR
   c. the sound is the UCS; fear to it is the CR
   d. the rat is the CS; fear to it is the CR

4. Lab monkeys show a fear of snakes:
   a. from birth; apparently the fear is genetic
   b. after watching a wild-born monkey show fear, even though the snake is out of sight
   c. after watching a wild-born monkey show fear, with the snake in sight
   d. only if they have been specifically conditioned to fear snakes with something like a shock as the UCS

5. The therapist is treating Susan's phobia of snakes by asking her to imagine herself at the bottom of a pit of 1,000 snakes. She cannot escape as they crawl all around on her and some bite her. The type of therapy is:
   a. flooding
   b. systematic desensitization
   c. similar to Skinner's shaping procedure
   d. b and c
   e. gradual exposure to the feared object via virtual reality

6. A person who constantly thinks about dying has:
    a. a compulsion
    b. an obsession
    c. a preparedness reaction
    d. a checker reaction
    e. a cleaner reaction

True/False
Select the best answer by circling *T for True* or *F for False*. Check your answers on p. 344.

1. **T or F** Research suggests that one reason a person may experience a checking compulsion is because they are less confident in their memory because of making previous checks.

2. **T or F** Systematic desensitization using virtual reality and flooding are effective therapies for treating phobias.

Module 16.2 Substance-Related Disorders
Answer these questions soon after reading the **Module 16.2: Substance-Related Disorders**. There are several formats to the assessments. Answers to all questions appear on pp. 345-346.

Fill in the Blank
Provide a term(s) which best completes the statement below. Answers appear on p. 345.

1. A drug taken to treat alcoholism, which makes the user physically ill if they drink is
    _____.

2. A common treatment for heroin addiction is _____ replacement therapy, which reduces cravings for opiate drugs.

3. When people find it difficult or impossible to stop using a substance and it interferes with their life they are experiencing _____.

Short Answer
The following questions require a short written answer (3-7 sentences). Answers appear on p. 345.

1. Discuss the things that make a substance addictive.

2. What are two ways in which the sons of alcoholic parents differ from the sons of non-alcoholic parents?

3. Describe the view of alcoholism and drug dependence as a disease. What is the alternative view?

4. Describe how methadone has been used to help people who are addicted to opiates.

Multiple Choice
Circle the best answer below. Check your answers on pp. 345-346. If your answer was incorrect, try to write why it was incorrect. Check your reasons on pp. 345-346.

1. Addictive substances:
   a. usually stimulate dopamine synapses in the brain
   b. enter the brain more slowly than non-addictive substances
   c. are addictive because of their characteristics, independent of the circumstances of use
   d. are more likely to cause addiction if they are eaten than if they are smoked

2. Sons of alcoholics:
   a. show less of a decline in stress when they drink alcohol than sons of nonalcoholics
   b. who sway more after drinking are more likely to become alcoholics later than those who sway less
   c. underestimate the amount of alcohol they have drunk
   d. who reported feeling intoxicated after drinking were more likely to become alcoholics than those who didn't feel intoxicated

3. Alcoholism:
   a. must be treated with total abstinence to prevent relapse
   b. may be treated with disulfiram, which produces a threat of sickness
   c. is clearly a progressive disease, because alcoholics always grow worse with time if they do not abstain
   d. is little affected by environmental factors, giving good evidence for the disease concept
   e. is best treated by controlled drinking

True/False
Select the best answer by circling *T for True* or *F for False*. Check your answers on p. 346.

1. **T or F** Although addicts once received a great deal of pleasure from taking a drug, now they get very little pleasure or liking from it but continue "wanting" the drug.

2. **T or F** Most addictive drugs stimulates dopamine receptors in the brain area called nucleus accumbens.

Fill in the Blank
Provide a term(s) which best completes the statement below. Answers appear on p. 346.

1. _____ psychotherapy has been shown to be as effective as medication in the treatment of mild to moderate depression.

2. A treatment for depression that involves inducing a seizure through electrical stimulation of the brain is _____.

3. A type of antidepressant that works by inhibiting the reuptake of serotonin describes _____ .

4. People with _____ disorder alternate between the episodes of mania and depression.

Short Answer
The following questions require a short written answer (3-7 sentences). Answers appear on pp. 346-347.

1. Discuss the risk factors involved in depression.

2. Explain how antidepressant drugs work.

3. Describe ECT and the conditions under which it is used today.

4. Describe seasonal affective disorder (SAD).

5. Describe the bipolar cycles in people with bipolar disorder.

Multiple Choice
Circle the best answer below. Check your answers on p. 347. If your answer was incorrect, try to write why it was incorrect. Check your reasons on p. 347.

1. Joe suffers from major depression; it is severe and has lasted for several months. Joe has always blamed himself for failure. Joe's depression is probably:
   a. a postpartum depression
   b. bipolar
   c. seasonal affective disorder
   d. related to a pessimistic explanatory style

2. A type of evidence that there is a genetic predisposition to depression is that:
   a. some women show postpartum depression following childbirth
   b. some types of depression respond better to drugs than to psychotherapy
   c. adopted children usually have more adoptive than biological relatives who are depressed
   d. relatives of depressed people are more likely to be depressed than other people

3. Each of the people below has just failed two tests. Given the explanatory styles below, which person is most likely to become depressed?
   a. Greg, who thinks he failed because the tests were bad
   b. Sally, who thinks she failed because she is stupid
   c. Mary, who thinks she failed because she did not study hard
   d. John, who thinks he failed because he partied all night

4. Cognitive therapy for depression:
   a. involves telling clients what to think
   b. was pioneered by Aaron Beck
   c. stresses interpretation of dreams
   d. uses bright lights to reduce depression
   e. is much less effective than drug therapy

5. The class of drugs called monoamine oxidase inhibitors:
   a. work by preventing the reuptake of serotonin
   b. block the reabsorption of serotonin, norepinephrine, and dopamine
   c. are made from natural substances that cannot be patented
   d. cause tardive dyskinesia as a side effect
   e. block the metabolic breakdown of serotonin, norepinephrine, and dopamine

6. Why would ECT be used rather than antidepressant drugs?
    a. antidepressant drugs decrease certain neurotransmitter molecules, but ECT increases them; an increase is helpful to some patients
    b. it has much more permanent effects than drugs
    c. drugs only help 20-30% of all depressed people
    d. ECT takes effect faster than drugs
    e. drugs produce side effects, such as nausea and blurred vision, even if the dose is only slightly greater than the recommended level

7. Rob recently quit his job and sold his house, and is building a sports shop in Aruba that will specialize in snow skiing. He thinks this is a great idea because there are no such shops on the tropical island of Aruba. Rob probably has:
    a. severe unipolar depression
    b. schizophrenia
    c. seasonal affective disorder
    d. mania

True/False
Select the best answer by circling *T for True* or *F for False*. Check your answers on p. 348.

1. **T or F** Antidepressant effects have been demonstrated for aerobic exercise, regular sleep habits, and just "doing something."

2. **T or F** SAD or seasonal affective disorder only causes depression during the winter.

3. **T or F** Maria is taking SSRI's. She is likely to experience less depression.

Module 16.4 Schizophrenia
Answer these questions soon after reading the **Module 16.4: Schizophrenia**. There are several formats to the assessments. Answers to all questions appear on pp. 348-349.

Fill in the Blank
Provide a term(s) which best completes the statement below. Answers appear on p. 348.

1. Individuals with _____ schizophrenia often have elaborate delusions and hallucinations that include feelings of grandeur and persecution.

2. _____ such as haloperidol are drugs are used to treat schizophrenia that work by blocking dopamine synapses in the brain.

3. High levels of _____ or negative and hostile comments from family members have been shown to be related to high rates of relapse in schizophrenia.

4. The _____ symptoms of schizophrenia are added onto a person's behavior after they become ill and include hallucinations, delusions, and thought disorder.

Short Answer

The following questions require a short written answer (3-7 sentences). Answers appear on p. 348.

1. What symptoms must a person show to be diagnosed as schizophrenic?

2. Discuss three characteristics of disordered thought in schizophrenia.

3. Discuss the evidence for a genetic predisposition to schizophrenia.

Multiple Choice

Circle the best answer below. Check your answers on pp. 348-349. If your answer was incorrect, try to write why it was incorrect. Check your reasons on pp. 348-349.

1. The term <u>schizophrenia</u> refers to:
   a. bipolar as compared with unipolar disorder
   b. split personality--a person who alternates between two or more personalities
   c. a split between emotional and intellectual aspects of personality
   d. a person who alternates between extreme happiness and extreme sadness

2. A patient who has been diagnosed as schizophrenic thinks that "they" are trying to control his mind. This person has what type of schizophrenia?
   a. undifferentiated
   b. paranoid
   c. catatonic
   d. disorganized
   e. delusion of grandeur

3. Schizophrenia is:
   a. more likely to be diagnosed in younger than older adults
   b. more common in women than men
   c. usually characterized by sudden onset
   d. develops in adults who had many friends as children
   e. probably caused by a bad mother

4. According to the Neurodevelopmental hypothesis of schizophrenia, which of the following is not likely to contribute to a person developing schizophrenia :
   a. Rh incompatibility between mother and child
   b. being born first as a twin
   c. being born in winter
   d. a difficult labor and delivery of the child

True/False
Select the best answer by circling *T for True* or *F for False*. Check your answers on p. 349.

1. **T or F** A diagnosis of a schizophrenia is likely to be accurate for a person suffering from infrequent delusions.

2. **T or F** Schizophrenia has become more common in men than in women.

3. **T or F** Research suggests that brain damage traditionally observed in schizophrenics may actually be the result of alcohol abuse or other conditions.

4. **T or F** Schizophrenics will always suffer relapse if they are exposed to expressed emotions by family members.

FINAL COMPREHENSIVE CHAPTER ASSESSMENT TEST

Check your answers on p. 349.

1. In panic disorder:
   a. people feel a strong state of anxiety in response to mild stress or exercise
   b. generalized anxiety attaches itself to a specific object
   c. people do not breathe deeply enough
   d. people do not show a physiological response to stressful situations
   e. the panic attack usually lasts several hours

2. Which of the following is true about phobias?
   a. systematic desensitization is an effective therapy
   b. they are easily treated by explaining that there is no reason to be afraid
   c. "irrational fears" is the best definition
   d. people rarely show any physical symptoms when they confront the object
   e. they are more common for objects that are part of technological societies (guns, cars) than for natural objects (animals, lightning)

3. Watson and Rayner's study with Little Albert showed that phobias:
   a. represent unconscious desires
   b. are only developed to objects that have caused injury
   c. develop any time one animal observes another animal showing fear
   d. are genetic in that people are born with a few intense fears
   e. can develop through learning

4. What was the conditioned stimulus in the Little Albert study?
   a. the loud sound
   b. the white rat
   c. trembling to the loud sound
   d. trembling to the white rat
   e. the sight of Watson

5. What would a therapist using flooding do to treat a phobia of snakes?
   a. first try to discover the origin of the phobia
   b. have the client imagine being in a place with many snakes
   c. attempt to identify which type of snake was the UCS
   d. have the client begin by imaging a small picture of a snake and gradually work up to a large realistic image or to an actual snake
   e. have the client try to understand what snakes represent so that the real problem can be discussed

6. Which of the following is <u>not</u> characteristic of both obsessive-compulsive checkers and cleaners?
   a. drugs that inhibit the reuptake of serotonin usually help
   b. realize that their rituals are inappropriate
   c. are usually average or above average in intelligence
   d. feel better after their rituals
   e. tend to be hard-working, perfectionist people

7. How do the memories of obsessive-compulsive people differ from those of normal people?
   a. Obsessive-compulsive people are less able to remember what they did and what they thought
   b. Obsessive-compulsive people are much slower to learn in avoidance learning
   c. Obsessive-compulsive people are less confident in their judgments of what they did and what they thought
   d. Obsessive-compulsive people show very fast extinction in avoidance learning
   e. Obsessive-compulsive people are overconfident in the accuracy of their memories

8. Alcohol addiction:
   a. may be more likely for sons of alcoholics because alcohol reduces stress more for them than for sons of nonalcoholics
   b. always gets worse and worse
   c. is best treated using the AA approach according to the research
   d. can easily be turned into controlled social drinking
   e. is independent of culture

9. Which of the following is true about the statement "alcoholism is a disease"?
   a. it is true because it fits all of the medical criteria for the term disease
   b. it is a bad definition because if makes alcoholics feel too guilty about their own role in their disorder
   c. it is true because alcoholism always gets progressively worse
   d. it is misleading because it downplays the role of environmental factors
   e. it is true because "controlled drinking" programs are unsuccessful

10. Why is methadone better as a morphine substitute than heroin?
    a. methadone does not produce the rush that heroin does and it does not produce rapid withdrawal symptoms
    b. methadone, when taken as a pill, is so fast-acting that it doesn't produce any rush, so addicts quickly stop using it
    c. methadone enters the brain faster than heroin
    d. methadone actually cures the addiction, heroin doesn't
    e. heroin is addictive, methadone is not

11. Why do women develop depression more often than men?
    a. women have more positive life events
    b. women ruminate more about depression whereas men distract themselves
    c. men are paid more money than women
    d. men are more religious than women

12. Most antidepressant drugs work by:
    a. altering the pattern of blood flow in the brain
    b. making people forget that they are depressed
    c. affecting the chemical pathways within neurons
    d. prolonging the stimulation of dopamine, norepinephrine, or serotonin synapses in the brain
    e. increasing the body's ability to use vitamins, such as B-1

13. One major <u>disadvantage</u> of using ECT for depression is that:
    a. its benefits develop more slowly than those of other therapies
    b. its benefits are less likely to last long
    c. it helps only the same people who respond well to drugs
    d. it works by impairing people's memories
    e. it increases the risk of suicide

14. A hospital removes all of the fire alarms from a floor because the patients continually pull them. The patients on this floor probably have:
    a. mania
    b. major depression
    c. learned helplessness
    d. an internal, stable, and global explanatory style
    e. seasonal affective disorder

15. John seems like two different people. One week he is extremely happy and uninhibited. The next month he is very depressed and can only think of suicide. John's disorder is:
    a. major depression
    b. learned helplessness
    c. suicidal tendencies
    d. multiple personality
    e. bipolar disorder

16. Lithium salts:
    a. are used to cure depression
    b. produce side effects including nausea and blurred vision
    c. have been aggressively marketed by drug companies in the U.S.
    d. are especially effective for undifferentiated schizophrenia
    e. decrease the amount of dopamine in the brain

17. Suicide:
    a. is the most common cause of death among people over age 50
    b. attempts are more common among men than among women
    c. is not usually committed by people who talk about it
    d. is often committed by people who are depressed
    e. will not be committed by someone who has tried and failed

18. The term schizophrenia:
    a. means split personality, another name for multiple personality
    b. is Latin for premature senility
    c. comes from the Greek terms meaning disordered thought
    d. refers to a split between emotional and intellectual parts of personality
    e. refers to a split between the situation and a person's reactions to it

19. A person who believes that she has been selected to receive messages from outer space that will ultimately save the world has:
    a. delusions of persecution
    b. catatonic schizophrenia
    c. manic-depressive disorder
    d. undifferentiated schizophrenia
    e. delusions of grandeur

20. Which of the following is true about the cause of schizophrenia?
    a. there is some brain damage in that cerebral ventricles are too small
    b. since effective drugs work by blocking dopamine receptors, schizophrenics may have too little dopamine in their brain
    c. confusing signals from the mother may cause schizophrenia
    d. schizophrenia has no genetic component
    e. prenatal infections may result in brain damage that leads to schizophrenia

ANSWERS AND EXPLANATIONS FOR CHAPTER MODULE ASSESSMENTS

Answers to the Fill in the Blank Questions -- Module 16.1

1. phobia (p. 617)

2. systematic desensitization (p. 621)

3. generalized anxiety disorder (p. 615)

4. agoraphobia (p. 616)

5. Benzodiazepines (p. 622)

Answers to the Short Answer Questions – Module 16.1

1. Superstitions are behaviors that cannot be expected to be effective. People persist in them because nothing goes wrong if they do them and, if something does go wrong, they assume that they did not try hard enough. Phobias are similar in that if people avoid the feared object, they never get hurt by it. Because they don't get close to it, they never learn that it really is harmless. (p. 617)

2. Lab-reared monkeys have no fear of snakes, but wild-reared monkeys show a strong fear of snakes. A lab-reared and a wild-reared monkey both saw a snake. Later, when the lab-reared monkey saw a snake, it showed fear. The lab-reared monkey had to see that it was a snake that the wild-reared monkey was afraid of; simply seeing the wild-reared monkey show fear was not enough for the lab-reared monkey to develop a fear. (pp. 619-620)

3. The person would first be taught to relax. Then, while in a relaxed state, she would be asked to imagine something that is not very frightening, such as looking at an elevator across the room. Then she would be asked to imagine gradually more frightening things until she is finally able to imagine being in an elevator that is stuck between floors. If the distress becomes too severe at some point, she would go back to imagining an easier scene. In the high-tech version, the client is given a helmet that displays a virtual-reality scene, so that the client can feel as if he or she is actually present in the scene. The therapist can change the scene to gradually expose the client to progressively more frightening situations, and the display can be turned off if the client becomes too fearful. (p. 621)

4. Obsessive-compulsive participants in one study took a memory test and estimated how many questions they answered correctly. Their actual percent correct was as good as average, but their estimates of their own performance were considerably less than average. So perhaps the obsessive-compulsive patients continue checking because they do not trust their memory that they have already checked. (p. 623)

Answers to the Multiple Choice Questions – Module 16.1

1. a. Incorrect. Her anxiety is not attached to a specific object
    b. Incorrect. Does not have repetitive thoughts or actions
    c. Correct! (pp. 615-616)
    d. Incorrect. Has not separated one set of memories from others
    e. Incorrect. Too much anxiety; persists when there is nothing to be anxious about

2. a. Incorrect. Normal; doesn't interfere with her life
    b. Incorrect. Her fear is not irrational; she's doing something about it
    c. Incorrect. Her fear is rational and limited to one situation
    d. Correct! (p. 617)
    e. Incorrect. See a, b, and c

3. a. Incorrect. Children naturally fear loud sounds, so that is the UCS; the rat is the CS
    b. Incorrect. Albert showed no natural fear of the rat, so fear to it is the CR; fear to sound is UCR
    c. Incorrect. Fear to sound is UCR
    d. Correct! (p. 619)

4. a. Incorrect. Lab-reared monkeys show no fear of snakes
    b. Incorrect. Lab-reared monkey has to see the snake also to develop the fear
    c. Correct! (pp. 619-620)
    d. Incorrect. Can be learned via observational learning; direct conditioning is not necessary

5. a. Correct! (p. 621)
    b. Incorrect. The feared stimulus would be exposed gradually and the person would remain relaxed while imagining
    c. Incorrect. b is similar to shaping, which involves gradual increases in mastery of the response
    d. Incorrect. See b
    e. Incorrect. Exposure here isn't gradual; it's sudden

6. a. Incorrect. Not unless repetitive behavior also occurs
    b. Correct! (p. 622)
    c. Incorrect. Means that some things are easily learned because of evolutionary influences; not relevant
    d. Incorrect. Not unless he constantly checks his body for physical symptoms
    e. Incorrect. Not unless he constantly washes and bathes

Answers to the True/False Questions – Module 16.1

1. **True**: New research suggests that people suffering from a checking compulsion check the thing so often that they have a hard time remembering when they last checked the item. (p. 623)

2. **True**: These therapies have been widely used to alleviate phobias (p. 621, Fig. 16.5-16.6)

Answers to the Fill in the Blank Questions – Module 16.2

1. Antabuse (p. 631)

2. methadone (pp. 632-633)

3. substance dependence (p. 626)

Answers to the Short Answer Questions – Module 16.2

1. One theory is that addictive substances all activate dopamine synapses and produce reinforcing effects. However, many substances can become addictive, as can gambling, which is not a substance at all. (p. 626)

2. Young men whose fathers were and were not alcoholics were placed in stressful situations. Half of the men were given alcohol to drink before the stressful situation. Drinking alcohol reduced heart rate and resulted in less reported anxiety. However, these effects were larger in the sons of alcoholics than in the other men. In a second study, sons of alcoholics and nonalcoholics drank varying amounts of alcohol. They then estimated how much they had drunk and how intoxicated they were. The sons of alcoholics underestimated how much they had drunk and how intoxicated they were. Later, men who had underestimated the most were the most likely to develop into alcoholics (pp. 629-630)

3. Those who view alcoholism and drug dependence as a disease believe that it will grow worse with time and that either a person has the disease or they do not have it. Calling it a disease also suggests that medical intervention is necessary. An alternative view is that it is not a disease but a condition since it does not necessarily grow worse over time. The condition is really a matter of degree and that medical intervention is not necessary for improvement. (p. 631)

4. Many addicts continue to have recurring urges to take opiates even after the withdrawal symptoms have subsided. Methadone can be taken in pill form, which does not produce the "rush" associated with opiates, but it does satisfy the craving. People using methadone are still addicted to opiates since opiate intake increases when methadone intake decreases (pp. 632-633)

Answers to the Multiple Choice Questions – Module 16.2

1.   a. Correct! (p. 626)
      b. Incorrect. Addictive substances enter it faster
      c. Incorrect. Depending upon how a substance is used, it may or may not be addictive; addiction is in the user
      d. Incorrect. Smoking is more likely to be addictive because the substance enters the brain faster

2.   a. Incorrect. They showed more decline in stress after alcohol
      b. Incorrect. It is the opposite; those who become alcoholic sway less
      c. Correct! (p. 630)
      d. Incorrect. It is the opposite; those who didn't feel intoxicated were more likely to become alcoholics

3.   a. Incorrect. Alcoholics treated with abstinence also relapse; some alcoholics decrease their use without abstaining
      b. Correct! (p. 631)
      c. Incorrect. Some don't grow worse
      d. Incorrect. Environmental factors, such as an improved family life and new interests, can help
      e. Incorrect. Controversial; such treatment may not work for many alcoholics

Answers to the True/False Questions – Module 16.2

1. **True**: Addicts continuing wanting the drug even thought they derive very little pleasure from using it. (p. 627)

2. **True**: Stimulation of these pleasure receptors which may contribute to addiction (p. 626)

Answers to the Fill in the Blank Questions -- Module 16.3

1. Cognitive (p. 639)

2. ECT (p. 640)

3. SSRIs (p. 638)

4. bipolar (p. 640)

Answers to the Short Answer Questions – Module 16.3

1. There is a genetic component, in that depressed people are more likely to have biological relatives who are depressed than are nondepressed people. Depression is more common in women than men. People suffering from events causing humiliation or guilt are also at an increase for depression. Depressed people may also focus on the unpleasant side of life and at the same time make internal attributions to explain failures. (pp. 635-637)

2. Tricyclic drugs block the reabsorption of dopamine, norepinephrine, and serotonin by the axon's terminal button. MAOIs block the conversion of these neurotransmitters into nonactive molecules. SSRIs, also known as serotonin reuptake blockers, block the reuptake of serotonin. Thus, each type of drug increases the time period in which these neurotransmitters can activate surrounding neurons. (p. 638, Fig. 16.13)

3. Electroconvulsive therapy consists of a brief electric shock across the head. People are usually given muscle relaxants and anesthetics. It is used when antidepressant drugs have been ineffective, for people with serious thinking disorders, and for people who are suicidal. It works faster than drugs, so it is effective in suicidal patients. (p. 640)

4. Most people with this disorder become depressed in the winter and are normal or slightly manic in the summer. They seem to respond to the amount of sunlight they see each day. The disorder can be helped by having people sit in front of lights to artificially lengthen the day. Annual summer depressions also occur in some people. (pp. 634-635)

5. Mood alternates between mania, being constantly active and uninhibited, and depression, feeling helpless, guilt ridden, and sad. In the depressive phase, people have trouble sleeping and often contemplate suicide. In the manic phase, people may either be angry or happy. They have trouble inhibiting their impulses. They may show rambling speech, jumping from one topic to another. Each mood may last for months or just a few days. (p. 640)

Answers to the Multiple Choice Questions – Module 16.3

1.   a. Incorrect. Women sometimes develop this after giving birth
    b. Incorrect. Must have manic phases also
    c. Incorrect. No mention of changes from one time of year to another
    d. Correct! (p. 637)

2.   a. Incorrect. May show a relation between depression and hormones, not genetics
    b. Incorrect. True, but not evidence for a genetic component
    c. Incorrect. It is the opposite; more depression among biological relatives
    d. Correct! (p. 635)

3.   a. Incorrect. External; his attribution is outside of himself
    b. Correct! (p. 637)
    c. Incorrect. Internal, but unstable; she can study more next time
    d. Incorrect. Can attribute failure to partying

4.   a. Incorrect. No, this is more likely in rational-emotive therapy
    b. Correct! (p. 638)
    c. Incorrect. This would occur in psychoanalysis
    d. Incorrect. Treatment for seasonal affective disorder
    e. Incorrect. Cognitive therapy is slightly more effective than drug therapy

5.   a. Incorrect. SSRIs do this
    b. Incorrect. Tricyclics for depression do this
    c. Incorrect. Lithium for bipolar disorder is a natural substance
    d. Incorrect. Side effect of neuroleptic drugs, used for schizophrenia
    e. Correct! (p. 638)

6.   a. Incorrect. Drugs increase these neurotransmitters; ECT may do the same
    b. Incorrect. The effects of ECT are temporary
    c. Incorrect. Drugs help 50-70%; placebos help 20-30%
    d. Correct! (p. 640)
    e. Incorrect. Side effects of lithium, used for bipolar disorder

7.   a. Incorrect. Is showing mania, so can't have unipolar depression
    b. Incorrect. No evidence that social relations and self-care have deteriorated
    c. Incorrect. He is not depressed, he's manic
    d. Correct! (p. 640)

Answers to the True/False Questions – Module 16.3

1. **True**: Research suggests all of these can have beneficial effects for people suffering from depression. (p. 637)

2. **False**: Although many suffer SAD during the winter some experience SAD during summer. (p. 635, Fig. 16.10)

3. **True**: SSRIs are one form of drug treatment used in the treatment of depression. (p. 638)

Answers to the Fill in the Blank Questions -- Module 16.4

1. paranoid (p. 647)

2. Antipsychotic drugs (p. 651)

3. expressed emotion (p. 652)

4. positive (p. 645)

Answers to the Short Answer Questions – Module 16.4

1. The person must show a deterioration in daily activities including work activities, social relations, and self-care. In addition, a person must show at least two of the following: hallucinations, delusions, incoherent speech, grossly disorganized behavior, thought disorders, or a loss of normal emotional responses and social behaviors. However, if a person shows severe hallucinations or delusions, no other symptoms are necessary. (p. 645)

2. <u>Use of loose associations and idiosyncratic associations</u>: Illogical leaps and misuse of words. <u>Difficulties in using abstract concepts</u>: Tendency to interpret everything literally. <u>Vague, roundabout ways of saying things</u>: Saying things in complex rather than simple ways. (pp. 646-647)

3. Adopted children who develop schizophrenia often have biological relatives who are schizophrenic. If one identical twin has schizophrenia, there is a 50% chance that the other one will, and both have an equal probability of having schizophrenic children whether or not both are schizophrenic. No one gene has not yet identified that causes schizophrenia. (pp. 648-649)

Answers to the Multiple Choice Questions – Module 16.4

1.
   a. Incorrect. Bipolar alternates between mania and depression; unipolar is depression only; neither is schizophrenia
   b. Incorrect. Multiple personality, a different disorder
   c. Correct! (p. 645)
   d. Incorrect. Bipolar disorder

2. a. Incorrect. Basic symptoms, but not delusion of persecution
    b. Correct! (p. 647)
    c. Incorrect. No movement disorders here
    d. Incorrect. No evidence for incoherent speech or silly behavior
    e. Incorrect. The patient may have delusions of grandeur, but that is not a type of schizophrenia

3. a. Correct! (p. 648)
    b. Incorrect. Equally common in men and women
    c. Incorrect. Usually gradual onset
    d. Incorrect. Opposite; schizophrenics had few friends as children
    e. Incorrect. Probably not; it develops after child is independent of mother and occurs even if child is adopted and raised by normal mother

4. a., c., d. Incorrect. All of these may increase the likelihood of developing schizophrenia
    b. Correct! (p. 650)

Answers to the True/False Questions – Module 16.4

1. **False**: A therapist should be very cautious diagnosing a person as schizophrenic if the person is only experiencing infrequent delusions or hallucinations. (p. 646)

2. **True**: According to current statistics schizophrenia is more common and severe in men than women. (p. 648)

3. **True**: Since schizophrenia frequently occurs with alcoholism, brain damage cannot be solely attributed to schizophrenia. (p. 650)

4. **False**: Expressed emotion looks less convincing than before as a cause of schizophrenia relapse. A parent's expressed emotion correlates better with the patient's previous behavior than with future behavior. (p. 652)

Answers to Final Comprehensive Assessment

1. a (p. 615)	11. c (pp. 635-636)
2. a (p. 621)	12. d (p. 638)
3. e (pp. 618-620)	13. b (p. 640)
4. b (p. 619)	14. a (p. 640)
5. b (p. 621)	15. e (p. 640)
6. d (p. 622)	16. b (p. 641)
7. c (p. 623)	17. d (p. 642)
8. a (pp. 629-630)	18. d (p. 645)
9. d (p. 628)	19. e (p. 646)
10. a (pp. 632-633)	20. e (p. 650)

GUIDE FOR NONNATIVE SPEAKERS

by Sally Gearhart
revised by Eric Bohman

The purpose of this guide for Nonnative Speakers of English is to provide still another resource for you as you move through the *Study Guide* that precedes this section and, of course, the course text, Kalat's **Introduction to Psychology.**

This particular section is broken down both in terms of lesson concepts and in terms of language to help you better comprehend the text material which may not be familiar to you. It includes the following features:

Prereading aids which give a sense of the direction or focus of each chapter:

Key verbs: Verbs taken from the text that can help the reader predict chapter concepts.

Chapter organization exercises focusing on headings, chapter divisions, and cues such as bold print and italics.

Key Idea: A focus point or central idea taken from the chapter, usually including important quotes from the author.

Paraphrasing and summarizing practice to help you, the student, analyze concepts and put the author's ideas into your own words.

Outlining exercises: Practice in outlining sections of text to get a clearer understanding of how concepts fit together.

Structural Clues: Exercises to help you understand signals the writer uses to indicate cause and effect, contrast, example, emphasis, etc.

Scanning activities: Exercises that help you focus on a specific kind of information and locate it quickly. *Skimming activities* help you get general overviews.

Vocabulary Exercises: **Word attack practice and rephrasing of idioms to help you build the vocabulary comprehension you need.**

Recommended procedure for using this guide with <u>Introduction to Psychology</u>:

1. <u>Without</u> referring to a dictionary, get a general idea of the assigned chapter of the text by *skimming* through its content, including introduction, module headings, illustrations, concept checks, and *In Closing*.

2. **Refer to this guide section for nonnative speakers to get an idea of how to approach the assigned chapter,** that is, what to focus on first.

3. Start reading the assigned text chapter more slowly, **referring to this guide to help you as you move through the various sections.**

4. **Review the chapter material by referring to the regular *Study Guide*,** which precedes this section for Nonnative Speakers.

5. **Complete the exercises in <u>both sections of the *Study Guide*</u>** to help you understand and remember material in Kalat's <u>Introduction to Psychology</u>.

CHAPTER 1: WHAT IS PSYCHOLOGY?

Before you begin Chapter 1: *Pay attention to the organization of this chapter* to predict what is coming.

Key Verbs: predict   assume   demonstrate   determine   influence   imply

Predicting: Seeing and Describing What is Coming Next:

A good way to understand a new topic is to *focus on what we already know about the topic.* Usually we have heard or seen words related to it before, and we have already formed some idea of what the subject covers.

Brainstorm the topic of **"psychology."** List your ideas below---in any order, using just simple words or phrases, not sentences. Note as many terms as you can in the space provided. Next, if possible, check with others to see if they agree. The list is started for you:

Ideas related to psychology:

Human behavior
Experiments

> >>>>>**KEY IDEA**:
> Now look at p.2 of the text, and underline the author's words, *"You have just encountered the theme of this book: Ask for the evidence."* How do the terms you wrote relate to this idea of getting "evidence"? How closely do your terms relate to the definition of psychology the author provides on p.3, *"the systematic study of behavior and experience"?*

Creating questions about content:
Asking questions is another way to help us think about a topic. The description of *determinism* tells us that scientists *"made an assumption.... that everything that happens has a cause...."* Make that into a question about what scientists believed, but couldn't prove:
Example:
What did scientists who believe in "determinism" assume?

Now look for the author's answer again. When you find it, underline it; and then copy it here.

_____

Go on in the chapter, paying special attention to questions the author is asking. Try to form an idea of the author's points of emphasis on the *relationship between the mind and the brain.*

Summarize the author's questions on the mind/brain connection here: *The author asks:*

_____

Can you find the answer to the question you wrote on the mind/brain relationship? Is there a definite answer?

*The answer I found seems to say......*_____

_____

Nature-Nurture: **Look over this section and copy the question that best <u>covers</u> <u>its points</u> here**: (Note: If you think the focus is only on sex differences, look again.)

_____
_____?

Write an answer for your question here:

_____

<u>Do the same question/answer pattern with the rest of the chapter</u>, which discusses different types of psychologists and their objectives. For each section, find a question that you can use, or, better, *form your own question by rewording, restating the questions in the text*. Then supply an answer based on your reading.

<u>Asking questions about text organization</u>:
Up to now we have been looking closely at ideas in the reading and asking questions about information within the example paragraphs. *Another kind of question to ask is about text organization*.

Ask yourself the following question: **"Is there any change in the focus of this section of the chapter as it moves from discussing research fields in psychology to another focus?"** What new, but related, focus did you find?   Where?

<u>Practice making questions with the summary terms</u>. <u>Then answer them</u> without looking at the answers in the text.

Practice your new skills to aid your understanding of new material: *Predict chapter content* within **"Psychology Then and Now." (See Module 1.2.) Use brainstorming to come up with ideas that might be discussed in this section.**

<u>**Psychology Then and Now:**</u>

Read the section and <u>underline</u> ideas that connect to your predicted terms. **Then list below some key questions that you could create about important persons and concepts discussed.** Try to form your own questions.

Example: **What were Wilhelm Wundt's most important contributions to psychology?** (Of course when you find the answer(s), underline them.)

Now look again at *text organization.* **What questions might you ask about the last part of the chapter after finishing the section on famous psychologists? Circle below some concepts that fit:**

More Recent Trends in Psychology:

What are changes in the field? What were common beliefs of the mid 1700's?

What did Darwin say? What did Titchener believe about the structure of the mind?

What is important today about human diversity?

Word Attack:

Word endings, suffixes, help us understand the form of a word. **Fill in the blanks for the suffix that fits the correct word category (part of speech) shown.** The first one is done for you:

Noun form +adjective suffix	Adjective Suffix: **(-al; -cal)**	Adverb Suffix: **(-ally; -cally)**
Biologist (**-cal**)	Biologi**cal**	Biologi**cally**
Psychologist (-cal)		
Development (-al)		
Environment (-al)		
Behaviorist (-al)		
Experiment (-al)		

Extending Your Vocabulary Knowledge

In addition to knowledge of word parts, knowledge of idioms and phrasal verbs is helpful. The phrases below **express relationships.**

--Write R next to those which express *result (effect).*
--Write C next to those which express only a *connection.*

___derive from   ___ stem from   ___ associated with

___ to be due to   ___ depend on   ___ relate to

CHAPTER 2: SCIENTIFIC METHODS IN PSYCHOLOGY

Note: <u>Before you begin Chapter 2:</u>

1. Review Ch. 1 of both the Kalat text and the Study Guide to be sure you have covered all key concepts and terms.
2. Next, pay attention to the organization of this section of the guide for <u>non native speakers of English</u>. It will give additional support as you move from chapter to chapter.

Key Verbs: claim   investigate   evaluate   measure   calculate   interpret

---

Predict what is coming in Chapter 2 by focusing on what you already know about the topic. **<u>Using the key words above to get you started, list a few phrases about</u>** *scientific methods*:

<u>Ideas related to</u> *scientific methods*:

claim = state unproven theory that needs careful *investigation*

procedures with statistics that systematically *measure*

>>>>>**KEY IDEA:**
Now look at the section of Ch.2 with the heading, "Steps for Gathering and Evaluating Evidence."
Underline the author's words, ***"When a dispute is indecisive, researchers collect new data, guided by a hypothesis, which is a clear predictive statement."*** How do the ideas you wrote relate to this idea of "a clear predictive statement?" How do your ideas connect with the author's points on **falsifiable** theories, p.31?

<u>**Creating questions about content**</u>: As in Ch.1 of this nonnative speakers' guide, one strategy presented to help you think about a topic is to form your own questions.
<u>**Create questions to fit the answers provided below:**</u>

<u>Answer</u>: The examples of perpetual motion machines, Clever Hans, the horse, and the example of ESP all show this principle.
Question: _____**?**

Try forming another question about chapter content, this time for the following answer:
<u>Answer:</u> "One kind of evidence consists of…people's reports of isolated events."
Question: _____**?**

Another answer: Hypothesis, methods, results, and interpretation are part of these procedures.
Your question:

_____
_____?

<u>Asking questions about text organization also helps you use text resources better</u>:

The Kalat text, <u>Introduction to Psychology</u>:

As in Ch. 1, you will notice that chapters are divided into different sections. **Ask yourself what the specific purposes of the subsections are** starting with "Summary" at the end of the first section of Ch.2. (In other words, ask yourself *why these sections are included.)*

<u>Utilizing the Study Guide</u> for the Kalat text:

1. **Create a question** for each of the first 3 subdivisions of Ch. 2 in the Study Guide, which are taken from the Kalat text. The first one is started for you:
    a. *How do scientists evaluate theories?*
    b.
    c.

 2. **<u>List the headings</u>** of the major sections of the Study Guide, Ch. 2, to guide you. **<u>Include a paraphrase</u>, your own words for the same idea. The first one is provided**.

    a. **Objectives** (outline of content)
    b. **Comprehension Check** (self-test of your understanding of chapter content)
    c.
    d.
    e.
    f.
    g.
    h.

Predict chapter content within the next section, "Methods of Investigation in Psychology," this time by previewing, that is, looking ahead, at the <u>Study Guide</u> outline for that section.

<u>Paraphrasing the Study Guide</u>: Focus on Module 2.2.
The Study Guide lists some key phrases about "Methods of Investigation..."**Another way of saying the same thing (a paraphrase) is also given for underlined phrases and terms:**

II. Research follows some <u>general principles</u>:
    Research follows some <u>basic steps.</u>

    A. <u>Variables</u> should be operationally <u>defined</u>:
       Things that vary results should be <u>identified</u> <u>and described.</u>

    B. Samples should be <u>representative and random</u>.
       Samples should <u>be chosen in specific ways to fairly represent the target group.</u>

    C. Observers and subjects should be "<u>blind</u>".
       Participants shouldn't know what results are expected.

Now *You* **try to paraphrase** some of the following. (Hint: You can also use the minor points and examples to help you understand major points. **In addition, you do <u>not</u> need to write every word, only key ideas. When you finish, reread Chapter 2 in the Kalat text.)**

III. Observational research designs don't show cause and effect relationships.

    Observational research= *research involving watching, observing, seeing*
    A. Naturalistic: *natural conditions*
    B. Case Histories: _____
    C. Surveys: _____
    D. Correlational Study: *research that studies relationship, not cause/effect*

IV. Experiments involve the manipulation of variables:
    Experiments: involve controlling and influencing things that vary results:
    A. Independent variables: _____ Dependent variables:_____
    B. Experimental groups: _____Control groups: _____
    C. Example of an experiment: *study of influence of TV violence on behavior*

    V. Demand characteristics may produce self-fulfilling prophecies : *Messages that show what behavior is expected can influence the behavior that results.*

VI. Ethical issues: _____

Now see the section, "Measuring and Reporting Results" in the <u>Study Guide</u>. You will see that Section VII A and B do not need paraphrasing. Move on to VIII, and <u>underline the author's paraphrase of "statistically significant."</u> **(Do you understand more than you thought?)**

<u>Word Attack</u>:

Note the suffix, *-ate*, for the first verb below; then fill in the same suffix to <u>change each of the following nouns to a verb.</u>

Replication: evaluation   calculation   indication   investigation   correlation
Replic**ate**: evalu____   calcul____   indic____   investig____   correl____

Note the suffix *–able* for the first adjective below; then fill in missing suffixes to <u>change verbs to adjectives.</u>
Vary: observe   falsify   conceive   compare   measure   depend
Vari**able** observ____   falsifi____   conceiv____   compar____   measur____   depend____

Write the *verb suffix* you practiced : _____

Write the *adjective suffix* you practiced:_____

Sentence examples:

CHAPTER 3: BIOLOGICAL PSYCHOLOGY

Before you begin Chapter 3:

l. *Review Ch. 2 of both the Kalat text and the Study Guide* to be sure you have covered all key concepts and terms.

2. *Next, pay attention to the organization of Chapter 3 to predict what is coming:*

Key Verbs:	control	interact	transmit	combine	activate	release

Add these nouns:	behavior	environment	chemicals	message	system

Predict chapter content:

Using the key words above, (both verbs and nouns), **and the following 2 terms, write phrases in notes and questions** to make connections. Do so in the following order:

       a. neurons (p.69)   *b. nervous system (p.78)*

Example of questions:
Do neurons control behavior?   Example of notes: *neurons > transmit messages*
Do neurons interact with chemicals?

>>>>>**KEY IDEA:**
Find the author's statement on p.68: *"We now know a great deal about how nerves work and how brains record sensory experiences. What we understand least is why and how brain activity produces conscious experiences."*
Look now at *In Closing,* p.90, to see how the author describes the relationship of the whole and independent parts of the brain.

Asking Questions About Text Organization: Text Cues: **Bold Print** and *Italics*:
In addition to headings, authors use **bold** print and *italics* to cue the reader something is important. Often these are found together in the Kalat text to signal important concepts and terms. Many of those appear again in the review activities at the end of each chapter.

Below, **write the meaning in italics for the bold terms on the pages listed**:
Example: central nervous system (p.78): *the brain and the spinal cord*
       peripheral nervous system (p.78):
       autonomic nervous system (p.78):

Now try listing the bold term for the meanings in italics:
Example: *nerve cells:* <u>neurons</u> (p. 69)

widely branching structures that receive transmissions from other (p. 69):_____

*a single, long, thin, straight fiber with branches near its tip (p. 69):*_____

Refer to the Study Guide for Ch. 3 to predict key concepts for this unit, using these strategies:

    l. Circle or highlight key terms, being careful **not to include all the words, only key words.**
    2. Look for these highlighted terms in the Kalat text. See the example below:

Practice: Highlight the key terms in this item from the Study Guide, Ch.3:

    B. Nerve impulses are called action potentials.
        l. Inflow of sodium ions makes inside of axon positive.

(**Hint**: Key terms to circle, underline or highlight might be <u>action potentials,</u> <u>sodium</u>, and <u>axon</u>. If you refer back to the Kalat text, you will see that the Guide is summarizing and paraphrasing the information in the text, Ch.3):

"When the **action potential** starts, *sodium gates open and allow sodium ions to enter. **As the sodium ions enter the axon, they drive the inside of the cell to <u>a slightly positive charge.</u>**"* (p.70)

(Notice that the Guide takes this idea about elimination of negative potential and phrases it as "makes inside of axon positive." However, <u>the idea is the same</u>.)

Study Strategy: Create your own textual cues: <u>Highlight key concepts as shown in the examples above:</u>

l. **Find and highlight key terms in the Guide.**
2.**Find and highlight corresponding terms and ideas in the text.**

After using the Kalat text chapter and the ***Study Guide***, check the review section at the end of the chapter in both texts. For example, reinforce your understanding through *Concept Check, Summary,* and *Key Terms* sections. See the following from the *Key Terms* section of the text, Ch.3:
The action potential: an excitation that travels along an axon at a constant strength, no matter how far it must travel. (Again, the focus is on the positive force="without loss of strength.")

Use all of your resources, <u>text, Study Guide, and this section for nonnative speakers</u> to help you understand and retain what you learn.

Other Study Strategies:
In addition to highlighting important words and concepts, another way to understand and remember that you might find useful is to illustrate the concepts you read in some way:

    l. Draw a picture of a process
    2. Draw a graphic representation, such as a chart or diagram
Practice:
Refer to the section of Ch. 3, "The Major Divisions of the Nervous System," p.78-83. On another paper make an illustration and label it for:

l. Forebrain
2. How the Cerebral Cortex Communicates with the Body
3. The Autonomic Nervous System and Endocrine System

Compare your illustration to the illustrations in the text to see if you understood the general ideas.

Use the strategies you have practiced to help yourself continue in Chapter 3:

1. Focus on **bold** print and *italics.*
2. Use both the Kalat text and the <u>Study Guide</u> to get key concepts.
    a.   Highlight only key terms
    b.   Look for the same ideas in all resources, including review sections.
3. Draw your own illustrations of concepts discussed and label them.

4. Compare your illustration to those in the text and make adjustments.
    ALSO: Don't forget to take chapter post tests in the Study Guide and check your answers.

<u>**Word Attack**</u>**: Idioms:**

To an extent: to a certain point; to a certain degree

To do so: to do things that specific/stated way

So far, so good: Up to this point, no problem.

CHAPTER 4: SENSATION AND PERCEPTION

Before you begin Ch. 4:

l. Review Ch. 3 of both the Kalat text and the Study Guide to be sure you have covered all key concepts and terms.

2. Next, pay attention to the organization of Chapter 4 to predict what is coming:

| Key Verbs: | convert | respond | adapt | perceive | stimulate | inhibit | detect |

Look for Chapter Themes or Main Ideas: Use chapter subheadings:

What can you predict about the contents of the following 3 major sections of Chapter 4, "Sensation and Perception"? **Write your ideas next to the subtitle:**

<u>**Example:**</u>   **Vision:**   **sight**   **about seeing**   **about eyes**   **how we see**

  *Nonvisual Senses:

  The Interpretation of Sensory Information:

Note: If you looked at all three subheadings before starting the first one, you probably noticed they all deal with one general topic, covered in the chapter title.

<u>**Write that general topic here, using other words than those of the title itself**</u>.
In other words, paraphrase the chapter title. "Sensation and Perception" covers information
on:_____

_____

> **>>>>>KEY IDEA: Notice the author's words at the top of page 97 in Ch. 4: "Our experiences** *translate* **the stimuli of the outside world into a very different representation."** What can you conclude from this comment?

<u>**Skimming**</u>: Although we have been practicing strategies that focus on specific ideas, we can do the opposite: get a general idea, without concentrating on specifics.

<u>Practice:</u>
Look over the Table of Contents of Kalat's text, <u>Introduction to Psychology</u>. **Get a general idea of chapter subjects without focusing on any particular one. Do that as quickly as you can, that is** <u>**skimming**</u>.

* Note: Compare your terms with terms the author uses to describe the senses.

Now do the following: **Skim the captions,** *the written explanation under illustrations throughout the chapter.* These are found with each numbered "figure" showing a diagram or drawing of some kind. Notice that these captions support key ideas connected to each heading.

l. Skim the first section of the chapter, Module 4.1, "Vision," and circle or underline the item below that best fits its general content in your opinion:

a. cones and rods
b. accommodation of the lens
c. how we focus in various situations
d. how brains construct the images we see

2. Skim the second section of the chapter, "The Nonvisual Senses," Module 4.2, and circle the item below that best fits its general content in your opinion:

a. different kinds of sounds the ear hears
b. definitions of sensory systems
c. how non visual sensory systems function
d. touch, taste, and smell

3. Skim the subheadings only for last section of the chapter, Module 4.3, "The Interpretation of Sensory Information," many of which are listed below.

Circle a <u>KEY WORD</u> (1 only) that best fits its general content:

I. Perception of Minimal Stimuli
      A. Sensory Thresholds and Signal Detection
      B. Subliminal Perception
      C. What Subliminal Perception Cannot Do
      D. What Subliminal Perception Can Do

II. Perception and the Recognition of Patterns
      A. The Feature-Detector Approach
      B. Do Feature Detectors Explain Perception?
      C. The Gestalt Psychology
      D. Similarities Between Vision and Hearing
      E. Feature Detectors and Gestalt Psychology

III. Perception of Movement and Depth
      (subcategories)

Note: If you circled the word **"perception,"** for I-III, you made a good guess. The last section's *In Closing* (p.144), says, "You have probably heard the expression, 'Seeing is believing.' The saying is true in many ways including that what you believe influences what you see."

Answers from the beginning of this section: (#1:d; #2:c.)

Paraphrasing Practice:
Now that you have a general idea of the chapter content, write your own paraphrase, your own words for the chapter title, without looking back at what you wrote at the beginning of this chapter:

The chapter **"Sensation and Perception" discusses**: _____

_____

Word Attack:

Change the nouns below to adjectives, based on the suffix in the following example:

Verb	Noun	Adjective
respond	Response	respons-*ive*
sense	Sense	sensit
interpret	Interpretation	interpret
conclude	Conclusion	conclus
perceive	Perception	percept
receive	Reception	recept
deduct	Deduction	deduct
adapt	Adaptation	adapt
elude	Elusion	elus

Idioms:

To draw a distinction: to distinguish one thing from another; differentiate

To be led astray: to be misled; to be deceived

To happen to deal with: to be about; to refer to

Even so: Even though this is true; nevertheless

To get locked into: To become convinced of something

CHAPTER 5: STATES OF CONSCIOUSNESS

1. *Review Ch. 4 of both the Kalat text and the Study Guide* to be sure you have covered all key terms and concepts.
2. *Look over the organization of Chapter 5* to predict what is coming next.

Key Verbs: alter   induce   impair   deprive   restore   tolerate   distinguish   abuse

Predict chapter content:

Chapter 4 has information that you have probably thought about or discussed with someone several times in your life. You will quickly recognize some topics from your own life experiences and those of other people you know.

Below, **check the terms and concepts that are already familiar to you,** even though only partially:

____ hallucinate
____ circadian rhythms ("morning people" and "evening people")
____ meditation
____ stages of sleep
____ withdrawal
____ stimulants
____ tranquilizers
____ sleep walking
____ hypnosis
____ repair and restoration
____ alcohol
____ sleep talking
____ insomnia
____ consciousness and unconsciousness
____ physical and/or psychological dependence
____ nightmares
____ energy conservation

Now organize the above terms into the 3 categories used by the author; some terms may fit in more than one category. Try to group them without using the text. See if you understand relationships of major topics and examples.

Sleep and Dreams:

Hypnosis:

Drugs and Their Effects:

Review:
Key Verbs: *alter   impair   deprive   restore   tolerate   distinguish   induce   abuse*

Vocabulary Practice: Using the "Key Verbs" listed above, <u>fill in the correct verb for each blank based on information drawn from the chapter topics</u>:

Many people have experienced some condition in which they were not aware of things in the same way as they normally would be. The author discusses various ways people change or _____ their sense of reality either consciously or unconsciously. During sleep, for example, the body works to _____ its functions. For most people, less than the typical amount of sleep can _____ the body of the rest it needs.   Not all sleep is satisfying, however, since interruptions such as nightmares or insomnia can _____ the individual's ability to move through the various sleep stages that are considered necessary for adequate rest.

Other "states" of altered consciousness described by the author are artificially created. One example is hypnosis, which can _____ a condition in which the individual follows suggestions more readily than otherwise might occur. However, the author cautions us to _____ between valid claims about hypnosis and hearsay, things people tell you that may not be based in fact.   Another example of altered states of consciousness occurs with drug and alcohol use. The author describes how different types of drugs affect users who may _____ more than normal amounts and therefore _____ the drug, suffering physical and/or psychological consequences.

>>>>>**KEY IDEA:**
The author's words on the first page of Chapter 5 summarize the message of the chapter:
"Consciousness relates closely to sensory experience, with an emphasis on the private, subjective aspect." He reinforces, that is, strengthens this argument by adding on the same page, *"We might simplify the definition of consciousness as the subjective experience of perceiving oneself and other entities."*

What is your paraphrase, your own words that explain the above comments?
_____
_____

Word Attack:

I. In each example below <u>choose the correct form of the word: noun, verb, or adjective</u>:

   l. East-coast people adjust to West-coast time more easily than West coast people adjust to East-coast time. Time _____ are difficult for people to make.
   (adjusted/adjustments)

   2.Sleep deprivation leads to _____ concentration and irritability; prolonged
                              (impaired/impairment)

deprivation can impair the function of the immune system and increase the risk of becoming ill.

3.We cannot draw cause-and-effect conclusions from correlational studies. We cannot say that just because one thing _____ with another that it therefore leads to or is
(correlates/correlation)
 a result of the other.

 4.Although people assume that hypnosis is somehow related to sleep, the connection is only superficial. In other words, that _____ is not completely accurate.
(assumed/assumption)

5.Research studies _____ changes that occur during experiments.
(document/documentation)

III. **Compare and fill in the missing word forms**:

Noun:	**Adjective:**	**Adverb:**
Hypnosis:	**hypnotic**	**hypnotically**
psychosis:		
neurosis:		

Answer key:

Vocabulary practice: alter; restore; deprive; impair; induce; distinguish; tolerate; abuse

Word Attack: adjustment; impaired; correlates; assumption; document

CHAPTER 6: LEARNING

Before you begin Chapter 6:

1. *Review Chapter 5 of both the Kalat text and the Study Guide* to be sure you have covered all key concepts and terms.
2. *Next, pay attention to the organization of Chapter 6* to predict what is coming:

Key Verbs: elicit   evoke   excite   provoke   acquire   reinforce   extinguish

What general idea is communicated by the following verbs:

         elicit   *evoke*   *excite*   *provoke*

elicit = to draw out, get
evoke = produce or call out
excite = raise strong feelings; cause to happen
provoke = to cause a feeling or action
The *general idea expressed by these verbs* is: _____
_____

Which **key verb** in the box above might express the *opposite* meaning?_____

Predict Chapter Content: Summarize Themes or Main Ideas

In each chapter of the text, the author begins with an introduction, which usually has some analogies or examples to help the reader understand the central idea of the chapter.

Read p.190 and 191 in Ch. 6, "Learning." Pay special attention to the paragraph on p.190 that begins, **"Psychologists have devoted an enormous amount of research to learning. One key finding is......"** Underline the key idea there. What can you predict about ideas coming in this chapter?

In the space below, briefly summarize the author's message from these first 2 pages:
_____

_____

>>>>>**KEY IDEA:**
      Use *In Closing* in Ch. 6 on p. 226 to find the author's central idea about conditioning and/or learning. <u>Then summarize it by doing the following:</u>

      a. Underline 1 or 2 key points.
      b. Paraphrase them.
      c. Write a one-sentence summary statement of your paraphrased idea:

<u>Ask questions about text organization</u>: **What terms or phrases show relationship between ideas?**
How do we know when the author is pointing out that one action affects another or is the opposite of another?

<u>Practice seeing relationships between ideas in order to understand the main ideas better.</u>

Below is a list of terms that show relationships. Match the purpose of the term (indicated by #1 or #2) to the appropriate phrase or word:

> ### Terms Showing Relationships
>
> 1. Cause and effect
> 2. Contrast or <u>un</u>expected result
>
> | | | | |
> |---|---|---|---|
> | _____ influence | _____produce | _____still | _____subject to |
> | _____ therefore | _____based on | _____lead to | _____except |
> | _____ consequently | _____instead | _____although | _____evidently |
> | _____depending on | _____despite | _____ rather | _____by contrast |
>
> With the following <u>excerpts</u> from the chapter, tell which shows #1 and which shows #2. In other words, decide what the relationship of the ideas is:
>
> _____1. The rats that had received shocks while drinking avoided only the tube that produced lights and noises. **Evidently**, rats...have a built-in predisposition to associate illness mostly with what they have eaten or drunk.
>
> _____2. You do not automatically imitate the behavior of someone else, even someone you admire. **Rather**, you imitate behavior that has proved reinforcing for that person.
>
> _____3. **Despite** widespread publicity about the consequences of driving drunk, using addictive drugs, or engaging in unsafe sex, many people ignore the dangers.
>
> _____4. Certain behavior can lead to certain rewards **while** other behavior can result in lack of reward as a reinforcement.
>
> _____5. **Instead**, reinforcement gradually increased the probability of one behavior.

Other words that show relationships:
The following words show *probable or possible relationships*, (although perhaps not cause and effect):

<u>Noun:</u>	<u>Verb:</u>	<u>General Meaning:</u>
1. tendency	to tend to	to tend/ be likely to/ predisposed to: expected to
2. likelihood	to be likely to	to be associated /correlate with= connected with
3. predisposition	to be predisposed to	
4. association	to be associated with	
5. correlation	to correlate with	

<u>Idioms:</u> Make note of the following idioms, which are used in Chapter 6:

In the long run: after enough time; in the end

"…but in the long run they made as many presses as did rats that never received any punishments" (p.209).

far-reaching: affects many; goes beyond

"If so, the implications are far-reaching" (p.200).

ANSWERS TO "WORDS SHOWING RELATIONSHIPS":

Influence: 1; therefore:1; consequently:1: depending on: 1 produce:1 based on: 1; instead:2 ; despite:2; still: 2; lead to: 1; although: 2: rather: 2: subject 2: 1: except: 2: evidently: 1: by contrast: 2

Answers to "excerpts": 1: 1; 2: 2; 3: 2; 4: 1; 5: 2

CHAPTER 7: MEMORY

<u>Before you begin Chapter 7</u>:

1. *Review Chapter 6 of both the Kalat text and the Study Guide* to be sure you have covered all key concepts and terms.
2. *Next, pay attention to the organization of Ch.7* to predict what is coming.

Key Verbs: memorize   interfere   store   retrieve   process   recall   decay   reconstruct

---

I. <u>Chapter Organization</u>: Turn to the initial page of Ch.7. Write your own prediction, your guess, about the focus of each section based on the subtitles.

<u>Look at both the **title** in bold print and the other **subtitles** that are not indented</u>.
<u>Example:</u>

1. Types of Memory (Note the key words: pioneering studies; methods; application)
        varieties of memory
The focus of this section is probably a discussion of _____

<u>Now you try:</u>
2. Long-Term Memory Storage   (Note the key words below)

        storage and processing   encoding   emotional arousal   mnemonic devices

The focus of this section is probably: _____

---

3. Retrieval of Memories: (Note the key words below)

        interference   reconstructing   "recovered memory" vs. "false memory"

The focus of this section is probably: _____

A sample summary sentence that explains the theme or central focus of this chapter:
Chapter 7 explains different kinds of memory and what affects how well we remember.

4. Amnesia: <u>Record below both key words and a summary sentence for the expected content of this chapter</u>:

II. Use Illustrations to help you understand chapter content

In addition to headings and subheadings, (and text organizers shown previously), **<u>illustrations and captions help us focus on key ideas</u>**.

Look over the illustrations and read the captions below each illustration in the first section, **Module 7.1**, of the chapter, **"Varieties of Memory."** **Then list the key terms and ideas from these textual aids below. (One is already provided for you.)**

Key terms: **Key ideas:**

Ebbinghaus

Note: Use the "Concept Check" section, p. 236, to see how much you already understood.

<u>**Related examples:**</u>

Now look again specifically at p.234. Why are Fig. 7.1 and 7.2 grouped together on this page? Can you summarize their main idea?

Now go back and read about Ebbinghaus, pages 233-234 to see if you were right.

Did you see anything in the text that connected to the main idea? Mark it. How did you remember where to find it quickly? Did you use any memory strategy? ***Read on in Module 7.1 of Ch. 7 to find out how you yourself remember.***

Use your skills with illustrations on the other sections of the chapter now.

Other Textual Cues: Bold print and italics.

Often, key terms related to important concepts are in <u>bold print</u> to focus our attention. <u>List below the bold print terms</u> you find <u>in the first section of the</u> **Memory** chapter.

P. 234: free recall and **cued recall**. (Definition in italics).
Note: *Recall* seems to be the key concept here, part of both terms. Look ahead in the chapter to find which testing method would be helpful for remembering the distinction between these two terms.

Other bold print examples:

Italics*:* In addition to bold print, ***italics*** are another way to focus reader attention. For example, italics are used for the term ***"phonological loop"*** on p. 242.

Can *italics* help you review? **Try "cued recall" with italics to remember key ideas**. Copy only the italicized terms in the Summary Section, p. 243-244. Then try to recall what they refer to after reading the chapter more carefully.

Review ways just shown to quickly locate chapter themes and key ideas:
--titles and subtitles with key words
--illustrations and captions
--bold print and italics

Use the ways you have learned in the first section of this chapter to remember main ideas:

In retrospect, that is, looking back, what do you recall the major points of the first section of Chapter 7 are? **(Review by writing two or three summary sentences based on key words in headings:)**
_____
_____
_____

Part II: Long-Term Memory Storage: Preview

Using illustrations and captions in Module 7.2, see if you can **find relationships to the key ideas expressed in the headings or subtitles.** (Find an illustration that is "meaningful" for you.)

Using **bold** print and *italics*, try to identify key terms of this section of the chapter. Then look again at the illustrations to find connections between them and the bold print or italicized terms, reinforcing main ideas.

Can you recall the **SPAR** method of memory improvement for understanding and remembering a text lesson? (See p.248)

Part III: Retrieval of Memories: Follow the same procedure you did for the previous sections of the chapter, making sure to carefully read the whole chapter when you finish to fully understand major themes and relationships.

Part IV: Amnesia: Follow the same procedure you did for the previous sections of the chapter, making sure to carefully read the whole chapter when you finish to fully understand major themes and relationships.

Word Attack: What relationship do you see between the following words based on their prefix, *re*:
recall; recognition; reconstruction; relearn; reinforcement; review:
The prefix "re" is usually used to indicate: _____

CHAPTER 8: COGNITION AND LANGUAGE

Before you begin Chapter 8:

l. *Review Ch. 7 of both the Kalat text and the Study Guide* to be sure you have covered all key concepts and terms.
2. *Next, pay attention to the organization of Chapter 8* to predict what is coming:

| Key Verbs: | categorize | link | imagine | recognize | rely | estimate |

Section I: Thinking and Mental Processes:

Note the introductory sentence on p. 273 in Module 8.1: Cognition is psychologists' word for *thinking, gaining knowledge, and dealing with knowledge.* Now answer this question based on the next sentence in the text: **What do cognitive psychologists study?**
Cognitive psychologists study _____.
_____
_____

One of the key verbs in the box above, ***imagine***, is found in many related forms in this unit, particularly in the first section, "Categorization and Attention" (Module 8.1).

Note the different word forms related to the verb "imagine":

image   imagery   imagination   imaginative   imaginary

Can you predict some of the content of the initial section of Chapter 8 based on these words? **Write your prediction here:**
Chapter 8 deals, at least partly, with _____
_____

>>>>>**KEY IDEA:**
Now look at the following statements from pages 272-273 of the chapter and <u>consider how the author might connect *imagination* to these points:</u>
"psychological researchers focus as much as possible on results obtained from carefully controlled experiments, not just on what people say they think ....." and
"People often claim that they have a clear mental image of some object but then cannot correctly answer simple questions about it."

A question to ask yourself :
If "people cannot correctly answer simple question" about a clear mental image, how does this relate, also, to "attention?"(See pages 277-279, Ch. 8, on "preattentive and attentive processes.")

Section II, Ch. 8: <u>Problem Solving, Expertise, and Error</u>.

Another key verb, *estimate,* is found in this second section of Ch. 8.
<u>Note the different forms related to the verb "estimate:"</u>

estimate   estimation   estimable   esteem

For these words, the dictionary refers to judgment or calculation of value given to something or someone. **When <u>problem solving</u>, people tend to *estimate* the value of ideas and specific information.**

> *"Psychologists study problem-solving behavior partly to understand the thought processes behind it and partly to look for ways to help people reason more effectively." (p. 285).*

  ...and....
"In short, experts are made, not born, and they are extremely impressive only in their area of specialization." (p. 286)
…and…
"Problem solving can be described in terms of four phases." (p. 287)
 Note: generating (producing) a *hypothesis* and testing it are among the phases.

The author seems to be saying that problem solving requires _____
_____
_____

Section III: Language:
Using what you have learned about problem solving, look again at **"Key Verbs,"** and *predict connections* between the remaining terms and *language:*

Recognize: to know someone or something that you have seen before; to accept and admit that something is true or real
Categorize: to put into groups according to type; classify
Link: to connect
Rely: to trust or depend on someone or something

Ch. 8, Section III "Language" probably discusses:_____
_____

<u>**Using available resources: Connecting with the Study Guide:**</u>

Using the *Study Guide*, focus on the outline form that is used to categorize concepts from the text, <u>Introduction to Psychology</u>.

Study the first section of the Study Guide outline for Ch. 8, "Categorization and Attention," taken from the Kalat text. Then close the *Study Guide* and fill in the missing parts of that outline for the second section, "Problem Solving, Expertise, and Error" shown here. Parts of the outline are provided for you. **Refer to the text for other parts, using short sentences or phrases. In other words, paraphrase where possible. <u>Start with VI:</u>**

VI. Expertise:
    A. Practice makes nearly perfect
        1. Experts have a lot of practice in their fields
    B. Expert pattern recognition
        1. Experts recognize common patterns in their fields quickly
            a. They remember organized material from their areas easily
        2. Experts solve problems quickly by selecting relevant information

---

Afterward try to outline the final section, "Language" on your own. Refer to the example.

Word Attack:

Prefixes can be whole words such as **over** (more than necessary) or **under** (less than necessary): In this chapter, we see several examples of words to which the prefix *over* is attached. **Complete the examples below**:

    Overestimate   _____**use:**   _____**confident**

Idioms:

Look at the definitions of the following idioms; find them in context in Chapter 8:

Approach the problem: p.288: to focus on answering a specific question or solving a specific problem

Lead us astray: p.293: persuade someone to believe something that isn't true or do something wrong

NOTE: Most of these idioms refer to interactions between people engaged in problem solving of some kind.

CHAPTER 9: INTELLIGENCE AND ITS MEASURMENT

Before you begin Chapter 9:

1. *Review Ch. 8 of both the Kalat text and the Study Guide* to be sure you have covered all key concepts and terms.
2. *Next, pay attention to the organization of Ch. 8* to predict what is coming:

Key Verbs: (**You** provide some below this time…before you even begin the chapter.)

Read the paragraph that begins in the second column of p.323, giving a summary of definitions of intelligence. **Next list the verbs that psychologists use to define intelligence (p. 323):**

adapt   judge   _____   _____   _____   _____

Read the rest of the paragraph and review the strategy you practiced for Ch. 2, for example: **Ask questions about content by changing some part of the following statement to a question:** "...Just as all the objects in the world are composed of compounds of 92 elements, most psychologists expect to find that all the kinds of intelligence are compounds of a few basic abilities. They have proposed several models of how intelligence is organized."

My question:

_____
_____?

Now answer your own question by outlining the information that follows on various views of intelligence. Remember to list major points and related subpoints (examples, etc.) Summarize each theory in one sentence or phrase. *Then check yourself by referring to the text and the Study Guide.*

I. Spearman's Psychometric Approach: all mental tasks share general ability
- A. General ability, called "g" factor, "rules" lesser abilities
- B. Suggested specific lesser abilities connect to "g"

II. Cattel's Theory:

III. Gardner's Theory:

IV. _____'s Theory:

Review *textual cues* as signals to relate ideas: Using the following, complete the sentences below to compare the theories and summarize them:

1. **Although** Spearman believed_____

Gardner suggested _____

2. Cattell suggested two kinds of ability; **however,** Gardner_____
_____

3.Sternberg's theory deals with three kinds of intelligence; **for example**, *the individual's own internal mental process,* _____
_____, and _____
_____

Continue making similar statements about relationships between IQ tests, the next section of the chapter:

1. The Weschsler test is helpful for measuring strengths and weaknesses; **in contrast**, the Stanford Binet test_____
_____

2. The Stanford-Binet and Wechsler tests are not suitable for testing persons of non English speaking cultures; Raven's Progressive Matrices do not require verbal responses. **Therefore,**
_____

3. The Progressive Matrices Test is fairer than the Stanford-Binet and Wechsler tests for nonnative speakers of English if they can take paper and pencil tests; **however,**
_____

4. The SAT, Scholastic Assessment Test predicts performance in college; **moreover,** it includes both a
_____
_____.

5. **Despite the fact** that existing IQ tests are one way to measure intelligence,
_____

>>>>>**KEY IDEA:**
Notice the author's words on p.332, *"If intelligence exists at all, it must be measurable, but it can also be measured incorrectly. The challenge is to evaluate the accuracy, usefulness, and fairness of IQ tests."*

Paraphrase the author's perspective of IQ tests in the preceding statement:
_____
_____

Read the section **"The Distribution of IQ Scores,"** and <u>**list the 2 math terms**</u> that you notice are key to the discussion of how people score across a range.
1. _____ **score: middle score**
2. _____ **measurement of how much scores vary from the middle.**

What is the *Flynn effect* **(p. 333)** and what does it demonstrate?

Fill in the appropriate math terms through the next section, *Evaluation of Tests*:

3. _____ : shows **correlation between scores on first test and on retest (repeatability of scores).**

4. _____ : demonstrates that **test items correctly measure what they are intended to measure.**

5. _____ : refers to **usefulness and practicality** of test.
(Note: Which of the above is more likely to reflect changes in results (fluctuations in scores) from one test to the next?)

Read further in "Heredity, Environment, and IQ Scores." **Summarize in one sentence what the author says about differences in scores among ethnic groups.**

_____

_____

Find the message of the section on *Family Resemblances* factors; follow the same procedure:
   l. Read and underline key points.
   2. Summarize the main message, the central idea.

Does the author draw a definite conclusion about the influence of heredity (genetic background of an individual) and environmental influences in determining level of intelligence? **Find and underline the author's opinion,** which repeats several places in this section.

What question might your instructor ask about *heredity* vs *environmental* influences? How would you answer it? Find several examples to support your answer.

Word Attack:

Idioms:

In a way (p.330): somewhat

Lose sight of the fact (p.337): to forget

Heated controversies (p.345): a very emotionally intense debate

CHAPTER 10: HUMAN DEVELOPMENT

Before you begin Chapter 10:

1. *Review Ch. 9 of both the Kalat text and the Study Guide* to be sure you have covered all key concepts and terms.
2. *Next, pay attention to the organization of Ch. 9* to predict what is coming:

Key Verbs:	**mature**	**infer**	**reason**	**assimilate**	**accommodate**	**fluctuate**

Predicting chapter content: Headings and key terms that "explain" chapter themes:

Hypothesis (p.353): suggested explanation for something not yet proven
Interpretation (p.354): one explanation for an event or action
Implications (p.357): suggestion of possible effects or results

Note that the author often indicates his interpretation of key concepts by the following headings:
 --Concept Check
 --In Closing
 -- Summary

>>>>>**KEY IDEA**:
What might you expect Chapter 10 to cover, based on the author's introduction to this chapter where he says, **"The goal of developmental psychology is to understand everything that influences human behavior "from womb to tomb."** (p.352)
What is the "womb"? What is the "tomb"? And what kinds of development might be included within that range of growth and experience?

Using textual cues to understand chapter content: **punctuation**

To distinguish various theories or their elements from one another, as in this chapter on "Development," the author often uses specific punctuation to signal some form of classification.

The colon (:) **a punctuation signal that prepares the reader for important information, often in list form,** *moving from general to specific.* **Note the following examples:**

The Development of Thought and Knowledge: Piaget's Contributions

Piaget's stages of intellectual development

"Piaget contended that children progress through four major stages of intellectual development:"
(See the four stages listed, p.367.)

The Sensorimotor Stage: Infancy (p.368)

The Preoperational Stage: Early Childhood (p.370).

What might come next in the stages of development of an individual moving from infancy (baby years) to adulthood? Notice that the author has covered only the early stages so far; the reader must continue looking for the next stages and their specific characteristics.
Punctuation is one way to see that a list has begun.

(Note: A colon also is used to introduce a definition. See reference to Gilligan's *caring orientation* on p. 380.)

<u>the dash</u> (--) **is another punctuation signal that prepares the reader for important information that is coming, ….moving, as with the colon, from general to specific.**

<u>**Example:**</u>
Kohlberg devised a series of moral dilemmas--problems that pit one moral value against another. (p.378)

….or moving from essential to non essential information.

<u>**Example:**</u>

<u>Using textual clues to understand chapter content</u>: <u>**transitions that signal conclusions**</u>:

That is: "That is, they show a sense of self..."

In other words: "In other words—and this is one of Piaget's central insights—children's thought processes are..."

In general: "In general, the progression from one stage of thinking to another appears to be gradual and not sudden."

Therefore: "Therefore, it is inefficient to expect children to rediscover the accumulated wisdom of humanity..."

In short: "In short, contrary to Kohlberg's views..."

<u>**Word Attack:**</u>

<u>**Fill in the noun suffixes -*a*nce or – *e*nce = a state or quality**</u>

<u>Verb</u>	<u>Noun</u>	
		maintenance
maintain	mainten(a)	_____
infer	infer(e)	_____
prefer	prefer(e)	_____

Fill in the verb ending : *ate*

<u>habitu**ate**</u>	habituation
assimil _____	assimilation
accommo _____	accommodation
fluctu _____	fluctuation
accultur _____	acculturation
associ _____	association

Idioms:

To tell the difference between: to know/recognize how 2 or more things are different

To have something going on: to have something happening

To point out: to emphasize some fact or stress some piece of information

To state something in terms of: to say how a particular fact or piece of information is related to something.

CHAPTER 11: MOTIVATION

Before you begin Chapter 11:

1. *Review Chapter 10 of both the Kalat text and the Study Guide* to be sure you have covered all key concepts and terms.
2. *Next, pay attention to the organization of Ch. 10* to predict what is coming.

Note: Chapter 11 <u>organization</u> is announced on p. 405 in the chapter headings: To focus on the author's categories for this chapter, **fill in the missing words below**:

> *We begin this chapter with an overview of_____*
> *_____*
>
> *Then we will study 3 different aspects of motivation:_____ ,*
> *_____ , and _____.*

Key Verbs: achieve	activate	direct	inhibit	reduce	maintain	arouse

How do the above verbs relate to *motivation? (Motivate=provide with strong reason for doing something.)*

Use the following comparison/contrast relationship to paraphrase the author's message about the 3 motivations discussed in this chapter:

Although _____ and _____ serve a biological need, _____ is based first on social needs related to competition.

<u>**Chart below the different categories of motivation discussed early in Chapter 11**</u>:

<u>**Contrasting Motivational forms**</u>:

Drive (from biological force)   *<u>incentive (from external stimuli)</u>*

Extrinsic (based on rewards or punishments)   _____

Primary (automatic, built-in process)   _____

>>>>>**KEY IDEA:** The author asks and answers many questions about *motivation*. Notice the verb "depends" appears repeatedly. The author seems to say that most motivation, either biologically induced or socially induced, depends on the interaction of various factors and represents a basic human response, the need to attain. Notice this comment from the ***Summary,*** p.411*: "Motivated behaviors vary from time to time, situation to situation, and person to person."…and "persist until the individual reaches the goal."*

Asking questions about content:

Since most readers feel the subject matter of biological and social drives is a familiar topic, it is useful to test yourself to see how much, in fact, you do or do not already know.

Preread the **Concept Check** and **Summary** section of Chapter 11, "Motivation." Underline statements or questions for which *you* need answers. Record them here, or create your own related questions.

1. List below key questions you need to answer about hunger motivation:

Example: *What is the relationship between insulin levels and hunger?*

Example: *What are some causes of being overweight?*

2. List below key questions you need to answer about sexual motivation:

Example: *How does testosterone affect the development of sexual orientation?*

3. List below key questions you need to answer about work motivation:

Example: *What difference is there, if any, between men and women in achievement needs?*

Now: Make notes on answers to your questions from the information given.

Using available resources: The *Study Guide*:

Check your understanding of the lessons in Chapter 11 by doing each of the following in the *Study Guide:*

Module Assessments
Final Comprehensive Assessment

Follow up each test with a review of answer keys provided to be sure you have understood.

Word Attack: Follow the suffix form shown, changing from adjective to noun:

Adjective form:	Noun form *(-ity)*	
Obese	obes	___obesity___
Variable	variabil	_____
Homosexual	homosexual	_____
Heterosexual	heterosexual	_____

CHAPTER 12: EMOTIONS, STRESS, AND HEALTH

Before you begin Chapter 12:

l. *Review Chapter 11 of both the Kalat text and the Study Guide* to be sure you have covered all key concepts and terms.

2. *Next, pay attention to the organization of Ch.12* to predict what is coming.

Key Verbs: perceive   function   produce   threaten   cope   contribute   control

Using various "Key Verbs" above and the chapter title to help you, write a sentence that uses many of the terms and concepts expressed. Such a sentence is provided for you:

Example:
How people perceive their emotions contributes to or threatens their health and how well they function and cope with events that they may or may not control.

Your Example:

_____

_____

_____

Previewing Chapter Organization:

Using the paragraph on the first page of Ch.12, starting with "In this chapter, we shall consider...." **list below the two main focuses of this chapter.** The third is supplied for you:

l. .

2.

3. **Ways people cope with emotions associated with stress**

>>>>>**KEY IDEA**: The author establishes a connection between emotion and decision making ability (emotional intelligence) on p.449 and suggests that emotions control our actions. He further suggests that emotions are *"related to the activity of the autonomic nervous system and....the body in general"* and adds that how people monitor and cope with stress is a factor in managing health and well being. However, the author's clear message is that psychologists have not been able to establish the range of emotions or agree on basic emotions that have been identified; furthermore, psychologists feel that health is affected by *both* emotions and genes.

Using Textual Cues: More practice with **transitions**: Work with the following signals.

Readers need to follow supporting points that relate to a central idea. Sometimes these points list *examples*, **sometimes** *contrasts* **or** *similarities,* **sometimes** *results,* **and sometimes only** *emphasis.*

<u>**Below fill in the purpose of the transition**</u> **for each example from the chapter**:

a. add an idea
b. result or reason
c. contrast or unexpected result
d. similarity
e. emphasis
f. example or illustration
g. summarize or generalization

___ also; furthermore; moreover; in addition
___ therefore; thus; consequently, in view of
___ however; nevertheless; still; yet; nonetheless
___ similarly; likewise; just as; in the same way
___ in fact; indeed; certainly; of course
___ that is; in other words
___ in short; in general; overall; in summary

1. ___ **Therefore**, critics argue, the epinephrine injections may have …

2. ___ **Furthermore**, the fact that people of all cultures can recognize...

3. ___ **Nevertheless,** whatever it is that these happiness reports measure...

4. ___ **Still**, even if certain disorders are associated with an increased risk...

5. ___ **Just as** they do with other kinds of criminals, psychologists...

6. ___ **In short**, people tell themselves, "I'm in control; my life is ...

<u>**Note:**</u> **In dependent (subordinate) clauses:**
   Contrast between ideas **is expressed with these**: ***although; even though; despite the fact that***; ***no matter***...

These expressions have the same purpose, though not the same grammar, as contrast transitions such as ***however, nevertheless, in contrast, yet***, etc.

<u>**Example**</u>: **(Dependent clause):** ***Although*** any kind of frustration or disappointment can…
<u>**Example**</u>: **(Transition):** Any kind of frustration or disappointment can…..; **however,**…..

Introductory phrase with acknowledgment or recognition of an idea: ***granted that; given that; in view of the fact that***

<u>**Example**</u>: ***Given this view***, the proper measure of stress would ...(p.478)

<u>**Word Attack:**</u>

Much of Chapter 12 focuses on ***how*** people behave as a result of emotions, in other words the ***manner*** in which actions happen. Adverbs are used to express the manner in which actions occur:

Change the adjective to the adverb form, (in most cases, the suffix -ly) based on the example provided:

> **Adjectives:**
> calm   rational   emotional   logical   intelligent   active   violent

calm<u>ly</u> rational__ emotional__ logical___intelligent__ active.__ violent___

Notice the change in spelling with adjectives that end in "y:" (add –i)

voluntary---voluntar*ily*   **unhappy---unhapp*ily***

Idioms with "**draw**":

To **draw a distinction**: to show a difference between two things

To **draw a conclusion**: to decide something is true after some consideration

To **draw on**: to use past experience to assist your present decision or action

CHAPTER 13: PERSONALITY

Before you begin Chapter 13:

1. Review Chapter 12 of both the Kalat text and the Study Guide to be sure you have covered all key concepts and terms.

2. Next, pay attention to the organization of Chapter 13 to predict what is coming.

Key Verbs: imitate   strive transform   represent   repress   modify   standardize

---

Predict the chapter content: Scanning:

Scanning allows the reader to look over a reading passage for only 1 specific kind of information. **Practice now locating only the following. Then list the answers:**

1. Names of prominent theorists (famous persons who developed theories) covered in the chapter:

a. Sigmund Freud= focused on sexual motivation

b.

c.

Hint: Check *In Closing*, p.504 to see if you were right.

2. Terms for key approaches to study of personality: (The first is supplied for you)

a. Psychodynamic Approach = personality related to interplay of conflicting inner forces, some unconscious

b.

c.

d.

3. Freud's "stages of psychosexual development:"

a. Oral stage = stimulation of mouth during infancy

b.

c.

d.

4. Freud's "defense mechanisms" (defense = a mental process of self protection)

a.

b.

c.

d.

e.

f.

g.

h.

Author's opinion of Freud's theories:

>>>>>**KEY IDEA:**
The author seems to state that, as with most areas of psychology, personality is full of variables. *In Closing* p.504, he states, **"...*most specialists in personality research neither accept any of those three theories nor attempt to replace with something better.*" And, "*these theories have produced both the questions and the hypotheses that have guided much of later research.*" (Can you find any evidence for that statement throughout this chapter?)**

Using textual cues to understand chapter content: Comparison and Contrast terms and expressions used like transitions:

Important: *The author often uses terms and expressions showing comparison to signal the reader those specific theories and theorists differ from one another.*

<u>**Scan for examples using the following terms to establish a contrast:**</u>

And yet (p.491)

Still (p.498)

Rather (p. 500)

<u>**Scan for key definitions:**</u>

In the section "Personality Traits," scan for the following:
<u>1.The definition of the word **"trait;"** write it below:</u>

Trait: _____

2. Five general personality traits:

a.

b.

c.

d.

e.

3. The author's conclusion on the results of studies of monozygotic and dizygotic twins:

4. The author's advice about personality tests in general: (Hint: See p.525-526.)

<u>Word Attack</u>:

Circle the words from the chapter that seem to describe your own personality traits.
Group the words by listing them in their appropriate category, *noun* **or** *adjective*. **Refer to the**
following pages for ideas: p.506-511 and the *Key Terms* **on p.527-528.**

neurotic   neurotics   agreeableness   agreeable   extroversion   extrovert

open   openness   conscientious   conscientiousness

sociability   ambition   sociable   ambitious   anxiety   anxious

<u>Nouns:</u>   <u>Adjectives:</u>

CHAPTER 14: SOCIAL PSYCHOLOGY

<u>Before you begin Chapter 14</u>:

l. *Review Chapter 13 of both the Kalat text and the Study Guide* to be sure you have covered all key concepts and terms.
2. *Next, pay attention to the organization of Ch. 14* to predict what is coming.

Key Verbs: attribute   reject   share   conform   lean   pressure   defeat   cooperate

---

Circle the verb **"attribute"** in the *Key Verbs* above. **Notice its definition**:
<u>Attribute:</u>
To believe something to be the result of; to say something is responsible for a specific action or quality.

Now read the author's definition of the term, **"social psychology:"** Social psychology "includes the study of attitudes, persuasion, self understanding, and almost all everyday behaviors of relatively normal people in their relationship with others."

Why might the key verb "attribute" be important in this chapter as we examine influences on behavior?

What kinds of connections can you find among the other key verbs? Consider the following:

> share   conform   pressure   cooperate

What happens when people share information and experiences? What happens to attitudes and behavior? Are the consequences positive or negative or possibly both? Can attitudes change over time? Why?

>>>>> **KEY IDEA**: The author summarizes the components of "attitudes" on p.543. Complete his statement below as you find it in the chapter by filling in the missing phrases:
Your attitudes include an emotional component (_____),
a cognitive component (_____), and a behavioral component
(_____).

<u>Using textual cues to understand chapter content</u>: **Reference:**

Often a writer makes a statement which refers back to a previous statement without repeating the previous statement. Notice the following examples:

<u>Example:</u>
Other things being equal, the first information we learn about someone influences us more than later information does...*This tendency*.... (p.533).
This tendency refers back to the concept just explained, that is, being influenced by first information most.

Example:

In contrast, when people listen to a message on a topic of little importance to them, they pay more attention to such factors as the speaker's appearance and reputation or the sheer number of arguments presented, regardless of their quality. *This superficial approach*…**(p.544).**

This superficial approach refers back to the concept just explained, that is, people's tendency to pay more attention to appearance and reputation of the speaker if the topic is not important to them.

Now you try to identify the core, or essential, idea to which the underlined reference applies. Underline *the key part* of that original idea to indicate the relationship.

---

1. On certain topics, however, many people form strong, unshakeable attitudes based on almost no information at all. <u>One such topic</u> is the death penalty.

2. Beginning in the 1930's the party's membership and support began to dwindle, until eventually the party stopped nominating candidates. Was <u>that</u> because the Socialists had failed?

3. We like people who resemble ourselves—in any way. In one striking illustration of <u>this tendency</u>, students were asked to read a very unflattering description of Grigori Rasputin, the "mad monk of Russia," and then rate Rasputin's personality on several scales such as…

4. You can probably think of examples in which a speaker began by stressing his or her resemblance to the audience. "I remember when I was a student like you.", "I grew up in a town similar to this one.", "I believe in family values, and I'm sure you do too." <u>This technique</u>…

5. The general principle is that if you get people to do something they would not otherwise do by means of a minimum reward or a tiny threat, so that they are acting voluntarily or almost voluntarily, they will change their attitudes to defend what they are doing in order to reduce cognitive dissonance. <u>This procedure</u> is a particularly powerful way of changing people's attitudes because people are actively participating, not just quietly listening to someone….

6. According to this approach, men prefer young women because women reach menopause and therefore stop being fertile at about age 40-50. Men have therefore evolved a tendency to find younger (probably fertile) women more attractive than older women. <u>This theory</u> sounds rather persuasive, although it is difficult to test.

Other textual cues: *Italics* **and bold print:**
Review the sections with italics and/or bold print. Most of them contain key chapter concepts.

Questions about chapter content: Review Pre reading questions **in each section of the chapter as well as questions in** *Concept Check* **and** *Summary* **sections. Create your own also.**

Word Attack: The prefix "self"+
You already, no doubt, know words like *self*-confident or *self*-interest. **Using the prefix** *self* **to form words from this chapter, fill in the appropriate choice for each blank.** Choose from the list provided:

self-defeating   self-monitoring   self-handicapping   self-serving   self-esteem

Self-defeating: preventing your own success
Self-monitoring: watching or checking on yourself to control behavior
Self-handicapping: creating a disadvantage for yourself
Self-serving: serving your own interests first
Self-esteem: valuing your own worth

1. Attributions that we adopt in an effort to maximize our credit for success and minimize our blame for failure are called _____biases (p.541).

2. People can also protect their image with _____ in which they when they intentionally put themselves at a disadvantage to provide an excuse for an expected failure (p.541).

3. Cognitive dissonance is a state of unpleasant tension that people experience when they hold contradictory attitudes or when they behave in a way that is inconsistent with their attitudes, especially if they perceive that inconsistency as a threat to their _____ (p.531).

Which two choices above are basically synonymous (have the same meaning)?

_____ and _____ .

CHAPTER 15: ABNORMALITIES, THERAPIES, AND SOCIAL ISSUES

Note: Before you begin Chapter 15:

1. *Review Ch. 1 of both the Kalat text and the Maki Study Guide* to be sure you have covered all key concepts and terms.
2. *Next, pay attention to the organization of Chapter 15* to predict what is coming.

> **Key Verbs: define   observe   regard   classify   diagnose   function   represent**

Circle all the terms above that deal with *putting something into a clear category*.

Are clear categories of human behavior always easy to establish? Why not?   Keep that concept in mind as you move through Chapter 15, a presentation on abnormal human behavior and types of therapy.

>>>>>**KEY IDEA:**
Look for ways the author *signals distinctions*, differences between specific types of behavior and forms of therapy; pay attention to the view point, stated in the following quote taken from the Chapter 15:
"Each time and place has interpreted abnormal behavior according to its own world view." **(p. 582)**

Explain the author's comments from the quote:

The author uses many expressions to differentiate/contrast theories, personality disorders, etc.
Knowing how such contrasts are introduced can help the reader.
Look at the following; then write the number for type of contrast that could follow:

> l. names/lists different examples
> 2. compares thinking/methods of different psychologists
> 3. contrasts thinking /methods of different time periods.
> 4. contrasts acceptable and unacceptable interpretations according to author's view

___at one time…/by the early 1990's…
___abnormal behavior has three major aspects:
___classify each patient along five separate axes (lists)
___In some types of psychotherapy…/in others…/still others
___At first, Freud…/He soon abandoned that approach…
___ Resistance can take many forms…
___ …but unlike psychoanalysts…
___ That ruling may sound reasonable, but
___ The problem is not …but…
___ What distinguishes family therapists is…
___ Table 15.3 contrasts five major types of psychotherapy…
___ Instead, they practice…
___ The advantage of this system is…/The disadvantage is…
___ Here we are not interested in…To draw a conclusion, we need…

___ And yet you know…
___ Until the 1950's…/With the advent of …
___ Several studies have compared…
___ Here we shall consider three examples…

Be an attentive reader: Be familiar with these ways of signaling a contrast coming.

Categorizing with charts:

The author uses illustrations of various kinds to contrast different information also. Take a moment to survey Chapter 15 to find what ways graphics are used to compare and contrast various behavior forms, related causes and therapies.

Keep these graphic aids in mind while making your own chart of contrasts you want to remember. See example for one type of categorizing activity below. Complete with the information from Ch.15. (Then try charting DSM-IV-TR categories **discussed in the chapter.**)

Example: Other Trends in Psychotherapy (p.596-598)
Brief Therapy: limited therapy -- client +therapist agree on length (eg., 2 mo.)
Advantage = less cost; disadvantage = not enough for those w/more problems
Group Therapy:
Self-Help Groups:

Note: If you are working with a classmate, be sure to share your charts to increase your understanding of the contrasts covered in this chapter.

Hint: **When charting information from a reading, list major categories in capital letters and supporting examples and details in smaller print, indented to catch your eye.** Later you can highlight, underline, asterisk (*star), check, circle, etc., the points you forget.

Word Attack:

Compound words derived from prefixes: **Two separate words combined to express a concept:**

Under+lying= underlying (adjective)= being the real explanation for some behavior whose cause is not obvious.

> Underlying **drives**
> Underlying **sexual motives**
> Underlying **power and superiority motives**

Used to describe unconscious behavior, *underlying* characteristics or behavior help explain the real reason why people act in specific ways.

Hyphenated words: two separate words joined by a hyphen (-) to express a concept in which one characteristic or concept is influenced by another.

Examples:
Anxiety + provoke = anxiety-provoking (adjective)
Self + help = self help (adjective or noun)
Life + threaten = life-threatening (adjective)
Person + center = person-centered (adjective)

Idioms:

To give a damn: to care about something (colloquial)
"But psychotherapy does little good unless a client gives the proverbial damn."

Other things being equal: Assuming that other factors do not change the situation…

To use a trial-and-error approach: To try to solve a problem or accomplish something without any specific plan.

CHAPTER 16: SPECIFIC DISORDERS AND TREATMENTS

Note: Before you begin Chapter 16:

1. *Review Ch.15 of both the Kalat text and the Study Guide* to be sure you have covered all key concepts and terms.
2. **Next, pay attention to the organization of this section of the guide for <u>non native speakers of English</u>.** It will give additional support as you move from chapter to chapter.

Key Verbs: avoid   cope   react   fear   embarrass   extinguish   reinforce   characterize

---

<u>**Chapter Organization**</u>: Categorization –a way to organize and remember

We have seen how key ideas are introduced through everything from headings to topic sentences to illustrations. Often main ideas are also repeated several times within a passage. Help yourself cope with the many descriptions and terms in this text. Summarize what you read. As in Ch.15, *creating charts to contain short, specific notes is one way to cope with many categories of information.*

>>>>>**KEY IDEA:**
In the introduction to Chapter 16, the author stresses the importance of understanding the differences between psychological disorders. He states, " *Medical progress ...has been marked by increasing ability to apply specific treatments aimed at specific disorders. "*...and *"therapists would like to distinguish one disorder from another and apply specific treatments aimed at particular disorders. "*

Brainstorm ways to categorize numerous psychological disorders using graphic illustrations that contain adequate room for notes on the specific characteristics of each disorder.

An example follows: PHOBIAS
                                        (+)   (-)
                          Present in Anxiety Disorder Absent in Anxiety Disoder

Features:
Learned behavior	+	
Avoidance behavior	+	
Cyclic (series of) occurrence:		---
Interferes with normal living	+	
Causes physical reaction	+	
Unpredictable/non specific fear		

You try: Add just l-2 more features to the list shown. (Limit the number to recall .)
Hint: Try including something on successful experiments or therapies.

Now practice writing a short description of *phobias*, based on the information in the grid (chart shown above).

> **Now: Refer back to the section of Ch.16 to check your description of this disorder.**
> On a paper, create other such organizing tools to help you remember characteristic features of the many disorders described in this chapter. **For example, chart and compare *phobias* with *panic disorders* or compare *obsessive compulsive disorders*.**

> *The Message*: **Throughout the Kalat text, the author has summarized central points for each section of the chapter in** *"In Closing."* Paraphrase the central point of the section on *Anxiety and Avoidance Disorders* from reading comments in *In Closing* on the relationship between specific disorders and an individual's cognitions (conscious thought) and emotions:
>
> _____

Other Organizational Aids: Outlining

In an earlier chapter, we practiced <u>outlining</u>, *that is ordering and categorizing major and minor points* **of information, putting** *main points first* **and** *examples and details next.*

Look over the following outline from the section on **"Mood Disorders."** Fill in the missing information, paying attention to *the order of the ideas.*

MOOD DISORDERS

VI. Depression
    A. Major depression is experienced most of each day for five months and involves little interest, little pleasure, and little reason for productive activity
        1. Affects sleeping pattern which in turn increases depression
        2. Cry less, affects 5% of adults within any year; 10-20% over lifetime
        3. SAD-depressed repeatedly during a season of the year
            a. Light therapy seemsto be effective for SAD
    B. Genetic Influences

Now: Try to create your own outline for the section on *Substance Related Disorders* or *Schizophrenia.*

Word Attack:

Literal vs. Figurative language:

In this chapter, the author discusses the communication problems that occur with schizophrenic individuals who cannot understand proverbs, for example, because they "take things literally." (Review the following illustrations from Ch.16, p.646, which show an example of such thinking.)

    Proverb: People who live in glass houses shouldn't throw stones.
    Interpretation: *It would break the glass.* (Actual meaning: *Don't criticize others.*)

    Proverb: All that glitters is not gold.
    Interpretation: *It might be brass.* (Actual meaning: *Some things are not what they appear.*)

In each case here, the person interpreting the proverb never thought of how the proverb was not being used to describe what the words actually said but rather as an example with deeper meaning. Native speakers understand proverbs need to be interpreted as analogies, comparisons.

Look over the following *idioms*, also used in this chapter. Note that their meaning is different than what the actual words mean individually but they do not represent a "life lesson" as do proverbs.

To run in families: to pass from one generation to the next through heredity
To address the question: to answer a specific question

Review: **Now use these special strategies for understanding and remembering this material, not only when you read your texts but also when reviewing for examinations.**